THE ARDEN SHAKESPEARE

GENERAL EDITORS: HAROLD F. BROOKS
HAROLD JENKINS AND BRIAN MORRIS

TWELFTH NIGHT

THE ARDEN EDITION OF THE
WORKS OF WILLIAM SHAKESPEARE

TWELFTH NIGHT

Edited by
J. M. LOTHIAN and T. W. CRAIK

LONDON
METHUEN & CO LTD

The general editors of the Arden Shakespeare have been
W. J. Craig (1899–1906), succeeded by R. H. Case (1909–1944)
and Una Ellis-Fermor (1946–1958).

Present general editors: Harold F. Brooks, Harold Jenkins
and Brian Morris.
Twelfth Night was first published in the Arden Shakespeare in 1906,
edited by Morton Luce.

This edition first published 1975
Editorial matter © 1975 Methuen & Co Ltd

ISBN (hardbound) 0 416 17950 9
ISBN (paperback) 0 416 17960 6

Printed in Great Britain by
Richard Clay (The Chaucer Press) Ltd,
Bungay, Suffolk

Distributed in the U.S.A. by
HARPER & ROW PUBLISHERS, INC.
BARNES & NOBLE IMPORT DIVISION

CONTENTS

PREFACE

THE death of Professor J. M. Lothian in October 1970, not long after his retirement from his personal chair of English in the University of Aberdeen, was much regretted by his friends and colleagues there (as well as by the many elsewhere), who had highly regarded his warmth of personality and his ripeness of judgment. He left incomplete this edition of *Twelfth Night* (a play which he greatly enjoyed), having prepared the text, assembled a collation and commentary, and begun to write an introduction: of this he had completed sections on the sources, date, and text, and was in course of composing his critical discussion of the play.

A few months after his death, at the request of his widow, I collected from her his papers and sent his unfinished work to Mr Peter Wait of Methuen and Company who, after first consulting Mrs Lothian and the general editors Professors H. F. Brooks and Harold Jenkins, asked me in the spring of 1971 to complete the edition. On this work I have been intermittently engaged from that time to the present.

I had at first hoped simply to put into final order the completed parts of Professor Lothian's edition and to expand his critical notes into a finished discussion, so that the 'new Arden' edition could be published as soon as possible and under his name alone. However, once I began to examine his manuscript and to work over the material in detail, I became convinced that, notwithstanding the value of what he had done, further revision was desirable, and that Professor Lothian would himself have undertaken it if he had lived long enough to do so; and therefore, with the consent of Mrs Lothian, the general editors, and the publishers, I undertook it myself. The text of the play remains very much as he left it, following the Folio except when emendation was evidently required, and altering the punctuation no more than was necessary to provide a modernized text. The collation also is very little changed: readings from editions which have appeared since its completion have been added, as have earlier readings where the commentary makes them desirable. The commentary has been thoroughly revised: about one-third of the annotations are Professor Lothian's, about one-third my own, and the remaining one-third are my expansions and modifications of his

ix

(thus making it impracticable to assign, for example by initials, each note to its author). The introduction is completely of my writing, but it includes almost everything that Professor Lothian designed to say: the section on stage performance was not part of his plan; in the other sections his work has been the nucleus of mine, although, as will be acknowledged in the remainder of this preface and in the footnotes, it has undergone considerable alteration because of the generous help given me by other persons.

It is at this point that I would wish to acknowledge the help given to Professor Lothian, but regret that, apart from Mrs Lothian and Mr James George of the University of Aberdeen, I do not know where acknowledgment is due: I therefore hope that his other helpers will take the will for the deed.

The editors upon whose work he and I have drawn most freely are H. H. Furness, M. Luce, G. L. Kittredge, J. Dover Wilson, and M. M. Mahood. To Professor Mahood, of the University of Kent, I am grateful not only for her published work but for sending me further information for which I asked; I am also grateful, for the same reasons, to Professor F. W. Sternfeld, of Exeter College, Oxford, who assisted her by transcribing and editing the songs. I am deeply indebted to Professor Robert K. Turner, Jr, of the University of Wisconsin-Milwaukee, for 'textual' information which extended very far beyond the limits suggested by that term, and also to his collaborator Professor Maurice Charney, of Rutgers University, who is engaged on the 'critical' part of their joint work (as yet unpublished: see Abbreviations); they both, with great generosity, sent me copies of their manuscripts, and commented most kindly and helpfully on my manuscripts which I sent them in return. To H. F. Brooks and Harold Jenkins, who have virtually had two editions to oversee, I also wish to express gratitude, on my predecessor's behalf as well as my own, for the unfailing clarity and charity which both of them showed in doing so.

My thanks are also due to Miss F. E. Richardson, of Trent Park College of Education, who brought to her examination of the entry (2 February 1602) in Manningham's diary much more familiarity with Elizabethan handwriting than I possess; to Mr D. S. Fuller, of the University of Aberdeen, for help in connection with the songs; to the library staffs of the British Museum and of the Universities of Aberdeen, Cambridge, Dundee, London (for the photographs of the Folio which served as copy-text for the play) and Oxford (for the photographs which served as copy-text for Appendix I); to those students of the

University of Dundee who performed the play in February 1974 under my direction and that of my co-producer Miss Valerie Reid, and thereby enabled me to learn much about it 'from the inside'; to Mrs Moira Anthony for expert copy-typing, and to Mrs Magdalen Pearce for expert copy-editing. I am, of course, responsible for all errors which may be discovered in this edition, and should be glad to be informed of them so that I may correct them at the first opportunity.

T. W. CRAIK

University of Dundee
December 1974

ABBREVIATIONS AND REFERENCES

I. EDITIONS AND MANUSCRIPT

F   *Mr. William Shakespeares Comedies, Histories, & Tragedies.* 1623.

F2   *Mr. William Shakespeares Comedies, Histories, and Tragedies.* 1632.

F3   *Mr. William Shakespear's Comedies, Histories, and Tragedies . . . The third Impression.* 1664.

F4   *Mr. William Shakespear's Comedies, Histories, and Tragedies . . . The fourth Edition.* 1685.

Douai MS.   Douai MS. 7.87 in the Douai Public Library: contains transcripts of *Tw.N.*, five other plays by Shakespeare, and one each by Lee, Dryden, and D'Avenant. See G. Blakemore Evans, 'The Douai Manuscript—Six Shakespearean Transcripts (1694–95)', *Philological Quarterly,* 41 (1962), 158–72.

Rowe   *The Works of Mr. William Shakespear . . . Revis'd and Corrected . . . By N. Rowe, Esq.* (Vol. 2) 1709.

Rowe[3]   *The Works of Mr. William Shakespear . . . With his Life, by N. Rowe, Esq.* (Vol. 2) 1714.

Pope   *The Works of Shakespear . . . Collected and Corrected . . . by Mr. Pope.* (Vol. 2) 1723.

Theobald   *The Works of Shakespeare . . . Collated with the Oldest Copies, and Corrected; With Notes . . . By Mr. Theobald.* (Vol. 2) 1733.

Theobald[2]   *The Works of Shakespeare . . . Collated . . . and Corrected: With Notes . . . By Mr. Theobald. The Second Edition.* (Vol. 3) 1740.

Hanmer   *The Works of Shakespear . . . Carefully Revised and Corrected by the former Editions.* (Vol. 2) Oxford, 1743–4.

Warburton   *The Works of Shakespear. The Genuine Text . . . settled By Mr. Pope and Mr. Warburton.* (Vol. 3) 1747.

Johnson   *The Plays of William Shakespear . . . To which are added Notes by Sam. Johnson.* (Second issue) (Vol. 2) 1765.

Capell   *Mr William Shakespeare his Comedies, Histories, and Tragedies* [ed. Edward Capell]. (Vol. 4) [1767]. *Notes,* 3 vols., 1779.

Var. '73   *The Plays of William Shakespeare . . . with the Corrections and Illustrations of Various Commentators. To which are added Notes by Samuel Johnson and George Steevens.* (Vol. 4) 1773.

Var. '78   *The Plays of William Shakespeare . . . The Second Edition, Revised and Augmented.* (Vol. 4) 1778.

Rann   *The Dramatic Works of Shakespeare . . . with notes by J. Rann.* (Vol. 2) Oxford, 1786.

Malone   *The Plays and Poems of William Shakespeare . . . With . . . notes . . . By Edmond Malone.* (Vol. 5) 1790.

Var. '93   *The Plays of William Shakespeare . . . The Fourth Edition.* (Vol. 4) 1793.

Var. '03   *The Plays of William Shakespeare . . . The Fifth Edition. Revised and augmented By Isaac Reed.* (Vol. 5) 1803.

Var. '13   *The Plays of William Shakespeare . . . Revised and augmented by Isaac Reed . . . The Sixth Edition.* (Vol. 5) 1813.

Var. '21   *The Plays and Poems of William Shakespeare . . . [with] a life of the poet . . . by the late E. Malone . . . [ed. J. Boswell].* (Vol. 11) 1821.

Harness   *The Dramatic Works of William Shakespeare; with notes . . . By the Rev. William Harness.* (Vol. 2) 1825.

Knight   *The Pictorial Edition of the Works of Shakspere. Edited by Charles Knight. Comedies.* (Vol. 1) [1839].

Collier   *The Works of William Shakespeare . . . with the various readings, notes . . . by J. Payne Collier.* (Vol. 3) 1842–4.

Collier²   *The Plays of Shakespeare: The text regulated by the old copies, and by the recently discovered Folio of 1632, containing early manuscript emendations. Edited by J. Payne Collier.* 1853.

Halliwell   *The Works of William Shakspere . . . from a New Collation of the Early Editions . . . James O. Halliwell.* (Vol. 7) 1853–65.

Delius   *Shakesperes Werke. Herausgegeben und erklärt von N. Delius.* (Vol. 6) Elberfeld, 1854–61.

Singer²   *The Dramatic Works of William Shakespeare . . . revised . . . by S. W. Singer.* (Vol. 3) 1856.

Dyce   *The Works of William Shakespeare. The Text revised by the Rev. Alexander Dyce.* (Vol. 3) 1857.

Collier³   *Shakespeare's Comedies, Histories Tragedies, and poems. Edited by J. Payne Collier.* (Vol. 2) 1858.

Staunton   *The Plays of Shakespeare. Edited by Howard Staunton.* (Vol. 2) 1859.

White   *The Works of William Shakespeare . . . edited . . . by Richard Grant White.* (Vol. 5) Boston, 1859–65.

Camb.   *The Works of William Shakespeare. Edited by William George Clark . . . and John Glover* [Vols. 2–9 edited by W. G. Clark and W. A. Wright]. *The Cambridge Shakespeare.* (Vol. 3) Cambridge and London, 1863–6.

Dyce²   *The Works of William Shakespeare . . . Second Edition.* (Vol. 3) 1863–7.

Globe   *The Works of William Shakespeare. Edited by W. G. Clark and W. A. Wright.* Cambridge and London, 1864.

Keightley   *The Plays of William Shakespeare. Carefully edited by Thomas Keightley.* (Vol. 2) 1864.

Hudson   *The Complete Works of William Shakespeare . . . edited by the Rev. Henry N. Hudson.* (Vol. 5) Boston, 1881.

Wright   *Twelfth Night. Edited by W. A. Wright.* Oxford, 1885.

Deighton   *Twelfth Night. Edited by K. Deighton.* 1889.

Camb.²   *The Works of William Shakespeare. Edited by William Aldis Wright.* (Vol. 3) 1891–5.

Furness   *Twelfe Night, or What You Will. Edited by Horace Howard Furness.* A New Variorum Edition of Shakespeare. Philadelphia and London, 1901.

Luce   *Twelfth Night; or, What You Will. Edited by Morton Luce.* The Arden Shakespeare. 1906. Fourth edition, revised, 1929.

N.C.S.   *Twelfth Night, or, What You Will. Edited . . . by Sir Arthur Quiller-Couch and John Dover Wilson.* The New Shakespeare. Cambridge, 1930. Second edition, 1949.

Kittredge   *Twelfth Night. Edited by George Lyman Kittredge.* Boston, 1941.

Alexander   *William Shakespeare. The Complete Works . . . edited . . . by Peter Alexander.* 1951.

Munro   *The London Shakespeare . . . edited by . . . John Munro.* (Vol. 2) 1958.

Ludowyk   *Twelfth Night, or What You Will . . . with notes by E. F. C. Ludowyk.* Cambridge, 1963.

Mahood   *Twelfth Night. Edited by M. M. Mahood.* New Penguin Shakespeare. Harmondsworth, 1968.

Musgrove   *Twelfth Night or What You Will. Edited by S. Musgrove.* Fountainwell Drama Texts. Edinburgh, 1969.

Honigmann   *Twelfth Night. Edited by E. A. J. Honigmann.* 1973.

Turner   *Twelfe Night, or, What You Will.* [Edition by Robert K. Turner, Jr, and Maurice Charney; awaiting publication.]

Charney   See Turner.

Wilson   See N.C.S.

2. OTHER WORKS

Abbott   E. A. Abbott. *A Shakespearian Grammar.* 1869, etc.

Badham   Charles Badham. 'The Text of Shakespeare'. In *Cambridge Essays.* Cambridge, 1856.

Bailey   Samuel Bailey. *On the Received Text of Shakespeare's Dramatic Writings, and its improvement.* 1862.

Becket   Andrew Becket. *Shakespeare's Himself Again: or the Language of the poet asserted: [etc.].* 1815.

Bradley   A. C. Bradley. 'Feste the Jester', in *A Book of Homage to Shakespeare,* edited by I. Gollancz, 1916. Reprinted in A. C. Bradley, *A Miscellany,* 1929.

Florio   John Florio. *Queen Anna's new World of Words, or, Dictionarie of the Italian and English tongues, [etc.].* 1611.

D.N.B.   *Dictionary of National Biography.* Edited by Leslie Stephen and Sidney Lee. 1908–9.

Daniel   P. A. Daniel. *Notes and Conjectural Emendations of certain Doubtful Passages in Shakespeare's Plays.* 1870.

Farmer   Richard Farmer. Contributions to Var '73.

Heath   [Benjamin Heath.] *A Revisal of Shakespeare's Text.* 1765.

Hotson   Leslie Hotson. *The First Night of 'Twelfth Night'.* London and New York, 1954.

Hulme   Hilda M. Hulme. *Explorations in Shakespeare's Language.* 1962.

Jonson   Ben Jonson. Edited by C. H. Herford and Percy and Evelyn Simpson. Oxford, 1925–52.

Lettsom   See Walker.

Lyly   *The Complete Works of John Lyly . . . Collected and edited . . . by R. Warwick Bond.* Oxford, 1902.

MSR   *Malone Society Reprints.*

Mason   J. Monck Mason. *Comments on the Last Edition* [Var. '85] *of Shakespeare's Plays*. Dublin, 1785.

N. & Q.   *Notes and Queries*.

Onions   C. T. Onions. *A Shakespeare Glossary*. Oxford, 1911, etc.

OED   *A New English Dictionary upon Historical Principles*. Oxford, 1884–1928.

RES   *The Review of English Studies*.

Seng   Peter J. Seng. *The Vocal Songs in the Plays of Shakespeare: A Critical History*. Cambridge, Mass., 1967.

Sh. Q.   *The Shakespeare Quarterly*.

Shakespeare's England   *Shakespeare's England. An Account of the Life and Manners of his Age*. [Edited by Sidney Lee and C. T. Onions.] Oxford, 1916.

Singer   Samuel Weller Singer. *The Text of Shakespeare* [*etc.*]. 1853.

Sisson   C. J. Sisson. *New Readings in Shakespeare*. Cambridge, 1956.

Thirlby   Styan Thirlby (1686?–1753), contributions to Theobald (1733) and annotations for an unpublished edition of Shakespeare. See Christopher Spencer and John W. Velz, 'Styan Thirlby: A Forgotten "Editor" of Shakespeare', *Shakespeare Studies*, VI (1970), 327–33.

Tilley   M. P. Tilley. *A Dictionary of the Proverbs in England in the Sixteenth and Seventeenth Centuries*. Ann Arbor, Michigan, 1950.

TLS   *The Times Literary Supplement*.

Tyrwhitt   [Thomas Tyrwhitt.] *Observations and Conjectures upon some Passages of Shakespeare*. Oxford, 1766.

Upton   John Upton. *Critical Observations on Shakespeare*. 1746. Second edition, 1748.

Walker   W. S. Walker. *A Critical Examination of the Text of Shakespeare* [ed. W. N. Lettsom]. 1860.

The abbreviations of the titles of Shakespeare's plays and poems are those of C. T. Onions, *A Shakespeare Glossary*. All quotations from Shakespeare (except from *Twelfth Night*) use the text and lineation of *Works*, ed. Peter Alexander (1951).

The place of publication, unless otherwise stated, is London.

INTRODUCTION

I TEXT

I THE PRINTER'S COPY

Twelfth Night was first printed in the Folio of 1623: that there
had been no quarto edition is implied by the play's being entered
in the Stationers' Register (8 November 1623) for Jaggard and
Blount, the printers of the Folio, along with fifteen other plays
hitherto unprinted.[1] The only authoritative text of the play is
accordingly that of the Folio, where *Twelfth Night* is the penulti-
mate play in the first section (Comedies), following *All's Well That
Ends Well* and preceding *The Winter's Tale*. It occupies pp. 255–75
inclusive (sigs. Y2 to Z6; Z6ᵛ is blank).

Charlton Hinman has shown that there was some delay in
securing for the compositors the copy for both *Twelfth Night* and
The Winter's Tale. After they had set quire X (taking *All's Well*
as far as p. 252) they did not proceed to quires Y and Z (thereby
completing *All's Well* and following it with the whole of *Twelfth
Night*) but instead set quires a and b (thereby beginning the
Histories with the whole of *King John* and, on sigs b6 and b6ᵛ, the
start of *Richard II*).[2]

The reasons for the delay must be matters of conjecture. It is
of more immediate consequence to try to establish the nature of
the copy that was eventually provided for the compositor
(Compositor B) of *Twelfth Night*.[3]

The text of *Twelfth Night* has been described as 'unusually

1. E. Arber (ed.), *A Transcript of the Register of the Company of Stationers of
London, 1554–1640* (1877), IV, 69.

2. C. Hinman, *The Printing and Proof-Reading of the First Folio of Shakespeare*
(1963), II, 521. Further evidence of the delay over the copy is the fact that the
last page of quire Z (Z6ᵛ, following the end of *Tw.N.*) is blank, as is the last
page of quire Cc (Cc6ᵛ, following the end of *The Winter's Tale*). This is unusual
in the Folio, where normally plays succeed one another on the following page,
whether recto or verso.

3. Hinman, *op. cit.*, II, 480–6; he points out (II, 522) that it was unusual for
only one compositor, instead of two, to be employed on a play. He finds no
evidence of proof-correction in quire Y (II, 481–2), nor in quire Z apart from
the knocking down of three inking space quads (II, 485), which may have been
accidental. The fact that the misprints and the wrong numbering of p. 265
(Z1) as 273 are uncorrected likewise suggests that no proof-reading took place
before or during the printing.

clean',[1] that is, remarkably free from textual corruption and obscurity, mislining of verse, and wrong attribution of speeches, though it has its share of evident misprints, many of which were corrected in the Second Folio of 1632, and though there are instances where the compositor misread his copy, notably at I. iii. 96 ('coole my' for 'curle by'), ii. v. 145 ('become' for 'borne'), and iii. iv. 70 ('langer' for 'tang'). At I. v. 168 S.D. he printed *Enter Violenta*, because (as R. K. Turner explains[2]) he had set the page in *All's Well* on which the name occurs (it had been Shakespeare's original name for Diana), and, beginning the typesetting of *Twelfth Night* with Y3^v, he expanded the *Viola* of the stage direction into *Violenta*. The copy's speech-headings, being presumably *Vio.* as they are in the Folio, did not show him his error.

This general cleanness of the text led Wilson[3] to conclude that the copy was 'a theatrical prompt-book or a transcript therefrom'; Greg, with some reservations, concurred, as have most later writers on the subject.[4] Turner, however, argues strongly against the possibility that the copy was a prompt-book, and gives two reasons for believing that it was a transcript of some kind.

1. The ends of Acts I, II, and IV are annotated *Finis Actus Primus*, etc. (At the end of Act III the notation was presumably overlooked.) These annotations must derive from copy, since they are almost unknown in the Folio.[5] Being 'more decorative than functional', they proceed either from author or scribe, and their absence from

1. W. W. Greg, *The Shakespeare First Folio* (1955), p. 296.

2. See Preface, p. x and List of Abbreviations, p. xv.

3. N.C.S., p. 89.

4. Greg, *op. cit.*, p. 296, pointing out that the directions at II. ii. S.D. (*Enter Viola and Maluolio, at seuerall doores*) and at IV. ii. 21 (*Maluolio within*) need not have come from the prompt-book but could equally well have been supplied by the author. Cf. W. T. Jewkes, *Act Division in Elizabethan and Jacobean Plays* (1958), p. 177: 'There does not seem to be much dispute that the copy from which the printer worked was probably a prompt-book or a transcript made for the printer.' Jewkes regards the longest directions, such as those at the beginning of I. i, I. iv, and II. ii, as 'probably originally the author's', while others, such as *Catch sung* (II. iii. 72), *Musicke playes* (II. iv. 14), *Musicke* (II. iv. 50), and *Maluolio within* (IV. ii. 21), 'are possibly the prompter's'. S. Musgrove (ed.), *Twelfth Night* (Fountainwell Drama Texts, 1969), p. 9, says that the copy 'may have been a prompt-book, but the clean text more probably suggests a transcript [i.e., from a prompt-book]'.

5. The only other instances are at the end of Act I of *LLL.*, and at the end of Act I of *Gent.* In the first instance, the *Finis Actus Primus* is a space-filler at the foot of a column and is not from the copy (Q 1598: cf. Greg, *op. cit.*, p. 223). In the second instance, *Finis* is probably from the copy, a transcript by Ralph Crane (*ibid.*, p. 217).

any texts (including quartos) derived directly from his foul papers shows that they 'did not originate with Shakespeare'.[1]

2. Orsino is always *Duke* in the stage directions and the speech headings, but though in the text he is called a duke three times in I. ii and a fourth time in the first line of I. iv, he is elsewhere called a count, twice in I. iii and fifteen times in the rest of the play (from I. iv. 9 onwards). It is most unlikely that Shakespeare or a prompter would normalize the directions and headings while allowing the discrepancy in the text to stand, and much more probable that the normalizing is the work of a scribe.[2]

Turner maintains that the transcript was not from a prompt-book but from Shakespeare's foul papers. He notes that the stage directions and speech headings are not more characteristic of prompt-book origin than they are characteristic of authorial origin. Greg has stated that the general characteristics of prompt-copy are 'the appearance of actors' names duplicating those of (usually minor) characters, possibly the general appearance of directions a few lines early, and warnings for actors and properties to be in readiness'.[3] The first of these characteristics is not found in *Twelfth Night*. The only significantly early entrance-direction (discounting, that is, Maria's insignificant one at II. v. 185, immediately prior to Sir Andrew's 'Nor I neither', with which her entrance coincides) is that of Malvolio at III. iv. 15.[4] By Greg's own showing

1. They could, of course, originate with a scribe copying a prompt-book and adding them on his own initiative. Turner is establishing that the prompt-book itself can hardly have been their source. He remarks that it was Compositor C who set the two *finises* mentioned in the preceding note and that Compositor B never uses the term except in *Tw.N.*, where he is therefore following copy.

2. Turner points out that it is only when Orsino is being mentioned by others that his title is used; when he is addressed, it is either 'by name or by such general honorifics as "my lord", "your lordship", or "sir"' (unless the Clown is punning on his ducal title when he says 'Put your grace in your pocket', v. i. 30). The copyist may well have understood that he was free to normalize the directions and speech headings but not to tamper with the text (unlike those eighteenth-century editors who consistently changed 'cousin' to 'uncle' every time Sir Toby's relationship to Olivia was mentioned, and who altered 'count' to 'duke' throughout the dialogue).

3. Greg, *op. cit.*, p. 142.

4. This misplaced entry can, I think, be most satisfactorily explained as resulting from the copyist's confusion while transcribing Shakespeare's foul papers. It is notable that the Folio's central placing of the entry makes Olivia's l. 14 into two lines (i.e., its second part returns to the left-hand margin as usually happens when a line is divided between two speakers). Assuming that Shakespeare did not trouble to write in Maria's *exit* (which is implied in Olivia's command), and that he wrote *Enter Malvolio* marginally, the scribe might naturally place that direction centrally and immediately after Olivia finishes speaking to Maria.

the technical directions might equally proceed from foul papers as from a prompt-book.[1] I agree with Turner that some of the directions are less precise than one would expect if the copy were the prompt-book or its transcript: such are *and other Lords* (I. i. S.D.), *and Saylors* (I. ii. S.D.), *and Attendants* (I. iv. 8 S.D.). Olivia's attendants are omitted altogether from I. v (in which Olivia once, and the Clown three times, bids them 'take away the fool'); and Maria at III. i. 85 S.D. is named simply as *Gentlewoman*.[2] There is a general, and in my opinion highly significant, carelessness about providing entrances and exits, not only for minor characters (Who calls forth the holy father at v. i. 140? Who pursues Malvolio and entreats him to a peace at v. i. 379?) but for major characters too. Malvolio's 'I'll be reveng'd on the whole pack of you!' (v. i. 377) is so obviously an exit-line that it would not need marking in a prompt-book. Maria's exits at III. iv. 14 and at IV. ii. 3 present no problem, being again obviously implied; but those at III. iv. 63[3] and III. iv. 202[4] are different. Similarly Fabian's exit and re-entry at v. i. 314 and 325 are obvious, but what of his unspecified exit with Sir Toby, the Clown, and Sir Andrew at v. i. 206?[5] The most problematical exit of all is the

---

1. See p. xix, n. 3, above, and R. B. McKerrow ('The Elizabethan Printer and Dramatic Manuscripts', *The Library*, 4th series, XII, 273–5), who says that a man of the theatre would tend to give stage directions 'in the form of directions to the actors (as they might appear in a prompt-book) rather than descriptions of action viewed from the front of the theatre. . . . Probably he would use either type of direction as it happened to occur to him.'

2. Possibly because she has no lines to speak on this occasion.

3. Since Olivia goes to meet 'Cesario', and Maria to fetch Sir Toby, it is desirable that they go out in different directions: possibly this is implied by giving Olivia an *exit* to show that Maria does not accompany her.

4. Since she takes no further part in the scene, Maria obviously goes out, but in the absence of any direction it is uncertain what the others do. Sir Toby and Fabian may either go out or merely retire, though I should have thought, by analogy with III. i. 94–5, 'Let the garden door be shut, and leave me to my hearing', that their presence anywhere on stage would be incongruous with Olivia's intimate dialogue with Viola; it may, of course, be fairly argued that III. i. 94–5 motivates Sir Andrew's jealousy and is introduced for that reason, and also because the dialogue is to continue till the end of the scene.

5. Fabian's exit at this point is by no means positively implied in the text (as is that of the Clown, who has entered supporting Sir Toby). It is arguable that editors introduce it in order to make sense of l. 278 S.D. (*Enter Clowne with a Letter, and Fabian* in F), for, unless Fabian leaves the stage with the wounded knights, he is still on stage, where indeed he has been since the beginning of the scene. I conjecture that Shakespeare originally intended to bring in Fabian (and Malvolio's letter) for the first time at l. 278 S.D., that the existing opening dialogue between him and the Clown, about the letter, was Shakespeare's

Clown's somewhere during II. iii (see commentary at II. iii. 117), where it looks as though Shakespeare decided towards the end of the scene that he should have got the Clown off stage earlier, leaving Sir Toby and Sir Andrew to finish it as they began it, but that he never went back over the scene to write in an exit for him. Doubtless the problem was discovered and solved in performance by Shakespeare's actors, as it has had to be by all actors since, but one would expect the solution, once found, to have been thereupon entered in the prompt-book.

I see in these places signs that Shakespeare was sometimes in two minds during the composition of the play, and these signs furnish more support for Turner's view that his foul papers, not the prompt-book, lie behind the transcript.[1]

The almost certain mislining at III. i. 122–7 strengthens the probability that the copy consisted of Shakespeare's foul papers in which the verse was revised *currente calamo* (see commentary).

An alteration of plan, this time involving the use of characters in the plot, seems to occur between II. iii. 173–5 (where Maria resolves that the Clown, as well as Sir Toby and Sir Andrew, shall observe Malvolio's construction of the letter she will drop in his way) and II. v. 1 (where the third watcher is actually Fabian, a new character, who will be put to further use later to perform functions the Clown cannot, as well as to prevent his too frequent appearances).[2]

---

afterthought, intended to give the Clown something to be doing on stage before being accosted by Orsino (he could hardly repeat the beginning of III. i); and that in writing the existing opening dialogue he forgot that, later in the scene, while the Clown was to exit and re-enter, Fabian was merely to enter. See n. 2 below.

1. A change of plan involving stage action may also underlie the question of whether Fabian and Viola do or do not leave the stage at III. iv. 277. See commentary.

2. Fabian is specially valuable as a 'straight man' with a twinkle of inner comedy in III. ii and III. iv (Sir Andrew's jealousy, Sir Toby's encounter with Malvolio, the preparations for the duel), and at the very end of the play, with his long speech, he is invaluable. Roy Walker, *Shakespeare Survey*, 12 (1959), 130, footnote 15 (reviewing productions of *Tw.N.* in 1958), remarks that Fabian's lines 'can mostly be plausibly distributed, or returned, to Feste, Sir Andrew and Maria. The opening of the final scene, v. i, is particularly suspect. Why introduce the business of the letter only to leave it aside for some 300 lines, during which Fabian neither speaks nor is spoken to and may or may not be on stage? Was not Maria, rather than Fabian, meant to say "myself and Toby / Set this device against Malvolio here" [v. i. 358–9]?' I think it unlikely that Maria was ever meant to speak verse. For the letter, see p. xx, n. 5, above. See also A. C. Sprague, 'Shakespeare's Unnecessary Characters', *Shakespeare Survey*, 20 (1967), 80: 'The indefiniteness of the role all but ceases when we

There must also be considered the inconsistency in the text as to Orsino's title: R. K. Turner states that the two titles are not employed synonymously by Shakespeare, pointing out that in his comedies his dukes always possess the dignity of rule and often of age, whereas his counts are younger and function primarily as lovers rather than as rulers or military leaders. He therefore concludes that Shakespeare 'either elevated or reduced Orsino in rank', and made him a count from I. iii onwards, the use of 'Duke' in I. iv. I being simply an authorial lapse. I have some difficulty in accepting this view, since Orsino's role as lover is fundamental to the story, and prefer to regard the inconsistency in the text between duke and count as one to which Shakespeare was indifferent, since his Orsino is in the unique position of being both the head of the state (with the power of life and death over enemy aliens like Antonio) and a young man in love.[1] Claudio in *Much Ado*, Bertram in *All's Well*, and Paris in *Romeo and Juliet* all have titled superiors (Don Pedro, the King of France, and the Prince of Verona), whereas Orsino has neither titled superiors nor titled inferiors: it is therefore possible that, in this play alone, Shakespeare did allow the same person to be both duke and count according as he exhibited the different aspects of his personality and office.

2 THE QUESTION OF REVISION

Another alleged inconsistency is the basis of the first of three arguments that Shakespeare rewrote some part or parts of the play either in the course of composition or after its production by his company.

(a) *The song and the dialogue surrounding it in II. iv*

The argument for revision here was forcefully expounded by J. Dover Wilson in the New Cambridge Shakespeare edition,[2] and, to my mind, no less forcefully refuted by S. L. Bethell in *Shakespeare and the Popular Dramatic Tradition*.[3] Wilson, following

---

reach the theatre and Fabian is embodied by a particular actor. In the theatre his enjoyment of the comic proceedings not only accompanies but intensifies our own.'

1. Viola's question 'Who governs here?' (I. ii. 24) is a very natural one, and, since Shakespeare's counts never govern, the answer she receives seems the only proper one, in which it would be impossible to substitute 'count'. It may be added that in Riche's story Apolonius is a duke, as was the contemporary Orsino who had recently visited England.

2. N.C.S., pp. 91–5.

3. Bethell, *op. cit.* (1944), pp. 137–44.

and quoting a suggestion originally made by F. G. Fleay in 1876,[1] drew attention to Viola's proposal to serve the Duke as a singer and an instrumentalist (I. ii. 55–9), a proposal which is never realized in the play; he interpreted II. iv. 2–3 as Orsino's request that Viola should sing the previous night's song, and interpreted Curio's statement that the proper singer is not present as Shakespeare's palpable substitution of the Clown for Viola; he also accepted Richmond Noble's conjecture that the substitution occurred because 'on the occasion of a revival there was no boy available capable both of taking such a part as Viola's and of singing', while there was a comedian highly talented as a singer, who was consequently allotted both this song and additional ones.[2] Bethell rejoined that Viola's proposal in I. ii is merely her means of entering the Duke's service and gives no grounds for assuming that she was originally meant to sing the song in II. iv; that Orsino was not asking her to sing the song but only to have it sung for him; that it is perfectly in character for him to plead where he might have commanded, to remember the song but not the singer, and to expatiate on its beauty to Cesario even though Cesario had heard it on the previous night; and that it is most unlikely that 'the company no longer had a boy-actor who could struggle through a song.' In preferring Bethell's view to Wilson's I rejoice to concur with M. M. Mahood's critical statement (which she amply supports by critical analysis):

> There are no awkwardnesses that suggest revision. . . . The scene is a dramatic climax, perfectly conceived and perfectly executed. . . . Shakespeare in fact speaks 'masterly' in this scene, and it is hard to believe that the writing of it was not part of his original inspiration.[3]

(b) The use of 'Jove' in the play

Wilson draws attention to the statute of 27 May 1606 whereby 'For the preventing and avoyding of the great Abuse of the Holy Name of God in Stageplayes, Interludes, Maygames, Shewes,

1. *Shakespeare Manual* (1876), pp. 227–9.
2. Richmond Noble, *Shakespeare's Use of Song* (1923), pp. 80–1, 87. Noble believed this 'final substantial' revision to have taken place between 1603 and 1606, and related the Clown's epilogue-song to the stanza with the same refrains in *Lr.*, III. ii. 74–7, which he regarded as reflecting the novelty and popularity of that song.
3. Mahood, *ed. cit.*, p. 19. Musgrove, *ed. cit.*, p. 10, agrees. Turner likewise judges that the Clown's participation contributes importantly to the mood of the scene, though (like Fleay and Wilson) he is uneasy about the prose (which I think Bethell fully justifies as 'a statement of hard fact: Orsino's passion may

and such like', a fine of £10 was decreed against anyone who in such performances should 'jestingly or prophanely speake or use the holy Name of God or of Christ Jesus, or of the Holy Ghoste or of the Trinitie',[1] and notes that 'the frequent use of "Jove" in the play where we should naturally expect "God"' is usually explained as its direct result, and hence as an aspect of revision;[2] he has, however, a fancy for revision of a different sort, and postulates that 'Shakespeare himself was handling the text' after the passing of the Act, and, in a jocular spirit, introduced additional apostrophes to Jove in the mouths of Malvolio (II. v. 173, 178; III. iv. 75, 83) and Sir Toby (IV. ii. 12, 'Jove bless thee, Master Parson').[3] R. K. Turner replies that 'the holy Name of God still appears, and about twice as often as the supposed substitute', and that Jove is not inappropriately invoked in Illyria (as by the Clown, III. i. 45, who also invokes Mercury, I. v. 97). There is, accordingly, no reason to believe that Shakespeare retouched the play after the passing of the Act, and if the printer's copy was a transcript of Shakespeare's foul papers there is no reason to believe that his original text had been altered by anyone else to comply with the Act.

(c) Possible topical allusions subsequent to 1601

Theobald's firm belief that Sir Toby's advice to Sir Andrew about his challenge to Cesario (III. ii. 43–4), 'If thou thou'st him some thrice, it shall not be amiss', was an allusion 'directly levelled at the Attorney-General Coke', who happened to use the insulting second-person form three times in succession at Raleigh's trial in November 1603, is, I think, now held by few.[4] Wilson

---

require the song, but the singer is not present'), and also remarks that 'oddly, Feste is called by name only here'. But Orsino's question 'Who was it?' makes it desirable to give him a proper name and something of a history, and this Curio's answer supplies. 'The Lady Olivia's clown, my lord' would seem too bald a reply, almost accusing Orsino of not noticing the obvious. (It is worth pointing out—what I do not think has been commented on—that a theatre audience never learns Viola's real name till less than two hundred lines from the end of the last scene, though it might have been introduced into Sebastian's dialogue with Antonio in II. i.)

1. Printed in Chambers, *The Elizabethan Stage* (Oxford, 1923), IV, 338–9.

2. In these instances Halliwell and Hudson independently regarded 'God' as Shakespeare's original word.

3. N.C.S., p. 97.

4. Theobald, *ed. cit.* (1733), *ad loc.* Wilson, N.C.S., who quotes Coke's words *ad loc.*, himself rejects the suggestion, though saying that 'many' accept it.

interprets III. i. 19–21 and 24–5 ('But indeed, words are very rascals, since bonds disgraced them' and 'words are grown so false, I am loath to prove reason with them') and III. ii. 12–13 ('I will prove it legitimate, sir, upon the oaths of judgment and reason') as referring to the Jesuit doctrine of equivocation current at the time of the Gunpowder Plot trial of Father Henry Garnett (March 1606).[1] But much simpler explanations are preferable, and Wilson's interpretation of the second passage is irrelevant, since Fabian is speaking about interpreting evidence, not about swearing to facts.[2] A third topicality, this time not political but personal, is proposed by Sisson by way of explaining Malvolio's cryptic 'example' of greatness achieved by, or thrust upon, a man of inferior social station (II. v. 39–40), 'The Lady of the Strachy married the yeoman of the wardrobe': he supposes the statement to refer to the wife of William Strachy (a shareholder in the Blackfriars theatre in 1606) and to the 'tireman' or wardrobe-master of the same theatre, whose name was David Yeomans.[3] Unfortunately, since nothing discreditable is known of these two persons as yet, Sisson's conjecture must remain no more than conjecture: the curious may, however, live in hope. It should be noted that, if the printer's copy was a transcript from foul papers, the insertion of any topical allusions after composition is as unlikely as that of alterations to comply with the Act against profanity of 1606: such changes to the text might find a place in a prompt-book, but there would be no point in inserting them into the papers from which the prompt-book was compiled.

3 CONCLUSION

The probability is that the printer's copy was a transcript of Shakespeare's foul papers, that these gave the text of the play as it was originally written, and that nothing was added with the exception of what may be called editorial decoration, namely the inscribing of the act-endings and of the headings of acts and scenes.

1. N.C.S., pp. 97–100.
2. See commentary, *ad loc*. Shakespeare does not even use the word 'equivocation' (as he does, quite non-politically, in *Ham.*, v. i. 134). Admittedly the word could hardly find a place in the dialogue, but I think it would be necessary if the spectators were to be directed towards the topical idea. His treatment of the 'equivocator' passage in *Mac.* (II. ii. 10–14) is completely different and obviously topical.
3. Sisson, *New Readings*, I, 188–91.

2 DATE AND TITLE

The latest limit of the play's composition is established by an entry in a small octavo notebook[1] kept by John Manningham when he was studying law in the Middle Temple. Though generally known as Manningham's Diary, it is better described as a book of memoranda of all sorts, the entries being made without systematic classification and without consistent chronology. The entry relating to *Twelfth Night* is the first entry for February 1601 (= 1602) and occurs about half-way down the page (f.10):

Febr: 1601/

at our feast
2/. wee had a play called [mid *crossed out*] Twelue night
    or what you will /./ / much like the com*m*edy of
    errors / or Menechmi in plaut*us* / but most
    like and neere to that in Italian called Inganni

    ———————

    a good practise in it to make the steward
    beleeue his Lady widdowe was in Loue wth him
    by counterfayting a lett[r] / as from his Lady in
    generall tearmes / telling him what shee
    liked best in him / and p*r*escribing his gesture
    in smiling his apparraile /&c /. And then
    when he came to practise making him beleeue
    they tooke him to be mad / : /

A line is drawn right across the page above the date-heading, and another after the entry, this being Manningham's usual way of separating the several entries one from another.

Though it has been suggested that J. P. Collier forged some entries in the diary,[2] R. K. Turner gives four convincing reasons for accepting this particular entry as genuine.[3] First, since Manningham's habit was to begin a month's entries by writing the month and year centrally, indicating days of the month by marginal numbers thereafter, he would not have left a space after this central heading if his first dated entry had been that marked 12/. referring to the arrest in London of a member of Manningham's family.[4] Secondly, Manningham's mistaken belief that Olivia was a widow must have originated in her costume (as Collier concluded in his edition of 1842), not from

1. B.M. MS. Harley 5353.
2. See S. Race, 'Manningham's Diary: the Case for Re-examination', *N. & Q.* 199 (1954), 380–3.
3. See Preface, p. x and List of Abbreviations, p. xv.
4. Collier could have not have forged the entry of 12 February, since the

any awareness of Manningham's that the corresponding character in Shakespeare's immediate source was indeed a widow,
since that source (Riche's tale of Apolonius and Silla) is not
mentioned in the entry. Thirdly, the Italian play which is mentioned, *Gl'Inganni*, was never stated to be Shakespeare's source by
Collier, who had as early as 1820 (in his *Poetical Decameron*, II, 134)
maintained the source to be Riche's tale. Fourthly, Collier
printed 'inscribing his apparraile' where others have read either
'in smiling' or 'in suiting'.[1] Turner's second, third, and fourth
points imply that, if Collier forged the entry, he practised an
extraordinarily obscure and devious deception. His first point,
in any case, proves irrefutably that the entry is genuine.

Manningham's reference to the Middle Temple performance
gives no reason to believe that this was the first production of
the play:[2] indeed, it gives three reasons for believing that it
was not. In the first place, if the play had been new Manningham
would probably have mentioned the fact. In the second place,
his deletion of 'mid' suggests that he had heard of the titles of both
A Midsummer Night's Dream and *Twelfth Night*, had hitherto
seen neither play, and hence made a momentary slip in beginning
to give the wrong title to the one he had just seen. In the third
place, his remarks about the play's resemblance to *Menaechmi* and
Gl'Inganni (meaning perhaps *Gl'Ingannati*, but quite possibly one
of the two later plays so called[3]) suggest that he had picked up
the information from somebody or other, and that therefore

---

diarist's name and circumstances were unknown until J. Hunter published his
discovery of them in *New Illustrations of Shakespeare* (1845), I, 375.

1. Collier, *History of English Dramatic Poetry* (1831), I, 327. (It is barely possible
that 'inscribing' is there a printer's error.) Hunter, *New Illustrations*, I, 365, and
J. Bruce (ed.), *The Diary of John Manningham* (Camden Society, 1868), p. 18,
read 'in smiling'. L. Hotson (*TLS*, 9 Sept. 1949, p. 585) and Jarold Ramsey
('The Importance of Manningham's Diary', *Shakespeare Studies*, 7 (1974),
328–9) read 'in suiting'. I have examined the MS. and am convinced that
Hunter and Bruce are right: the letter which Hotson and Ramsey take for a t is
clearly looped (Manningham, as far as I could ascertain in two hours' examination of the MS., never loops a t), and the angular stroke passing through this
loop in a NW/SE direction bears no resemblance to the way he crosses a t (when
he does so, he usually forms the cross-bar by returning up the downstroke);
it appears to be merely an unintended pen-mark.

2. J. Dover Wilson (N.C.S.) believes that the play was written for an Inns of
Court audience because 'the prose-scenes are full of legal jests' (p. 95). However,
legal jests are not infrequent in Shakespeare, and some of Wilson's legal
interpretations strain the natural sense of the passages where they occur (see
commentary).

3. See below, pp. xl–xli.

Twelfth Night had been on the stage long enough for there to have been talk about its sources, perhaps among the Middle Temple students when it became known what play they were going to have at their feast: any grammar-school-educated Elizabethan might have read Plautus' play, but the odds against his knowing Italian playwrights' work at first hand were much longer, unless he were a particularly avid reader of Italian plays (as, no doubt, some students were).

The question, then, if we infer that *Twelfth Night* was not new when Manningham saw it, is how new, or how old, it was.

In attempting to answer this question, the only available evidence is internal evidence (from the play itself). There is no extant piece of external evidence relating to its date apart from the entry already quoted from Manningham's notebook. It is necessary to insist upon this fact, since Leslie Hotson has made much use of contemporary records to support his contention that *Twelfth Night* was written for a first performance on the evening of 6 January (Twelfth Night, the final night of the traditional twelve days of Christmas festivities) 1601. On that evening the Queen's guest of honour was Don Virginio Orsino, Duke of Bracciano, an accomplished and brave young nobleman then aged twenty-eight, who wrote to his wife that he was entertained with 'a mingled comedy, with pieces of music and dances [*una commedia mescolata, con musiche e balli*]'.[1] The Lord Chamberlain (Lord Hunsdon, the patron of the company to which Shakespeare belonged) had written a memorandum in readiness for 'the play after supper':

> to confer with my Lord Admirall and the Master of the Revells for takeing order generally with the players to make choyse of [the] play that shalbe best furnished with rich apparell, have great variety and change of Musicke and daunces, and of a Subject that may be most pleasing to her Majestie,[2]

and in consequence the Lord Chamberlain's Men received payment for a play 'showed before her highnes' on 'Twelfth day at night'.[3] It will be noted that the play is nowhere named, nor is any hint given as to its subject: it is not even known to have been one of Shakespeare's. Hotson's assumption that the play was

---

1. L. Hotson, *The First Night of 'Twelfth Night'* (1954), p. 202. The information which he gives about the visit itself is of considerable interest.

2. *Ibid.*, pp. 180–1.

3. David Cook (ed.), *Dramatic Records in the Declared Accounts of the Treasurer of the Chamber, 1558–1642* (*Malone Society Collections VI*, Oxford, 1962), p. 31.

Twelfth Night is therefore wholly conjectural,[1] and ultimately rests upon the occurrence in it of the name Orsino, and upon a multitude of supposedly topical allusions to persons,[2] to the place of performance (the royal palace at Whitehall), and to 6 January as the Feast of the Epiphany (the visit of the Three Kings to Bethlehem to worship Christ). Weighty objections can be brought against his assumption. There are no dances, nor opportunities for dances, in *Twelfth Night*;[3] there is no certainty whatever that its subject, in particular the use made of her guest's name, would be at all pleasing to her Majesty; and it is most unlikely that Shakespeare could have composed it and the actors rehearsed it between 25 December 1600 (when the date of Orsino's visit became known) and 6 January 1601, or that the Lord Chamberlain would have risked so tight a schedule for so important an occasion.[4]

Though Hotson's conclusion as to the occasion (and hence the date) of *Twelfth Night* is unacceptable, Orsino's visit has long been connected with the name which Shakespeare chose for the Duke in the play,[5] and there is no good reason to suppose this choice merely accidental:[6] Shakespeare, indeed, may have been

1. The conjecture had been previously made, simply on the basis of Orsino's visit, by J. W. Draper, *The 'Twelfth Night' of Shakespeare's Audience* (1950), pp. 258–9.

2 There is no sound basis for regarding Malvolio as a satirical personal portrait of Sir William Knollys (Hotson, pp. 93–118) or of any other individual. A. Thaler, 'The Original Malvolio?', *Shakespeare Association Bulletin*, VII (1932), 57 ff., who proposes William Ffarington, mentions other identifications which have been put forward.

3. If we are to assume (as is likely enough) that it was one of Shakespeare's comedies which was performed, *Much Ado About Nothing* is a strong candidate. It has two songs ('Sigh no more, ladies', II. iii, and 'Pardon, goddess of the night', v. iii) and two dances (the masked ball in II. i, and the final dance demanded by Benedick), and could be called *'una comedia mescolata'*, not only in the sense of mingling high- and low-comedy characters, but also in that of mingling wholly comic elements with much more serious and potentially tragic ones (the villainy of Don John, and Claudio's consequent repudiation of Hero in IV. i).

4. A further objection to Hotson's opinion is that the Lord Chamberlain would have been, in this event, commissioning a new play, not choosing an existing one (as is implied in his memorandum). While it is true that plays have been written in less than a fortnight, Shakespeare's average output appears to have been two plays a year; it is worth remembering that Jonson considered his own rapid writing of *Volpone* a notable piece of work: ' 'Tis knowne, fiue weekes fully pen'd it' (Prologue, l. 16).

5. G. Sarrazin, 'Zur Chronologie von Shakespeares Dichtungen', *Shakespeare Jahrbuch*, XXXII (1896), 168.

6. The name Orsino does not occur in any of the play's known possible sources; though Hunter drew attention to its occurrence in a bound-up volume

one of the actors who performed before the Queen and her guest, and may have carried away a vivid impression of the handsome nobleman who bore 'a generall report of a very courtlike and compleat gentleman'.[1] It is, of course, arguable that he was already composing *Twelfth Night* before Orsino's visit, and named his Duke in the course of composition, but the fact that Orsino's name appears as early as I. ii. 28 (in a line of verse) makes it more likely that composition began some time in or after January 1601. This conjecture is consistent with the internal evidence, which will be taken in the order in which it appears in the play.

1. The ludicrous sung dialogue between Sir Toby and the Clown, beginning 'Farewell, dear heart, since I must needs be gone' (II. iii. 102), is so closely based on a song first extant in Robert Jones's *First Booke of Songes and Ayres* (published in 1600)[2] as to suggest that the song was new and popular and that for this very reason Shakespeare gave it an incongruous context and made the appropriate alterations: by 1601 he could have satisfied himself of the song's popularity.

2. There are two references to 'the Sophy' or Shah of Persia. After witnessing Malvolio's reading of the letter, Fabian exclaims 'I will not give my part of this sport for a pension of thousands to be paid from the Sophy' (II. v. 180–1) and in the duel scene Sir Toby sums up the skill of Sir Andrew's opponent by telling him 'They say he has been fencer to the Sophy' (III. iv. 283–4). These are generally accepted as allusions to a subject of topical interest between the summer of 1598 and the end of 1601, the journey of Sir Anthony Sherley (or Shirley) to the Sophy's court. Sir Anthony's project was known by 2 June 1598, when one of his men mentioned it in a letter.[3] Between November 1599 and April 1601 he made visits, purportedly as the Sophy's ambassador, to Moscow, to Prague and to Rome (where Will Kempe saw him),[4] meantime leaving his brother Robert in Persia as a hostage and also as a military adviser. His exploits

---

of Italian plays which included *Gl'Ingannati* (see below, p. xli, n. 2), there is no historical evidence that Shakespeare saw the volume.

1. *The Letters of John Chamberlain*, ed. Norman Egbert McClure (Philadelphia, 1939), I, 115.

2. Its absence from the Stationers' Register makes it impossible to establish an earliest limit for its publication within the year 1600.

3. Samuel C. Chew, *The Crescent and the Rose* (New York and Oxford, 1937), p. 243. R. K. Turner kindly directed my attention to this book.

4. Chew, p. 275, citing the diary of William Smith of Abingdon (B.M. Sloane MS. 414), fol. 56. It is quoted by E. K. Chambers, *The Elizabethan Stage*, II, 326.

were recorded in two publications, *A True Report of Sir Anthonie Shierlies Journey* and *A New and Large Discourse of the Travels of Sir Anthony Shirley*: the first of these, ascribed on its title page to two of his party who had accompanied him in his earlier travels, was published in September 1600 and ordered to be suppressed on 2 October and again on 7 September of the following year;[1] the second was written by William Parry, another member of Sherley's expedition, and was published late in 1601. While it cannot be proved, from either of Shakespeare's phrases, that he had read either book, his first allusion comes as a surprise and has every appearance of being inserted for its topicality, since there is no other reason why the Sophy's munificence should come into Fabian's mind; the second allusion, besides being a follow-up to the first, fits more naturally into its context (a duel in Illyria), and there is no need to relate it specifically to Robert Sherley's military employment in Persia. It would seem, then, that the existence of one or both of the published accounts was known to Shakespeare and to his audience, which would suggest a date no earlier than the autumn of 1600, and probably rather later.[2]

3. The Clown, agreeing to announce Viola's arrival to Olivia, remarks

> My lady is within, sir. I will conster to them whence you come; who you are and what you would are out of my welkin. I might say 'element', but the word is overworn. (III. i. 56–60)

In Dekker's *Satiromastix* the phrase 'out of his element' is several times treated as a verbal mannerism of Jonson (represented in the play by Horace, 'the humorous poet'). It was suggested in 1887[3]

1. Wilson, N.C.S., p. 96, attributes the suppression to Sherley's being 'a strong adherent of the Essex party', but the fact that Parry's book was not similarly suppressed suggests that the suppression was due to the first book's not being entered under licence in the Stationers' Register, as Parry's was on 11 Nov. 1601 (Arber, *op. cit.*, III, 195).

2. R. K. Turner is more cautious and declines to argue for a more limited date than 1598–1601 on the basis of the evidence.

3. By R. W. Boodle (*Shakespeariana*, March 1887, IV, 116, quoted by Furness in his commentary on the passage in *Twelfth Night*: 'Speaking of Captain Tucca, he says, "'tis out of his element to traduce me; I am too well ranked, Asinine, to be stabbed with his dudgeon wit." [I. ii. 134–6] Asinius, Horace's friend, also uses the expression as a favourite one with "his ningle" (*i.e.* Horace): "Marry, for reading any book, I'll take my death upon't (as my ningle says) 'tis out of my element." [I. ii. 186–8] Lastly, the words are among the things that Horace is forced to abjure: "*Sir Vaughan*: Thirdly, and last of all saving one, when your plays are misliked at Court, you shall not cry mew like a puss-cat, and say you are glad you write out of the courtiers' element. *Tucca.* Let the element alone, 'tis out of thy reach." [V. ii. 324–7]' Boodle's quotations

that the Clown's reference to the word's being overworn depends for its humour on the audience's familiarity with Dekker's play, and this interpretation has won general acceptance. *Satiromastix* was performed by the Lord Chamberlain's Men and the Children of Paul's in 1601, as a rejoinder to Jonson's *Poetaster* (late spring, 1601), and entered in the Stationers' Register on 11 November of that year.[1] The allusion is accordingly consistent with a date of 1601 for *Twelfth Night*.

4. Fabian, insisting that Olivia showed favour to Orsino's page in Sir Andrew's sight in order to provoke her suitor to show his wit and valour, describes her disdain in the following figurative language:

> you are now sailed into the north of my lady's opinion, where you will hang like an icicle on a Dutchman's beard . . .
> (III. ii. 24–6)

It is universally agreed that the reference is to the Arctic voyage of William Barentz or Barents, a Dutchman from Friesland, round the north of Nova Zembla in 1596–7. An English translation of Gerrit de Veer's account of the voyage was entered in the Stationers' Register on 13 June 1598, having a title almost a full quarto page in length which goes into details of 'the feirce Beares and other Sea monsters and mervelous could [i.e., cold] and howe in the last voyage the shippe is besett in Iyce and thatt owr men beinge vnder 76 degrees of Nova sembla built them a howse and Remayned there 10 monethes . . .'.[2] The voyage and its hardships must have been common knowledge when Shakespeare wrote *Twelfth Night*, and the early date of this account does not assist in the precise dating of the play.

5. Maria's equally grotesque image of Malvolio—'he does smile his face into more lines than is in the new map with the augmentation of the Indies' (III. ii. 75–7)—is generally agreed to be taken from a map first published in 1599[3] and reissued in the

---

have been given references from the edition of Fredson Bowers, Vol. 1 (1953), and, in his second, 'my' is corrected to 'any' from the same edition: again I am indebted to R. K. Turner for these references and the correction.

1. Chambers, *The Elizabethan Stage*, III, 293, for the date of *Satiromastix*; III, 366, for that of *Poetaster* (cf. C. H. Herford and P. and E. Simpson's edition of Jonson, IX, 189).

2. Arber, *op. cit.*, III, 118: Furness believes that this book furnished Shakespeare with 'stories of icicles on Dutchmen's beards'. The first extant edition (that of 1609), however, contains no such detail.

3. C. H. Coote, *New Shakespeare Society Transactions*, 1877–9, p. 88 (14 June 1878), who confirmed H. Hallam's identification (1839) of the map as this one,

following year with minor additions. The augmented Indies are the East Indies (not America, as stated by Wilson),[1] shown on the first issue in full with the added northern coastline of New Holland (Australia), and the lines 'are the rhumb-lines which form a very striking feature of the map—radiating out from their centres exactly like wrinkles about eyes'.[2] This map could still be called 'new' within a few years of its appearance (in fact as long as it continued to be the latest map), so its existence in 1599 does not increase the possibility of a date before 1601 for *Twelfth Night*.

R. K. Turner bases an attractive theory upon the fact that *Twelfth Night* is the only one of Shakespeare's plays to have two alternative titles, and that the second of these, *What You Will*, is also the title of a play by Marston, which in all probability appeared early in 1601, between Jonson's *Cynthia's Revels* (Winter, 1600) and *Poetaster* (late Spring, 1601).[3] He proposes that '*What You Will* may have been Shakespeare's working title, one adopted before Marston preempted it in the Spring of 1601 and one which required modification before the play was made public', and adds that Marston plays upon the phrase 'what you will' half a dozen times in his dialogue. His theory, it must be allowed, omits to explain why Shakespeare did not abandon the title *What You Will* altogether upon the appearance of Marston's play, but this omission presents no objection to its acceptance. On the contrary, in my opinion, it is very possible that Shakespeare retained the original title in order to make it absolutely clear to his audiences that the new title *Twelfth Night* bore no more significance than had the casual titles of his two previous comedies, *Much Ado About Nothing*[4] and *As You Like It*, and that it was (as Pepys was later

---

describes it in detail (quoted by Furness). It is reproduced in *Shakespeare's England*, 1, 174. The one possible objection to the identification is that 'the new map with the augmentation of the Indies' sounds like a title but is not printed on the map itself; but W. A. Wright (quoted by Furness), who raised the point, did not press it.

1. N.C.S., p. 148; but see Coote.
2. Wilson, *ibid.*
3. Chambers, *The Elizabethan Stage*, III, 364 (for the date of *Cynthia's Revels*); Herford and Simpson's Jonson, I, 27 (for that of *What You Will*).
4. I agree with R. A. Foakes (ed. *Ado*, New Penguin Shakespeare, 1968, p. 125), that the title is 'deliberately puzzling' and that its direct reference is to the events of the Claudio–Hero plot; but I disagree with his acceptance of P. A. Jorgensen's contention (*Redeeming Shakespeare's Words*, Berkeley, 1962) that it contains a pun on 'noting' and hence refers to 'people observing and overhearing one another'. The word 'note' occurs in only five passages of the play, and only in Don Pedro's dialogue with Balthazar (II. iii) is it punned upon; 'noted' and 'notable' occur only once each, again with merely literal

to complain) irrelevant to the story and to performance on 6 January (on which date he saw it in 1663). If so, the whirligig of time has brought in its revenges, since Shakespeare's capriciousness has exposed both titles to attempts at explanation: on the one hand, the sense of 'What You Will' (i.e., whatever you like to call it) has been strained into 'What you desire', the 'you' being either the spectators or the characters;[1] on the other 'Twelfth Night' has been subjected both to super-subtlety (in the search for allusions to the Epiphany)[2] and to downright simplicity ('it was got up on purpose to be Acted on Twelfth Night').[3] It seems to me that for a Twelfth Night play there could be no title more barren than *Twelfth Night*. If we believe that Shakespeare used *Gl'Ingannati*[4] as a source we may also believe that he took his title from a phrase in its prologue.

> The story is new and taken from nowhere but their [the authors'] own industrious pates whence also are taken your lots on Twelfth Night [footnote: *la notte di beffana* (Epiphany)] . . .[5]

Yet even if Shakespeare had read the passage and had recognized 'la notte di beffana' as meaning 'Twelfth Night', there is nothing in the context of that prologue to lead him towards choosing this title for his comedy, and I prefer to think that he chose it merely for its general festive associations.

To sum up: in the absence of any allusions which would have lost their point by 1601, there is nothing against taking Don Virginio Orsino's visit as the *terminus a quo* and the Middle Temple performance as the *terminus ad quem*. The apparently firm connection with Dekker's *Satiromastix*, which 'had probably been on the stage not long before'[6] its entry in the Stationers' Register on 11 November 1601, and which must have been acted recently enough for the allusion in *Twelfth Night* III. i. 56–60 to be generally understood, suggests that Shakespeare was writing

---

meaning. Reference to any concordance will show that these seven occurrences are not a high score for a Shakespeare play; he used the words frequently.

1. S. Nagarajan, 'What You Will: a suggestion', *Sh. Q.*, 10 (1959), 61–7, argues that the title relates to the theme of self-deception, and of the conflict between will and reason. Hotson, p. 158, sees a reference to Rabelais's Abbey of Theleme (*Gargantua*, bk I, ch. 57) with its motto 'Fay ce que vouldras'.

2. Hotson, pp. 145–8.

3. John Downes, *Roscius Anglicanus or, an Historical View of the Stage* (1708), p. 32.

4. See p. xxv below.

5. G. Bullough, *Narrative and Dramatic Sources of Shakespeare*, II (1958), 287.

6. Chambers, *The Elizabethan Stage*, II, 207.

the play by the middle of the year, with *Satiromastix* at least in rehearsal and probably in production,[1] and that he completed it before the year's end, with the approach of the Christmas holiday period perhaps suggesting, but not dictating, its title.

3 SOURCES

The ultimate source of Shakespeare's story in *Twelfth Night* is an Italian play, *Gl'Ingannati* (The Deceived Ones), written and presented at Siena by the Academy of the Intronati in 1531, first published at Venice in 1537, and frequently reprinted: its prologue claims, probably truthfully, that it is a wholly original composition written in three days. An immediate source is Barnabe Riche's prose tale of Apolonius and Silla, which is the second of eight 'histories' forming *Riche his Farewell to Militarie Profession* (1581), and which derives indirectly from the play by way of other prose narratives by Bandello and Belleforest, the latter being Riche's own source.[2] Shakespeare had certainly read 'Apolonius and Silla',[3] and it supplied parts of his story which are absent from *Gl'Ingannati* and from any of its known derivative versions either dramatic or narrative. Whether he had also read *Gl'Ingannati* is a matter of conjecture, and so is the question of possible influence from that play, from those plays which are translations or close imitations of it, from other Italian plays of similar type, and from the narratives which preceded Riche's.[4]

1. There was no summer closure on account of plague in 1601; 'probably during 1588–91, and certainly during 1595–1602 and 1610–16, plague was so far absent as to be practically negligible' (Chambers, *ibid.*, I, 329).

2. Riche omits, for brevity's sake, a 'long and dolorous discourse' of the heroine's, which is one of Belleforest's additions to Bandello (G. Bullough, *Narrative and Dramatic Sources of Shakespeare*, II (1958), 276).

3. Juliet's impatience for nightfall (*Rom.*, III. ii. 1–4) follows Silvio's, who 'had thought the statelie Steedes had been tired, that drawe the Chariot of the Sunne, . . . and wished that *Phaeton* had been there with a whippe' (Appendix I, p. 168). In the main source of *Rom.*, Arthur Brooke's *Romeus and Juliet*, ll. 821–6, Shakespeare found a hint ('. . . if they might have . . . The sunne bond to theyr will, if they the heavens might gyde, / Black shade of night and doubled darke should straight all over hyde.' Bullough, I, 307), but not the image of Phaeton as waggoner with a whip.

4. The sources of *Tw.N.* have been discussed by H. H. Furness, Variorum ed. (1901), pp. xiv–xxi, 326–77; M. Luce, Arden ed. (1906), pp. ix–xviii, 177–190; M. Luce, ed., *Rich's 'Apolonius and Silla', an Original of Shakespeare's 'Twelfth Night'* (London, 1912); K. Muir, *Shakespeare's Sources*, I (1957), 66–77; G. Bullough, *Narrative and Dramatic Sources of Shakespeare*, II (1958), pp. 269–372; R. Pruvost in *Études Anglaises*, XIII (1960), 1–9; J. Satin, *Shakespeare and his Sources* (Boston, 1966); and D. Orr, *Italian Renaissance Drama in England before 1625* (Chapel Hill, University of North Carolina Press, 1970), pp. 41–4.

GL'INGANNATI AND OTHER PLAYS

The plot of *Gl'Ingannati* is as follows.[1]

An old man, Virginio, has a daughter named Lelia and a son named Fabrizio. In the Sack of Rome (1527) he lost his son but took his thirteen-year-old daughter to Modena. Lelia is now (1531) sought in marriage by another old man, Gherardo, who has her father's consent. She, however, loves a young gentleman, Flamminio, and has done so since she came to Modena; he at first returned her love, but, during her absence for a year with her father, he has transferred his love to Gherardo's daughter Isabella, who does not return it. Lelia has escaped from the convent where her father has temporarily placed her, and now serves Flamminio (unrecognized) as a page called Fabio, carrying his love-messages to Isabella. Isabella has fallen in love with Fabio, who requires her to repulse Flamminio. Lelia's brother Fabrizio now arrives in Modena, with a pedant-tutor and a greedy servant. The old men mistake him for the escaped and disguised Lelia, and lock him in Isabella's room; she too mistakes him for Fabio and they both make the most of their opportunity. Flamminio meanwhile has heard that Isabella loves Fabio, but his revengeful feelings are mollified when Lelia's nurse (who has had a prominent part in the play) tells him a long story of the constancy of a woman who proves to be Lelia. He marries Lelia, and Fabrizio marries Isabella. In a subplot of three scenes, Isabella's comic suitor, a Spaniard called Giglio, is tricked out of a valuable rosary by her maid Pasquella.

Gl'Ingannati is essentially a Plautine comedy of mistaken identity. Little attempt has been made to develop the romantic aspects of its plot, Flamminio's love for Isabella, Isabella's for Lelia as Fabio, and Lelia's for Flamminio: the first of these is merely a *datum*, the second is given only one short scene (II. vi) in which the comic overhearing servants have as much to say as the principals, and only the third is dramatically exploited in two scenes (II. i, vii) in which the master tells his page that he no longer loves Lelia; in the later scene Lelia is so grieved that she nearly faints, Flamminio treats her with great solicitude and she is left to a short and disconsolate soliloquy. But much more of the play is taken up with the old men's folly, the nurse's resourcefulness, the servants' jealousy of their new fellow the page, the

1. Bullough, pp. 286–339, translates the play, omitting only the scenes wholly irrelevant to Shakespeare's (references are to this version); Furness, pp. 341–359, also prints a translation (T. L. Peacock's, expurgated) of the important scenes.

rivalry of two innkeepers for Fabrizio's custom, the mutual abuse of the Pedant and Fabrizio's servant, the comic greed of the latter, and the maidservant's tricking of the Spaniard. 'The tone is light, colloquial, at times bawdy' (Bullough, II, 273), and the indecency extends to Isabella (whose forcible discovery that Fabrizio is a man is salaciously related by Pasquella)[1] and even to Lelia, who begins her part by contemplating her risk of rape in going about disguised so early in the morning,[2] and ends it off stage in bed with Flamminio while the nurse's daughter Cittina reports to the audience the words and other sounds she hears. This is very un-like Shakespeare's treatment of Viola, which, though sometimes lighthearted, is never salacious.

The sentimental element of *Twelfth Night* is closer to that of an entertainment called *Il Sacrificio*, which the Intronati performed on the same occasion, though not on the same day, as *Gl'Ingannati*. The prologue of the play refers back to the entertainment, and both were usually printed together under the title of the latter, so that if Shakespeare read one he probably also read the other. In *Il Sacrificio* the Intronati professed themselves rebels against Cupid and followers of Minerva, and each delivered to the priest in charge of the sacrificial rite some object associated with his lady-love (such as a tear-stained handkerchief, a ring, a chain, a scarf, a pair of spectacles, an image of Cupid), and recited or sang a poem. It has not, however, been claimed that Shakespeare directly borrowed anything from *Il Sacrificio*.[3]

Many things in *Gl'Ingannati* have been thought to have pro-vided direct suggestions for *Twelfth Night*.[4] Before listing some of them, it should be said that none of them carries irresistible con-viction.

In the first place, some scholars have supposed that Shakes-peare created his characters by amalgamating traits from those of *Gl'Ingannati*: this is a theory too flimsy to bear handling.

Secondly, resemblances of incident and idea have been sought. There are overhearings: of Lelia's leave-taking of Isabella by the former's fellow-servants (pp. 307–8), and of Gherardo's dialogue

1. Bullough omits about six lines of this speech; J. Satin, p. 369, gives it in full. Both Bullough and Satin omit Cittina's short soliloquy mentioned later in this sentence (though that is no more indelicate).
2. Her whole dialogue with the nurse is vigorously worldly. In the course of it the nurse asks what Lelia would do 'if some night, seized with the accursed temptation', the master invited the page to his bed (p. 297).
3. With the one doubtful exception of the name Malvolio (see below, p. xl).
4. Bullough has noted all these instances except that of the 'gallows' (see below, p. xxxviii, which I do not think has been noticed before.

with the nurse by his own servant, who derides his old master's folly (pp. 299–300). But overhearings are common to most comedies, and neither of these is a deliberate eavesdropping like that in the letter scene of *Twelfth Night*. Talk of madness is equally common ground to many more plays than those two: the servant's pretended anxiety that his old amorous master is going mad (pp. 298–9) is just an indirect way of telling him he is a fool, while Fabrizio's belief that anyone who takes him for a woman must be mad (pp. 318–21) goes back to Plautus and to *The Comedy of Errors*; these need not have respectively suggested Olivia's genuine anxiety over the smiling cross-gartered Malvolio, and Sebastian's reaction to being attacked by Sir Andrew in mistake for Cesario. The servants' casual plan to get at the food and drink so that they can enjoy the carnival with some girls (p. 307: not shown in action) hardly connects with Sir Toby's revelry which provokes Malvolio's austerity. Nor does the nurse's hint that old Gherardo should dress fashionably to please Lelia (pp. 299–300: nothing in the play suggests that he later does) foreshadow Malvolio's important change of costume.

This leaves, thirdly, verbal resemblances. Gherardo's claim that he is 'as strong in my legs as when I was twenty-five years old' (p. 289) is an old man's sexual boast; Sir Andrew's 'strong' leg qualifies him as a dancer, not as a lover, and when he declares that he has the back-trick 'simply as strong as any man in Illyria' (I. iii. 120–1) Shakespeare is unlikely to be remembering Gherardo's anticipation of a marriage which will give him 'the finest time of any man in Modena' (p. 297), having already made Dogberry call himself 'as pretty a piece of flesh as any is in Messina' (*Ado*, IV. i. 80). We come closer to parallel passages when Gherardo's servant, overhearing his follies, exclaims 'O for a truncheon!' (p. 300), which does somewhat resemble Sir Toby's wish for a stone-bow and the other talk of beating, pistolling, and cudgelling in the letter scene. When Flamminio asks his page why he stayed so long at Isabella's he uses the image 'You thought you'd stay fixed like a gallows, eh?' (p. 309: *Tu vorrai diventar un forcasi*. Literally, 'You wanted to become a gallows, yes?'),[1] and Lelia replies that she stayed hoping that she could speak to Isabella: this may have suggested Viola's imagery (reported by Malvolio) in the same situation: 'he says he'll stand at your door like a sheriff's post, and be the supporter to a bench, but he'll speak

---

1. I have used the Venice edition of 1543 (Cambridge University Library, Syn. 8. 54. 212). The reading '*un forcasi.*' is, I take it, a double error for *una forca, si?* It is marginally glossed, in a contemporary hand, 'a gallow[es]'.

with you' (I. v. 149–51). The verb *accostare* (to come closer) is used three times in Lelia's scene with Isabella (pp. 307–8), but without any mistake corresponding to Sir Andrew's over 'accost' (I. iii. 51–4), which, though evidently a fashionable word, had been current for a few years before *Twelfth Night* was written.[1] When Isabella's maid invites the supposed page to visit her mistress, and Lelia refuses, Pasquella says 'Truly and seriously, Fabio, you are too proud [*tu sei troppo superbo*]' and warns the page that 'this beauty of yours will not last for ever. Your beard will grow; your cheeks will not always be so glowing nor your lips so red' (p. 305). This has been compared with Viola's rebuke to Olivia's pride, and with her preceding speech about Olivia's beauty and her cruelty in not perpetuating it by marriage (I. v. 244–6). On the other hand, the ideas and language are traditional, and the two situations very different. A closer resemblance of situation exists between Lelia's words to Flamminio, 'Isn't there in all this city some lady or other who deserves your love as much as she? Has no other woman pleased you but Isabella?' (p. 310), and Viola's

> Say that some lady, as perhaps there is,
> Hath for your love as great a pang of heart
> As you have for Olivia: you cannot love her:
> You tell her so. Must she not then be answer'd?
> (II. iv. 90–3)

Bullough suggests that the phrase 'You tell her so' may recall the sequel to the speech in *Gl'Ingannati*, where Flamminio, by immediately declaring that he loves Lelia no longer, plunges her into sorrow: it seems, however, that 'You tell her so' is purely hypothetical ('suppose you were to tell that lady so'), and therefore different in effect (since Orsino has no knowledge that Viola, as Viola, exists). It is stated that Lelia was aged thirteen at the Sack of Rome (p. 290; Bandello's Nicuola was fifteen), and perhaps Shakespeare was recalling this fact when he made Viola's father die on her thirteenth birthday (v. i. 242–3). With these verbal correspondences may be included possible hints for the title and for two (or perhaps three) of the characters' names. The prologue to *Gl'Ingannati* mentions the drawing of lots on Twelfth Night ('*la notte di beffana*', i.e., the night of Epiphany, p. 287); Lelia's assumed name of Fabio may have supplied that of Fabian;

1. As a naval term ('to go alongside of') in 1578 (*OED*). Metaphorically, as here, in Marlowe, *Hero and Leander*, I. 198 (before 1593): Shakespeare knew *Hero and Leander*, in MS., at least as early as *MND.*, H. F. Brooks reminds me.

and the name of one of the participants in *Il Sacrificio*, Messer Agnol Malevolti, has been more dubiously regarded as the origin of Malvolio's, or alternatively (being variously interpreted by Luce and Bullough as 'ill-favoured' and 'ache-faces') of Sir Andrew Aguecheek's.

Gl'Ingannati was a successful play and was translated or adapted into other languages, as *Les Abusés* (by Charles Estienne, 1543, first printed as *Le Sacrifice*), *Los Engaños* (by Lope de Rueda, 1556, printed 1567), and *Laelia* (authorship unknown, based on *Les Abusés*, performed at Cambridge probably in 1595, but possibly written much earlier and performed in 1546 or 1547; unpublished before *Twelfth Night*). There is no substantial evidence for regarding any of these as a source of *Twelfth Night*.[1]

Two other Italian plays, *Gl'Inganni* ('1547' on title-page; really 1551?; printed 1562) and *L'Interesse* (1547?; printed 1581), both by Nicolò Secchi, contain the situation in which a woman is disguised as a man and in that disguise helps the man she loves to woo the woman he loves. In both—unlike *Gl'Ingannati*, where her speech is clearly meant and taken as alluding to Lelia—she speaks to him about another woman whom he does not know: in *Gl'Inganni*[2] it is a woman who loves him, and whom he is recommended to love instead of the courtesan with whom he is infatuated; in *L'Interesse*[3] it is a woman whom the pretended youth says he loves. Both employ similar dramatic irony, with dialogue such as 'Would it be easy to go to her?' 'As easy as to come to me.' (*Gl'Inganni*); and 'Is she young?' 'About your age.' 'Is she beautiful?' 'A charming face, and good-looking as yours is.' (*L'Interesse*). Both may therefore be compared with Viola's dialogue with Orsino in II. iv, in which, as Cesario, she admits to loving one 'of your complexion' and 'about your years' and later tells the story of her sister who

> lov'd a man,
> As it might be perhaps, were I a woman,
> I should your lordship.

It is possible, though no more than possible, that these plays were known to Shakespeare;[4] but the possibility is not increased

1. The case for *Laelia* as a possible source is argued by G. C. Moore Smith in his edition (Cambridge, 1910), where he also discusses the date, and by Luce, *Apolonius and Silla*, pp. 26, 90–1.

2. Translated extract in Bullough, pp. 340–2.

3. Translated extract in Bullough, p. 344.

4. Helen A. Kaufman, 'Nicolò Secchi as a Source of *Twelfth Night*', *Sh. Q.*, 5 (1954), 271–80, maintains Shakespeare's indebtedness. See also R. C. Melzi,

by talk of a duel between the disguised heroine and the man she loves in *L'Interesse*, for this duel turns out to be merely a sexual metaphor,[1] whereas that in *Twelfth Night* surely originated in Sir Andrew's cowardice (as did his name?).

In a second play called *Gl'Inganni* and based upon Secchi's, the author (Curzio Gonzaga, 1592) changed the heroine's false name from Ruberto to Cesare, which may have suggested the name Cesario. But this again is no more than a possibility, like the possibility that Shakespeare took the Duke's name from 'Orsino innamorato', a character in *Il Viluppo* (Girolamo Parabosco, 1547)—a play which Joseph Hunter[2] discovered bound up with Gonzaga's, a 1585 edition of *Gl'Ingannati*, and two other plays; for there is no evidence that Shakespeare ever saw this volume, and so its existence may testify equally to the force of coincidence.

'APOLONIUS AND SILLA' AND OTHER NARRATIVES

The main story of *Gl'Ingannati* (shorn of the Giglio subplot, the innkeepers, the Pedant, and all the servants except the indispensable nurse and maid) was retold as a prose tale by Matteo Bandello in his *Novelle*, part II, no. 36 (1554); by Pierre de Belleforest, who had it from Bandello, in his *Histoires Tragiques*, part IV, no. 59 (1570); and by Barnabe Riche, who had it from Belleforest, as the tale of Apolonius and Silla in *Riche his Farewell to Militarie Profession* (1581). These narratives reduced the Plautine characteristics of the play, and developed in their place romantic ones. Thus Bandello, while retaining the error as to the identity of the heroine's twin brother, modifies the form it takes: instead of being locked by two old men into the same room as the woman he eventually marries, he is invited by her into her house in mistake for his disguised sister. Bandello also dwells on the heroine's feelings of unrequited love. He makes one important change: she does not hinder her master's courtship as Lelia hinders Flamminio's, though she does acquiesce in being preferred to him, and is relieved by this setback of his courtship. He also writes new dialogue for her encounters with her master and the other woman.

'From Lelia to Viola', *Renaissance Drama*, 9 (1966), 67–81: he discusses the dates of Secchi's plays, makes an inconclusive case for Giovan' Battista Della Porta's *La Cinthia* as a source for *Tw.N.*, and suggests that Shakespeare may have encountered Italian plays through *commedia dell'arte* versions.

1. Bullough, p. 344.

2. J. Hunter, *New Illustrations of the Life, Studies, and Writings of Shakespeare*, 2 vols. (1845), I, 393, 398.

It is in these dialogues that parallels have been sought with the corresponding dialogues in *Twelfth Night*. Reproving her master's inconstancy to herself, the disguised heroine says to him, 'Who knoweth but this fair damsel yet loveth you and liveth in sore affliction for your sake? More by token that I have many a time heard say that girls, in their first loves, love far more tenderly and with much greater fervour than do men. My heart forebodeth me this hapless lass must needs languish for you and live a life of anguish and misery.'[1] (Compare *Twelfth Night*, II. iv. 90–3, 111–19; there is no corresponding passage in Riche.) Viola's simile in this latter passage ('concealment, like a worm i' th' bud') has been compared with a metaphor Bandello uses earlier in his story, 'the worm of amorous wistfulness still gnawed at her heart and fretted it with the utmost affliction';[2] but an important difference is that Bandello's image is an emblem of painful emotion itself (the serpent gnawing the heart), while Shakespeare's is a symbol of such emotion's effect, the blighting of beauty and promise (the grub in the flower; cf. *Romeo and Juliet*, I. i. 145–51, where the same image occurs, again in connection with concealed passion), so the resemblance is probably coincidental.[3]

Belleforest made some interpolations and omissions when he translated Bandello's tale, but only one phrase looks close enough to be a possible influence on Shakespeare. This occurs during the supposed page's interview with the lady, when the latter says, '*Je ne sçay, mon amy, qu'est-ce que tu as fait en mon endroit, mais j'estime que tu m'as enchantée.*' The words closely follow Bandello's except in adding 'en mon endroit', which is perhaps followed in Olivia's line 'After the last enchantment you did here' (III. i. 114).[4]

1. p. 378. References to the text of John Payne's translation (London, 1890: reprinted [expurgated] in Furness, pp. 362–75). Bullough does not give a text of Bandello, though he quotes this passage in a different translation, p. 275. There is an edition of Bandello's *Novelle* in the original Italian by G. Brognoligo (Bari, 1910–12): this story is in vol. III (1911), 252–79.

2. Bullough's translation: Brognoligo, p. 257: '*l'amoroso verme voracemente con gravissimo cordoglio le rodeva il core.*' Luce, *Apolonius and Silla*, p. 28, and Bullough, p. 275, read '*veracemente*' and '*grandissimo*'; Luce, ed. *Tw.N.*, pp. 183–4, also reads '*rodena*', in which he is followed by Muir, p. 69.

3. As is probably the resemblance between Malvolio's name and the phrase '*mala voglia*' (ill will) which occurs seven times in Bandello's tale; '*per il mal ch'io vi voglio*' (through the ill will I bear you) is also found in the Prologue to *Gl'Ingannati*. But since Shakespeare could easily have invented the name (compare Benvolio in *Rom.*) it is likely that he did so.

4. Belleforest is quoted by Luce, p. 184. Bandello (Brognoligo, p. 263) has '*Io non so a la fe di Dio cio che tu m'abbia fatto, e penso per certo che tu m'abbi incantata*' (I know not, by my faith in God, what thou hast done to me, and I believe for sure that thou hast enchanted me). I see no reason why Shakespeare's 'here'

In my opinion, then, no clear indebtedness either to Bandello or to Belleforest can be established.

Riche's tale of Apolonius and Silla[1] requires summary and quotation for two reasons: it differs materially from the story as related by Bandello and Belleforest, and it is known to have been read by Shakespeare (whose departures from it may be as significant as his debts to it).

Duke Apolonius ('a verie yong man'), on his way home after a year's distinguished service in the Turkish wars, was forced by a storm to take refuge in Cyprus, and, while his ships were refitting, was nobly entertained by Duke Pontus the Governor. Pontus had two children: a son named Silvio, at that time serving in the wars in Africa, and a daughter named Silla. Silla fell in love with Apolonius, but failed (in spite of maidenly efforts) to attract his interest: his mind was preoccupied with the late wars and the immediate tasks in hand. Presently he sailed away for his home in Constantinople. Silla then enlisted the help of her trusty servant Pedro, who secured a passage for himself and her—she pretending to be his sister—on a ship bound for that city. The captain invited Silla first to be his mistress, then his wife, both of which she refused; he then threatened to take her by force; she secured a respite till night, and meanwhile prepared to kill herself, but was saved from this desperate remedy by a storm which wrecked the vessel. Pedro, like the rest, was drowned, but Silla saved herself by clinging to a sea-chest of the captain's. Cast on shore alone, and realizing the danger to which her sex exposed her, she dressed herself in clothes taken from the chest, assumed her brother's name, and made her way to Apolonius' court and (still unrecognized) into his service, where she rapidly gained his special favour: '*Siluio* pleased his maister so well, that aboue all the reste of his seruauntes aboute hym, he had the greatest credite, and the Duke put him moste in trust.'[2] Since returning from the war, Apolonius had become suitor to Julina, a wealthy widow of great beauty; he had already learned the first lesson in the school of love, 'that is, to speake pitifully, to looke ruthfully, to promise largely, to

---

should not be coincidental. The notion of love as an enchantment was sufficiently familiar for Shakespeare to have spontaneously referred to it; cf. Egeus' complaint against Lysander: 'This man hath bewitch'd the bosom of my child' (*MND.*, I. i. 27).

1. *Riche his Farewell to Militarie Profession: conteining verie pleasaunt discourses fit for a peaceable tyme* [etc.], 1581. Reprinted by Bullough, pp. 344–63, and (expurgated) by Furness, pp. 328–39. Reprinted as Appendix I, pp. 157–79.
2. Appendix I, p. 164. Cf. *Tw.N.*, I. IV. 1–15.

serue diligently, and to please carefully', and was now learning
the second lesson, 'that is to reward liberally, to giue bountifully,
to present willyngly, and to write louyngly'; and he employed
'Silvio' as his messenger. (It is in this part of Riche's story that
Shakespeare's interest seems to have been greatest, if one may
judge from echoes which cluster about this point, as quotation
may conveniently show.)

> Now gentilwomen, doe you thinke there could haue been a
> greater torment deuised, wherewith to afflicte the harte of
> *Silla*, then her self to bee made the instrumente to woorke
> her owne mishapp, and to plaie the Atturney in a cause, that
> made so muche againste her self. But *Silla* altogether desirous
> to please her maister, cared nothyng at all to offende her self,
> [?and] followed his businesse with so good a will, as if it had
> been in her owne preferment.[1]

> *Iulina* now hauyng many tymes, taken the gaze of this yong
> youth *Siluio*, perceiuyng hym to bee of suche excellente perfecte
> grace, was so intangeled with the often sight of this sweete
> temptation, that she fell into as greate a likyng with the man,
> as the maister was with her self:[2] And on a tyme *Siluio* beyng
> sent from his maister, with a message to the Ladie *Iulina*,
> as he beganne very earnestly to solicet in his maisters behalfe,
> *Iulina* interruptyng hym in his tale, saied: *Siluio* it is enough
> that you have saied for your maister, from henceforthe either
> speake for your self, or saie nothyng at all.[3] *Silla* abashed
> to heare these wordes, began in her minde to accuse the blind-
> nesse of Loue, that *Iulina* neglectyng the good will of so noble
> a Duke, would preferre her loue vnto suche a one, as Nature it
> self had denaied to recompence her likyng.[4]

At this point the real Silvio, travelling in search of his sister (whom
he believed Pedro had abducted), arrived at Constantinople,
where he happened to meet Julina in a 'pleasaunte greene yarde'
outside the city walls. She mistook him for the Duke's messenger
and renewed her courtship, to which he responded, whereupon
she invited him to supper next day. He eagerly kept the appoint-
ment and stayed the night at her house, where she came to his bed
(and, in consequence, conceived a child). Certain in his mind

---

1. Cf. *Tw.N.*, I. iv. 40–2: 'I'll do my best / To woo your lady: [*Aside*] yet,
a barful strife! / Whoe'er I woo, myself would be his wife.'

2. Cf. *Tw.N.*, I. v. 298: 'Unless the master were the man'.

3. Cf. *Tw.N.*, III. i. 109–12: 'I bade you never speak again of him; / But
would you undertake another suit, / I had rather hear you to solicit that, / Than
music from the spheres.'

4. Appendix I, pp. 165–6. Cf. *Tw.N.*, II. ii. 37–8: 'As I am woman (now alas
the day!) / What thriftless sighs shall poor Olivia breathe?'

that Julina had mistaken him for someone else, Silvio next day
left the city ('for feare of further euilles') and continued his search
for his sister. Apolonius now making his final offer of marriage,
Julina took the opportunity to tell him that she belonged to another
'whose wife I now remaine by faithfull vowe and promise', and
(hoping to save Silvio from his displeasure) asked his consent,
to which he returned a disappointed answer and departed. Soon
afterwards, when he learned indirectly that one of Julina's
servants 'neuer sawe his Ladie and mistres, vse so good countenaunce to the Duke hym self, as she had doen to *Siluio* his
manne',[1] he was very angry and put 'Silvio' in prison. Julina
was finally forced, by her advancing pregnancy and her concern
for Silvio, to reveal to the Duke the condition to which her love
of Silvio had brought her. This convinced Apolonius that 'Silvio'
had been disloyal to him, while 'Silvio' continued to deny the accusation in spite of Julina's insistence that they were virtually married
by a pre-contract: 'therefore (as I saied before) *Siluio* is my
housbande by plited faithe. . . . Feare not then my *Siluio* to
keepe your faith and promise, whiche you haue made vnto me.'[2]
Finally, to Silla's astonishment, Julina claimed her as the father
of the unborn child,[3] which so incensed Apolonius that he drew
his sword and threatened to kill 'Silvio' there and then unless
he married her:[4] Silla thereupon begged for a private interview
with Julina, in which she revealed her true identity and the
reason for her disguise. Julina told the Duke. He admired Silla's
courage and devotion, and married her with great splendour.
The remarkable story soon reached the real Silvio, who immediately returned to Constantinople and was welcomed by his new
brother-in-law the Duke, from whom he learned of Julina's part
in the events and of her present situation. Stricken with remorse,
he willingly married her. 'And thus *Siluio* hauyng attained a noble
wife, and *Silla* his sister her desired houseband, thei passed the
residue of their daies with suche delight, as those that haue accomplished the perfection of their felicities.'

In turning Riche's tale into his own play, Shakespeare simpli-
fied and shortened its story, concentrating it from a loose nar-

1. Appendix I, p. 170. Cf. Sir Andrew's complaint, *Tw.N.*, III. ii. 4–6.

2. Appendix I, p. 173. Cf. *Tw.N.*, v. i. 144–8: 'Alas, it is the baseness of thy
fear . . . As great as that thou fear'st.'

3. Lamenting her situation, 'that haue so charely preserued myne honour,
and now am made a praie to satisfie a yong mans lust' (Appendix I, p. 176). Cf.
Tw.N., III. iv. 203–4: 'I have said too much unto a heart of stone, / And laid
mine honour too unchary out.'

4. Cf. Orsino's differently motivated inclination to kill Cesario, v. i. 123–9.

rative into a tightly organized plot: he omitted all the action preliminary to Silla's shipwreck, and the anticlimax of Silvio's
return; instead he shipwrecked brother and sister together,[1] thus
allowing various confusions of identity to take place from III. iv
onwards and to be unravelled concurrently in the general encounter of the final scene. He also changed the mood, especially
in the parts involving the widow Julina (for whom he substitutes
the unmarried Olivia): her hasty meeting, feasting, and bedding
of Silvio is refined into Olivia's equally hasty but decorous mar-
riage-ceremony, and in consequence there is no pregnancy, no
desertion, and no imprisonment of the heroine; all that survives
of this rather sensational element of Riche's tale is Orsino's
violent impulse, to slay Olivia or to sacrifice Viola, in Shakespeare's last scene. At the same time, the essentials of Riche's
situation are retained—the arrival of the brother, his reception
by the lady the Duke is courting, her claiming of the disguised
sister as her husband, and the consequent discovery of the disguise
and the winning of the Duke by the sister—and, since these last
events are not in Bandello nor Belleforest, nor in any other known
version, dramatic or narrative, of this story which originated in
Gl'Ingannati, Shakespeare's use of Riche's tale as his main source
may be safely assumed.

Besides this story itself, and the resemblances of detail which
have been noted in summarizing Riche's tale, *Twelfth Night* may
include other debts to *Riche his Farewell to Militarie Profession*.
The most important, if it is a debt and not a coincidence, concerns the conspirators' pretence that Malvolio is mad. This trick
is played by a husband upon his shrewish wife in the fifth of
Riche's 'histories'.[2] The story is more brutal (the wife's leg is
chained, and her arms bound with cords and scratched with
brambles), but the pious exhortations of her neighbours, and their
joining with the dissembling husband in prayer, which further
enrages her, have their counterpart in the dialogues of III. iv.
85–126 and IV. ii. 21–62 and 75–132. The other correspondences
are entirely verbal. Four words which are rare in Shakespeare's

---

1. A twin brother (Gaio) and sister (Giulia) are separated by shipwreck
from each other (and from their father) at the beginning of a story (v. 8) in
Giraldi Cinthio's *Hecatommithi* (1565), but thereafter the story (summarized
by Luce, p. 186) is different from Riche's and from Shakespeare's; Muir is
incorrect in calling it 'the story of Lelia' (p. 70).

2. Text reprinted by Bullough, pp. 34–44, as a possible source of the buck-
basket incident in *Wiv.* The part relevant to *Tw.N.* is on pp. 43–4. This part
is also reprinted by Luce, *Apolonius and Silla*, pp. 84–5.

plays[1] can be found in Riche (but none of them is peculiar to
him or first used by him), and Riche's dedicatory epistle includes
a jocular passage in which he mentions 'Measures', 'Galliardes'
full of 'trickes and tournes', a 'Sinquepace', a 'Capre', and a
'Ieigge' (also 'these braules' and a 'Rounde'—but not a coranto)
which may underlie Sir Toby's and Sir Andrew's dialogue in
I. iii. 117–31.

The names Olivia and Viola have sometimes been thought to
come from Olivia and Violetta (the latter a girl disguised as a
page, though there is no other resemblance of story) in Emanuel
Forde's prose romance *Parismus, the Renowned Prince of Bohemia*
(1598).[2] This possibility, like the borrowing of names from Italian
plays, must remain conjectural.

SHAKESPEARE'S OWN PLAYS

Whatever use Shakespeare made of the writings of others,
he also drew upon his own earlier comedies for ideas and treatment.

Manningham[3] noticed the resemblance between *Twelfth
Night* and Plautus' *Menaechmi*, which is itself the source of *The
Comedy of Errors*. In that play Shakespeare altered Plautus' story
considerably, giving twin servants to the twin masters and also
introducing romantic elements (Antipholus of Syracuse's courtship of Luciana, and Aegeon's pathetic situation which frames
the main action); but he kept—and, with the twin servants,
increased—its essentially farcical basis of mistaken identity.
The love-interest itself is built upon this basis, for Luciana resists
the courtship of Antipholus of Syracuse because she mistakes
him for her sister's husband.

One prominent cause of error is a gold chain which Antipholus of Ephesus has ordered from a goldsmith named Angelo,
and which Angelo gives by mistake to Antipholus of Syracuse
(III. i). Immediately afterwards (IV. i) Angelo is arrested at the
suit of a Merchant to whom he owes just as much money as
Antipholus of Ephesus owes him for the chain; so, when Antipholus of Ephesus now enters, Angelo asks him for the money,
which Antipholus of Ephesus refuses, denying with perfect truth

1. Coisterell, garragascoynes, pavion, galliarde. These appear in F as
Coystrill (I. iii. 40), gaskins (I. v. 24), panyn (v. i. 198; for pauyn), Galliard
(I. iii. 117, 125). They were noted by Luce (*Apolonius and Silla*, p. 48); Muir, p.
70 (unlike Luce), says they are not found in Shakespeare's other plays, but
coistrel is also in *Per.* (IV. vi. 164), and galliard in *H5* (I. ii. 252).

2. Extract in Bullough, pp. 363–71.

3. See above, p. xxvi.

that he has received the chain, whereupon Angelo in his turn has Antipholus of Ephesus arrested for debt. In the next act (v. i) Angelo and the Merchant meet Antipholus of Syracuse wearing the chain and reproach him for what they imagine to have been his earlier lie: passions run high and swords are drawn. The prevailing mood of these scenes is farcical, sparkling the brighter for the indignation of the parties; but the mistakes anticipate Antonio's in *Twelfth Night* (III. v; v. i), when he accuses Cesario of withholding the money he lent to Sebastian. Antonio's firm friendship for Sebastian has already been stressed, and his indignation is fittingly more poignant than that of Angelo and the Merchant, who have only a business relationship with Antipholus of Ephesus; it comes closer to Aegeon's momentary pathos in 'but perhaps, my son, / Thou sham'st to acknowledge me in misery' (being unrecognized by Antipholus of Ephesus, whom he takes to be Antipholus of Syracuse, v. i. 320–1). This final recognition scene anticipates its counterpart in *Twelfth Night* in other ways. The Duke tells Aegeon that Antipholus has lived in Ephesus for twenty years, just as Orsino tells Antonio that Cesario has lived at court for three months, and each Duke accuses the complainant of madness. And when the twin brother appears (accompanied by the twin slave), the speeches of the Duke in *The Comedy of Errors*,

> One of these men is genius to the other;
> And so of these. Which is the natural man,
> And which the spirit? Who deciphers them?   (v. i. 331–3)

and of Antipholus of Syracuse,

> Aegeon art thou not? or else his ghost?   (v. i. 336)

are transmuted in *Twelfth Night* from mere puzzlement into something rich and strange (v. i. 224–36).[1]

In the sub-plot of *Twelfth Night* other echoes of *The Comedy of Errors* are heard. Though Sir Toby, Fabian, Maria, and later Feste only pretend to believe that Malvolio is mad (III. iv, IV. ii), their dialogues with him resemble that of Adriana, Luciana, the

---

1. Similarly, Antipholus of Syracuse reacts to Adriana's addressing him as her husband (*Err.*, II. ii. 180–5, 211–12) as Sebastian does to Olivia's addressing him as Cesario (*Tw.N.*, IV. i. 59–62) by wondering whether he is awake or dreaming (compare also Christopher Sly in *Shr.* Ind. ii. 66–71); he later accepts the goldsmith's chain (*Err.*, III. ii. 177–81) as readily as Sebastian accepts Olivia's hand in marriage (*Tw.N.*, IV. iii. 32–3) or Sly his translation to gentility. The differences are as important as the resemblances, but the resemblances are there. Riche's Silvio, in similar circumstances, perceives that there is some mistake, but never doubts the reality of his present or past experience in the way Shakespeare's characters do.

Courtesan, and Pinch with Antipholus of Ephesus, whom the
other four really do think possessed by the devil (*Err.* iv. iv). It
is possible that Shakespeare took the false accusation of madness
from Riche's fifth story; it is certain that he treated it in the manner of his own earlier play. When Antipholus of Ephesus has
escaped from his bonds 'in a dark and dankish vault', he appears
before the Duke (v. i. 190–252) clamouring for

> ample satisfaction
> For these deep shames and great indignities

(of which his imprisonment was the culmination), somewhat in
Malvolio's manner. A great difference, of course, is that Antipholus' comic misfortunes (like everyone else's in this play) have
come in battalions and are virtually unrelated to his personality
(except insofar as they provide fuel for his choleric temperament),
whereas Malvolio is the victim of a single conspiracy directed at
his self-conceit and ambition.

The disguise of the heroine as a young man, though in *Twelfth
Night* it is taken from the particular story-tradition culminating
in 'Apolonius and Silla', was already an established ingredient
of Shakespearean comedy. In *The Two Gentlemen of Verona*,
Julia enters her lover Proteus' service as a page and is sent with a
love-token to Silvia, for whom he has forsaken her; in *The
Merchant of Venice*, Portia plays the lawyer to save her husband's
friend, and incidentally to get her husband's ring so that she can
later pretend to be jealous; in *As You Like It*, Rosalind lives in the
Forest of Arden as a 'shepherd youth', and in that character
invites Orlando's courtship by pretending to act the part of his
Rosalind; she is also herself beloved by the shepherdess Phebe,
who repulses her own faithful lover Silvius and does not penetrate
the supposed youth's disguise. Shakespeare found all these
materials in his sources for these plays. In dramatizing them, he
exploited the dramatic irony of the situations. This is agreed by
all readers, though there is less agreement about the emotional
effects which his treatment produces. However, it is agreed (even
by those who, in my opinion wrongly, cannot take *The Two
Gentlemen of Verona* at all seriously) that Julia's situation evokes a
sentiment and a pathos (of whatever kind) which are not evoked
by Portia's or Rosalind's. Her lover's faithlessness ensures that
this is so, and her own references to the absent Julia reinforce the
feeling: she pities Julia, she tells Proteus,

> Because methinks that she lov'd you as well
> As you do love your lady Silvia, (iv. iv. 75–6)

and in speaking to Silvia, she pictures herself (by an ingenious invention involving the page's wearing the lady's gown in a play) as an Ariadne deserted by a false Theseus (IV. iv. 154–68). Something of the same pathos, though without its element of reproach, is in Viola's scene with Orsino, when she speculates,

> Say that some lady, as perhaps there is,
> Hath for your love as great a pang of heart
> As you have for Olivia,   (II. iv. 90–2)

and relates how her father's daughter 'never told her love'. Thus one aspect of Viola's situation, her concealed love for Orsino, recalls Julia's for Proteus. But another aspect of it, Olivia's misdirected love for her, recalls Phebe's for Rosalind[1]— though again there are great differences between Shakespeare's treatments of these similar errors.

The primary influences on *Twelfth Night*, then, appear to have been Riche's story (the direct source, though much modified by Shakespeare in his use of it) and the earlier comedies which Shakespeare had written. That he consulted other versions of the story, both narrative and dramatic (including the ultimate source, *Gl'Ingannati*), is possible, but there is no irrefutable evidence that he did. The degree of possibility must be left to each reader to determine.

4 THE CRITICISM OF *TWELFTH NIGHT*

The earliest appreciative comments are on the gulling of Malvolio. Manningham's praise of it as 'a good device', and Digges's statement (in his verses prefixed to Shakespeare's *Poems*, 1640)[2] that '*Malvoglio* that crosse garter'd Gull' packed the theatre, foreshadow the eighteenth-century editors' remarks. Rowe (1709) found 'something singularly Ridiculous and Pleasant in the fantastical Steward *Malvolio*', and Johnson (1765), who thought it unfair to mock Sir Andrew's 'natural fatuity', allowed that 'the soliloquy of *Malvolio* is truly comick; he is betrayed to ridicule merely by his pride'.[3]

---

1. It is, Harold Jenkins points out to me, even more reminiscent of Celia's love for Felismena in the *Diana Enamorada*, the source of *Gent.* (see Bullough, I, 225–53): Shakespeare must have been aware of the dramatic potentialities of this situation at the time when he was writing *Gent.*, even though he did not use it there.

2. Quoted by Chambers, *William Shakespeare*, II, 233.

3. Quoted by Furness, p. 378. Subsequent quotations from critics to the end of the nineteenth century are taken from Furness's longer extracts, pp. 377–407.

With Johnson's short notice also begins the critical appreciation of *Twelfth Night* as a work of art: he thought it 'in the graver
part elegant and easy, and in some of the lighter scenes exquisitely
humorous'. Unlike Pepys, who saw it three times and dismissed it
as 'silly' and 'weak',[1] Johnson obviously enjoyed the play, but
he had misgivings about its lack of verisimilitude and consequently
of seriousness:

> The marriage of *Olivia*, and the succeeding perplexity, though
> well enough contrived to divert on the stage, wants credibility,
> and fails to produce the proper instruction required in the
> drama, as it exhibits no just picture of life.[2]

He here raised a number of questions to which later critics were
to reply in different ways.

In the nineteenth century, it began to be noticed that the graver
and lighter parts are fused together by a common theme. A. W.
Schlegel (1811), after remarking that Shakespeare often, and in
much of this play, 'treats love more as an affair of the imagination than of the heart', pointed out that the 'ideal follies' of the
main plot are provided with a contrast in the 'undisguised
absurdities' of the wholly comic characters arising 'in like manner
under pretence of love'.[3] Schlegel's is essentially a factual statement that Olivia is sought in marriage by Sir Andrew and by
Malvolio as well as by Orsino. With F. Kreyssig (1862) begins
the explicitly moral interpretation of the dramatic design, and the
claim that the play is indeed instructive: for, beneath the grada-
tions of 'amorous folly or foolish amorousness' from Sir Andrew
up to Orsino and Olivia,

> we do not fail to hear the lovely ground-tone, which at first
> softly sounding, at last rises triumphantly above the chaos of
> clashing tones, and in the most delightful way harmonises
> all discords; I mean the portrayal of deep and true love in
> sound healthy natures.[4]

Following the same line of thought, H. J. Ruggles (1870) saw
in Viola perfection, in Sir Toby and Malvolio gross imperfection,
and in Orsino and Olivia the subtle imperfection of characters
'marked by grace and gentility both inborn and acquired, but
who, grounding their affections upon mere external beauty, are

1. Furness, pp. 377–8.
2. Furness, p. 378.
3. *Lectures* (transl. J. Black, 1815). Furness, p. 378.
4. *Vorlesungen über Shakespeare* (Berlin). Furness (in translation), p. 381.

devoid of all restraints in the indulgence of their fancies and passions'.[1] Orsino had already come under criticism as a sentimen-
talist: G. G. Gervinus (1850) seems to have first pronounced him
to be 'more in love with his love, than with his mistress' (it is
no exaggeration to say that this has been repeated in print fifty
times), and he pressed the charge to the point of deducing that
this was why Olivia refused the Duke.[2]

Not all critics embraced the moral interpretation. E. Montégut
(1867) stressed the element of masquerade, festival, topsyturvey-
dom, and ambiguity, and resisted the moralists. The only
'philosophy' he extracted was that 'we are all, in varying degrees,
insane', the slaves either of our peculiar defects and follies or else
of our dreams and hopes: 'some have a graceful poetic madness,
others a madness grotesque and trivial', and those who achieve
their dreams do so not through their good sense but because
their dreams are acceptable to Nature as graceful, poetic, and
beautiful.[3] By this argument Montégut derived satisfaction from
what had dissatisfied Johnson.

Though Montégut and Ruggles were morally poles apart, they
united in finding the play delightful. Ruggles declared,

> Beside the air of elegance it possesses, it is filled to the brim
> and overflowing with the spirit that seeks to enjoy this world
> without one thought or aspiration beyond. It jumps the here-
> after entirely. Every scene of it glows with the warmth and
> sunshine of physical enjoyment.[4]

This was a general nineteenth-century feeling about *Twelfth
Night*. A. C. Swinburne (1880) found a 'sunny identity of spirit'
between it and *As You Like It*.[5] Even when (as by F. J. Furnivall,
1877) attention was drawn to its elements of pathos and danger,
and to the absence of Beatrice's or Rosalind's vivacity from Viola's
part, it was 'still one of the comedies of Shakspere's bright, sweet
time'.[6] This phrase reflects the growing interest in Shakespeare's
dramatic career as a whole, and the knowledge that he would
next write the tragedies and the 'dark comedies'. In the present
century this knowledge has pressed more and more heavily upon
Twelfth Night: it is Shakespeare's 'Farewell to Comedy' (A. T.

---

1. *The Method of Shakespeare as an Artist* (New York). Furness, pp. 384–5.
2. *Shakespeare* (Leipzig). Furness (in translation), p. 379.
3. Introduction to *Œuvres complètes de Shakespeare*. Furness (in translation), pp. 382–4.
4. *Op. cit.* Furness, p. 385.
5. *A Study of Shakespeare*. Furness, p. 386.
6. Introduction to *The Leopold Shakspere*. Furness, p. 385.

Quiller-Couch, 1930),[1] it has 'a silvery undertone of sadness'
(J. Middleton Murry, 1936),[2] its poetry is of 'an almost elegiac
quality' (T. M. Parrott, 1949).[3] It is probably true to say that a
twentieth-century reader, suddenly invited to recall *Twelfth
Night*, will think first of Viola's scenes with Olivia and Orsino (I.
v and II. iv), and in particular of her 'willow cabin' and 'Patience
on a monument' speeches, whereas for Furnivall in 1877

> The self-conceited Malvolio is brought to the front, the drunk-
> ards and the Clown come next; none of these touches any
> heart; and it's not till we look past them, that we feel the
> beauty of the characters who stand in half-light behind.[4]

The difference is one of focus rather than of interpretation: the
same things are noticed, but are given different prominence.
Feste, to be sure, began to touch twentieth-century hearts:
A. C. Bradley (1916), without missing his humour, made him
the subject of a whole sympathetic essay,[5] and Middleton
Murry compared his final loneliness on stage to that of the old
servant Firs at the end of Chekhov's *Cherry Orchard*, quoting Adam's
line from *As You Like It* (II. iii. 42): 'And unregarded age in
corners thrown'.[6] The influence of this mood is still strongly with
us, for when readers remember Feste they think first of his last
song (pathetically interpreted) and of 'Come away, death': it
costs them some effort to remember him playing Sir Topas.
Malvolio, in the last century and in the present, has sometimes
been seen as a man too ill-used for our comfort.[7] But whether the
play's gaiety or its pathos is placed in the foreground, it is assumed
in all this criticism that Shakespeare's heart is in them both.

An innovation in more recent twentieth-century criticism has
been to regard *Twelfth Night* not merely as a farewell to comedy
but as a positive rejection of mirth and romance. The extremity
of this view has been stated in characteristically extreme terms by

1. N.C.S., p. xi.
2. *Shakespeare*, p. 225.
3. *Shakespearean Comedy*, p. 187.
4. *Op. cit.* Furness, p. 385.
5. 'Feste the Jester', in *A Book of Homage to Shakespeare*, ed. I. Gollancz;
reprinted in *A Miscellany* (1929) and in D. J. Palmer (ed.), *'Twelfth Night': A
Casebook* (1972).
6. *Op. cit.*, p. 228.
7. W. Hazlitt, *Characters of Shakespeare's Plays* (1817: Furness, pp. 378–9), first
remarked that 'poor Malvolio's treatment is a little hard', merely as an afterthought, having quoted with relish his soliloquy before he finds the letter (II.
v. 23–80); he does not seem to have intended to suggest that this upsets the
comic balance of the play.

W. H. Auden (1957) and by Jan Kott (1965). For Auden, 'Shakespeare was in no mood for comedy, but in a mood of puritanical aversion to all those pleasing illusions which men cherish and by which they lead their lives';[1] for Kott, 'with all its appearances of gaiety, it is a very bitter comedy about the Elizabethan *dolce vita*, or at any rate about the *dolce vita* at every level and in every wing of the Southampton residence.'[2] Another critic who finds the play 'uncomfortable' is Philip Edwards (1968), whose discomfort extends to Viola's marriage with Orsino, and whose consolation is her recognition scene with Sebastian, which foreshadows for him the final scenes of *Pericles* and *The Tempest*: 'It is so much greater, in this play, than the ritual of converging lovers, which seems sardonically treated in comparison. There was something here to hold on to, when the celebration of achieved love may have wearied Shakespeare.'[3] E. C. Pettet (1949) and Clifford Leech (1965) express more moderately their sense of 'Shakespeare's detachment from romance',[4] or, at least, his less-than-complete commitment to it. Pettet stresses the element of robust prose comedy which *Twelfth Night* has in common with *Much Ado*, the element of exaggeration in Orsino's speeches about his passion and in Viola's conveying of it to Olivia, and the absence of romantic courtship-dialogues between Viola and Orsino and between Olivia and Sebastian, but finds 'not the slightest discord'[5] between the romance and the broader comedy of the play (which, in this respect, he considers much more successful than *Much Ado*). Leech's position is somewhat different: Orsino's closing couplet leaves us 'securely in the world of make-believe', but only for a moment, before Feste's song recalls us to reality:

> Yet the transition is bridged by music. . . . Shakespeare here dismisses his comedy and our acceptance of it, but the total effect is not harsh. We leave the theatre with a tune in our ears, and the harmony of *Twelfth Night* is after a fashion maintained.[6]

Indeed, for Leech, the balance, though achieved, is of the most delicate and precarious kind: the play gives 'delight', and creates

1. 'Music in Shakespeare', *Encounter*, IX (1957); reprinted in *The Dyer's Hand* (1962 ed.), p. 520.
2. *Shakespeare our Contemporary* (revised ed., 1967, transl. B. Taborski), p. 229. The reference is to Fellini's film *La Dolce Vita*, 1959.
3. *Shakespeare and the Confines of Art*, p. 69.
4. E. C. Pettet, *Shakespeare and the Romance Tradition*, title of ch. 5.
5. *Ibid.*, p. 133.
6. '*Twelfth Night*' *and Shakespearean Comedy*, p. 55.

at the same time an uneasy sense that this delight is 'vulnerable';
we rejoice in the life it presents, yet we are kept conscious that
real life is not like this. Like many modern critics, Leech prefers
Shakespeare's later work (he singles out *Troilus and Cressida* and
The Winter's Tale), in which he finds 'a larger vision of comedy'.[1]

Meanwhile, twentieth-century criticism has pursued its purpose of demonstrating the unity of *Twelfth Night* and the coher-
ence of Shakespearean comedy. The thematic approach is the
most characteristic, and has taken various forms with various
critics. What may be called the moral analysis of *Twelfth Night*
has laid particular stress upon the self-deception practised by
Orsino, Olivia, and Malvolio (and sometimes by others), and
upon the related question of whether they do or do not acquire
self-knowledge. It has been applied by some critics with the
crudest rigour;[2] by others with sensitivity and discretion, as by
J. H. Summers (1955).[3] J. R. Brown (1957) is also illuminating,
for his discussion of the play is part of an 'attempt to define the
implicit judgement' which informs the comedies and to 'determine
Shakespeare's ideals of romantic love', which Brown recognizes
to be the main motive of most of them.[4] At a still more philosophical—and more abstract—level, the self-deceptions, decep-
tions, and mistakes have been related to an examination of
appearance and reality, conspicuously by Frank Kermode
(1961), who concludes that *Twelfth Night* is 'a comedy of identity,
set on the borders of wonder and madness'.[5] The emotional and
imaginative unity of the romantic part of the play has been
asserted by G. Wilson Knight (1932), pointing to a thematic
pattern of 'music, love, and precious stones, threaded by the
sombre strands of a sea-tempest and a sea-flight', leading
finally to 'love, reunion and joy'; he finds similar elements in
other Shakespearean plays.[6] Northrop Frye (1949), whose concern is with comedy as a genre, with particular reference to its
traditional and mythic nature and to its celebration of 'the

---

1. *Ibid.*, p. 87.
2. Herbert R. Coursen, Jr, 'Shakespeare in Maine: Summer, 1970' (review
of productions), *Sh. Q.* xxi (1970), 488. Herschel Baker, *Twelfth Night*, Signet
ed. (New York, 1965), p. xxviii, calls Orsino 'a narcissistic fool'.
3. 'The Masks of *Twelfth Night*', *University of Kansas City Review*, 22 (1955);
reprinted in L. F. Dean (ed.), *Shakespeare: Modern Essays in Criticism* (New York,
1961), pp. 128–37.
4. *Shakespeare and his Comedies*, p. 44.
5. 'The Mature Comedies', in J. R. Brown and B. Harris (eds.), *Stratford-upon-
Avon Studies 3: Early Shakespeare*, p. 227.
6. *The Shakespearian Tempest*, p. 126.

triumph of life over the waste land', maintains that Shakespearean comedy expresses this triumph by transferring the action 'from the normal world to the green world and back again': this green world, which opens up an idealized prospect of life, is a forest if the play contains one, and, if not, its greenness (as of Portia's Belmont) is metaphorical; thus *Twelfth Night* 'presents a carnival society, not so much a green world as an evergreen one'.[1] C. L. Barber (1959), with a closer relevance to the festive element as it is actually presented in *Twelfth Night*, examines in this and earlier Shakespearean comedies 'the way the social form of Elizabethan holidays contributed to the dramatic form of festive comedy' by means of dance, disguise, merriment, and licence.[2] Finally, a contemporary social theme, the Elizabethan pursuit of 'social security', has been extracted from the play by J. W. Draper: he regards the contention for Olivia's hand as the 'major plot', and stresses the social motivation of Sir Andrew and Malvolio (Shakespeare's additions to his source), along with that of Sir Toby and Maria.[3]

This necessarily compressed account of critical developments must not be taken to imply that the new has driven out the old. *Twelfth Night* is still numbered among Shakespeare's 'Happy Comedies' by J. Dover Wilson (1962),[4] and, I believe, by most readers and spectators; the characterization continues to be praised; and Shakespeare's dramatic technique, which any Shakespearean critic neglects at his peril, has not been neglected even by critics whose principal interests have lain elsewhere. In his useful study of dramatic irony in the comedies (itself reaching out to wider questions) Bertrand Evans (1960) has an important and detailed chapter on *Twelfth Night*;[5] and two well-balanced essays, both beginning by relating *Twelfth Night* to its sources and to Shakespeare's earlier comedies, have been written by L. G. Salingar (1958)[6] and Harold Jenkins (1959).[7]

1. 'The Argument of Comedy', in *English Institute Essays 1948* (New York, 1949). More recently (*A Natural Perspective*, 1965), Frye has transferred this symbolic importance from the carnival society to the sea (cf. G. Wilson Knight's emphasis): Viola and Sebastian emerge from the sea as strange ambiguous beings who fulfil a restorative function.

2. *Shakespeare's Festive Comedy* (Princeton, N.J.).

3. *The 'Twelfth Night' of Shakespeare's Audience* (Stanford and London, 1950).

4. *Shakespeare's Happy Comedies.*

5. *Shakespeare's Comedies* (Oxford).

6. 'The Design of *Twelfth Night*', *Shakespeare Quarterly*, IX (1958), pp. 117–39.

7. Shakespeare's '*Twelfth Night*', *Rice Institute Pamphlet*, XLV (1959); reprinted in K. Muir (ed.), *Shakespeare: The Comedies* (*Twentieth-Century Views*, Englewood Cliffs, N.J., 1965): page-references (below) are to this volume.

No general comments upon the critical history, or upon the play itself in the light of it, can hope to be comprehensive, yet it is proper to attempt a few. A suitable starting-point is J. R. Brown's survey of the interpretation of the comedies in the first half of this century.[1] He mentions the danger of excessive pre-occupation with character, which has led readers (for example) to neglect the early comedies, to belittle the Claudio–Hero plot of *Much Ado*, and to consider the ends of *The Two Gentlemen of Verona*, *Much Ado* and *Twelfth Night* 'precipitous and unsatis-fying'; and he comments that 'there does seem to be something wrong with a theory of Shakespeare's comedy which implies that all his successes are so considerably blemished'.[2] This remark recalls Johnson's objection to Olivia's marriage, and some modern critics' dissatisfaction with Viola's. Another modern critic, Alexander Leggatt, counters the objection and the dis-satisfaction:

> The ending takes little account of the reasons for particular attachments; it is, on the contrary, a generalized image of love.
> As such, its significance is limited. We can easily think of Rosalind and Orlando married and producing children, for they think of themselves that way; but the union of lovers in *Twelfth Night* is more a freezing of the moment of romantic contemplation, before the practical business of marriage: Viola is to be 'Orsino's mistress, and his fancy's queen' . . . The happiness they have achieved is more stylized and conventional [than Rosalind's and Orlando's]. It is also more miraculous and exclusive: it cannot touch the ordinary world.[3]

Marriage in Shakespeare, as Nevill Coghill had said, is 'an image of happiness that ends his comedies almost as invariably as death ends a tragedy';[4] Shakespeare's comic vision is 'the firm asser-tion of basic harmony'.[5] Not that at the end of *Twelfth Night* this harmony is achieved without reference to character; the char-acter which creates it, as Stopford A. Brooke recognized, is Viola's:

1. 'The Interpretation of Shakespeare's Comedies, 1900–1953', *Shakespeare Survey*, 8 (1955), 1–13.
2. *Ibid.*, p. 7.
3. *Shakespeare's Comedy of Love* (1974), p. 251.
4. 'Comic Form in *Measure for Measure*', *Shakespeare Survey*, 8 (1955), p. 18.
5. N. Coghill, 'The Basis of Shakespeare's Comedy', *Essays and Studies* (1950), p. 13.

The atmosphere of love is round all that Viola is; and it creates love in whomsoever it touches. It infects Olivia. It has already infected the Duke. He loves Cesario; he needs only one touch of circumstance to love Viola.[1]

If Viola is regarded in this way, as the centre of the main plot, there is less danger of over-stressing or misinterpreting the irony with which Orsino and Olivia are regarded:

> Shakespeare gives the love intrigue the necessary remoteness, by the poetic charm with which he invests it, and the delicate irony with which he touches it. Viola must have her Orsino, and Olivia finds a substitute for her Cesario; and this Shakespeare achieves without provoking criticism by any realistic treatment of the story's improbabilities.[2]

The irony, indeed, can be seen to be serving an artistic purpose (the maintaining of lightness of mood because of their amusing unawareness that Viola is a woman, loves Orsino, and will eventually marry him) much more than any moral purpose of exposing Orsino's and Olivia's defects of character.

The other principal dramatic interest, the scheme against Malvolio, has also been viewed in different ways. It is, of course, the secondary interest, though sometimes treated by actors and readers as the primary one. 'The distortion of emphasis this implies is a tribute to Shakespeare's invention of the most novel situation in the play',[3] as is the sympathy which Malvolio has sometimes excited. He is often compared to Shylock, as an unpleasant character who is nevertheless credibly human, perhaps so human as to disturb the balance of the comedy in which he appears and to make us uneasy at his discomfiture. The comparison is not unreasonable, though it should be borne in mind that Shylock is a danger and Malvolio merely a nuisance.[4] It is when

---

1. *Ten More Plays of Shakespeare* (1913), p. 47.

2. Peter Alexander, *Shakespeare's Life and Art* (1939), p. 137.

3. H. Jenkins, *op. cit.*, p. 83. He points out that the main plot of the play is developed before this secondary one is set in motion.

4. To call him so is not to diminish his importance in the play. It is true that 'while Shylock is a threat to life itself, Malvolio is a threat to the enjoyment of it' (Harold Jenkins, privately). Though diligent in his stewardship ('I would not have him miscarry for the half of my dowry', III. iv. 62–3), he is officious and uncharitable, and therefore hostile not merely to Sir Toby but also to the Clown and to the disguised Viola. In a comedy, and one which is called *Twelfth Night*, he must be defeated; and accordingly, though Sir Toby has to submit to Olivia's authority (IV. i. 44–50), he is allowed to triumph over Malvolio.

Malvolio is treated as a madman that uneasiness is felt, an uneasiness which Manningham evidently did not share,[1] and which
(though it may be unsafe to measure Shakespeare by his times)
perhaps distinguishes modern sensibilities from Elizabethan:
L. Cazamian points out that

> having to prove their sanity is a pet nightmare with many,
> and we do not like to be reminded how the insane were then
> treated.[2]

It is also possible to pity Malvolio for what he is, as well as for
what he suffers:

> But he is certainly pathetic, if one thinks about it, because he is
> so utterly cut off from everyone else by his anxious self-love.[3]

This view (as the phrase 'if one thinks about it' suggests) comes
from reflecting on Malvolio rather than from experiencing the
impact of his personality while hearing or reading his lines: he
remains well pleased with his self-love, and though he could be
content to marry Olivia as a means to becoming Count Malvolio,
he does not crave the love of her or of anyone else. It is clear from
his letter to Olivia (which 'savours not much of distraction') that
his confinement to the dark room has not broken him, as it is
sometimes wrongly represented as doing; and the fact is clearer
still when he reappears, upbraids Olivia with having done him
'notorious wrong', learns how he has been gulled, and makes an
angry and implacable exit. This exit, again, may be seen as disturbing the final harmony, and so in a sense it does, by providing
a discord; yet the Duke's command, 'Pursue him, and entreat
him to a peace', carries sufficient weight to resolve the discord,
within the framework of the play. Shakespeare always knows
who can and who cannot be included in the final reconciliations
on the stage, and this is partly what makes them so satisfying:
'He avoids what would falsify them, and so they are not
false.'[4]

The Malvolio scenes have been called 'Jonsonian',[5] and there is
some justice in this epithet. Both Malvolio and Sir Andrew are

1. See p. xxvi. E. E. Stoll, *Shakespeare Studies* (New York, 1962 ed.), p. 313,
declares that 'the invitation to hilarity' is 'plain and clear'.

2. *The Development of English Humour* (Durham, N. Carolina, 1952), p. 215.

3. Barber, *op. cit.*, p. 256.

4. H. F. Brooks (privately). See pp. lxxix, xcviii.

5. C. H. Herford (ed.), *Plays of Ben Jonson* (The Mermaid Dramatists),
1893–5, I, xliii.

'gulls',[1] and Sir Toby is, as far as Sir Andrew is concerned, a cheat who exploits his gullibility. Yet if these scenes are Jonsonian, they are so in a Shakespearean way. As for Sir Andrew, 'no one expects or desires his reform',[2] and his 'natural fatuity' (which Dr Johnson thought an unfit subject for ridicule)[3] marks him as one of Shakespeare's delightful idiots, like Verges or Slender.[4] Malvolio, complacently thanking Jove for his good fortune, was well described by Rowe as 'fantastical',[5] and his encounter with Sir Toby is one of the comic highlights of the play, not because it is satirical but because it is absurd. His traits of personality— his hostility to revelry, his social ambition, his self-love which is at the root of both these and of his churlishness to the Clown and to Viola—may be, indeed, considered not primarily as means of exposing him to our moral criticism but as means of exposing him to the trick which is played upon him for Sir Toby's pastime[6] and our own. Sir Andrew's quarrelsomeness, while it is the mark of the fool positive, is also Shakespeare's instrument in contriving the duel scene, to be followed by the coward's comic hubris and nemesis which are shown in rapid succession when he tries to beat Sebastian. There is poetic justice, but of a lightweight sort, when he and Sir Toby get bloody coxcombs at the end of the play: it does not, any more than Malvolio's anger, darken the final joy, and we are over-sensitive on Sir Andrew's behalf if Sir Toby's irritable rejection of him causes us pain.

I have dwelt on characterization, in relation to plot-construction and mood, because these are the fundamentals of drama. Shakespeare begins with a borrowed story which he modifies and builds upon; he adds a sub-plot, links it to the main plot both structurally and thematically (chiefly by the courtship theme and by that of false appearances), and calls out our emotional response by presenting character through situation, action, and speech. The style of *Twelfth Night* is not easily summarized: G. Wilson

---

1. 'Gull him into a nayword' (II. iii. 135–6); 'my noble gull-catcher' (II. v. 187); 'yond gull Malvolio' (III. ii. 66); 'a thin-faced knave, a gull' (v. i. 205); 'the most notorious geck and gull' (v. i. 342). There are only seven other occurrences of 'gull' in Shakespeare's writings.

2. O. J. Campbell, *Shakespeare's Satire* (1943), p. 84.

3. See p. l.

4. See commentary, I. iii. 114–15.

5. See p. l. As Harold Jenkins points out (privately), Rowe's epithet 'suggests a point of correspondence between Orsino and Malvolio in that each is dominated by the fantasies of his own mind' (cf. I. i. 15), though Orsino's fantasy springs from romantic illusion and Malvolio's from the illusions of ambition.

6. III. iv. 139.

Knight has called attention to some of the dominant images,[1] but there is 'no recurrent group of associations for the imagery'[2] as there is in *A Midsummer Night's Dream* with its fairies and its moonlit wood, and the versification is generally designed for fluency rather than for any patterned effects.[3] The prose (which accounts for more than half the lines of this play, so 'poetic' in the feeling of the main plot) is vivacious and often brilliant.

> She did show favour to the youth in your sight only to exasper-
> ate you, to awake your dormouse valour, to put fire in your
> heart, and brimstone in your liver.[4]

'Brimstone in your liver' is a delightfully unexpected parallel to the conventional 'fire in your heart', and the use of 'dormouse' as an epithet is a stroke of genius. *Twelfth Night* is remarkable for its combination of romantic comedy with boisterous comedy, and for the imagination which has created both.

5 CRITICAL ANALYSIS BY ACTS AND SCENES

[I. i] The reading of plays backwards is a kind of blasphemy against drama. No matter how complete the unity of a play, no matter how much reflected light the later scenes may throw on the earlier, the earlier scenes come first, and our view of character, action, and theme is widened as the later ones follow. Admittedly, in interpreting Shakespeare we are all wise after the event: it is impossible to suspend our knowledge of what is coming, nor would it be desirable to do so if we could, for his plays never depend on mere surprise for the satisfaction they give, and, moreover, the earlier scenes have been designed to prepare us for the later ones. Yet the dangers of over-familiarity remain, and we should be armed against them. One danger is misplaced emphasis,[5] another is premature judgment. These dangers are heightened when the critical tradition is almost as familiar as the play.

The opening scene of *Twelfth Night* is a case in point. We are shown Orsino's love for Olivia, and are told of her seven years'

1. See p. lv.

2. B. Ifor Evans, *The Language of Shakespeare's Plays* (1952), p. 115.

3. Pattern is not absent: it contributes to the rhetoric of Viola's 'willow cabin' speech with the line-beginnings 'Make me . . . And call . . . Write . . . And sing . . . Halloo . . . And make . . .' (I. v. 272–7).

4. III. ii. 16–19.

5. If, for example, while watching a performance of the trial scene in *Mer.V.* we are chiefly waiting to see how Shylock will take his disappointment.

vow of mourning, for which reason she refuses to receive the messenger of his courtship; but whether or not he will finally win her is left an open question. What we are offered is a situation: the irresistible force (Orsino's passion) opposing the immovable object (Olivia's self-seclusion).

This does not mean that Shakespeare offers us a situation and nothing more; obviously he must clothe its bones with the flesh of language, and in doing this he must characterize the speaker, and may do other things besides.[1] There is, however, a widespread assumption that this first scene is designed chiefly to exhibit, if not to expose, the nature of Orsino's love. To regard Orsino as though he were predestined to sentimentality, so that his every word confirms his reprobation as a lover, is not the way into the scene or the play. We must allow 'the richness and ardency' of his fancy,[2] even if we do also suspect him of luxuriating in it. In short, his speeches raise another open question, whether (the play being a comedy) his love will persist in its present extreme form.[3]

Olivia's vow gives us more definite expectations. In comedy, vows like hers are made to be broken; but we are invited to wonder what will make her break it, rather than to leap to the judgment that she was a fool to make it. Orsino's admiring comment points in the former direction ('How will she love . . .!'), while his commendation of her 'heart of that fine frame' (even allowing for his bias as her lover) reflects credit on them both, not least because it is this very vow of hers which frustrates his love.

[ii] Viola's arrival in Illyria is essentially a cheerful scene, in spite of her shipwreck and her separation from her brother. Though she feels his loss (her 'Elysium' lines are deeply touching), hope emerges from her distress, and the Captain's speech, while picturing a real shipwreck, is very reassuring.[4] It creates a noble

1. The contribution made by the music, and by the sensuous imagery (including a reference to the sea, which looks forward to the next scene), is noticed by every reader.

2. The phrase is from J. R. Brown, *Shakespeare and his Comedies* (1957), p. 165, who is much aware of Orsino's limitations.

3. He may, for instance, be another Valentine (*Gent.*) who gets his lady in the end. Valentine survives the light mockery of his servant, as Orsino does that of the Clown. (If Shakespeare had wished to expose Orsino, he had Valentine and Curio ready to hand for an opening dialogue.)

4. Viola must be kept in at least nominal doubt of Sebastian's survival, so that the final recognition scene is properly moving, yet she must feel it to be probable, so that her adventures in Illyria do not appear to us too lively for her pathetic situation.

vigorous brother for Viola (the 'Arion' simile also serving to sustain the poetic mood of I. i). His characterization of Orsino ('A noble duke, in nature as in name') and Olivia ('A virtuous maid') confirms their real merit, which nothing in the previous scene should have made us doubt, and his neutral account of Orsino's courtship and Olivia's vow gives us no reason to regard the latter as an affectation of sorrow or as a device to avoid an unwelcome suitor. Viola's remark about Orsino, 'He was a bachelor then', is Shakespeare's way of introducing the Captain's information, and not of hinting any ambition in Viola, for he makes it clear that her original plan is to serve Olivia, not Orsino; thus her disguise appears a natural step and neither a deep-laid scheme nor an irresponsible caprice.[1] Yet her intention of singing and playing to the Duke already begins faintly to suggest to us (after the previous scene's emphasis on music) the possibility of love between the two. The scene ends with the first of several hints that time will resolve whatever may chance to happen.

The contrast with the first scene is marked, but can be over-interpreted. The comfort Viola takes despite her brother's loss does not reflect adversely on Olivia's mourning for a brother who really is dead,[2] nor does Sebastian's activity as a shipwrecked passenger reflect on Orsino's passiveness as an unrequited lover (a passiveness to which the plot confines him if he is to employ Viola as his messenger). What is certainly suggested is that the apparent deadlock of the first scene is presently to be broken.

[iii] Both the first two scenes have been placed in the world of romance. In the third, with its bolder contrast, we 'step down-stairs'.[3]

What a plague means my niece to take the death of her brother thus? I am sure care's an enemy to life.

Sir Toby's first words tell us who he is and what he is, Olivia's kinsman and a reveller. This scene, familiarizing us with Sir

1. 'Till I had made mine own occasion mellow' will pass in the theatre. There is, and can be, no sound reason given for her taking service with either Olivia or Orsino: this is simply required by the plot, from which Shakespeare has dropped the original motivation of the heroine's disguise (to serve the man she secretly loves).

2. Olivia's vow of seven years' mourning is often, and rightly, compared with the lords' vow of three years' study in *LLL.*, I. i, but it should also be compared with the Princess's vow of one year's mourning for her father, *LLL.*, v. i. It is, of course, very possible that Viola's loss of her brother put into Shakespeare's head the reason for Olivia's vow.

3. G. Gordon, *Shakespearean Comedy and Other Studies* (Oxford, 1944), p. 50.

Toby, his dupe Sir Andrew, and the lively Maria, is also a preparation for things to come, talk of Sir Andrew's quarrelsomeness anticipating his challenge to Cesario, and his eager 'Shall we set about some revels?' anticipating their conflict with Malvolio's austerity.

[iv]   As a ludicrous suitor to Olivia, Sir Andrew gives scale to the noble Orsino, who now reappears. First we are shown that Viola has become Cesario and has in three days gained Orsino's favour. Shakespeare takes the opportunity to put in another good word for the Duke, who is not 'inconstant in his favours', and Orsino's imagery confirms that the page is his friend as well as his confidant:

> I have unclasp'd
> To thee the book even of my secret soul.

Their dialogue foreshadows the next scene: Viola is to break through Olivia's barrier, and, that done, to act Orsino's woes (when the impression made by her youthfulness may be greater than Orsino would desire). The Duke's dwelling on the page's womanly appearance launches the dramatic irony of their future relationship, and his closing lines hint both at its happy conclusion and at the apparent logical impossibility of that conclusion:

> Prosper well in this,
> And thou shalt live as freely as thy lord,
> To call his fortunes thine.

The double hint is not present when the words are uttered, but they are still echoing when Viola's love is sprung upon us by her aside, in a couplet that also concludes the scene:

> I'll do my best
> To woo your lady: yet, a barful strife!
> Whoe'er I woo, myself would be his wife.

[v]   Between Viola's leaving Orsino and her encountering Olivia, Shakespeare introduces the Clown and builds up our picture of Olivia's household. He also prepares for later scenes, since the Clown's reported absence without leave prevents our surprise when we later see him at Orsino's, and the first hint is dropped of Maria's ultimate marriage with Sir Toby. When Olivia enters, attended by Malvolio, the dialogue (as usual) serves several purposes. The Clown regains Olivia's approval and increases our own. His 'proof' that she is a 'fool' redirects our

attention to her rash vow (sympathetically and not contemptu-
ously), and other speeches of his obscurely foreshadow its aban-
donment and her marriage.[1] Olivia's generous readiness to be
pleased with him sets off Malvolio's gratuitous hostility, which
displays his 'self-love' (his master passion, and the ground of his
gulling) and which also motivates the Clown's revenge. Viola's
entry is carefully prepared in advance (with further exhibition
of Sir Toby and of Malvolio), since her embassy, and its effect
upon Olivia, will be the heart of this important scene.

Olivia's veil,[2] the symbol of her vow and hence of her inac-
cessibility to Orsino, allows Viola (whose assurance, already reported by Malvolio, is our reassurance that the 'barful strife'
of I. iv. 41 will give her and us no deep distress) to expatiate on
her own prepared 'speech' which 'is poetical'; its removal, dis-
playing Olivia's beauty, allows Viola to launch instead into the
spontaneous poetry of her attack upon Olivia's refusal to marry
and to requite Orsino's love. The balance between lightness and
gravity, with the dramatic irony of Viola's situation underlying
both, is finely maintained: wit and feeling continually overlap.[3]
There is flippancy in Olivia's conceits upon 'divinity', 'picture',
and 'schedules', her prose throwing Viola's verse into relief.
Viola's faithful utterance of Orsino's love for Olivia carries with
it all the force of her own love for him, and this adds a dimension
to the adorer's conventional plaint, which, as she delivers it, far
transcends the conventional: the hyperbolical 'groans that
thunder love' and 'sighs of fire', the antithetical 'deadly life'
of unrequited love, and the beautifully expressed sentimental
actions in the 'willow cabin' speech, combine to make Orsino's
feelings both conventional in themselves and held with passionate
sincerity by him.[4] That love is an irresistible passion, whether it

1. 'As there is no true cuckold but calamity, so beauty's a flower.' 'Thou hast
spoke for us, madonna, as if thy eldest son should be a fool: whose skull Jove
cram with brains.' (The latter remark is also, of course, a bridge to the next
sentence, introducing Sir Toby.)

2. Which should surely be black. Whether she is to change her mourning
costume later in the play is not made clear: not, one would think, before her
interview with Malvolio, III. iv; perhaps between IV. i and IV. iii.

3. As in Olivia's 'If I do not usurp myself, I am', and Viola's rejoinder.

4. We are, by now, expecting that he will finally marry Viola, but we need
not therefore be hypercritical of his passion for Olivia. Viola has no expectation
that his mind will change; nothing she says ever hints that she considers his
passion less than genuine and lasting. Olivia, while insisting that she 'cannot
love him', pays tribute to his merit (I. v. 262–6), which renews the value
already set upon him.

be Orsino's for Olivia, Viola's for Orsino, or Olivia's for the disguised Viola, is fundamental to the play.

'You might do much': Olivia's words are the turning-point of
the scene. We instantly see what Viola does not yet see; and
we see, too, how her spirited refusal of the purse, with her rhymed
exit-line, clinches the new situation:

> Love make his heart of flint that you shall love,
> And let your fervour like my master's be,
> Plac'd in contempt. Farewell, fair cruelty.

Olivia, having now recognized her own feelings, and sent the
ring which shall make them known to Orsino's messenger,
abandons herself and the situation to a stronger power:

> Fate, show thy force; ourselves we do not owe.
> What is decreed, must be: and be this so.

[II. i] The next scene opens with two new characters, one of
whom presently identifies himself as Viola's brother Sebastian.
He informs Antonio (his rescuer and now his friend) of his parentage and history. This scene, the counterpart of i. ii, is very different from it. Viola had good hope of her brother's safety (the
play required to be firmly grounded as a comedy); he despairs
of hers (but we know better), and praises the beauty of her mind
(praise with which we readily concur). Viola did not go into inappropriate and premature detail about their being identical
twins, but such detail is appropriate and timely here, when the
shipwreck is a thing of the past, and the plot has just been complicated by Olivia's love for Viola, whom she supposes to be a
young man.[1]

Yet the scene does not give too much away. We are so conscious of Sebastian as Viola's loving brother and Antonio's beloved friend that we are not impelled to see in him Olivia's
future husband. Even his statement that he is 'bound to the
Count Orsino's court', with its obvious promise of situations of
mistaken identity, is overshadowed by Antonio's soliloquy, which
ends the scene by promising an element of danger and enmity
quite new to the play.

1. Bertrand Evans, *Shakespeare's Comedies* (Oxford, 1960), p. 122, remarks
that Sebastian's appearance is much earlier than is strictly necessary, and that
it is conspicuously placed between Olivia's sending the ring and Viola's receiving
it (events which, he thinks, would normally be juxtaposed by Shakespeare).
This is, he argues, 'our assurance that all is well and will end well, an assurance
which contradicts Viola's distress on recognizing what seems a hopeless entangle-
ment'.

[ii]   Malvolio, with characteristic churlishness, delivers Olivia's ring to Viola, who concludes in soliloquy that her 'outside' has 'charm'd' Olivia.[1] Her response is to pity the lady, for in her own character she can show her a fellow-feeling which she cannot as Cesario; her general reflections about women's 'frailty' similarly associate Olivia and herself, and prevent our giving all our sympathy to the one and none to the other. This soliloquy is the pivot of the play, summing up the complicated and fantastic situation, attributing it to 'fortune', and leaving it to 'time' to resolve. The final couplet is ambiguous in its effect: on the one hand, Viola abandons the 'knot' as 'too hard'; on the other, her words invite us (having just seen Sebastian) to entrust it confidently to time.[2]

[iii]   Having thus fully matured the situation on which his main plot turns, Shakespeare sets about developing his secondary plot. The scene opens in a festive, relaxed spirit, with Sir Toby and Sir Andrew each fooling after his fashion, and the Clown contributing his professional nonsense and a song which introduces the play's leading theme of love into this scene of 'good life'; the song also brings in the catch, and the catch brings in Malvolio.[3] Malvolio has his orders from Olivia, but he carries them out in exactly the same churlish manner as he returned the ring to Viola: his first speech consists wholly of aggressive rhetorical questions, off which it is a pleasure to see Sir Toby score,[4] and the tart antitheses of his second one are in his own style and not in his lady's. That Sir Toby and the Clown pursue the argument

    1. It is not necessary to suppose that, in replying to Malvolio 'She took the ring of me', Viola has instantly deduced Olivia's love and is therefore concealing her deduction: she may be merely concealing from Malvolio the difference between Olivia's message and the facts (thereby avoiding giving Olivia the lie in her steward's hearing, and avoiding also an unseemly wrangle with him about the facts). She responds as the Duke's messenger might well respond if the facts were as Malvolio states them (that is, if the Duke really had sent Olivia a ring which she had accepted but on second thoughts returned). Moreover, even if she has formed a shrewd suspicion of Olivia's motive in sending the ring, she cannot express it until she is alone; and then 'what means this lady?' need not show bewilderment, but merely surprise that Olivia should act (and feel) in this way.

    2. Contrast Hamlet's:

            The time is out of joint. O cursed spite,
            That ever I was born to set it right!

where, the play being a tragedy, we feel more apprehension than confidence.

    3. With Maria to prepare his coming. The Clown's earlier mention of him (l. 27) has put him and his austerity in mind. The catch, too, is first mentioned the moment the Clown appears.

    4. By his usual form of wit, the quibble: cf. i. iii, his first two replies to Maria.

in song, reducing him to indignant interjections, adds to his sourness, which he vents on Maria as he withdraws. He has thus given offence to all of them, and their conspiracy against him begins the moment he leaves the stage. Shakespeare's handling of the rest of the dialogue, as of the whole scene, is artfully natural.[1] Sir Andrew's witless proposal of an abortive challenge taken up by Sir Toby prepares for his challenge to Cesario, as his zeal to beat Malvolio[2] for being a puritan prepares for his disastrous attempt to beat Sebastian. Meanwhile Maria, unfolding her more promising plan, brings in by the way a reminder that Olivia 'is much out of quiet' after her interview with Viola, to explain why she sent Malvolio to suppress the singing. Thus scenes are connected, plausibility is strengthened, and the direct course of this scene (forward to the letter scene, II. v) is disguised. It is reiterated that Malvolio's weakness is self-conceit, and a full display of this is promised when he finds the forged letter. When Maria goes, the knights subside into their usual element, drink, but not without further reminders of Sir Toby's and Maria's mutual appreciation, and of Sir Andrew's courtship of Olivia, so unprofitable to himself.

[iv] From the small hours at Olivia's house the play moves to morning at Orsino's, from a foolish wooer to a noble one, and from 'caterwauling' and 'coziers' catches' to an 'old and antic song'. This is our first sight of Viola with Orsino since she confided her secret love in an aside and a soliloquy. How successfully she will continue to conceal it from him will accordingly occupy our chief attention.

The delay while the singer is found allows them two dialogues instead of one: expansiveness is gained without risking tedium, and Viola's love is covertly expressed in two different ways, as Cesario's love for a lady of the Duke's years and complexion, and as Cesario's sister's love for a man to whom she never told it.[3] Over both dialogues, as over the play's first scene, hangs emotive

1. Compare, for an earlier instance of natural presentation, the way that when Sir Toby calls out for Maria to bring wine, it is the Clown who comes in. A difficulty, however, is that the Clown takes no further part in the scene after l. 117, and that by ll. 173–4 he seems to be off stage. Possibly his last line was his exit line and the direction has dropped out. Since he is to reappear in Orsino's court midway through the next scene, it is doubly unlikely that Shakespeare meant him to remain, with nothing to do or say, till the end of the present scene. See p. xx–xxi above.

2. Pursued in II. v. 33: ''Slight, I could so beat the rogue!'

3. I express it thus for brevity's sake. This is how it appears to Orsino: but everything Viola says is directly applicable to herself in her real person.

music, prompting both speakers to express their feelings; in contrast to this prevailing spirit of sentiment, the Clown is allowed to interject his mild mockery of Orsino's melancholy and capriciousness of mood; while the dialogues themselves are opal and changeable taffeta, the dramatic irony most delicately balanced between the humour (of Orsino's unawareness that Cesario is a woman and loves him) and the pathos (of Viola's inability to enlighten him).

The emphasis of the scene is upon Viola, for we already know all there is to know about Orsino's love for Olivia. In the dialogue before the song she says little, just enough to prompt Orsino's generalized observations and finally to cap his couplet with one which hints at her latent sadness and also introduces the remoter sadness of the song. In the second dialogue she is brought so much nearer to disclosing her love and her identity that for a moment we almost expect her to do so:

> *Viola.*   Ay, but I know—
> *Duke.* What dost thou know?
> *Viola.* Too well what love women to men may owe:
>   In faith, they are as true of heart as we.
>   My father had a daughter lov'd a man . . .

With the full line and its rhyme all is safe again; with the next, she is once more keeping up the fiction of the man-to-man conversation about love and women; and with the third, she is beginning to tell her own story as if it were someone else's. Her self-restraint adds to the poignancy of the well-known lines that follow: she ends half-humorously with a generalization of her own about how 'we men' behave. Orsino's question,

> But died thy sister of her love, my boy?

expresses more than curiosity: he is moved by the story and by its telling, and in this double sympathy for his page and his page's sister he comes as close as the situation permits to loving Viola herself. Her reply is:

> I am all the daughters of my father's house,
> And all the brothers too: and yet I know not.

The first line we might have anticipated. The second, totally unprepared by anything in the scene, wonderfully deepens the feeling: it is far more than a reminder of the 'twins' theme; it expresses a sense of loss and loneliness, yet in the same instant it arrives at hope and resilience, and leads on to the brisk closing lines of the scene, in which Viola sets off again for Olivia's.

[v]　With another strong contrast, the action returns to the conspiracy against Malvolio. Like the previous and very different scene, this scene is varied, prolonged, and developed far beyond expectation. Before he sees the letter (even before he appears) Malvolio is indulging his ambitious and substantial daydreams; they include not only marrying Olivia and thereby becoming Count Malvolio, but also, from that exalted position, reproving his kinsman Toby;[1] consequently Sir Toby adds unexpected comedy to the scene with his robust indignation at what he never looked to overhear. The letter itself is added fuel to an already blazing imagination. Yet its riddling verse slows Malvolio down to a ludicrous deliberateness, a tortoise-like advance upon its meaning. Then 'follows prose', prose designed to be recalled by the audience when it is quoted (III. iv) and requoted (v. i); and to its anonymous declaration of love it adds commands—opposition to Sir Toby (we almost hope to see the fancied interview, complete with the 'blow o' the lips'), yellow stockings, cross-gartering—all of which Malvolio proposes to perform 'even with the swiftness of putting on'. 'Jove and my stars be praised!—Here is yet a postscript'—with perhaps the most incongruous command of all:

> thy smiles become thee well. Therefore in my presence still smile, dear my sweet, I prithee.[2]

As Malvolio hurries away to make sure of Olivia and greatness, Sir Toby voluntarily gives up his liberty to Maria, followed in the offer, as in all things, by Sir Andrew, who seems to have forgotten that he is a suitor to Olivia. The whole mood is one of hilarious gaiety, with every prospect of a sequel to match it.

[III. i]　The first three scenes of Act III are mainly devoted to preparing for the fourth scene, the climax and finale of the act.

Viola's quibbling exchange with the Clown has every appearance of a warming-up after a theatrical interval.[3] It adds nothing to the plot, and the Clown's remark about universal folly is of

1. Whose 'Art any more than a steward?' (II. iii. 113–14) has, no doubt, rankled.

2. This takes up another aspect of Malvolio's vanity: 'quenching my familiar smile with an austere regard of control' (ll. 66–7). His familiar smile! (He is, of course, thinking of the affable—and condescending—smile which he will bestow on the household when, as Count Malvolio, he is the head of it.)

3. In view of this impression—and the length of Viola's dialogue before Olivia appears—I doubt Evans's suggestion that 'Maria's promise of the ludicrous spectacle that is to be the highest point of hilarity in all the action thus

debatable importance.[1] His side-strokes at Olivia, Orsino, and Viola herself ('your wisdom') are equally part of his act, like his proving Olivia a fool in I. v and his ironical compliment to Orsino in II. iv (though both those observations have their relevance); so are his cynicism about marriage (which is certainly not the play's view of it) and the saucy roughness of 'but in my conscience, sir, I do not care for you.' All this he evidently delivers without the least ill-will, for Viola takes it in good part, gives him money when she calls a halt, and, in her soliloquy, approves his discretion in suiting his jests to his hearer.[2] Act III will call for the lively, rather than the pathetic, aspect of Viola, and so the tone is set from the first (when the Clown wishes her a beard, her ironical reply treats her secret love lightheartedly), and is maintained when she is accosted by Sir Toby and Sir Andrew. Sir Toby's extravagant style ('taste your legs') permits more quibbling ('understand'), and makes a smooth transition to Viola's complimentary style, which both impresses Sir Andrew and contributes to his later jealousy.

When Viola and Olivia are left alone, fine speaking gives way to plain speaking. Olivia brushes aside the formal compliment,[3] declares her love, and entreats an answer. It is she, not Viola, who is pitiable in this scene, blushing for her forwardness in having sent the ring, struggling to accept Viola's indifference stoically, at last pouring out her love; and Viola does pity her. Her situation would be positively painful to witness if Shakespeare had not kept the emotion under control by putting it into typical couplets like those of *A Midsummer Night's Dream*, by preluding it with a cryptic line-by-line exchange which concentrates on the recurring irony of Viola's disguise ('I am not what I am'),[4] and by rounding it off with Viola's couplets, which reinforce this irony.

---

hangs over the tender scene' (*Shakespeare's Comedies*, pp. 128–9), and that there is any felt connection between Olivia's passion for Cesario (which, he allows, is sympathetically treated) and Malvolio's ambition for Olivia because both are 'preposterous' (*ibid.*, p. 132).

1. I think it is far less relevant to the main action of this play than Puck's 'Lord, what fools these mortals be!' is relevant to that of *MND*.

2. Wilson's notes on 'She will keep no fool, sir, till she be married' and 'your wisdom' suggest, on the contrary, that the Clown is hitting at Cesario's evident progress in Olivia's affections.

3. Which is also, with a transient dramatic irony, a statement of Viola's love for Orsino: 'Your servant's servant'.

4. Cf. the Clown's earlier 'who you are and what you would are out of my welkin' (ll. 58–9), which itself recalls Viola's first visit and Olivia's questions 'What are you? What would you?' (I. v. 215–16).

[ii]   Sir Toby encourages Sir Andrew to send 'the Count's youth' a challenge, and Maria reports that Malvolio 'does obey every point of the letter' and is even now on his way to Olivia. Although we are again reminded that Sir Toby gets money out of Sir Andrew (and therefore has an interest in turning his despair into rivalry), his project of the duel is a piece of mischief-making for sheer fun's sake, and, by association, the gulling of Malvolio becomes one as well: Sir Toby and Fabian are invited not to feed their revenge but to laugh themselves into stitches, an invitation which goes for the audience too.

[iii]   Antonio has followed Sebastian to Orsino's city, as he resolved to do in II. i. His loyalty (too well-motivated, by his concern for Sebastian's safety, to appear as dotage) and Sebastian's gratitude stress the theme of friendship, which (as treated in this play) becomes another aspect of love. The verse expresses the earnestness of both men, and fits the graver subject of Antonio's own danger; his history marks him as the brave, impetuous, but not lawless, man that the future action will require him to be. At the end of the scene he gives Sebastian his purse, a deed which sticks in our minds. But, like their earlier appearance, this one reveals nothing prematurely. The previous scene has not shown us Viola, so we are not driven to anticipate an imminent mistake of identity. Even Sebastian's gratitude, a foreshadowing of Antonio's charge of ingratitude, is introduced before his receiving of the purse, and kept well apart from it by Antonio's story.

[iv]   This scene exploits the dramatic ironies which Shakespeare has been preparing for some time: it is composed of 'four principal situations':

> first, that in which Malvolio's delusion is central; second, that in which Olivia's unawareness of 'Cesario's' identity is central; third, that in which Viola and Sir Andrew's unawareness of Toby's practice is central; fourth, that in which Antonio's mistaking of 'Cesario' for Sebastian is central.[1]

The second of these situations can be developed no further, and is simply reintroduced as the necessary means of linking up the three others.[2]

---

1. Evans, *Shakespeare's Comedies*, p. 133.

2. Hence the greater part of the dialogue is supposed to take place off stage, which both frees Shakespeare from the need to write it and allows him to remove Olivia and let Sir Toby deal with Malvolio. There has been no suggestion at the end of III. i that Viola intends to see Olivia again (quite the contrary), or that Olivia will send after Viola to recall her.

Maria has already (III. ii. 79) relished the idea of the melancholy Olivia confronted with the smiling Malvolio. The real cause
of Olivia's present melancholy heightens our own relish, since she
is indeed in love, though not, as Malvolio fancies, with him:

> I am as mad as he,
> If sad and merry madness equal be.

It is, of course, in spite of her professed sadness, a wholly comic
interview, vigorously and economically dramatized. Its keynote
is Malvolio's invincible assurance: he does not even begin to perceive that he is made an ass. His soliloquy lets us enjoy it in retro-
spect and anticipate his clash with Sir Toby:

> she sends him on purpose, that I may appear stubborn to him;
> for she incites me to that in the letter.

But when Sir Toby comes, if we expected roughness from him,
we are given what is much funnier, diplomacy and cajolery.
Malvolio is allowed to stalk off; we do not see him taken to his
dark room, nor do we worry about when or how Sir Toby's
decision is carried out, for the whole incident is already manifest
fantasy, much larger than life:

> If this were played upon a stage now, I could condemn it
> as an improbable fiction.

With that, in comes Sir Andrew with 'Here's the challenge, read
it'. There is hardly a moment's respite between one absurdity
and the next.[1]

Sir Toby's mischief-making has by this time become the motive
force of the scene: though Maria invented the plot against
Malvolio, Sir Toby is now directing both that and the duel.
He describes each adversary to the other with inventive gusto.
Sir Andrew's comic discomfiture, as the sender of the challenge,
makes him the butt of the joke. Viola shows a natural and
feminine anxiety, but not terror, which would distress us for her.
Even so, and though we know she is in no danger from Sir
Andrew, we shall feel relief when the duel is called off: its object,
in terms of comedy of character (to make Sir Andrew ridiculous),
is already achieved, and it would be embarrassing to see her forced

---

1. Just enough, however, for Sir Toby to give us any reassurance we may
need that they will 'have mercy' on Malvolio when their 'pastime' is 'tired out
of breath'.

lxxiv TWELFTH NIGHT

to handle a sword.[1] A further reason for our relief is added just
as the swords are to be drawn:

> Pray God defend me! A little thing would make me tell them
> how much I lack of a man.

It has never till this moment entered our heads that the duel
could expose Viola's disguise, and we do not want it to happen;
we want the knot untied, not cut.

Therefore, for every reason, Antonio's intervention is welcome.
It is a relief; it is a surprise; and, in beginning to unite Viola's
adventures with Sebastian's, it is neat. Nor is this all, for no sooner
has Antonio appeared than the officers come in to arrest him,
a fresh surprise even though we have been informed of his danger
in Illyria, and one which modifies our pleasure in recognizing
that he has mistaken Viola for Sebastian. When he now asks for
the return of his purse, and Viola denies all knowledge of it or
of him, our emotional response is surely meant to be mixed.
Antonio is a high-principled man and a loving friend, and his
indignation commands our sympathy, yet we are very conscious
that it is all a mistake, so that there is an element of detachment
even in our involvement.[2] Besides, we are still seeing the situation
very much from Viola's point of view, emotionally speaking
(though we do not share her bewilderment), so we are content
to leave Antonio to his future enlightenment, and to share in
Viola's joy in the dawning hope of Sebastian's safety.[3]

With the last few lines of the scene the balance is tipped back

1. This, I think, would be no less true in Shakespeare's theatre with the part
played by a boy, because Viola's femininity has been so thoroughly established.
Producers who make a prolonged farcical spectacle of the duel go directly
against the spirit of the scene, and against its dramatic technique too, since it is
plain from the text that, the moment the opponents draw, Antonio comes in
(for, if he does not come in at once, no stage business can supply him with a
reason for ever doing so). I take it that it is the sight of 'Sebastian' ready to fight
a duel which draws Antonio to take part, not the sight of an absurd reluctance
on the part of both duellists, nor the clash of swords (since Antonio is anxious to
be inconspicuous in Orsino's 'adverse town'), though it is doubtless the clash
of his and Sir Toby's swords which attracts the officers' attention.

2. Permitting us, for instance, to notice how the situation makes Viola's own
high principles look like hypocrisy to Antonio. Evans suggests that perhaps,
despite her innocence and her eagerness to help Antonio, she 'is singed with
an involuntary flash of our resentment' (*Shakespeare's Comedies*, p. 138): I think
this is going too far.

3. She can, in any case, hardly fail to put two and two together, and, if she
did not, we should be asking why not, so Shakespeare has this reason also for
introducing her deduction—though at the end of the play it will be convenient
for him and us to forget it.

towards a broader and simpler comedy. Sir Andrew cannot be allowed to beat Viola, so he must be going to encounter Sebastian.

[IV. i]   This scene hastens on the encounter. The Clown is a well-chosen interlocutor for Sebastian: his natural sharpness indulges itself in ironies (which are comically unconscious truths: 'No, I do not know you . . .'); he thus wears Sebastian's patience thin and puts him in a fit state to deal with Sir Andrew; and he comes in handy to fetch Olivia to the quarrel.[1] Sebastian defies Sir Toby manfully, Olivia dismisses him with dignity; and though the comic mood persists in her mistaking Sebastian for Viola—to his amazement—the short scene ends with delight and harmony. No sooner have the mistakes of identity begun than the romantic knitting up begins too.

[ii]   This being so, the scene of Malvolio's imprisonment appears as an interlude. It is less Malvolio's scene than the Clown's: in the 'Pythagoras' dialogue, for example, the interest lies in seeing how the Clown will manage to retort upon sense, and his 'bay-windows' speech gives him a new vent for his folly when he delivers it as if it were reason. His skipping versatility, in being first Sir Topas and then himself and then for a while both together, carries the scene along briskly, but, as Sir Toby's wish to be 'well rid of this knavery' shows, this part of the play is being allowed to run down after its climax in III. iv, though the letter which Malvolio is about to send Olivia may be expected to produce a final burst of comedy.

[iii]   Sebastian's soliloquy takes up his aside near the end of IV. i, with its mingling of wonder and delight reinforced by the imagery of 'the glorious sun' and 'this accident and flood of fortune'. His tribute to Olivia's 'smooth, discreet, and stable bearing' colours her speech, in which the haste of her marriage is far less important than her religious sincerity, on which the heavens shine approvingly. The scene has to be short,[2] but it is not perfunctory.

[v. i]   The last act consists of one great scene.

It begins lightly and in prose: Malvolio's letter is introduced less as a reminder than as a way of getting the scene quietly started, like the Clown's characteristic performance for Orsino

---

1. These benefits more than compensate for the lack of connection (cf. that between III. i and III. iv, above) between Olivia's parting from Viola in the previous scene and her having now sent the Clown to fetch her.

2. They cannot have a long dialogue without noticing, or conspicuously failing to notice, the mistake about Sebastian's identity.

which follows it. Orsino's natural benignity, his good humour, is a foil to the passions he will soon be called upon to show, and his dialogue with Antonio (who is now brought before him) begins to prepare for them. Orsino is stern, but still not angry; he generously and eloquently acknowledges his enemy's past bravery ('That very envy and the tongue of loss / Cried fame and honour on him'). Antonio reiterates his charge against the supposed Sebastian, with this difference from III. iv, that his speech re-creates the original shipwreck, so that we begin to have a sense of the wheel's coming full circle at last. The 'three months' for which both Antonio and Orsino insist that they have had the young man's company also seem to be bringing on the dénouement through the very fact of their inconsistency.

Olivia's entry precludes premature investigation of the point ('But more of that anon'), and substitutes a last agonizing of the characters' emotions. Her final refusal of Orsino's suit precipitates his outburst: his first impulse is to kill her (though 'had I the heart to do it' shows that this impulse is rejected before it is expressed), his second to kill Viola:

> I'll sacrifice the lamb that I do love,
> To spite a raven's heart within a dove.

Viola responds to his mood and to its expression:

> And I most jocund, apt, and willingly,
> To do you rest, a thousand deaths would die.

This is frankly theatrical, even melodramatic, but it is an ingredient which Shakespearean romantic comedy has already shown itself well able to digest.[1] Though the whole play is our reassurance against the threat's being carried out, the whole play equally demands that we take the threat seriously, for this is Viola's supreme moment of self-sacrifice. Shakespeare's style makes acceptance easy, because the couplets which end Orsino's blank-verse tirade are both a crystallizing and a distancing of the emotions: they clinch the position, and they fix it in an artistic tableau. The next moment we are past the momentary crisis, and again the couplets control our response:

> *Olivia.* Where goes Cesario?
> *Viola.*   After him I love
> More than I love these eyes, more than my life,
> More, by all mores, than e'er I shall love wife.

1. For example in *Gent.* and *Mer.V.*

With that last line we are on the way back to situation comedy,[1] and at last within sight of the goal, for it is this speech which prompts Olivia to disclose her marriage. Her disclosure, however, does not at once release the whole tension: the Priest's weighty statement allows the fact of the marriage to sink into Orsino's mind, and, when he next speaks, flaming passion has given way to a smouldering resentment which, if it looked likely to be sustained, would create a distress on Viola's account which the threat of death did not create. Yet now we can even enjoy Viola's predicament, bewildered between Orsino and Olivia, for all that we are waiting for is Sebastian's entry.

But what we are given is Sir Andrew's. His appeal for a surgeon is addressed to Olivia, and his amazement when he sees Viola is one of the play's excellent comic moments (''Od's lifelings, here he is!'), for he has obviously run away from Sebastian as fast as his legs will carry him. Now Viola's bewilderment is directed to Sir Andrew; the earlier tension has been thoroughly and instantly released. This is finely managed, with a good final appearance for Sir Toby, and an effective joint disappearance for him and Sir Andrew.[2]

Sebastian's apology for wounding Sir Toby permits his spontaneous mention of the marriage, yet his entry does not lead into a burst of explanations but into his reunion first with Antonio (Sebastian's love redeeming all Antonio's sorrows in a moment) and then with Viola, whom he does not see till the others' amazement has directed his attention to her. The joyful mood of their recognition is tempered with mystery and even with awe.[3] The

---

1. Cf. III. i. 149–66, with its couplets.

2. Considered rationally, Sebastian must have had a second encounter with Sir Andrew and Sir Toby after IV. i, but this is not the way to consider the matter. What Shakespeare has provided is an alternative version of the same encounter (as is proved by Sir Andrew's 'We took him for a coward', which could not be true after their experience in IV. i). As so often, he sacrifices rational consistency for dramatic effect, knowing that the inconsistency will go unnoticed in the theatre. (The inconsistency is pointed out by Wilson in his note on the passage, but is ascribed by him to revision.)

3. Viola half-believes that it is Sebastian's ghost she sees, even though this is only a fleeting feeling and though the emphasis on his clothes keeps the tone from inappropriate heaviness. In taking Viola's bewilderment as genuine throughout the scene (and as a further example of Shakespeare's deliberate and artistic inconsistency) I part company with Evans, who, denying that Shakespeare 'sacrifices plausibility', maintains that since Viola deduced Sebastian's survival earlier she is merely 'feigning ignorance' now, for subtle reasons which he analyses (*Shakespeare's Comedies*, p. 141). I agree with him that plausibility is not sacrificed, for I distinguish between consistency and plausibility.

length of this dialogue, with its return to loveliness and romance after Sir Andrew's ridiculous interruption, allows Olivia time to accept, in silence, her mistake as a happy one (it is Sebastian's speech which does this on her behalf, his mention of his virginity reinforcing the beauty and purity with which Shakespeare has carefully invested their marriage). It also allows Orsino time to arrive, by an equally discreet process of silence, at the position from which he can begin proposing marriage to Viola (and, again, it is the stress on Viola's love for him—an emotion which we have always believed in—that makes it easy to believe i n his own transference of affection).[1]

One piece of unfinished business remains, Malvolio's enlightenment. This is brought in by way of the Captain's reported imprisonment at his suit, a connection so delightfully shameless in its artificiality that it predisposes us to good humour,[2] even while it reminds us (not too seriously) of Malvolio's habitual ill-will and so provides further retrospective justification for the trick played on him. The keynote of his letter (the production of which gives the Clown yet another opportunity to use his talents) is indignation; and indignation, not pathos, is the keynote of his speech when he appears. Its blank verse (Malvolio's only verse in the play) matches its argumentative, aggressive course, and leads on, by way of Olivia's calm and conciliatory explanation, to Fabian's manly appeal for a general amnesty to preserve the harmonious 'condition of this present hour'.[3] Why, then, is the Clown permitted his prose jeer, stressing the malicious element in the 'sportful malice' of which Fabian has stressed the sportiveness? Various explanations suggest themselves: it is true to life; it completes Fabian's otherwise comprehensive account of the

1. Clifford Leech (one of many critics who point to 'the Duke's insufficiency as an adult being') says that 'he proposes marriage in what are, after all, slightly chilly terms' ('Shakespeare's Comic Dukes', *Review of English Literature*, v, i, April 1964, pp. 110, 109). Yet one can imagine the critical outcry against his sentimentality had he spoken more passionately. And how could he have done so without indirectly reflecting on his love for Olivia and thereby insulting her?

2. Shakespeare is given to such gestures near the end of other comedies too: cf. Portia's production of the letter notifying Antonio of his renewed prosperity at the end of *Mer.V.* ('You shall not know by what strange accident / I chanced on this letter'), and Duke Frederick's reported conversion by the hermit at the end of *AYL*.

3. D. R. Preston, 'The Minor Characters in *Twelfth Night*', *Sh. Q.*, xxi (1970), 174–5, well analyses Fabian's role in this scene and the play. It is convenient that Sir Toby is off stage, as is also, apparently, Maria: she could have entered with Olivia's other attendants, but Olivia's speech (ll. 344–54) reads more naturally if she is absent.

trick; it unifies the play by reminding us of how Malvolio and the Clown quarrelled at their first appearance; and it allows Malvolio a strong exit line in which he shows his implacable rage (far more consistent with his personality than a generous forgiveness would have been). This angry exit of Malvolio's, far from disturbing the general cheerfulness, heightens it by putting a sharper edge on it (Olivia's line, 'He hath been most notoriously abus'd', echoing his indignant vocabulary, is surely spoken merrily), and is made to appear as no more than a temporary impediment to universal goodwill; for the sake of that goodwill we acquiesce in Orsino's hopeful line, 'Pursue him, and entreat him to a peace'. Orsino's whole speech is full of harmony, looking forward to the 'golden time' when

> A solemn combination shall be made
> Of our dear souls.

yet kept from over-solemnity by his half-jesting reference to Viola's disguise, one last reminder of all the dramatic irony. His final couplet rounds off this fanciful, moving, and very beautiful play.

The Clown's song is the epilogue. It contrasts with the closing speech of the play proper, and, in so doing, it prepares the theatre audience to take leave of the make-believe world of romantic Shakespearean comedy and go home. How much more, or how little more, it does is a matter for critical contest of which there appears no end. All I will contribute to the debate is a reminder that the last line of his song is

> And we'll strive to please you every day.

6 *TWELFTH NIGHT* IN THE THEATRE

The following selective account is concerned, first, with the vicissitudes of Shakespeare's text in the theatre; secondly, with the general history of stage performance, with special reference to setting and costume; and thirdly, with various theatrical interpretations of the play, and of particular scenes and characters.

1. The only recorded performance of *Twelfth Night* in Shakespeare's lifetime is that at the Middle Temple on 2 February 1602 witnessed by John Manningham. Performances at court by the King's Men took place on 6 April 1618 (as *Twelfth Night*) and on 2 February 1623 (as *Malvolio*).[1] When the theatres reopened after

1. E. K. Chambers, *William Shakespeare: Facts and Problems* (Oxford, 1930), II, 346. In Charles I's copy of the 1632 Folio (at Buckingham Palace), the name

the Restoration, *Twelfth Night* was in the repertory of D'Avenant's company (the Duke of York's) and was in production by 11 September 1661, when Charles II saw it and Pepys was also in the audience. Pepys saw the play again on 6 January 1663 and 20 January 1669. The performances he saw (no text survives) may have been adapted by D'Avenant. In 1703 Charles Burnaby published his *Love Betray'd: or, the Agreable [sic] Disapointment [sic]*;[1] 'Part of the Tale of this Play, I took from Shakespear', he wrote in his preface, 'and about 50 of the Lines', these including the opening words and Viola's image of patience on a monument. His play (which was not a success) is of no importance to the history of *Twelfth Night* in the theatre (most of Shakespeare's design being changed beyond recognition), though it is of some interest in confirming the un-Shakespearean temper of its time, at least with regard to Shakespearean romantic comedy (Pepys had a low opinion of *Twelfth Night*). Shakespeare's comedy itself, after a long period of neglect, returned to the London stage in 1741, with Macklin playing Malvolio at Drury Lane, and thereafter it continued to be regularly performed until in 1820 it was again briefly supplanted by a thoroughly altered version, this time a musical production devised by Frederick Reynolds (who had in 1816 and 1819 presented similarly 'operatic' renderings of *A Midsummer Night's Dream* and *The Comedy of Errors*); it contained 'Songs, Glees, and Choruses' selected from Shakespeare's other plays and poems and set by various composers, chiefly Henry Bishop, who was responsible for the vocal and orchestral arrangements.[2] Since that time there have been no such thoroughgoing transformations of *Twelfth Night*, though omissions, additions and transpositions have been frequent. The Clown's songs in II. iii and II. iv, for example, were omitted from Bell's acting edition (printed from prompt-books, 1773–5), along with their context of dialogue, but it is more usual to find them (and others) in unexpected places and sung by unexpected persons. One would nowadays hardly expect Olivia to sing, though

---

Malvolio is written opposite the title in the list of contents. This is a memorandum, not an alternative title: cf. 'Pyramus and Thisby' opposite the title of *MND*.

1. The fullest account of the plot is given by G. C. D. Odell, *Shakespeare from Betterton to Irving* (New York, 1920), I, 81–3; a shorter one by H. Child, N.C.S., p. 174; D. J. Palmer (ed.), '*Twelfth Night': a Casebook* (1972), gives a short extract from the text.

2. 'It was a wretched piece of business, but, as it is not printed, it is impossible to point out the quantum of its demerits': P. Genest, *An Account of the English Stage, 1660–1830* (Bath, 1832), IX, 99 (quoted by Furness, p. 407).

in 1771 Mrs Abington did so; still less Sebastian, for whom Henry Bishop supplied a song in 1818 and 1819 (in the 'operatic' age of Reynolds, admittedly).[1] As recently as 1932 Olivia joined the Clown in the final verse of his final song, and in the same production Orsino had 'Come away, death' sung to him in the opening scene (not by the Clown).[2] Acting upon many readers' conviction that because Viola declares in I. ii that she can sing to the Duke she must have been originally intended to do so, Eduard and Otto Devrient gave 'Come away, death' to her in 1893 at Carlsruhe.[3] This change, though I think it misconceived, was at least based on a theory of dramatic propriety. The merely ornamental introduction of songs, however—a relic of the 'operatic' period— reappeared as late as Daly's production of 1894, where (in an otherwise wordless scene following III. iv) Orsino's musicians serenaded Olivia with 'Who is Olivia? What is she?' adapted from the serenade to Silvia in *The Two Gentlemen of Verona* and sung to Schubert's deservedly famous setting. It is true that Daly had here contrived a dramatic and romantic context which may well be defended on its own terms,[4] but his opening of the play, with the two 'shipwreck' scenes II. i. and I. ii preceded by 'Come unto these yellow sands', was an incongruity wholly indefensible.[5]

Songs—omitted, interpolated or transferred—are a relatively unimportant alteration to the text (however seriously they may affect the mood), provided that Shakespeare's dialogue and his scene-order are preserved. Alterations to these, though often made with good intentions or for compelling reasons, are capable of affecting the play more drastically. In fact, the verbal alterations

1. For Bell, see Odell, *op. cit.*, II, 29. Child, *op. cit.*, pp. 175–6, notes that from 1799 the Drury Lane playbills advertise 'the original epilogue song'. This was possibly Vernon's air, published in 1772 (see Appendix II). The implication seems to be that the final song had been omitted, rather than sung to some other tune. For Mrs Abington (date from W. Winter, *Shakespeare on the Stage*, 3rd series, New York, 1915, p. 20) and Mr Duruset (Sebastian), see Child, *ibid.*

2. How Orsino's opening speech was accommodated to this song's inclusion I cannot imagine. See G. Crosse, *Shakespearean Playgoing, 1890–1952* (1953), p. 115; J. C. Trewin, *Shakespeare on the English Stage, 1900–64* (1964), p. 134.

3. Furness, p. 411: she was alone with the Duke at this time (II. iv), having begun the scene with her soliloquy from II. ii. Helen Modjeska as Viola in the U.S.A. in the 1880s also sang the song, to a harp accompaniment (Winter, *op. cit.*, p. 62).

4. Odell, *op. cit.*, p. 442. See J. R. Brown, *Shakespeare's Plays in Performance* (Penguin, 1969), p. 244, for a contemporary reviewer's full description of the incident.

5. Odell, *ibid.* The singers were 'fishermen and peasants, strolling by the seashore' (Winter, *op. cit.*, p. 65). But this was no worse an incongruity than opening the play with a shipwreck and some phrases from *The Tempest*, followed by I. ii and II. i, in New York, 1955 (*Sh. Q.*, VI (1955), 425).

have been few and unobjectionable.[1] One can sympathize with Kemble's excision of 'Castiliano vulgo' from I. iii. 42–3 on the evident grounds of its unintelligibility;[2] one can understand his rewriting of Viola's lines, I. ii. 55–6, as

> I'll serve this duke;
> Thou shalt present me as a page unto him,
> Of gentle breeding, and my name Cesario:—
> This trunk, the reliques of my sea-drown'd brother,
> Will furnish man's apparel to my need,

since it gets rid of her embarrassing word 'eunuch', prepares the audience for her assumed name, and undertakes to explain how she came to be dressed just like her brother—though all these points may well be trivial or even superfluous.[3] His omission of her line (v. i. 134)

> More, by all mores, than e'er I shall love wife

is an interesting pointer to his judgment (he probably thought 'by all mores' an eccentric phrase and the whole line dangerous to the seriousness at which he was presumably aiming in Viola's asseveration of her love for Orsino). Finally, his interpolation later in the same scene (v. i. 384: between 'We will not part from hence' and 'Cesario, come') is specially interesting because it shows his awareness, as a man of the theatre, that Orsino and Antonio must quench their enmity during the final speeches of the play:

> —Go, officers,
> We do discharge you of your prisoner. [*Exeunt officers.*
> Antonio, thou hast well deserv'd our thanks:
> Thy kind protection of Cesario's person,
> Although thou knew'st not then for whom thou fought'st,
> Merits our favour: Henceforth, be forgotten
> All cause of anger: Thou hast a noble spirit,
> And, as Sebastian's friend, be ever near him.—[4]

1. The worst has been the editorial transference of the three words 'save I alone' (III. i. 162) from Viola to Olivia by Hanmer.

2. *Shakespeare's 'Twelfth Night; or What You Will': a comedy. Revised by J. P. Kemble; and now published as it is performed at the Theatre Royal.* 1815. (Kemble cut the knot by reading '. . . like a parish-top.—See, here comes Sir Andrew Ague-face.')

3. For 'Viola's luggage', see A. C. Sprague, *Shakespeare and the Actors* (Cambridge, Mass., 1945), p. 3, and A. C. Sprague and J. C. Trewin, *Shakespeare's Plays Today* (1970), pp. 28–9: 'Later she says that she imitated the fashion of her brother's clothes, not that she wore them.' Kemble's suppression of 'eunuch' compelled him to omit the Captain's final cheerful couplet.

4. Antonio cannot leave the stage still apparently under arrest at the end. Shakespeare, I imagine, simply forgot the Officers' presence (and possibly,

This production of Kemble's was the first to reverse the order
of the first two scenes, a regrettable change often made since, and
occasionally found even today. There are at least three reasons
why the order of Shakespeare's scenes has been, on various occasions, altered. One is the desire to improve on Shakespeare's
dramatic art. A second is the need to get late-comers seated
without their or other spectators' missing, or suffering distraction
from, the first appearances of the more important characters:
thus Daly's 1894 production began with ii. i (Antonio and Sebastian) before i. ii (Viola) and i. i (Orsino).[1] A third is the fact that,
in the nineteenth-century theatre, relatively unlocalized scenes
were conventionally presented before a lowered front curtain
which was afterwards raised to disclose a representational stage-
set (such as Orsino's palace, even though this was required for
only forty lines); it was chiefly for this reason that so many productions, from Kemble's time onwards, began with 'What
country, friends, is this?—a question to be asked indeed when
nothing indicated the answer.[2]

2. Changes of elaborate scenery (accompanied by many and
long intervals) were characteristic of the nineteenth-century

---

after the recognition scene, Antonio's as well). Orsino can give the Officers
a mute signal to depart (though there is no point in the dialogue where such a
signal can be easily introduced or the Officers' exit be other than a distraction),
or alternatively (since Antonio can no longer be under physical restraint when
he and Sebastian greet each other) they can merely join in the general final
exit, while Antonio is welcomed by either of the betrothed couples (assuming
that he leaves the stage with the rest of the party and does not make a solitary
exit in the opposite direction, as in John Barton's Stratford-upon-Avon production of 1969).

Another alteration to the final scene, far less justifiable in my opinion, is
recorded of Wilhelm Oechelhauser's production of 1881 (Furness, pp. 386–7):
Viola had an exit arranged in order to change into her 'maid's garments',
thus obviating the interruption of the romantic conclusion by Malvolio's entry,
and also the unromantic spectacle of the Duke embracing a page.

1. Odell, *op. cit.*, II, 406. Of the 2684 lines Daly cut about 600 for his 1893–4
production. He also reversed the positions of 'O mistress mine' and 'Come away,
death', and eventually omitted the latter.

2. For proposals for a typical Victorian production in four acts, 'each con-
taining one set scene', see Furness, pp. 408–9 (extract from article by E. W.
Godwin, F.S.A., in *The Architect*, 24 April 1875). The division is as follows.
Act I, Olivia's house (interior): I. iii, I. v, II. iii. Act II, Orsino's palace (interior):
II. ii, II. iv. Act III, Olivia's house (exterior, with garden and garden-house):
II. v, III. i, III. ii, III. iv, IV. ii. Act IV, The street before Olivia's house: IV. i,
IV. iii, V. i. The remaining scenes 'may be described . . . either by the characters
or in a prologue'; the coast scenes 'may be retained in their entirety where there
is a good proscenium, and acted before the curtain or act-drop, which should
then, of course, be painted for the purpose'.

theatre; the principal set of Tree's 1901 *Twelfth Night* was Olivia's terraced garden, copied by Hawes Craven from a picture in *Country Life*,[1] while Sir Barry Jackson refers to an unspecified production ending with 'a double marriage ceremony in the Illyrian Cathedral'.[2] The basic stage requirements of *Twelfth Night* are, of course, minimal: no appearances 'above', no 'discoveries' or 'concealments', no trap-door entrances or exits, are called for, and, apart from the 'box tree' where the overhearers hide (II. v) and the exterior of the 'dark room' where the supposedly mad Malvolio is confined 'within' (IV. ii), place never needs to be visually suggested, and stage furniture, if used at all, needs only to be of the most elementary kind. A fundamentalist return to Elizabethan simplicity, as he conceived it, was made by William Poel in 1895. Though coldly received by Max Beerbohm,[3] Poel's similar production of 1903 prepared the way for Granville Barker's of 1912, in which the settings were formal and uncluttered; while the 'twisted pink barley-sugar pillars' of Orsino's palace and the 'Noah's-ark trees'[4] of Olivia's garden might look affected to us today, these settings were well fitted to Barker's sense of dramatic rhythm. Since then, splendour of setting has never been allowed to obstruct the flow of the play. In terms of setting and costume, the theatrical treatment of *Twelfth Night* has been prevailingly 'Elizabethan'. Wheatley's 1774 drawing of the duel scene (III. iv) shows Fabian wearing the deep lace collar and cuffs of the Caroline period, and Sir Toby in a small ruff, a laced jerkin, and the boots to which he refers in I. iii, though Sir Andrew's dress, apart from ruffles at the wrists and rosettes on the shoes, is that of the 1770s, and Viola's, more ornate and worn under a long cape, is similar, the only Illyrian touch consisting in her turban-like hat with an ostrich plume.[5] The nineteenth century saw a steady movement towards consistency, though Malvolio's cross-gartering was often misinterpreted as extending to his ankles, and though there was a tendency to clothe Viola

1. Trewin, *op. cit.*, p. 18.

2. 'Producing the Comedies', *Shakespeare Survey*, 8 (1955), 76.

3. Trewin, *op. cit.*, p. 26.

4. *Ibid.*, p. 55. A reviewer's comment, 'all is over at the Savoy in three hours' (*The Nation*, 23 Nov. 1912, quoted by G. Ll. Evans, *Shakespeare in the Limelight* (1968), p. 115), shows how ponderous earlier productions must have been. Yet William Winter (*op. cit.*, pp. xxvii–xxviii), a judicious critic, was inclined (from 'what I have read and heard about them') to dismiss Granville Barker, Max Reinhardt and Gordon Craig as all 'eccentric pretenders to originality'.

5. Reproduced in Odell, *op. cit.*, I, facing p. 412.

in a tunic, belted at the waist, such as is shown in many photo-graphs[1] of actresses in the role (a concession, perhaps, to the con-fusion of Messaline in the play with Mitylene in Greece, but more probably to a feminine sense of what was 'becoming': one feels sorry for the male Sebastians of these productions). An interesting and very satisfactory compromise between the androgynous and the Elizabethan appears in the two 'Cesario' costumes for Granville Barker's *Twelfth Night* preserved in the London Museum.[2] Naturally, in the present century, producers have experimented with other times and place than the England of Shakespeare, though it is very rare indeed to find the play done in familiar 'modern dress': indeed, the usual motivation of experi-ment seems to be the creation of an unfamiliar world in order to make the 'unrealistic' main plot more acceptable (hence the use of the French eighteenth century, or the English Regency, or the late Victorian periods). However, as John Russell Brown has shown, *Twelfth Night* returns again and again in its language and action to 'English countryside and domesticity', and, as he says, the stage picture can help to establish this world, 'not insistently, but with subtlety'.[3] Despite occasional references to shipwreck on the Illyrian coast, eunuchs and mutes, 'the Count his galleys', the 'rough and unhospitable' manners of the natives to strangers, and the Italianate names of most of the characters, the greater part of the action takes place in and near Olivia's house, which is the typical great household of Shakespeare's day, with its lady, her waiting-gentlewoman, her steward, and her fool. Sir Toby Belch (her kinsman) and Sir Andrew Aguecheek are no strangers in this society, as are Sir Politic and Lady Would-be in the Venice of *Volpone*, but are indigenous. Dogberry and Bottom similarly confirm the Elizabethan Englishness of the air they breathe, though it will rightly be replied that Messina and Athens, and Illyria, have also (whenever it suits Shakespeare's purpose) romantic atmospheres of their own, in which Antonio's idealistic loyalty to the friend he adores finds its natural element, as do Orsino's ardent despair and (near the end of the play) his fierce jealousy. Sir Toby's remark about 'the bed of Ware in England',

1. See, in particular, W. Winter, *op. cit.,* pp. 1–106 *passim,* and Odell, *op. cit.,* facing p. 262.
2. Both are described, and one illustrated, in M. R. Holmes, *Stage Costume and Accessories in the London Museum* (London, H.M.S.O., 1968), p. 63 and plate XXVI. Viola's cloak (I. ii) is also described (p. 63), as are Irving's two costumes as Malvolio in 1884 (p. 43 and plate XIV). Granville Barker's costume-designer was Norman Wilkinson.
3. *Op. cit.,* p. 230: 'Directions for *Twelfth Night*'.

like Trinculo's 'Were I in England now, as once I was',[1] is designed to keep us simultaneously and humorously aware of both worlds at once. Both are, of course, in their different ways, Elizabethan, and call for Elizabethan costume.

Nothing is known for certain of how the roles were distributed among the original performers. Even Robert Armin's taking the part of the Clown is not an established fact but merely a probability, based on the considerations that Will Kempe had left the company and that Armin may have had musical talent.[2] It is, of course, unsafe to suppose that because he was familiar with his fellow-actors, Shakespeare had his mind's eye continually upon them in creating his characters. Though Kempe had left, Sir Toby is a Kempe part, and he and Sir Andrew recall the Kempe-and-Cowley pairing of Dogberry and Verges. Sir Andrew is never explicitly said to be thin, though this may perhaps be deducible from his surname, from the 'flax on a distaff' simile (I. iii. 99), and also from the word 'anatomy' (III. ii. 61) if it is descriptive, as it had been when applied to the 'hungry lean-faced' Pinch in *The Comedy of Errors* (v. i. 238). He has, it is true, much in common with Slender in *The Merry Wives of Windsor*, but then Slender's wit is quite as slender as his body could possibly be. John Sincklo, who played the thin Beadle in *2 Henry IV* (v. iv),[3] seems unlikely to have taken so large a part as Sir Andrew's, and, in any case, Shakespeare had a fancy for 'thin man' jokes whether or not they demand a specially thin actor.[4] It would be specially valuable to know who played Malvolio.

It is not part of my purpose to give later cast-lists (which can be found elsewhere).[5] It is, however, interesting to find that (as one man in his time plays many parts) in the eighteenth century Richard Yates graduated from the Clown to Malvolio, and John Palmer from Sebastian to Sir Toby, while in our own century

1. *Tp.*, II. ii. 30.

2. See Chambers, *The Elizabethan Stage*, III, 326 (for Kempe's departure from the Lord Chamberlain's Men: he sold his share in the Globe early in 1599), and 300 (for Armin's probable engagement as Kempe's replacement). Armin's musical talent is an inference from the songs given to the Clown in this play and in *King Lear*, so the argument is circular.

3. See A. R. Humphreys's note on the scene, in the New Arden edition. Sincklo also played one of the two Keepers in *3H6*, III. i (not a 'thin man' part): see A. S. Cairncross's note in the New Arden edition.

4. *John*, I. i. 92, 138–42 (Robert Falconbridge); *LLL.*, v. ii. 600–16 (Holofernes); *Rom.*, v. i. 37–84 (the Apothecary).

5. For example, in Winter, *op. cit.*; Child, N.C.S., pp. 173–9; G. C. D. Odell, *op. cit.*; C. B. Hogan, *Shakespeare in the Theatre: a record of performances in London, 1701–1800* (Oxford, 1952, 1957).

Leon Quartermaine has been first the Clown and later Sir Andrew, and Laurence Olivier has been successively Sir Toby and Malvolio, a part which John Laurie filled after beginning (like Yates) as the Clown. When Shakespeare's company acted *Twelfth Night* at court in 1618 and 1623, the casts would, in all probability, be different (certainly as regards the boys) and might include similar graduations from one role to another.

John Palmer's majestic figure must have suited Sir Toby far more than Sebastian, and how the lack of resemblance between him as Sebastian and the actress playing Viola was made endurable it is hard to guess.[1] When Ben Jonson visited William Drummond of Hawthornden in 1619, he confided to him (with doubtful seriousness?) that

> he had ane intention to have made a play like Plaut[us'] Amphitrio but left it of, for that he could never find two so like others that he could persuade the spectators they were one.[2]

Although Viola and Sebastian must not be wildly unlike (a bearded Sebastian would be the ultimate absurdity, and therefore, no doubt, we shall see so much if we live so long), it is in fact the natural difference between the actors in this and similar plays which prevents the spectators' sharing in the general confusion and makes them able to distinguish the twins as the other characters cannot. As far as I know, identical twins have never taken the roles (to be truly identical they would need to be of the same sex, which would not be impossible if a boy were to play Viola or a girl Sebastian). On the professional stage, the parts have sometimes been taken by sister and brother; by Mrs Jordan and Mr Bland in 1790, and by Mrs Henry Siddons and William Murray at Edinburgh in 1815.[3] A more daring venture is for one actress to double the two parts. This has occurred from time to time in the past century or so: first in a German translation of the play at Dresden in 1851 (Henry Crabb Robinson, the diarist, noted that Mme Baier Bürick adopted a manliness of voice and step as Sebastian);[4] later by Kate Terry in 1865, and Jessica Tandy in 1937,[5] and also by the actress (whose name I have not been able to discover) in a French version by Jean Anouilh in

1. See below, p. lxxxix.
2. Jonson, ed. Herford and Simpson, I, 144.
3. See Sir Walter Scott's complimentary reference to the latter pair in *Waverley*, ch. xxi.
4. Winter, *op. cit.*, p. 35.
5. Kate Terry at the Olympic, London; Jessica Tandy at the Old Vic, London.

1961. On all these occasions the audience must have anticipated
the final scene with apprehension. In the production of 1851,
another person, who managed to hide his (or her?) face, came on,
and in 1961 the reunion took place in silhouette behind a screen;
Anouilh's solution had the limited merit that the actress was able
to speak both parts. Yet however the end is contrived, the experi-
ment is a dramatic perversity, memorably condemned by A. S.
Downer in his review of Anouilh's production:

> For four and a half acts the complex structure of *Twelfth
> Night* prepares the audience for the confrontation of the twins.
> Shakespeare rewards our patience with seventy lines of anag-
> norisis, a long and gratifying tribute to the comic view of life.
> It is a *necessary* scene, and Shakespeare does not cheat even
> when improbability might have tempted him to do so. To share
> in the triumph of the improbable is the true delight of *Twelfth
> Night*, but Anouilh will be tinkering.[1]

In short, if spectators are reluctant to embrace theatrical illusion
in the theatre, they had better stay away. Strong resemblance
of costume, and tolerable resemblance of personal appearance,
are quite enough to preserve this particular theatrical illusion in
Twelfth Night.[2]

3. It is perhaps best to discuss the stage interpretation of the
characters before proceeding to specially important scenes,
though it is evident that the two go together; the reports of the
earlier productions commonly dwell on how this or that actor
played his part, and it is only later that detailed accounts of the
treatment of whole scenes can be found. Generally speaking, it
seems that eighteenth- and nineteenth-century audiences gave
their special attention to Viola, Sir Toby, Sir Andrew, and
Malvolio. Before the present century one hears little of Orsino
and Olivia, and little of the Clown (who has been called several
times the centre of the play).[3]

Sir Toby and Sir Andrew have traditionally been recognized
as a pair of united broad-comedy parts (Sir Andrew never has a

1. *Sh. Q.*, xii (1962), 228.
2. '[Peter Hall's] choice of Cavalier costume [at Stratford-upon-Avon,
1958] gave the maximum thematic contrast with Malvolio's Puritan habit,
served the opposition of amours and austerity, and brought out what is most
English in Shakespeare's Never-Never-Land of Illyria. It also eased the problem
of the identical twins, with a hair-style equally suitable to boy or girl.' (Roy
Walker, *Shakespeare Survey*, 12 (1959), 128.)
3. *Ibid.*, p. 126 (quoting Sir Arthur Quiller-Couch, N.C.S., p. xxvi, and
L. G. Salingar, *Sh. Q.*, ix (1958), 135–6).

scene without Sir Toby, and Sir Toby only two without Sir Andrew),[1] with Sir Andrew as Sir Toby's 'anvil', as Theobald well described him.[2] It was also traditional that Sir Toby should be Falstaffian and Puckish, Sir Andrew tractable and idiotic. Lamb's brilliant account of James Dodd's performance of Sir Andrew stresses the genius with which he made 'slowness of apprehension' the natural product of Sir Andrew's mental metabolism ('He seemed to keep back his intellect, as some have had the power to retard their pulsation'), not a grotesque exhibition.[3] In the role of drunken Sir Toby (according to another critic) 'Palmer's gigantic limbs outstretched seemed to indicate the enjoyment of that physical superiority which Nature had given him, even while debasing it to the lowest of all vices',[4] though Lamb felt that John Palmer 'did not quite fill out' Sir Toby's 'solidity of wit' and put too much 'swaggering gentility' into the part.[5] Early actors and reviewers alike seemed in no doubt as to the nature and relative simplicity of both characters: it was a matter of how well the agreed features were portrayed. To say this is, of course, to speak rather too generally: even Sir Andrew has his moments of pique and disillusionment, and neither he nor Sir Toby is all of a piece throughout. But in the present century we have seen a larger range of interpretation, with Sir Toby sometimes conspicuous for his glazed and fuddled dignity,[6] sometimes for his vivacity,[7] sometimes even for his tenacious maintenance of his place at Olivia's (with consequent bitter hostility to Malvolio who seems to threaten it in II. iii);[8] and 'a melancholy Sir Toby', compensating himself for his sense of failure in life, is not quite impossible (though I feel this conception

1. If we count the first part of III. iv, with Malvolio, as one of these; the other is IV. ii.

2. In his editorial footnote to I. iii.

3. *The Works of Charles and Mary Lamb* (ed. T. Hutchinson, 1908), I, 642: 'On Some of the Old Actors' (*The Essays of Elia*, 1823).

4. The American critic William Dunlop, quoted by Winter, *op. cit.*, p. 20.

5. Lamb, *op. cit.*, I, 646. 'He was as much too showy as Moody (who sometimes took the part) was dry and sottish.'

6. Cedric Hardwicke (Crosse, *op. cit.*, p. 131; Trewin, *Shakespeare on the English Stage*, p. 211).

7. Laurence Olivier (Trewin, *op. cit.*, p. 164: 'like a veteran Skye terrier, ears pricked for mischief'), Patrick Wymark (Brown, *op. cit.*, pp. 223–4: 'Young and spry with a sense of style; for this, "she's a beagle, true-bred" was most appropriate language, and his easy confidence in "consanguinity" with Olivia and expertise in swordplay were natural accomplishments').

8. S. Wells, *Literature and Drama* (1970), p. 113. 'Sir Toby's wrath against Malvolio was the more impressive in that it was clear that he knew he was endangering his own position.' (Of the Stratford-upon-Avon *Tw.N.*, 1969.)

goes against the grain of the play and of most of his lines).[1]
'Sir Andrew Aguecheek can be patient, sunny, feckless, gormless,
animated or neurotic', or even a 'paranoid manic-depressive,
strongly reminiscent at times of Lucky in *Waiting for Godot*';[2]
he has been equipped with a Scottish accent and bagpipes,[3] presumably on the strength of his Christian name, but this is carrying
inventiveness too far (and I doubt whether he could have mastered
the pipes any more than the viol-de-gamboys, since he has not
studied the arts). The more natural the touches, the better, like
his 'vanity of authorship' when Sir Toby reads aloud his challenge.[4]

Audiences have always recognized in Malvolio the centre of
the play's conspicuously comic scenes, and actors have interpreted him in a variety of ways. It is of great historical importance
that the first notable Malvolio, Charles Macklin in 1741, also
played Shylock:[5] the two parts (each of them the leading unromantic part in a romantic comedy) have often been in one
actor's repertoire, and there is a long-standing critical tradition
(more long-standing, perhaps, than well-grounded) of treating
them as comparable. Malvolio, though at the centre of the play's
broadest comedy, is no part for a clown. After Macklin, though
David Garrick never played him, important actors like Robert
Bensley and John Henderson (who also played Hamlet) did so.
Everyone is familiar with Lamb's eulogy of Bensley's performance
('He looked, spake, and moved like an old Castilian'), and even
though the performance may have been amended by Lamb's
imagination, it must have included solid respectability as well as
fantastical vanity.[6] Whatever faith we may place in Lamb's

1. Brown, *op. cit.*, p. 224. Contrast Crosse, *op. cit.*, p. 57, who found Robert
Atkins in 1920–5 'rather too sombre for that merry and mischievous old soul',
but added 'It has since become one of his best parts.'

2. Brown, *op. cit.*, pp. 224–5. The quotation is from a contemporary review of
Richard Johnson's performance in 1958. In the early 1920s Sir Andrew had
been 'a tinnily-squeaking doll in a starched ruff' (Sprague and Trewin, *op. cit.*,
p. 94).

3. At Stratford-upon-Avon, 1969: *Shakespeare Survey*, 23 (1970), 134.

4. Evans, *op. cit.*, p. 115 (of Leon Quartermaine). Crosse, *op. cit.*, p. 40, commends a momentary effect in Norman Forbes's performance in Tree's 1901
production: 'On his first entrance his startled look, when he caught sight of
Maria over Sir Toby's shoulder as the knights embraced, was itself worth the
money.'

5. For a detailed account of his Shylock see Brown, *op. cit.*, pp. 83–8.

6. Lamb, *op. cit.*, I, 641. Sylvan Barnet, *Philological Quarterly*, XXXIII (1954),
178–88, produces evidence conflicting with Lamb's and suggesting that there
were farcical elements in Bensley's performance. Of course, the different
opinions of reviewers as to what is farcical come into the matter. Brown,

account, it is clear that by his time the opportunities offered by
the role were being explored. Samuel Phelps, in 1857, emphasized
the steward's 'self-love' by regarding the world through eyes
'very nearly covered with their heavy lids'; his thoughts were
turned inward. 'Walled up in his own temple of flesh, he is his
own adorer': Henry Morley's phrase captures the impassiveness
with which this versatile actor (whose parts included Hamlet
and Christopher Sly) played the part to the very end. Morley
had clearly read Lamb's essay, and his description suggests that
Phelps had read it too: 'Few who have seen or may see at Sadler's
Wells the Spanish-looking steward of Countess Olivia, and
laughed at the rise and fall of his *château en Espagne*, will forget him
speedily.'[1] Henry Irving, in 1884, likewise aimed at consistency
and credibility. He too played with half-shut eyes, and with
beard of pointed Spanish cut, but he exploited his lean and intel-
lectual appearance to evoke a more genuine dignity than that
which Phelps had attempted. A reliable contemporary account
makes it clear that Irving conceived the character humorously
(in the lightness of his steward's wand there was 'something
of fantastic symbolism'), though essentially as an exhibition of
real personality.[2]

Later actors seem to have generally presented Malvolio as
human rather than fantastic, with the exception of Beerbohm
Tree who played him in the vacuous-vain tradition, with pom-
pous gestures and a quizzing-glass. At his first entry (followed
by the attendants whom the Clown bids 'Take away the lady'—
four smaller copies of himself)[3] he fell down a flight of steps—a

---

op. cit., p. 242, comments that Bensley succeeded Thomas King in the role and
that King (who played the Gravedigger, Stephano, and Touchstone) never
took back the part from Bensley, who played 'straight' roles such as Banquo
and Prospero; he concludes that it was not 'the cult of the misunderstood'
which made Malvolio 'more than a comic butt'. This is true, yet by 1777 the
romantic approach to Shakespeare had begun, and the interest in psychology
was developing fast. Lamb remarks (p. 639) that 'John Kemble thought it no
derogation to succeed to the part'; but according to Child, N.C.S., p. 175, he
seems to have played it only once.

1. *The Journal of a London Playgoer from 1851 to 1866* (1891 ed.), pp. 139–40.
2. Sir Edward Russell, *The Fortnightly Review*, 1 Sept. 1884, p. 403 (quoted by
Furness, p. 400). The Viola of Irving's production, Ellen Terry, revealed (in
The Story of My Life, quoted by Winter, *op. cit.*, p. 34) that Irving told her he
should never have put on the play 'without three great comedians'; but whether
he included Malvolio among the comic trio or was thinking of the two knights
and the clown is not clear.
3. The 'fellows' and 'gentlemen' (ll. 37, 70) of the text have sometimes been
replaced by ladies. A photograph of the Old Vic production of 1950 (*Shakespeare Survey*, 5 (1952), Illustration IIIB) shows three ladies and Olivia all veiled,

feature of his elaborate garden setting—without losing his composure. Tree also, according to Crosse, set the fashion for Malvolio 'to wear a night-gown in the kitchen scene, a refinement that has been adopted by most of his successors'; yet Crosse, though 'refinement' is obviously ironical, commends his whole performance, particularly in 'Malvolio's loyalty to Olivia, and his reluctance to give her away' towards the end.[1] Most Malvolios of this century may be very roughly classified into the old kill-joys and the young upstarts. Granville Barker had in the part Henry Ainley, pallid, middle-aged, and convincing;[2] John Laurie, in the 'Victorian' Stratford-upon-Avon production of 1939, was 'consumed by a wintry ambition and by gout';[3] Ernest Thesiger was in 1944 a 'sour Grey Eminence',[4] Michael Hordern in 1954 a tortured, El-Greco-like figure,[5] and of Roger Mitchell (at the Colorado Shakespeare Festival, 1960) it was well said that 'when he read the line where Malvolio is instructed to smile, you could hear the ice crack in his lips'.[6] By contrast John Abbott, a brisk young Malvolio in Tyrone Guthrie's Old Vic production of 1937, 'might have been seconded from the Illyrian foreign office'.[7] One of the most distinctive younger Malvolios was Laurence Olivier's in 1955 at Stratford-upon-Avon, 'whose speech suggested his origin by an affected, lisping veneer that flaked away suddenly to reveal the barrow-boy vowels'.[8] He was not the first to hint at a Cockney background (Maurice Evans had done so in 1939), nor the last (Ian Holm followed in 1966): Robert Speight remarks, 'The new convention insists that Malvolio comes from the

presumably to justify Viola's query as to which is 'the honourable lady of the house'. It looks like a reminiscence of *LLL.*, v. ii, in which the Princess and her three ladies are in masks (l. 127). Sometimes Maria puts on a veil for the same reason. However, the scene plays better with only Olivia veiled, and with Viola knowing well that she is the Lady: the veil then adds comic point to 'I pray you tell me if this be the lady of the house, for I never saw her' (ll. 172–3), and to the immediately preceding tribute to her beauty.

1. Crosse, *op. cit.*, p. 40 (for the night-gown, see below p. xcvi). See also Sprague, *op. cit.*, p. 4, and Trewin, *op. cit.*, p. 19, who mention only the opening appearance. Tree's Malvolio is illustrated in G. Wilson Knight's *Shakespearian Production* (1964), facing p. 208.

2. Trewin, *op. cit.*, p. 55 (with long quotation from the *Morning Post* of 16 Nov. 1912); see also Evans, *op. cit.*, p. 115.

3. Trewin, *op. cit.*, p. 180.

4. Sprague and Trewin, *op. cit.*, p. 94.

5. Brown, *op. cit.* (quoting an unspecified review), p. 223.

6. R. L. Perkin in *Sh. Q.*, XI (1960), 465.

7. Trewin, *op. cit.*, p. 164.

8. *Illustrated London News*, 23 April 1955, quoted by Sprague and Trewin, *op. cit.*, p. 95.

"suburbs [by] the Elephant"',[1] but, of course, the idea has not hardened into a rigid convention, and Malvolios continue to appear in great variety.

Space forbids equally full treatment of the Violas. At the risk of over-simplifying, it may be said that Viola is a character universally attractive to audiences and to performers, and it would be a sorry day for *Twelfth Night* if any producer were so perverse as to take a whim to dislike her. The only problem—though it requires delicate judgment to solve—is how to balance the liveliness and the poignancy in the moods and situations created by her disguise. Beatrice is sad only for Hero's sake; there is hardly a cloud in Rosalind's sky; but Viola's opening lines strike a pathetic chord; yet on her embassy to Olivia she is confident and able to brush aside impediments; and yet again her newly disclosed and newly discovered love for Orsino hangs over the dialogue with Olivia (whom it is not quite correct to call her rival). This juxtaposition, and even combination, of moods runs right through the play. The sort of traps that exist for the unwary, or the challenges that can be created by the audacious, lie in phrases like 'Excellently done, if God did all' (I. v. 239) or

> And make the babbling gossip of the air
> Cry out 'Olivia!'   (I. v. 277–8)

It is clear that the first of these should not be shouted crudely or delivered maliciously, and even the 'graceful impudence' of Ellen Terry (commended by Clement Scott)[2] has its evident danger. As to the second, a Peggy Ashcroft can bring off the effect of 'a hastily remembered substitution' of the name Olivia for the name Orsino,[3] but it is not, I am sure, an effect that naturally grows from the scene or the speech or from the Shakespearean attitude to women in the comedies: 'We should be woo'd, and were not made to woo.'[4] The soliloquy in II. ii is a kind of test

1. *Sh. Q.*, XVII (1966), 398.
2. *From 'The Bells' to 'King Arthur'* (1896), p. 271. It is quoted by Furness (in his note on the line), who remarks that 'Olivia had invited the suspicion that her beauty was fictitious by asking, "Is it not *well done?*" and there is more of tragedy than comedy in Viola's reply. She knew that God had done all, but replied merely in Olivia's vein while her admiration was gathering itself into that earnest tribute, which follows, to the exquisite beauty of her rival.' This seems to me an admirable comment, though the word 'tragedy' (doubtless used by Furness for rhetorical effect) is a trifle too strong.
3. In the Old Vic production by Hugh Hunt, 1950; the quotation is from a review by R. David, *Shakespeare Survey*, 5 (1952), 121–4, where he praises this particular effect.
4. *MND.*, II. i. 242 (Helena to Demetrius). My point is that Viola's whole

piece for Violas, who must choose whether to make a comic point of 'I am the man' (and, if so, *how* to make it) or to let the verbal irony do its own work.[1] So, above all, is the scene with Orsino (II. iv):

> When she said, 'I am all the daughters of my father's house', her manner and the despairing sadness of her tone almost revealed her sex to the Duke, and, as Orsino turned towards her with a look of mingled surprise and inquiry, she rapidly, confusedly, and also *comically*, added, 'a—a—and all the *brothers* too!'—thus obtaining a laugh instead of a tear.[2]

A laugh so bought costs the scene dear. Of course, the femininity of Viola must be stressed where it is possible to stress it (to attempt a convincing male impersonation in all the Cesario scenes is fatal to the play),[3] but not in such inappropriate ways as this. It is always salutary to remember the boy actor, though no actress could be expected to reconstruct his performance, nor would it be desirable for her to try to do so. The great thing to remember is that Viola's part culminates in her eloquent avowal of her love for Orsino, and in her reunion with her brother, which Peggy Ashcroft made so memorably beautiful:

> At the end, as Sebastian faces his sister, he cries: 'What countryman? What name? What parentage?' There is a long pause now before Viola, in almost a whisper (but one of infinite rapture and astonishment), answers: 'Of Messaline'.[4]

Olivia, as has been concisely pointed out by Sprague and

'willow cabin' speech embodies a man's passionate courtship of a woman, and that therefore she cannot be so carried away as to put herself unconsciously into the wooer's place.

1. Adelaide Neilson (1877, New York), who combined an underlying pathos with a 'lovely smile' and 'exuberant vitality', was 'affluent in pretty bravado and demonstrative glee'. 'The mock ruefulness and bubbling merriment with which she delivered the speech culminating with "*I* am the MAN!" were delicious, both as an outburst of humour and a dramatic effect' (Winter, *op. cit.*, pp. 41–4). Ellen Terry added to this gaiety of tone 'a charming and laughing assumption of a mannish walk' (*Saturday Review*, 12 July 1884, quoted by Furness *ad loc.*, who adds that, though retaining this effect in later performances, she supplied a new tone of pathos for 'Poor lady, she were better love a dream').

2. Winter, *op. cit.*, p. 73 (his italics), of Ada Rehan in Daly's long-running London production (111 performances), 1894.

3. It has been attempted (by Viola Allen in 1904): see Winter, *op. cit.*, pp. 80–1; he rightly objects that 'the scheme [of Viola's disguise] is a delightful fiction, and it cannot be successfully treated as a bald fact'.

4. J. C. Trewin's review of her Old Vic (1950) performance, *John O'London's Weekly*, 8 Dec. 1950 (quoted by Brown, *op. cit.*, p. 225).

Trewin, has, in the twentieth century, changed from 'a stately Countess' to a young and often foolish girl.[1] Though partly connected with the riper age of leading ladies in the past, the change is more obviously attributable to a general trend in twentieth-century criticism and production which may be called anti-romantic, a trend towards extracting the potentially ironical and ridiculous in Shakespeare's dramatic situations, which I regard as wholly regrettable. Young she must be, if she is to marry Sebastian, but apart from her passing levity of response to the Duke's messenger in I. v there is nothing to suggest frivolity in her character, and there are both the Captain (I. ii. 36) and Sebastian (IV. iii. 16–20) to testify to her virtue and her discretion as ruler of her household.

Meanwhile, as the same writers notice, Feste has been growing older. Granville Barker's own Feste in 1912 was Hayden Coffin, then aged fifty.[2] Occasionally, as with Robert Eddison's Old Vic performance of 1948, there is a mystic sadness about him.[3] More usually, however, he is merely ageing and has seen the best of his time, 'retained not for his wit but for his length of service'.[4] He is also, nowadays, often insecure as to his future employment, and we are sometimes allowed to think that in his epilogue-song he is out of a job.[5] Gone (with happy exceptions, usually on the amateur stage) are the days when 'Mr John Laurie, like Frank Rodway, let us see that Feste was a human being as

1. *Shakespeare's Plays Today*, p. 95. This goes back at least as far as Hugh Hunt's 1950 production (see his *Old Vic Prefaces*, 1954, p. 73: 'Behind the veil there is more than a hint of a self-willed, temperamental flirt', though he maintained that she should be attractive as well as affected). The Olivia of Peter Hall's Stratford-upon-Avon production of 1958, Geraldine McEwan, presented the new Olivia in the most exaggerated form.

2. *Shakespeare Survey*, 12 (1959), 130, note 15. Granville Barker's own preface to his Players' Edition of the play (quoted by Sprague and Trewin, p. 96) diagnoses failure in life as the source of the Clown's persistent irony.

3. Sprague and Trewin, *op. cit.*, pp. 96–7.

4. *Sh. Q.*, VIII (1957), 512 (in Tyrone Guthrie's 1957 production at Stratford, Ontario). See note in commentary on II. iv. 11–12. Perhaps the Clown in *All's W.* has influenced the portrayal of the one in *Tw.N.*

5. As in Hugh Hunt's 1950 production and several others. The critical history is relevant: 'Unscathed by the slaps and side-blows of the plot, in the end he gets dismissed out into the cold: and that is Shakespeare's last word of irony—as it is with his last word on the poor loyal Fool in *Lear*' (Quiller-Couch, introduction to N.C.S., p. xxvi: this was written in 1930). I regard this as pure sentimental fantasy. Though Maria threatens him with dismissal, he fools his way back to the favour of Olivia, who defends him against Malvolio, in I. v: and in v. i, after Fabian's appeal for general clemency, he can taunt Malvolio (a taunt which suggests security, not desperation).

well as a professional funny man, and also that he thoroughly enjoys his own fooling'.[1] In 1960 Tom Courteney's performance was criticized because the part needed 'more weariness and weight of middle age'.[2]

Orsino and Maria are pretty straightforward, and highly actable, roles. Orsino's nobility (I. ii. 25), despite his lovesickness, should be never in question.[3] Nor should Maria's youth and liveliness: the ageing Maria of John Barton's 1969 production at Stratford-upon-Avon, to whom (and not to Sir Andrew) Sir Toby most incongruously addressed the phrase in his last speech in II. iii, ' 'Tis too late to go to bed now', should have retorted, parodying Marlowe, 'Never too late, if Toby will consent'. Her social status, as Olivia's gentlewoman, needs to be made clear; she is socially a fit match for Sir Toby.

Of the performance of particular scenes much has already been implied in considering the portrayal of the characters. Only on one or two of them a little needs to be added.

The humour of the so-called 'kitchen scene' (II. iii) has often been buried beneath gross stage business, sometimes supposedly arising from the text (as in 'Sir Toby, there you lie', l. 107)[4] but usually quite extraneous, involving flapping of arms, crowing, and the blowing-out of candles and throwing of tobacco-pipes.[5] Malvolio's night-gown (allegedly introduced by Tree) has already been referred to; in fact a prompt-book of 1864 for a performance at Brooklyn already specifies the night-gown, night-cap and slippers.[6] Sprague and Trewin rightly insist that Malvolio gives offence, not suffers it, in this scene as written by Shakespeare, and remind us that the only line referring to Malvolio's dress

1. Crosse, *op. cit.*, p. 115, of Sydney Carroll's production of 1932.

2. Robert Speaight on the Old Vic production, in *Sh. Q.*, XII (1961), 427. In the previous year, it is fair to add, he had said that Max Adrian's interpretation was too heavy and that he 'had drawn his pathos from a canvas by Georges Rouault' (*ibid.*, XI (1960), 450).

3. I totally agree with G. Wilson Knight's short sub-chapter on Orsino in his *Shakespearian Production* (revised ed., 1964), pp. 80–3. This also appeared in the earlier editions of Knight's book as *Principles of Shakespearian Production* (1936, 1949).   4. See note in commentary.

5. Winter, *op. cit.*, pp. 102–3, instances the use, in 1914, of a particularly 'asinine device' for ending the scene, with the Clown frightening the two knights with a 'ghost' made of a sheet.

6. See Sprague and Trewin, *op. cit.*, pp. 83–4, and Sprague, *Shakespeare and the Actors*, pp. 6–7. There is an illustration from Ben Greet's 1904 production (reproduced from *New York Theatre*, April 1904) facing p. 81 of the former book. Winter, *op. cit.*, p. 88, says of this same scene that (despite Malvolio's costume) it was 'acted with natural jollity and almost entirely without horseplay'.

invites him to rub his chain with crumbs, thus implying that he has appeared in full ceremonial costume to put down the revelry.

The 'duel scene' (latter part of III. iv) is traditionally, and rightly, taken as comic, but it need not therefore be farcical. It is a great test of a producer's discretion. Even Sir Andrew's terror should not be overplayed,[1] and to demand similar fooleries from Viola (even though on a smaller scale) is pernicious.[2] Self-control, like that of Dorothy Tutin at Stratford-upon-Avon in 1958 and 1960, is what she should show,[3] though her lines sufficiently express her feelings of alarm.

By contrast, the 'prison scene' (IV. ii) has often, with the emphasis placed on a pathetic Malvolio, been pushed towards the painful.[4] Despite the Folio's unambiguous direction *Malvolio within*, audiences have often been treated to a sight of him manacled, or 'stretched on the straw of a dungeon worthy of *Fidelio*'.[5] How he and the Clown are thus to share the stage, unless it is partitioned into left and right halves, I cannot imagine.[6] In any case, this is the Clown's scene rather than Malvolio's: he should have the whole of the stage to himself. A modern way of granting him this and also providing a part-visible and clearly-audible Malvolio is to situate the 'dark room' under a grating (that is, beneath a trap), through which Michael Hordern's hands are shown protruding in a photograph of 1954.[7]

1. Sprague, *op. cit.*, pp. 8–9, records his climbing variously up part of the proscenium arch, up a tree, and up a rope ladder.

2. 'That the humours of the duelling scene will ever be brought back within the text of Shakespeare, and the limits of *becoming* mirth, is more than we can hope.' J. Spedding, *Fraser's Magazine*, Aug. 1865 (quoted by Furness, at greater length, p. 242).   3. Brown, *op. cit.*, p. 225.

4. Daly cut out the 'prison scene' from his New York production of 1893 (and, I presume, from his London one of 1894), explaining to Winter (*op. cit.*, p. 68) that audiences found it 'painful and tiresome'. They would find some Malvolios much more painful than others. Phelps, for example, played the scene somewhat phlegmatically, 'sustained by his self-content, and by the honest certainty that he has been notoriously abused' (Morley, *op. cit.*, p. 140).

5. Sprague, *op. cit.*, p. 10 (Irving's production); he cites a prompt-book of 1864 for the 'chains on wrists'. The custom survives: I saw the scene so performed (manacles and all) by a professional company at Perth in October 1974, without a divided stage, so that Maria's 'he sees thee not' was true merely because Malvolio did not choose to look at 'Sir Topas', and the Clown's later monologue for two voices was utterly unconvincing.

6. It is so divided in the pictorial frontispiece to the play in Rowe's edition (1709), reproduced in W. M. Merchant, *Shakespeare and the Artist* (1959, plate 9(c)); but there is no need to accept Merchant's conjecture that the engraving follows theatrical practice, since (as he allows, p. 50) *Twelfth Night* was not at that time in the repertory, being revived only in 1741.

7. R. Wood and M. Clarke, *Shakespeare at the Old Vic* (1954), p. 31.

The dominant interest of the play's closing minutes is Malvolio's enlightenment. J. R. Brown has an excellent paragraph on the effectiveness of Malvolio's silence during which the deception is explained to him, the emotions which he may register, and the pent-up dramatic expectation which is released with his single exit-line, 'I'll be reveng'd on the whole pack of you!'[1] Various pieces of business which have accompanied this line—Tree tore off his steward's chain, Sothern tore the forged letter[2]—serve both to concentrate the audience's attention on a material object and to indicate Malvolio's state of mind. The speaker's intonation and general manner are also of great importance, and can range from Phelps's expression of undented pride[3] to Olivier's utterance of the line as 'the cry of a man unmade'.[4] Perhaps Olivier's manner, though highly effective at the moment, alienated Malvolio so completely from the rest of the characters as to undermine the Duke's assumption that he could be entreated to a peace, and hence to damage the tone of the ending. A merely angry Malvolio might—if it was made worth his while—relent. Tree's tearing off of his chain also perhaps damaged the ending, by its suggestion that Malvolio is giving up his post: no doubt Olivia's household could carry on without him and a replacement be found, but at the end of *Twelfth Night* one does not like to be asked to look beyond the conclusion of the action. This is a further reason why the Clown should not end his part as an outcast, especially since no one has cast him out. The final mood should surely be one of harmony. Not every reader, I am well aware, will agree with this; but, even though we may take our pleasures differently, we may unite to agree with Gordon Crosse that 'a really good performance of *Twelfth Night* is the perfection of pleasure that Shakespearean acting can give, at any rate in comedy'.[5]

1. *Op. cit.*, pp. 76–7.
2. Sprague, *op. cit.*, p. 10.
3. '. . . and when at last he, for once, opens his eyes on learning how he has been tricked, they close again in happy self-content, and he is retiring in state without deigning a word to his tormentors, when, as the fool has twitted him by noting how 'the whirligig of time brings in his revenges', he remembers that the whirligig is still in motion. Therefore, marching back with as much increase of speed as is consistent with magnificence, he threatens all—including now Olivia in his contempt—"I'll be reveng'd on the whole pack of you!"' (Morley, *op. cit.*, p. 140). The inclusion of Olivia in the 'whole pack' is surely a mistake: the term is too derogatory. Besides, she has explained that she has been no party to the plot.
4. Brown, *op. cit.*, p. 222.
5. Crosse, *op. cit.*, p. 116. Annual reviews of Shakespearean productions appear in *Sh. Q.* and *Shakespeare Survey*.

TWELFTH NIGHT:
OR, WHAT YOU WILL

DRAMATIS PERSONÆ] This ed. (subst. as Mahood); not in F.
12. *kinsman*] *N.C.S.; Uncle | Rowe.*

Dramatis Personæ] first printed by Rowe (though a list is given in Douai MS.).

1. *Orsino*] For Don Virginio Orsino, Duke of Bracciano, see Introduction, pp. xxviii–xxx.

Duke] For F's use of the titles Duke and Count, see Introduction, pp. xix, xxii.

12. *Sir Toby . . . kinsman*] 'The word "uncle" does not appear in the play. and though Olivia is often called his "niece" this is a vaguer term in Shakespeare's day than ours and she herself addresses him as "cousin", a vaguer term still' (Wilson). Maria, speaking to Olivia, calls him her 'kinsman', I. v. 105; and Malvolio, writing to her, calls him her 'drunken cousin' (v. i. 301). His own use of 'niece' (e.g. I. iii. 1, 38, 41, 50), taken up by Sir Andrew (I. iii. 103, III. ii. 4), perhaps presumes that he has more influence with her than he has in reality; its use by Maria (II. iii. 160), by Fabian (III. iv. 199), by Malvolio (II. v. 71), and by Viola (III. i. 77, answering Sir Toby's l. 75), clearly implies that he is older than she is. In all other plays of Shakespeare's 'niece' is always used in its modern sense. In *Twelfth Night* it might degrade Olivia to give her such an uncle, and her angry speeches to him (IV. i. 44, 46–50) might appear unseemly in their language to so close a relative.

13. *Aguecheek*] so called from his leanness (I. iii. 99–101, v. i. 205; cf. *John*, III. iv. 85, 'As dim [i.e., pallid] and meagre as an ague's fit'; *Caes.*,

II. ii. 113, 'that same ague which hath made you lean') and his cowardice (I. iii. 31, III. iv. 278–317; cf. *Cor.*, I. iv. 37–8, 'faces pale | With flight and agued fear'; *R2*, III. ii. 190, 'This ague-fit of fear is overblown.').

14. *Malvolio*] so called from the 'ill-will' he bears to the Clown (I. v. 73–88), Sir Toby and Maria (II. iii. 87–123) and Fabian (II. v. 6–8). The formation of his name is analogous to that of Benvolio in *Rom.*, a man of goodwill. For attempts to derive it from the name of a person (Malevolti) in *Il Sacrificio*, and from an Italian phrase in the prologue to *Gl'Ingannati*, see Introduction, pp. xl, xlii (n. 3). Hotson, taking Malvolio to be a satire on Sir William Knollys, adds the improbable interpretation 'Mall-voglio', i.e., 'I want Mall [Mary Fitton]' (p. 108).

15. *Fabian*] Since Sir Toby calls him 'Signior' (II. v. 1, III. iv. 261) and Olivia calls him 'sirrah' (v. i. 300), his status is doubtful. He addresses Sir Toby familiarly as 'man' (II. v. 6), and, speaking to Olivia, he calls him plain 'Toby' (v. i. 358). Rowe calls him a 'servant', Wilson a 'gentleman'; I follow Mahood.

16. *Clown (Feste)*] named only once (II. iv. 11), when Orsino's question requires him to have a personal name. In the text he is usually called 'fool'; in the directions and prefixes invariably 'Clown', which is therefore retained.

20–1. *and . . . Adriatic*] to take account of II. i, which (as III. iii. shows) is located outside Orsino's duchy.

2

DRAMATIS PERSONÆ

ORSINO, *Duke of Illyria.*
VALENTINE,
CURIO, } *gentlemen attending on the Duke.*
FIRST OFFICER,
SECOND OFFICER, } *in the service of the Duke.*   5
VIOLA, *later disguised as Cesario.*
SEBASTIAN, *her twin brother.*
CAPTAIN *of the wrecked ship, befriending Viola.*
ANTONIO, *another sea-captain, befriending Sebastian.*
OLIVIA, *a countess.*   10
MARIA, *Olivia's waiting-gentlewoman.*
SIR TOBY BELCH, *Olivia's kinsman.*
SIR ANDREW AGUECHEEK, *Sir Toby's companion.*
MALVOLIO, *Olivia's steward.*
FABIAN, *a member of Olivia's household.*   15
CLOWN (FESTE), *jester to Olivia.*
SERVANT *to Olivia.*
PRIEST.

Musicians, Lords, Sailors, Attendants.

SCENE: *Illyria, and another state further along the coast of*   20
the Adriatic.

3

TWELFTH NIGHT: OR, WHAT YOU WILL

ACT I

SCENE I

[Music.] Enter ORSINO, *Duke of Illyria,* CURIO, *and other Lords.*

Duke. If music be the food of love, play on,
    Give me excess of it, that, surfeiting,
    The appetite may sicken, and so die.
    That strain again, it had a dying fall:
    O, it came o'er my ear like the sweet sound   5

ACT I
Scene 1

Title. TWELFTH NIGHT: OR, WHAT] F (Twelfe Night, Or what).   ACT I
SCENE 1] F (*Actus Primus, Scæna Prima.*).   [*Location.*] *The Palace. Rowe; A
Room in the Duke's Palace. Capell; not in F.*   S.D. [*Music.*]] *Mahood; Musick
attending. Capell (after Lords); not in F.*   5. sound] *F; wind Rowe;* south *Pope;*
sough *conj. anon. apud Camb.*

1–3. *food of love . . . excess . . . sur-feiting . . . appetite*] The emphasis is on (1) the intensity, (2) the instability, of the appetites love creates. Wilson interprets: 'Appetite' means not 'love' as is generally assumed, but 'love's appetite for music'. But surely Orsino, like other lovers, may wish also to have the pangs of love itself allayed. For music, cf. *Ant.,* II. v. 1–2, 'music, moody food / Of us that trade in love'; for the appetites, cf. *Gent.,* II. iv. 137–8, 'Now can I break my fast, dine, sup, and sleep, / Upon the very naked name of love.'

2. *surfeiting*] related grammatically to 'appetite'; logically also to 'me'.

4. *dying fall*] final cadence (with *diminuendo?*).

5. *sound*] F's reading is defensible

if 'sound' is freely interpreted to mean either the sound of a sweet wind or that of sweet music borne on the wind (preferably the former, since odour is given to the violets as well as stolen from them). Yet Hudson's objection, 'It is as much as to say, "The sweet sound came o'er my ear like the sweet sound",' has force, and makes the citation of Milton's simile of sound and scent (*Comus,* ll. 555–7) irrelevant. Pope's *south* is now generally rejected because (1) Shakespeare often speaks in uncomplimentary terms of the south (wind) (e.g. *AYL.,* III. v. 50; *2H4,* II. iv. 350; *Troil.,* v. i. 17, *Cor.,* I. iv. 30, *Cym.,* IV. ii. 350; cf. 'south-fog', *Cym.,* II. iii. 131, and 'south-west', *Tp.,* I. ii. 323), though favourably in *Wint.,* v. i. 161; (2) sound/south

5

That breathes upon a bank of violets,
Stealing and giving odour. Enough, no more;
'Tis not so sweet now as it was before.
O spirit of love, how quick and fresh art thou,
That notwithstanding thy capacity   10
Receiveth as the sea, nought enters there,
Of what validity and pitch soe'er,
But falls into abatement and low price,
Even in a minute! So full of shapes is fancy,
That it alone is high fantastical.   15
Curio. Will you go hunt, my lord?
Duke.   What, Curio?
Curio. The hart.
Duke. Why so I do, the noblest that I have.
   O, when mine eyes did see Olivia first,
   Methought she purg'd the air of pestilence;   20
   That instant was I turn'd into a hart,

---

11. sea,] *Rowe*³; Sea. *F.*

---

confusion is 'graphically difficult' (Wilson). Yet it may be defended (1) by citing (with Steevens) Sidney's *Arcadia* (ed. 1598, bk 1, p. 2, 'Her breath is more sweete than a gentle South-west wind, which comes creeping ouer flowrie fieldes and shadowed waters in the extreme heate of sommer') and by comparing *Cym.*, iv. ii. 172–4, 'as gentle / As zephyrs blowing below the violet, / Not wagging his sweet head': see zephyr, *OED*, 2, 'a soft mild gentle wind or breeze' (not necessarily the west); and (2) by supposing that, if transcribing from a blotted or damaged first page of foul papers (see Introduction, pp. xix–xxi), the scribe was led by the general context to supply 'sou[nd]'. Wilson, who had 'sound' in his first ed. (1930), changed the reading to 'south' in his second (1949), and though I retain F's reading I do so without firm conviction.

   9. *quick and fresh*] keen and hungry: *OED*, quick, iii. 20, fresh, 11.b (Wilson).

11. *as the sea*] Cf. ii. iv. 101–2, 'But mine is all as hungry as the sea, / And can digest as much', and *Tp.*, iii. iii. 55, 'The never-surfeited sea'.

   12. *validity*] value.

   pitch] height, hence 'value'; *OED*, 18, the height to which a falcon soars.

   13. *abatement*] lowering; cf., for the thought, Bacon, *Essays*, 'Of Love': 'It is a strange thing to note the excess of this passion, and how it braves the nature and value of things.'

   14–15. *So full . . . fantastical*] Cf. *MND.*, v. i. 4–17, on 'The lunatic, the lover, and the poet'. Love (fancy, Onions, *sb.* 2) creates many 'shapes' (imaginary forms) and yet tires immediately of each, so that 'it alone [above all other passions] is high fantastical' (imaginative in the highest degree). Cf. also *LLL.*, v. ii. 751, where Love is 'Full of strange shapes, of habits, and of forms'. For further discussion of 'fancy' in *Tw.N.*, see v. i. 387.

   17–21. *hart*] For the hart/heart quibble (common in Shakespeare),

And my desires, like fell and cruel hounds,
E'er since pursue me.

Enter VALENTINE.

How now? what news from her?
Val. So please my lord, I might not be admitted,
But from her handmaid do return this answer: 25
The element itself, till seven years' heat,
Shall not behold her face at ample view;
But like a cloistress she will veiled walk,
And water once a day her chamber round
With eye-offending brine: all this to season   30
A brother's dead love, which she would keep fresh
And lasting, in her sad remembrance.
Duke. O, she that hath a heart of that fine frame
To pay this debt of love but to a brother,
How will she love, when the rich golden shaft   35
Hath kill'd the flock of all affections else
That live in her; when liver, brain, and heart,

---

23. S.D.] *As Dyce; after* her? *F.*   26. years' heat] *Harness;* yeares heate *F;*
years hence *Rowe*[3].   37. her;] *F* (her.).

cf. IV. i. 58. Similar allusions to the
story of Actaeon's transformation by
Diana (Ovid, *Metamorphoses*, III. 138
ff.) as typifying hopeless passion, were
common: cf. Daniel, *Delia*, Sonnet 5.

26. *element*] air, sky; cf. I. v. 279.

heat] Some take this as a participle
(=heated); but more probably it is a
sb. (=the heat of summer, so that the
phrase=seven hot summers): cf.
Mer.V., II. vii. 75, *R2*, I. iii. 299, and
2H6, I. i. 76 ('In winter's cold and
summer's parching heat'). The idea
is that Olivia's face will be veiled as if
to protect it from the summer sun.

28. *cloistress*] a nun cloistered from
the world.

30. *eye-offending brine*] salt water
(tears) which hurts the eyes; cf. II. i.
29–31.

season] preserve (as in brine); cf.
All's W., I. i. 43–4.

31. *A brother's dead love*] either (1)
'the love which her [dead] brother

bore to her', or (2) 'her love for a
dead brother'. The former seems preferable, since her mourning is called a
'debt', l. 34; for the latter sense, cf. I.
ii. 39, 'for whose dear love'.

32. *remembrance*] pronounced 're-
memberance' (*q.v.* in *OED* as a now
obsolete form).

35. *golden shaft*] Cupid's golden-
tipped arrow caused love, his leaden-
tipped one aversion; cf. Ovid,
Metamorphoses, I. 468–71, and *MND.*,
I. i. 170.

36. *flock*] Cf. 'the flock of vnspeak-
able virtues laid up delightfully in
that best builded folde [her body]',
(Sidney, *Arcadia*) which follows the
passage quoted in note to l. 5 (Wilson).

affections] feelings.

37–9. *when liver . . . self king*] The
liver was supposed the seat or 'throne'
of passion, the brain that of thought,
and the heart that of emotion. Orsino
hopes for a time when 'these several

These sovereign thrones, are all supplied, and fill'd
Her sweet perfections with one self king!
Away before me to sweet beds of flowers!   40
Love-thoughts lie rich when canopied with bowers.

Exeunt.

SCENE II

Enter VIOLA, *a* CAPTAIN, *and Sailors.*

Viola. What country, friends, is this?
Captain. This is Illyria, lady.
Viola. And what should I do in Illyria?
  My brother he is in Elysium.
  Perchance he is not drown'd: what think you, sailors?
Captain. It is perchance that you yourself were sav'd.   6
Viola. O my poor brother! and so perchance may he be.
Captain. True, madam, and to comfort you with chance,

38. supplied, and fill'd] *Rowe* (supply'd, and fill'd); supply'd and fill'd *F.*
39. Her sweet perfections] *F;* (O sweet perfection!) *conj. Warburton;* (Her
sweet perfection) *Capell.*   40. flowers!] *F* (Flowres,).

Scene II

SCENE II] *F* (*Scena Secunda.*).   [*Location.*] *The Street. Rowe; The Sea-coast.
Capell; not in F.*

thrones' within the sweet and perfect
Olivia will be 'supplied, and fill'd'
by one and the same 'king', himself.
For 'perfections', cf. i. v. 300. Rowe's
punctuation is followed in order to
give 'perfections' a related participle.
'Thrones' and 'perfections' are not
synonymous (therefore Capell's reading cannot stand), but 'supplied and
fill'd' is a typically Shakespearean
tautology, and, when the passage is
read aloud, 'fill'd' is linked to both
'supplied' and 'perfections'.

Scene II

2. *Illyria*] 'This name for what is
now Yugoslavia conjures up the world
of the late Greek romances, but the
local colour of the play is all English'

(Mahood): but see note to l. 56.
Shakespeare may have remembered a
line from Golding's translation of
Ovid's *Metamorphoses*, iv. 701: 'Upon
the c[o]ast of Illirie his wife and he
were cast' (Cadmus and his wife, in
ignorance that their daughter and
her child had been saved from perish-
ing in the sea, by being turned into
sea-deities). I owe this suggestion to
H. F. Brooks.

4. *Elysium*] the abode of the blessed
after death: here=heaven. 'An antithesis to Illyria suggested by the sound'
(Wilson).

5–6. *Perchance*] (1) perhaps, (2) by
mere chance.

8. *chance*] what may have happened.

Assure yourself, after our ship did split,
When you and those poor number sav'd with you   10
Hung on our driving boat, I saw your brother,
Most provident in peril, bind himself
(Courage and hope both teaching him the practice)
To a strong mast that liv'd upon the sea;
Where, like Arion on the dolphin's back,   15
I saw him hold acquaintance with the waves
So long as I could see.

Viola. For saying so, there's gold:
Mine own escape unfoldeth to my hope,
Whereto thy speech serves for authority,   20
The like of him. Know'st thou this country?

Captain. Ay, madam, well, for I was bred and born
Not three hours' travel from this very place.

Viola. Who governs here?

Captain. A noble duke, in nature as in name.   25

Viola. What is his name?

Captain. Orsino.

Viola. Orsino! I have heard my father name him.
He was a bachelor then.

Captain. And so is now, or was so very late;   30
For but a month ago I went from hence,
And then 'twas fresh in murmur (as, you know,
What great ones do, the less will prattle of)
That he did seek the love of fair Olivia.

Viola. What's she?   35

Captain. A virtuous maid, the daughter of a count
That died some twelvemonth since; then leaving her
In the protection of his son, her brother,

---

15. Arion] *Pope; Orion F.*   25. duke, in nature] *Dyce;* Duke in nature, *F.*

---

11. *driving*] driven by the storm, with the suggestion of both speed and helplessness; cf. *Per.,* III, Chorus, 50, 'So up and down the poor ship drives'. Seaman's term.

14. *liv'd*] floated (seaman's term: cf. Ralegh, *Discovery of Guiana,* quoted in Furness).

15. *Arion*] Arion, by his music on board ship, charmed a dolphin along-side, which carried him ashore when he leapt overboard to escape being murdered; cf. Ovid, *Fasti,* II. 79–118.

19–21. *Mine own escape . . . The like of him*] 'My own escape encourages me in the hope, which is warranted by what you have just said, that he also has escaped' (Mahood).

32. *murmur*] rumour.

Who shortly also died; for whose dear love
(They say) she hath abjur'd the company   40
And sight of men.
Viola.   O that I serv'd that lady,
And might not be deliver'd to the world,
Till I had made mine own occasion mellow,
What my estate is.
Captain.   That were hard to compass,
Because she will admit no kind of suit,   45
No, not the Duke's.
Viola. There is a fair behaviour in thee, Captain;
And though that nature with a beauteous wall
Doth oft close in pollution, yet of thee
I will believe thou hast a mind that suits   50
With this thy fair and outward character.
I prithee (and I'll pay thee bounteously)
Conceal me what I am, and be my aid
For such disguise as haply shall become
The form of my intent. I'll serve this duke;   55
Thou shalt present me as an eunuch to him.
It may be worth thy pains; for I can sing,

---

39. love] *F;* loss *Dyce², conj. Walker.*   40–1. company / And sight] *Hanmer;* sight / And company *F.*   42. world,] *Rowe;* world *F.*   43. mellow,] *Hanmer;* mellow *F.*   50. will] *F;* well *conj. Walker.*

40–1. *the company | And sight*] Hanmer's transposition restores the metre; it also intensifies Olivia's seclusion, though Sisson (who associates 'company' with courtship and marriage disagrees (1, 185).

42–4. *be deliver'd . . . estate is*] be publicly made known ('deliver'd', Onions, 3) in my true station ('estate') until I considered that the time was ripe. 'Mellow' is an adj., not a transitive vb (as might be supposed from F's punctuation).

44. *compass*] contrive.

45. *suit*] petition.

48–9. *And though that . . . pollution*] a familiar Shakespearean observation: see any Concordance, e.g., under *outside, outward,* and cf. III. iv. 378–9. Cf. Matthew xxiii, 27 ('whited sepulchres').

50. *will*] am prepared to; emendation is unnecessary.

51. *character*] appearance.

54–5. *haply shall . . . intent*] may chance to fit my purpose; 'form' = shape, physical appearance: cf. v. i. 233.

56. *eunuch*] After this scene no further reference is made to this part of the plan. Shakespeare associates eunuchs, as singers, with Eastern Mediterranean courts, *MND.*, v. i. 45 ('an Athenian eunuch') and *Ant.*, I. v. 9–10 (of Mardian). The Duke's attitude to Cesario in II. iv shows that Viola has not entered his service in this character but as a page. For discussion of the opinion that the play was revised, see Introduction, pp. xxii–xxiii.

And speak to him in many sorts of music,
That will allow me very worth his service.
What else may hap, to time I will commit; 　　　　　60
Only shape thou thy silence to my wit.
Captain. Be you his eunuch, and your mute I'll be:
When my tongue blabs, then let mine eyes not see.
Viola. I thank thee. Lead me on. 　　　　　*Exeunt.*

SCENE III

Enter SIR TOBY BELCH *and* MARIA.

Sir To. What a plague means my niece to take the death
of her brother thus? I am sure care's an enemy to
life.
Maria. By my troth, Sir Toby, you must come in earlier
o' nights: your cousin, my lady, takes great excep- 　　5
tions to your ill hours.
Sir To. Why, let her except, before excepted.
Maria. Ay, but you must confine yourself within the
modest limits of order.
Sir To. Confine? I'll confine myself no finer than I am. 　10

Scene III

SCENE III] F (*Scæna Tertia.*). [Location.] *Olivia's House. Rowe.* 　5. o' nights] F
(a nights). 　7. except,] *F;* except *Hanmer.*

58. *many sorts of music*] instrumental as well as vocal.
59. *allow*] prove.
61. *wit*] ingenuity (referring to her proposal).
62–3. *Be you . . . not see*] a witty rejoinder, referring both to Viola's request for his secrecy and to her own proposed disguise.
62. *mute*] dumb servant in a Turkish court; cf. *H5*, I. ii. 232, 'Like Turkish mute, shall have a tongueless mouth'. The Captain alludes to the employment of eunuchs as guards in Turkish harems (cf. *LLL.*, III. i. 189, 'Though Argus were her eunuch and her guard'), and of mutes as their subordinates.

Scene III

1, 5. *niece, cousin.*] See note on Dramatis Personæ: *Sir Toby.*

7. *except, before excepted*] *exceptis excipiendis* (excepting those things [i.e., former items] which are to be excepted): a legal phrase. Sir Toby quibbles on 'exceptions' (ll. 5–6), having, as F's punctuation suggests, refused to take notice of Olivia's disapproval.

9. *modest*] moderate.

10. *Confine? . . . than I am*] another rejection of Maria's advice, turning to a tipsy quibble whereby 'confine' is made to mean 'dress myself up'.

These clothes are good enough to drink in, and so
be these boots too: and they be not, let them hang
themselves in their own straps.

Maria. That quaffing and drinking will undo you: I
heard my lady talk of it yesterday; and of a foolish   15
knight that you brought in one night here to be her
wooer.

Sir To. Who, Sir Andrew Aguecheek?

Maria. Ay, he.

Sir To. He's as tall a man as any's in Illyria.   20

Maria. What's that to th' purpose?

Sir To. Why, he has three thousand ducats a year.

Maria. Ay, but he'll have but a year in all these ducats.
He's a very fool, and a prodigal.

Sir To. Fie, that you'll say so! he plays o' th' viol-de-   25
gamboys, and speaks three or four languages word
for word without book, and hath all the good gifts
of nature.

Maria. He hath indeed all, most natural: for besides
that he's a fool, he's a great quarreller; and but   30
that he hath the gift of a coward to allay the gust he

---

18. Aguecheek] *F (Ague-cheeke).*   29. indeed all, most] *Mahood, conj. Furness;*
indeed,—all most *Collier², conj. Upton;* indeed, almost *F.*

12–13. *let them . . . own straps*] playing with the proverb (Tilley, G42)
'He may go hang himself in his own
garters'; cf. *1H4*, II. ii. 43–4, and
MND., v. i. 349–50.

18. *Aguecheek*] See note on Dramatis
Personæ.

20. *tall*] (1) valiant (Onions, 3),
Sir Toby's meaning; (2) of great
height, Maria's deliberate misunderstanding.

22. *ducats*] gold coins; in Shakespeare's time, variously worth between
a fifth and a third of a pound.

23. *he'll have . . . ducats*] He'll waste
all that money in a year. Sir Andrew
could lose his income by selling his
land (cf. Roderigo in *Oth.*, I. iii. 376)
and wasting the proceeds.

25–6. *viol-de-gamboys*] viola di
gamba, so called 'because men hold it

betweene or vpon their legges'
(Florio, 1611: *gamba*, Ital.=leg); a
bass-viol.

27. *without book*] Sir Toby's intended praise suggests that Sir
Andrew has merely learned foreign
phrases by heart, and prepares us for
his ignorance at ll. 90–3 (which suggests that he has no accomplishments,
linguistic or musical).

29. *all, most natural*] Maria repeats
Sir Toby's 'all', and develops his
'nature' into 'natural' (sb., Onions,=
idiot): i.e., Sir Andrew has every
quality of folly. Furness compares
with the F reading the line 'Fairies be
gone, and be alwaies [all ways=in
all directions] away' (*MND.*, IV. i. 38)
as printed in Qq and Ff. Cf. III. i. 93.

31, 33. *gift*] (1) talent, (2) present.
Wilson gives currency to E. A. Mere-

  hath in quarrelling, 'tis thought among the prudent
  he would quickly have the gift of a grave.

Sir To. By this hand, they are scoundrels and substractors that say so of him. Who are they?　　　35

Maria. They that add, moreover, he's drunk nightly in
  your company.

Sir To. With drinking healths to my niece: I'll drink to
  her as long as there is a passage in my throat,
  and drink in Illyria: he's a coward and a coistrel　　40
  that will not drink to my niece till his brains turn o'
  th' toe, like a parish top. What, wench! *Castiliano*
  vulgo: for here comes Sir Andrew Agueface.

    Enter Sir Andrew Aguecheek.

Sir And. Sir Toby Belch! How now, Sir Toby Belch?

Sir To. Sweet Sir Andrew!　　　　　　　　　　　45

41–2. o' th'] *F* (o'th), *F3*.　　42–3. *Castiliano vulgo:*] *F*; *Castiliano volto*; *Hanmer,
conj. Warburton; Castiglione voglio; conj. Sir H. Thomas (TLS, 4 June 1933);
Castigliano volgo; conj. L. Hotson (TLS, 1 October 1947); Castiliano, vulgo— Mahood.*

dith's conj. 'gift' for 'gust' (=relish),
l. 31; but, as Furness points out, this
word is followed by 'in', not by 'of',
as is 'gift' twice in the passage.

 34–5. *substractors*] perversion of
'detractors' (Onions). No other example is given in *OED*, which does,
however, give 'substract' and 'sub-
straction' as archaic forms of 'sub-
tract' and 'subtraction'. Sir Toby's
word allows Maria's quibble on 'add'
in l. 36 (cf. 'addition'=mark of distinction, Onions).

 40. *coistrel*] base fellow; literally,
groom.

 42. *parish top*] 'whipping-top kept
for the exercise of parishioners'
(Onions). Wilson adds S.D. *he seizes
her by the waist and they dance a turn*
(after Nicholson: see Furness, who
gives good reasons for rejecting it).

 42–3. *Castiliano vulgo*] The sense
is obscure and the accuracy of the
text in doubt. Explanatory attempts
include (1) *Castiliano volto*: Spanish,
i.e., solemn, face (Warburton and

Hanmer, independently); (2) *Castiglione voglio*: I want some Castiglione
or Lacrima Christi, a costly wine
(Thomas); (3) *Castigliano volgo*: I am
thinking of a Spanish ducat, i.e., of
Sir Andrew's money (Hotson, p. 115);
(4) *Castiliano, vulgo—*: Talk of the
devil [and he will appear], Castiliano
being a devil's assumed name in *Grim
the Collier of Croydon, c.*1600, and *vulgo*
being interpreted as 'in the common
tongue' (Mahood). Steevens (quoted
in Furness) gives instances of Castilian,
Castile, and Castiliano as words used
in a colloquial way, twice in obvious
connection with drinking: 'And Rivo
will he cry and Castile too' (*Look
About You*, 1600), and 'Hey, *Rivo
Castiliano*, a man's a man' (Marlowe,
The Jew of Malta). See also Humphreys's note on '*Rivo*! says the
drunkard' (*1H4*, New Arden ed.,
II. iv. 108–9). Sir Toby's 'What,
wench!' may be interpreted either as
a caution or as a commanding request
(cf. II. iii. 14 and 119); I incline to

Sir And. Bless you, fair shrew.

Maria. And you too, sir.

Sir To. Accost, Sir Andrew, accost.

Sir And. What's that?

Sir To. My niece's chambermaid.   50

Sir And. Good Mistress Accost, I desire better acquaintance.

Maria. My name is Mary, sir.

Sir And. Good Mistress Mary Accost—

Sir To. You mistake, knight. 'Accost' is front her,   55
board her, woo her, assail her.

Sir And. By my troth, I would not undertake her in this
company. Is that the meaning of 'accost'?

Maria. Fare you well, gentlemen.

Sir To. And thou let part so, Sir Andrew, would thou   60
might'st never draw sword again!

Sir And. And you part so, mistress, I would I might
never draw sword again. Fair lady, do you think
you have fools in hand?

Maria. Sir, I have not you by th' hand.   65

Sir And. Marry, but you shall have, and here's my
hand.

Maria. Now, sir, thought is free. I pray you bring

---

51. *Sir And.*] *F2 (An.); Ma. F.*   54. Mary Accost—] *Theobald;* Mary Accost.
Rowe³; *Mary,* accost. *F.*

the latter (i.e., seeing Sir Andrew
approach, Sir Toby calls for wine).

46. *shrew*] (1) a shrew-mouse, (2)
an ill-tempered woman. Possibly a
maladroit compliment in the first
sense (cf. mouse, I. v. 61), without
recognizing the second.

48. *Accost*] pay court, address with
courtesy (cf. *OED, v.,* 6, deriving
from nautical 'go alongside', *OED
v.,* 3; cf. l. 56, 'board'.

49. *What's that?*] What does that
mean?

50. *My niece's chambermaid*] intended by Sir Toby as the object of
his imperative verb; misunderstood
by Sir Andrew as a reply to his
question.

55. *front*] confront.

57. *undertake*] to take in hand to deal
with (a person), *OED,* 5.c (giving
this example). Here used with sexual
innuendo, through misunderstanding
'assail'. Shakespeare is perhaps recol-
lecting his innuendoes in *Shr.,*
IV. iii. 154–5 ('Take up my mistress'
gown for thy master's use!') and *Wiv.,*
IV. ii. 124–5 ('Will you take up your
wife's clothes?').

57–8. *in this company*] before the
spectators. Sir Andrew and Sir Toby
are downstage, Maria upstage.

64. *in hand*] to deal with.

68. *thought is free*] proverbial (Tilley,
T244); cf. Lyly's *Euphues and his
England* (1580), 'Why then, quoth he,

your hand to th' buttery bar and let it drink.

Sir And. Wherefore, sweetheart? What's your meta- 70
phor?

Maria. It's dry, sir.

Sir And. Why, I think so: I am not such an ass but I can
keep my hand dry. But what's your jest?

Maria. A dry jest, sir.   75

Sir And. Are you full of them?

Maria. Ay, sir, I have them at my fingers' ends: marry,
now I let go your hand, I am barren.   *Exit Maria.*

Sir To. O knight, thou lack'st a cup of canary: when
did I see thee so put down?   80

Sir And. Never in your life, I think, unless you see canary
put me down. Methinks sometimes I have no more
wit than a Christian or an ordinary man has: but
I am a great eater of beef, and I believe that does
harm to my wit.   85

doest thou thinke me a foole, thought
is free my Lord quoth she' (Lyly, II,
60); cf. *Tp.*, III. ii. 118.

68–9. *bring . . . drink*] Furness quotes
Kenrick's (1865) explanation 'A
proverbial phrase among forward
Abigails , to ask at once for a kiss and a
present'. But it seems merely to prepare for her next remark.

69. *buttery bar*] the ledge on the top
of the buttery-hatch or half-door, to
rest tankards on (Onions).

72. *dry*] (1) thirsty (cf. I. v. 41),
(2) not moist, and therefore implying
sexual insufficiency like that of age
(contr. *Oth.*, III. iv. 33–5, and cf.
Ado, II. i. 102).

73–4. *I am not . . . hand dry*] Wilson
refers this to the proverb 'Fools have
wit enough to keep themselves
[come in] out of the rain' (Tilley,
F537). Sir Andrew unconsciously
implies that he is a fool ('ass'), and
takes Maria's sense literally.

75. *dry*] (1) stupid (cf. I. v. 38,
but here glancing at Sir Andrew's
stupidity), (2) ironical (*OED*, a.,
II.14), (3) depending on the word
'dry'.

77. *at my fingers' ends*] (1) always
ready, (2) 'by th' hand', l. 65.

78. *barren*] empty of jests (replying
to his 'full'); cf. I. v. 82.

79. *canary*] sweet wine, fortified like
sherry, originally from the Canary
Islands.

80, 82. *put down*] (1) defeated (in
repartee; cf. I. v. 82), (2) laid flat
(with drink). For the pun, cf. *Ado*,
II. i. 252–5.

83. *a Christian or an ordinary man*] i.e.,
an average man. Mahood suggests
that, to avoid tautology, an ordinary
man may mean a man who eats at
the 'ordinary' (table providing a stock
meal at a fixed price). But to make a
distinction without a difference is
characteristic of Sir Andrew (cf.
III. iv. 152), as is the idiotic implication that he is not a Christian.

84–5. *eater of beef . . . wit*] beef,
being gross and heavy, was supposed
to dull the brain; cf. *Troil.*, II. i. 13,
'beef-witted', and *H5*, III. vii. 130–47.
Sir Andrew is perhaps indirectly
claiming to be valiant.

Sir To. No question.

Sir And. And I thought that, I'd forswear it. I'll ride
home to-morrow, Sir Toby.

Sir To. Pourquoi, my dear knight?

Sir And. What is *pourquoi*? Do, or not do? I would I   90
had bestowed that time in the tongues that I have
in fencing, dancing, and bear-baiting. O, had I
but followed the arts!

Sir To. Then hadst thou had an excellent head of hair.

Sir And. Why, would that have mended my hair?   95

Sir To. Past question, for thou seest it will not curl by
nature.

Sir And. But it becomes me well enough, does't not?

Sir To. Excellent, it hangs like flax on a distaff; and I
hope to see a housewife take thee between her legs,   100
and spin it off.

Sir And. Faith, I'll home to-morrow, Sir Toby; your
niece will not be seen, or if she be, it's four to one
she'll none of me: the Count himself here hard by
woos her.   105

Sir To. She'll none o' th' Count; she'll not match
above her degree, neither in estate, years, nor wit;
I have heard her swear't. Tut, there's life in't,
man.

Sir And. I'll stay a month longer. I am a fellow o' th' 110
strangest mind i' th' world: I delight in masques
and revels sometimes altogether.

---

96. curl by] *Theobald;* coole my *F.*   100. housewife] *F* (huswife).

91. *tongues*] (1) languages, (2)
curling-tongs, in Sir Toby's quibble,
where he also contrasts 'arts' (l. 93)
and 'nature' (l. 97).

100. *housewife*] (1) woman who
keeps house (Onions, 1), (2) prostitute (Onions, 2; cf. *H5*, v. i. 74,
'Doth Fortune play the huswife with
me now? and cf. *Ham.*, II. ii. 487, 'Out,
out, thou strumpet Fortune'). Pronounced 'hussif' (cf. F spelling, and
modern 'hussy').

99–101. *like flax . . . spin it off*] Sir
Toby's   simile   (cf.   Chaucer's

Pardoner's hair in *Canterbury Tales*,
Prologue, ll. 675–6) leads to a *double
entendre*: (1) a housewife might treat
the thin Sir Andrew as a distaff and
his hair as the flax on it, (2) a prostitute might take him between her legs
and give him venereal disease which
would, according to Elizabethan
belief, make his hair fall out; cf. *Tim.*,
IV. iii. 159, 'Make curl'd-pate ruf-
fians bald'.

108. *there's life in't*] proverbial
(Tilley, L265; and L269, 'While
there's life there's hope').

Sir To. Art thou good at these kickshawses, knight?

Sir And. As any man in Illyria, whatsoever he be, under
the degree of my betters; and yet I will not com-   115
pare with an old man.

Sir To. What is thy excellence in a galliard, knight?

Sir And. Faith, I can cut a caper.

Sir To. And I can cut the mutton to't.

Sir And. And I think I have the back-trick simply as   120
strong as any man in Illyria.

Sir To. Wherefore are these things hid? Wherefore
have these gifts a curtain before 'em? Are they
like to take dust, like Mistress Mall's picture?

---

113. kickshawses] *F* (kicke-chawses); kicke-shawses *F3*; kick-shaws *F4.*

113. *kickshawses*] trifles: the plural
form of 'kickshaws' (*2H4*, v. i. 26:
= Fr. *quelque chose*).

114–15. *under . . . betters*] 'Betters'
may mean 'social superiors', but the
whole phrase is probably as absurd
as Verges' claim to be 'as honest as
any man living that is an old man and
no honester than I' (*Ado*, III. v. 13–15).

116. *an old man*] perhaps 'an old
hand' (Wilson, citing *OED*, old, *a.*,
5); or possibly a maladroit compli-
pliment to Sir Toby as his elder
(Furness). The former is the more
probable: cf. *Ado*, v. i. 118–19 (Don
Pedro speaking of his and Claudio's
quarrel with Leonato and Antonio),
'Had we fought, I doubt we should
have been too young for them',
where 'young' seems to play upon
the double meaning of 'old' (= (1)
aged, (2) experienced).

117. *galliard*] a lively dance in
triple time, consisting of five steps,
with a 'caper' before the fifth (Naylor,
p. 122, quoted by Furness).

119. *cut the mutton to't*] Sir Toby
quibbles on 'caper': (1) leap, (2) spice
berry used to make sauce for mutton.
No evident quibble on 'mutton'
(prostitute, cf. Onions, 2).

120. *back-trick*] not known as a
technical term. Presumably a backward step or series of steps. If it is

coined by Sir Andrew, there may be
unconscious indecency (Mahood),
especially in association with 'strong':
this would be comic after Maria's jest
about his 'dry' hand. Charney compares Sir Epicure Mammon's boast
'a back . . . as tough / As Hercules',
to encounter fiftie a night' (Jonson,
The Alchemist, II. ii. 37–9). Kittredge
compares *The Birth of Hercules*
(*MSR*, 1911, ll. 457 ff.): 'We had
dauncing I faith . . .; I never see
the lyke without minstreles in my lief.
They talke of the backe tricke; I
faith our Shipp fetcht the backe trick
backward and forward to[o].' The
date of the play is uncertain (Harbage,
Annals of English Drama, rev. Schoenbaum, 1964, dates it conjecturally
1604 and gives its limits as 1597–
*c.*1610), so the allusion may derive
from *Tw.N.* rather than from a
phrase in common use.

123. *curtain*] to protect a picture
from dust; cf. I. v. 236–7.

124. *Mistress Mall*] probably 'a
mere impersonation, like "my lady's
eldest son" [*Ado*, II. i. 9]' (Singer²).
'Undoubtedly a topical allusion'
(Wilson). Various Marys have been
put forward: Mary Frith *alias* Moll
Cutpurse (Steevens), Mary Ambree
(Barnett), Mary Carlton (Grey) (for
details see Furness), Moll Newberry

Why dost thou not go to church in a galliard, and   125
come home in a coranto? My very walk should
be a jig; I would not so much as make water but in
a sink-a-pace. What dost thou mean? Is it a world
to hide virtues in? I did think, by the excellent
constitution of thy leg, it was formed under the   130
star of a galliard.

Sir And. Ay, 'tis strong, and it does indifferent well in
a damned coloured stock. Shall we set about
some revels?

Sir To. What shall we do else? were we not born under   135
Taurus?

Sir And. Taurus? That's sides and heart.

Sir To. No, sir, it is legs and thighs. Let me see thee
caper. Ha, higher! Ha, ha, excellent!   *Exeunt.*

---

133. damned coloured] *F* (dam'd colour'd); flame-colour'd *Rowe*³; dun-coloured *Collier*²   set] *Rowe*³; sit *F*.   137. That's] *F3*; That *F*.

(Wilson), Mary Fitton (Hotson), Maria in this play (Luce).

126. *coranto*] a 'running' (Ital.), i.e., rapid, dance.

128. *sink-a-pace*] i.e., cinquepace, a five-step (*cinq pas*) dance like the galliard; perhaps quibbling on 'sink' =sewer, *OED*, *sb.*, 1.1.b (Mahood).

130–1. *formed . . . galliard*] destined for dancing; cf. Beatrice's astrological reason for her gaiety, *Ado*, II. i. 302.

132. *indifferent well*] well enough (said with complacency).

133. *damned coloured*] conceivably a gratuitous oath (cf. III. iv. 184, 'let me alone for swearing'); otherwise a reference to a colour. 'Flame-coloured' (Rowe³) occurs in *1H4*, I. ii. 11. Wilson rejects it on graphological grounds, and reads 'dun' [spelled perhaps 'dunne' or 'donne' in MS.] after Collier²; if this is right,

the humour comes from Sir Andrew's unadventurous taste in stockings.

136. *Taurus*] the Bull in the Zodiac, the twelve signs being supposed to govern various parts of the body. Whether Sir Toby corrects or misinforms Sir Andrew is debatable. Wilson follows E. B. Knobel (*Shakespeare's England*, 1916, I, 460) who quotes as 'authoritative' the *Liber Novem Iudicum*, 1509, where Leo is said to govern sides and heart, Taurus *crura et pedes* (this is shanks and feet, not legs and thighs). But in the normal astrological correspondence (beginning with Aries at the head and ending with Pisces at the feet) Taurus governs neck and throat. (Cf. Lyly, *Gallathea*, III. iii. 58, where the Astronomer says 'Then the Bull for the throte.') It is characteristic of Sir Andrew to err involuntarily and of Sir Toby to do so perversely.

SCENE IV

Enter VALENTINE, *and* VIOLA *in man's attire.*

Val. If the Duke continue these favours towards you,
Cesario, you are like to be much advanced: he hath
known you but three days, and already you are no
stranger.

Viola. You either fear his humour, or my negligence,   5
that you call in question the continuance of his love.
Is he inconstant, sir, in his favours?

Val. No, believe me.

Enter DUKE, CURIO, *and Attendants.*

Viola. I thank you. Here comes the Count.

Duke. Who saw Cesario, ho?   10

Viola. On your attendance, my lord, here.

Duke. [*To Curio and Attendants*] Stand you awhile aloof.
    [*To Viola*] Cesario,
Thou know'st no less but all: I have unclasp'd
To thee the book even of my secret soul.
Therefore, good youth, address thy gait unto her,   15
Be not denied access, stand at her doors,
And tell them, there thy fixed foot shall grow
Till thou have audience.

Viola.   Sure, my noble lord,
If she be so abandon'd to her sorrow
As it is spoke, she never will admit me.   20

Duke. Be clamorous, and leap all civil bounds,
Rather than make unprofited return.

Viola. Say I do speak with her, my lord, what then?

Scene IV

SCENE IV] F (*Scena Quarta.*).   [*Location.*] *The Palace. Rowe.*   12. [*To Curio
and Attendants*]] *Mahood; not in F.*   [*To Viola*]] *Mahood; not in F.*   15. gait]
F (gate), *Capell.*

3. *but three days*] For the passage of   16. *access*] accented on the second
time, see v. i. 92.   syllable.
    5. *humour*] capriciousness.   21. *civil bounds*] the limits of normal
    15. *address thy gait*] direct your steps.   courtesy.

Duke. O then unfold the passion of my love,
 Surprise her with discourse of my dear faith; 25
 It shall become thee well to act my woes:
 She will attend it better in thy youth,
 Than in a nuncio's of more grave aspect.
Viola. I think not so, my lord.
Duke.   Dear lad, believe it;
 For they shall yet belie thy happy years, 30
 That say thou art a man; Diana's lip
 Is not more smooth and rubious: thy small pipe
 Is as the maiden's organ, shrill and sound,
 And all is semblative a woman's part.
 I know thy constellation is right apt 35
 For this affair. Some four or five attend him;
 All, if you will: for I myself am best
 When least in company. Prosper well in this,
 . And thou shalt live as freely as thy lord,
 To call his fortunes thine.
Viola.   I'll do my best 40
 To woo your lady: [*Aside*] yet, a barful strife!
 Whoe'er I woo, myself would be his wife. *Exeunt.*

33. shrill and] *F* (shrill, and)*;* shrill in *White;* shrill of *conj. Hudson.*
41. [*Aside*]] *As Capell; not in F.*

25. *Surprise her*] take her [heart] by force (military image).

dear] used intensively (cf. 'dear love', I. ii. 39), and also reinforcing 'passion' and 'woes'.

28. *nuncio*] messenger.

aspect] accented on the second syllable.

30. *belie . . . years*] misrepresent your fortunate youthfulness.

32. *rubious*] ruby-red: a Shakespearean coinage (Onions).

pipe] voice, i.e., boyish treble; cf. *Cor.*, III. ii. 113–15, 'a pipe / Small as an eunuch or the virgin voice / That babies lulls asleep', and II. ii. 56 above ('eunuch').

33. *shrill and sound*] clear and unbroken (cf. *Ham.*, II. ii. 422, 'not cracked' [of the boy actor's voice], and *LLL.*, v. ii. 415, 'sound, sans crack or flaw'). See note on l. 34, *a*

woman's part. Sisson (I, 186) argues that 'and' is an erroneous expansion of 'a' (=of).

34. *semblative*] like: a Shakespearean coinage (Onions).

a woman's part] a woman's attributes; possibly with a quibble on a theatrical role: cf. *Gent.*, IV. iv. 156, where Julia (as Sebastian, a page) says that when 'Our youth got me to play the woman's part' she wore Julia's gown.

35. *constellation*] disposition and destiny (by astrological influence).

39–40. *live as freely as . . . thine*] either 'live in equal plenty with thy lord' or 'live to call thy lord's fortune thine as freely as he calls it his'.

41. *a barful strife*] a labour full of impediments.

SCENE V

Enter MARIA *and* CLOWN.

Maria. Nay, either tell me where thou hast been, or I
   will not open my lips so wide as a bristle may
   enter, in way of thy excuse: my lady will hang
   thee for thy absence.

Clown. Let her hang me: he that is well hanged in this   5
   world needs to fear no colours.

Maria. Make that good.

Clown. He shall see none to fear.

Maria. A good lenten answer. I can tell thee where that
   saying was born, of 'I fear no colours.'   10

Clown. Where, good Mistress Mary?

Maria. In the wars, and that may you be bold to say in
   your foolery.

Scene v

SCENE v] *F* (*Scena Quinta.*).   [*Location.*]   *Olivia's House. Rowe.*

1. *where thou hast been*] 'By thus
stressing Feste's truancy, Shakespeare prepares his audience for the
rather awkward presence of Olivia's
Fool at Orsino's palace' (Wilson).
But surely his visit there would not
be a hanging matter (though doubtless Maria exaggerates), nor could it
have been as long as Maria suggests,
l. 16.

6. *fear no colours*] fear no foe; proverbial (Tilley, C520), origin obscure,
probably military, as Maria explains
below, l. 12: colours=standards,
ensigns (*OED*, 7, first reference
given 1590, and, for the phrase, *OED*,
7.c). There is also, after 'hanged', a
pun on colours/collars (Wilson); cf.
1H4, II. iv. 315–16, where Prince Hal
puns on choler/collar, using 'halter'
as the latter's synonym.

7. *Make that good*] Justify that.

9. *lenten answer*] thin repartee
(Lent being a season of fasting).

Maria's comment suggests that
Wilson's ingenious explanation of it
(that drawing and quartering followed a brief hanging in the execution
of traitors) is wrong, and that the
Clown means no more than that a
man well hanged will see no colours
because he will be dead. There is no
reason to suppose with Hotson (p.
168) that the Clown meant 'well
hanged' indecently and that Maria
here reproves his answer.

12–13. *In the wars . . . foolery*] Wilson
interprets 'Say you have been in the
wars; that's an excuse your Foolship
may venture upon.' But if 'that' refers
not to 'in the wars' but to 'fear no
colours', Maria means that this would
be indeed a 'bold' reply to Olivia's
displeasure, since it needs courage to
say 'I fear no colours' when one really
is 'in the wars', which is precisely
where the Clown will be when he
confronts his Lady.

Clown. Well, God give them wisdom that have it; and
    those that are fools, let them use their talents.   15
Maria. Yet you will be hanged for being so long absent;
    or to be turned away—is not that as good as a
    hanging to you?
Clown. Many a good hanging prevents a bad marriage:
    and for turning away, let summer bear it out.   20
Maria. You are resolute then?
Clown. Not so, neither, but I am resolved on two points.
Maria. That if one break, the other will hold: or if both
    break, your gaskins fall.
Clown. Apt, in good faith, very apt. Well, go thy way: 25
    if Sir Toby would leave drinking, thou wert as
    witty a piece of Eve's flesh as any in Illyria.
Maria. Peace, you rogue, no more o' that. Here comes
    my lady: make your excuse wisely, you were best.

                                  [*Exit.*]

16–17. absent; . . . away—] *Malone (subst.)*; absent, . . . away: *F.*   29. [*Exit.*]]
Pope; *not in F.*   29 S.D. [*and Attendants*]] *Capell (subst.)*, *Staunton*; *not in F.*

14. *God . . . have it*] a nonsense-
ejaculation, since one would expect
'lack it'; perhaps based on 'To him
that hath shall be given' (Mahood, cf.
talents, l. 15).

15. *use their talents*] literally, use
their skills; but also alluding to the
parable of the talents, Matthew xxv
(Deighton, Mahood), again nonsensi-
cally: 'let the fools lay out their folly
profitably and increase it.' A talents/
talons pun, as in *LLL.*, IV. ii. 61–2
(Halliwell), does not seem intended.

16–17. *Yet . . . away*] To be 'turned
away' is to lose one's employment
and hence to face destitution, which
is why Maria regards it as tanta-
mount to being hanged. Furness
(enlarging on Wright) defends the F
punctuation by Shakespearean and
contemporary parallels in which 'to'
is inserted before the second infinitive,
but, in view of the speech's continua-
tion, Malone's punctuation is followed here.

19. *Many a . . . bad marriage*] The
antithesis of 'good hanging' and 'bad

marriage' takes up Maria's ll. 17–18,
and has proverbial force (Tilley,
H130 'Better be half hanged than ill
wed'; cf. W232, 'Wedding and hanging go by destiny'): both proverbs
represent marriage as a dangerous
undertaking. There is no likelihood
that the Clown here anticipates
Maria's marriage with Sir Toby, as
Bradley (looking ahead to ll. 26–7)
suggests.

20. *bear it out*] make it (i.e., destitution) endurable; or perhaps the
whole phrase 'let summer bear it out'
means 'may the fine weather hold'
(Mahood).

22. *points*] (1) matters, (2) tagged
laces attaching breeches to doublet.
Hence Maria's reply. For the pun,
cf. *1H4*, II. iv. 238–9, where the
'points' are those of swords.

24. *gaskins*] wide breeches.

26–7. *as witty . . . in Illyria*] Cf. *Ado*,
IV. ii. 79, where Dogberry calls himself 'as pretty a piece of flesh as any is
in Messina'.

29. S.D.] Bradley maintains that

Enter Lady OLIVIA, *with* MALVOLIO [*and Attendants*].

Clown. Wit, and't be thy will, put me into good fooling!   30
   Those wits that think they have thee, do very oft
   prove fools: and I that am sure I lack thee, may
   pass for a wise man. For what says Quinapalus?
   'Better a witty fool than a foolish wit.' God
   bless thee, lady!   35
Olivia. Take the fool away.
Clown. Do you not hear, fellows? Take away the lady.
Olivia. Go to, y'are a dry fool: I'll no more of you.
   Besides, you grow dishonest.
Clown. Two faults, madonna, that drink and good   40
   counsel will amend: for give the dry fool drink, then
   is the fool not dry: bid the dishonest man mend
   himself, if he mend, he is no longer dishonest;
   if he cannot, let the botcher mend him. Anything
   that's mended is but patched: virtue that trans-   45
   gresses is but patched with sin, and sin that amends
   is but patched with virtue. If that this simple
   syllogism will serve, so: if it will not, what remedy?
   As there is no true cuckold but calamity, so beauty's

the Clown's ensuing speech is for his own diversion, Wilson that it is meant to be heard by Olivia and that the Clown greets her with feigned surprise.

30. *Wit . . . will*] Wit (i.e., intelligence, wisdom) is often contrasted with will (=passion), hence the wit of the Clown's invocation.

33. *Quinapalus*] a philosopher invented by the Clown by Rabelaisian example (cf. Pigrogromitus, II. iii. 23), as a mock authority, perhaps by analogy with Quintilian (Charney). Hotson, p. 157 (interpreting *quinapalo* as mock-Italian for 'there on the stick'), suggests that the Clown pretends to interrogate the carved head on his bauble: this seems unnecessary.

38. *dry*] barren (of jests); cf. I. iii. 72–8, and l. 82 below. The Clown in his reply (like Maria in

I. iii) quibbles on the word's two meanings.

39. *dishonest*] undutiful (with reference to his truancy).

40. *madonna*] my lady (Ital.); used only by this speaker in Shakespeare, as Wilson notes.

42, 43, 44. *mend*] (1) amend, (2) repair (leading on to 'patched' l. 45).

44. *botcher*] one who professionally mends clothes.

45. *patched*] 'alluding to the patched or parti-coloured garment of the fool' (Malone, quoted Wilson).

48. *syllogism*] argument, to prove that 'no man is either absolutely good or bad, but of motley morality' (Wilson).

49–50. *As there is . . . a flower*] Rather than 'purposely rattling off bewildering nonsense' (Furness), the Clown insinuates that Olivia's sorrow will not last (cf. 'wedded to calamity',

a flower. The lady bade take away the fool, there-   50
fore I say again, take her away.

Olivia. Sir, I bade them take away you.

Clown. Misprision in the highest degree! Lady, *cucullus
non facit monachum*: that's as much to say, as I wear
not motley in my brain. Good madonna, give me   55
leave to prove you a fool.

Olivia. Can you do it?

Clown. Dexteriously, good madonna.

Olivia. Make your proof.

Clown. I must catechise you for it, madonna. Good my   60
mouse of virtue, answer me.

Olivia. Well sir, for want of other idleness, I'll bide
your proof.

Clown. Good madonna, why mourn'st thou?

Olivia. Good fool, for my brother's death.   65

Clown. I think his soul is in hell, madonna.

Olivia. I know his soul is in heaven, fool.

Clown. The more fool, madonna, to mourn for your
brother's soul, being in heaven. Take away the

69. soul, being] *F;* soul being *Rowe.*

Rom., III. iii. 3) and advises her to
enjoy the flower of her beauty, before
it fades, by marrying (Luce compares
Nashe, *Summer's Last Will and Testament,* 'Beauty is but a flower / Which
wrinkles will devour'); cf. II. iv. 38–
39. 'Calamity is a cuckold because
those who are "wedded" to it are always faithless, just as beauty (equally
inconstant) always fades' (H. Jenkins, privately).

53. *Misprision*] (1) misunderstanding (the usual Shakespearean
sense, Onions 1), (2) misdemeanour,
wrongful action (the original legal
sense, *OED,* 1). The phrase 'in the
highest degree' adds to the first
meaning the judicial weight of the
second.

53–4. cucullus ... monachum] 'The
hood makes not the monk': proverbial
(Tilley, H586). The Clown probably
points to his fool's cap as he proceeds.

54. *as much to say, as*] Shakespeare

has both this form (*2H6,* IV. ii. 16)
and the more usual 'as much as to
say' (*Gent.,* III. ii. 299, *Ado,* II. iii. 239,
III. ii. 47, *2H4,* II. ii. 125). Furness
gives examples from other writers.

58. *Dexteriously*] an Elizabethan
variant of 'dexterously'. J. O. Wood,
N. & Q., July 1966, cites 'dexterious'
from a pamphlet of 1597: *OED*'s first
example is dated 1629.

60–1. *Good my mouse of virtue*] my
good little dear (Wilson); 'mouse'
is a frequent Elizabethan term of
endearment (*OED,* 1.3a; so in *LLL.,*
v. ii. 19; *Ham.,* III. iv. 183); the
tautology of 'good' and 'of virtue' is
allowable because of the idiomatic
style, and Furness's conjectural
punctuation 'Good,' (cf. 'Good now',
Ham., I. i. 170) seems unnecessary.

62. *idleness*] pastime; not used
pejoratively.

69. *soul, being*] F's punctuation
makes Olivia mourn for her brother's

fool, gentlemen. 70

Olivia. What think you of this fool, Malvolio, doth he
not mend?

Mal. Yes, and shall do, till the pangs of death shake
him. Infirmity, that decays the wise, doth ever
make the better fool. 75

Clown. God send you, sir, a speedy infirmity, for the
better increasing your folly! Sir Toby will be sworn
that I am no fox, but he will not pass his word for
twopence that you are no fool.

Olivia. How say you to that, Malvolio? 80

Mal. I marvel your ladyship takes delight in such a
barren rascal: I saw him put down the other day
with an ordinary fool, that has no more brain than a
stone. Look you now, he's out of his guard already:
unless you laugh and minister occasion to him, he 85
is gagged. I protest I take these wise men, that crow

soul, which is, however, in heaven;
Rowe's makes her mourn for the
fact that it is in heaven.

72. *mend*] improve, i.e., grow more
amusing, less 'dry' (l. 38 above).
Wilson interprets 'make amends'
(cf. ll. 42, 43). Malvolio uncharitably
replies as though she meant 'grow
more foolish'.

78. *fox*] here used as the type of
cleverness, and in antithesis with the
alliterating 'fool'. Wilson suggests
that the Clown refers to Sir Toby's
view of Malvolio as a sly, ingratiating
knave, and mentions him 'because
he knows that Malvolio hates him'.
But this is more than the audience
yet knows. The allusion to Sir Toby
seems rather to prepare for his entrance and ultimately for the quarrel
in II. iii.

83–4. *ordinary fool . . . stone*]
'ordinary' here (contrast I. iii. 83)
means 'performing in a tavern'.
Mahood points out that Stone, a well-
known Elizabethan jester, is called 'a
tauerne-foole' in Jonson's *Volpone*,

II. i. 53–4, and that the reference here
may be to him. This is very probable:
a stone in Shakespeare usually typi-
fies lack of feeling, not lack of intellect;
Stone's name seems deliberately
brought in. Perhaps Jonson, in the
passage cited, was recalling *Tw.N.*,
because the speaker immediately
goes on to say of Sir Politic Would-be,
his hearer, that if he were brought
on stage, the author of the comedy
would be 'thought to faine / Extremely, if not maliciously'. This recalls Fabian's remark, III. iv. 128–9.
Yet 'He has no more wit than a stone'
was proverbial (Tilley, W550).

84. *he's out of his guard*] literally, 'he
has used up all his tricks of fence'
(Wilson); thus 'he is at a loss for a
repartee.' Wilson suggests that the
Clown has shrugged his shoulders or
turned away.

86. *wise men*] men who have their
wits (as opposed to fools), not men
conspicuous for wisdom.

crow] laugh stridently (as Jaques
at Touchstone, *AYL.*, II. vii. 30).

so at these set kind of fools, no better than the
fools' zanies.

Olivia. O, you are sick of self-love, Malvolio, and taste
with a distempered appetite. To be generous, 90
guiltless, and of free disposition, is to take those
things for bird-bolts that you deem cannon-
bullets. There is no slander in an allowed fool,
though he do nothing but rail; nor no railing
in a known discreet man, though he do nothing 95
but reprove.

Clown. Now Mercury endue thee with leasing, for thou
speak'st well of fools!

Enter MARIA.

Maria. Madam, there is at the gate a young gentleman
much desires to speak with you. 100

Olivia. From the Count Orsino, is it?

Maria. I know not, madam: 'tis a fair young man, and
well attended.

Olivia. Who of my people hold him in delay?

Maria. Sir Toby, madam, your kinsman. 105

Olivia. Fetch him off, I pray you: he speaks nothing
but madman. Fie on him! [*Exit Maria.*] Go you,

107. [*Exit Maria.*]] Capell; not in F.

87. *set*] lacking spontaneous wit;
uttering memorized jests.

88. *zanies*] assistants, imitators.

91. *free*] As adjective qualifying 'disposition', this means 'magnanimous'
(Onions, 1: cf. l. 264 below), or
'innocent' (Onions, 2, citing this passage); yet by following 'guiltless' it
partakes of this latter sense as well as
the former (cf. *Ham.*, II. ii. 557, 'Make
mad the guilty and appal the free').

92. *bird-bolts*] flat-headed arrows
for shooting birds.

93. *allowed*] licensed, having the
right to jest without restraint.

94–6. *nor no railing . . . reprove*] Is
this spoken to Malvolio by way of
appeasement (or, as Furness suggests,
of irony), or to the Clown by way of
showing her impartiality?

97–8. *Now Mercury . . . fools!*] May
Mercury (the god of cheating) teach
you to lie, since you speak well of
fools (and in order to do that, one
must needs lie).

106–8. *Fetch him off . . . Malvolio*]
Since Maria's exit is not marked in
F, it is possible (cf. Mahood, here
and at l. 130) to interpret Olivia's
speech as a change of plan, sending
Malvolio instead of Maria. But it is
unlikely that Sir Toby would obey
Malvolio, and very likely that he
could be humoured by Maria; I
therefore assume that Malvolio is
sent off, after Maria's exit, to interview Orsino's messenger. 'Go you' is
certainly emphatic, but may equally
well mean 'too' as 'instead'.

107. *madman*] madman's talk; cf.

Malvolio. If it be a suit from the Count, I am
　　sick, or not at home. What you will, to dismiss
　　it.　　　　　　　　　　　　　*Exit Malvolio.*　110
　　Now you see, sir, how your fooling grows old, and
　　people dislike it.
Clown. Thou hast spoke for us, madonna, as if thy eldest
　　son should be a fool: whose skull Jove cram with
　　brains, for here he comes, one of thy kin has a　115
　　most weak *pia mater.*

Enter SIR TOBY.

Olivia. By mine honour, half drunk. What is he at the
　　gate, cousin?
Sir To. A gentleman.
Olivia. A gentleman? What gentleman?　　　　　　120
Sir To. 'Tis a gentleman here—[*Belches.*] A plague o'
　　these pickle-herring! How now, sot?
Clown. Good Sir Toby!

115. for here he comes, one] *Malone;* for heere he comes. *Enter Sir Toby.* | One
F; for here comes one *Rowe*[3]; for—here he comes—one *Camb.*　　116. S.D.
Enter Sir Toby.] *As Rowe*[3]; *after* comes. *F.*　　121. gentleman here—] *Rann;*
Gentleman heere. *F;* gentleman. Here,—*Theobald;* gentleman:—(hiccups) |
Capell. [Belches.]] *Theobald; not in F.*

Oth., II. iii. 271, 'Drunk? and speak
parrot?'
　　111. *old*] stale.
　　115. *for . . . one*] The sense given by
Malone's reading is 'for here he
comes, one of thy kin [who] has a
most weak *pia mater*'; cf. Abbott
§244, and *Meas.,* II. ii. 34, 'I have a
brother is condemn'd to die.' F's
punctuation is clearly wrong; it was
used possibly because Sir Toby's
entrance-direction had to be fitted
in, but more probably because the
scribe, observing this direction, added
his own punctuation in the belief
that 'for here he comes' was the end
of a sentence. There seems no reason
to suppose that he also added the 'he',
for if his copy had not had it he would
not have introduced the full stop,
but would have been likely to interpret as Malone does. The parenthetic

punctuation of the Cambridge edd.,
though retaining all the words, is
rather harder to speak: Dyce[2] commented that it 'would have surprised
Shakespeare'.
　　116. *pia mater*] brain: literally
'meeke mother', 'milde mother' (the
Elizabethan translation is quoted
from *Batman vppon Bartholome De
Proprietaribus Rerum,* 1582, by Furness),
the softer of two membranes enclosing
the brain.
　　121. *here*] The word possibly
stands for a belch (cf. Capell's
reading), but more probably means
'at the gate'. The reference to pickle
herring makes the unwritten direction supplied by Theobald clear
enough.
　　122. *sot*] (1) fool (French origin),
(2) drunkard: therefore appropriate
both to speaker and hearer.

Olivia. Cousin, cousin, how have you come so early by
     this lethargy?   125
Sir To. Lechery? I defy lechery. There's one at the
     gate.
Olivia. Ay, marry, what is he?
Sir To. Let him be the devil and he will, I care not:
     give me faith, say I. Well, it's all one.   *Exit.*
Olivia. What's a drunken man like, fool?   131
Clown. Like a drowned man, a fool, and a madman:
     one draught above heat makes him a fool, the
     second mads him, and a third drowns him.
Olivia. Go thou and seek the crowner, and let him sit o' 135
     my coz: for he's in the third degree of drink;
     he's drowned. Go look after him.
Clown. He is but mad yet, madonna, and the fool
     shall look to the madman.   [*Exit.*]

Enter MALVOLIO.

Mal. Madam, yond young fellow swears he will speak   140
     with you. I told him you were sick; he takes on
     him to understand so much, and therefore comes
     to speak with you. I told him you were asleep;
     he seems to have a foreknowledge of that too,
     and therefore comes to speak with you. What is   145

130. *Exit.*] F; *Exit Sir Toby, followed by Maria. Mahood.*   139. [*Exit.*]] *Rowe;
not in* F.

126-7. *There's one at the gate*]
Rossiter, *English Drama from Early
Times to the Elizabethans* (1950), p. 10,
suggests that Sir Toby means an
incarnation of lechery, a 'smart
young gallant' and morality-play
character; but more probably—and
more humorously—he is merely
making an announcement, having
already forgotten Olivia's question
and his attempt to answer it. His
next remark, which Rossiter connects
with this one, is just Sir Toby's
drunken mind swaggering off at a
tangent: Wilson's comment that he
relies on faith rather than on works

is also over-subtle. Furness aptly
remarks: 'Toby's drunkenness is
here a dramatic necessity. Maria has
been sent to "fetch him off", and
Malvolio to dismiss the Duke's messenger. Some time must be given to
Malvolio's altercation with Viola at
the gate; Sir Toby must obey the
summons, but must not anticipate
any portion of Malvolio's report.
This is attained by representing him as
so intoxicated that he can tell nothing.'

133. *above heat*] above the normal
body warmth; cf. *Tim.*, I. i. 263, 'to
see . . . wine heat fools'.

135. *crowner*] coroner.

to be said to him, lady? He's fortified against any
denial.

Olivia. Tell him, he shall not speak with me.

Mal. 'Has been told so: and he says he'll stand at
    your door like a sheriff's post, and be the sup-   150
    porter to a bench, but he'll speak with you.

Olivia. What kind o' man is he?

Mal. Why, of mankind.

Olivia. What manner of man?

Mal. Of very ill manner: he'll speak with you, will   155
    you or no.

Olivia. Of what personage and years is he?

Mal. Not yet old enough for a man, nor young enough
    for a boy: as a squash is before 'tis a peascod, or a
    codling when 'tis almost an apple. 'Tis with him   160
    in standing water, between boy and man. He is
    very well-favoured, and he speaks very shrewishly.
    One would think his mother's milk were scarce
    out of him.

Olivia. Let him approach. Call in my gentlewoman.   165

Mal. Gentlewoman, my lady calls.   *Exit.*

---

149. 'Has] *Dyce*[2]; H'as *F*; He has *Pope*; Has *Dyce*.

150. *sheriff's post*] Large decorated posts were erected at the doors of mayors and sheriffs to mark the residence of authority.

153. *of mankind*] Furness considers this (and 'ill manner', l. 155) as 'quibbling' which is out of keeping with Malvolio's sedate character. Mahood interprets as 'fierce', comparing *Wint.*, II. iii. 67, 'A mankind witch!', but this seems strained, as Viola has been merely persistent. Malvolio probably means no more than 'ordinary' (i.e., a man like any other man—which we, however, know that Viola is not), and in 'ill manner' supposes himself to be answering Olivia's question, his mind still being full of Viola's refusal to do his bidding.

159. *squash*] unripe pea-pod (*peascod*).

160. *codling*] unripe apple (originally, a hard kind of apple).

161. *in standing water, between boy and man*] at the turn of the tide, midway between two ages. H. F. Brooks (privately) compares Golding's description of sixteen-year-old Narcissus (tr. Ovid, *Metamorphoses*, III. 438). 'For when yeares three times fiue and one he fully lyued had, / So that he seemde to stande betweene the state of man and Lad, / The hearts of diuers trim yong men his beautie gan to moue, / And many a Ladie fresh and faire was taken in his loue.'

162. *shrewishly*] sharply, and perhaps also shrilly (cf. I. iv. 33).

163–4. *his mother's milk . . . him*] proverbial (Tilley, M1204).

Enter MARIA.

Olivia. Give me my veil: come, throw it o'er my face.
　　We'll once more hear Orsino's embassy.

Enter VIOLA.

Viola. The honourable lady of the house, which is she?
Olivia. Speak to me, I shall answer for her. Your will?　170
Viola. Most　radiant,　exquisite,　and　unmatchable
　　beauty—I pray you tell me if this be the lady of the
　　house, for I never saw her. I would be loath to cast
　　away my speech: for besides that it is excellently
　　well penned, I have taken great pains to con it.　175
　　Good beauties, let me sustain no scorn; I am very
　　comptible, even to the least sinister usage.
Olivia. Whence came you, sir?
Viola. I can say little more than I have studied, and
　　that question's out of my part. Good gentle one,　180
　　give me modest assurance if you be the lady of the
　　house, that I may proceed in my speech.
Olivia. Are you a comedian?
Viola. No, my profound heart: and yet, by the very

---

168. S.D. *Viola*] *F2; Violenta F.*　　172. beauty—] *Rowe;* beautie. *F.*

167. *Give . . . veil*] Since it is Olivia's
custom to wear a mourning veil
(I. i. 28), this will be attached to her
tire (headdress); Maria is not to
bring it in as though she had a fore-
knowledge of Olivia's wish.
　168. S.D. Enter Viola.] On F's
reading see Introduction, p. xviii.
　170. *answer for her*] deliberately
ambiguous: (1) reply for myself, (2)
substitute myself for her.
　175. *con*] learn.
　177. *comptible . . . usage*] sensitive
to the slightest incivility; *comptible*
(*OED* countable, 1.c, this example
only) is glossed 'Liable to answer to,
sensitive to'.
　181. *modest*] moderate, reasonable.
　183. *comedian*] actor. 'Olivia is

insulting, but the word follows
naturally upon Viola's talk of con-
ning her speech and studying her
part' (Wilson)—so naturally that
probably no insult is intended; it is a
direct question, which incidentally
allows the irony of Viola's reply.
　184. *my profound heart*] always taken
by editors as addressed to Olivia and
meaning 'my most wise lady', either
banteringly or in the high complimentary style of Viola's 'speech'
(l. 174); but surely too familiar a
form of address to be used in either
way? It seems rather to be an excla-
matory asseveration ('No, in all
sincerity'). For 'my profound heart',
cf. *Ham.*, III. ii. 78, 'In my heart's
core, yea, in my heart of heart'.

fangs of malice I swear, I am not that I play. Are   185
you the lady of the house?

Olivia. If I do not usurp myself, I am.

Viola. Most certain, if you are she, you do usurp yourself: for what is yours to bestow is not yours to
reserve. But this is from my commission. I will   190
on with my speech in your praise, and then show
you the heart of my message.

Olivia. Come to what is important in't: I forgive you
the praise.

Viola. Alas, I took great pains to study it, and 'tis   195
poetical.

Olivia. It is the more like to be feigned; I pray you
keep it in. I heard you were saucy at my gates,
and allowed your approach rather to wonder at
you than to hear you. If you be mad, be gone: 200
if you have reason, be brief: 'tis not that time of

---

185. fangs] *F* (phangs), *Rowe*³; pangs *Rowe.*   200. mad] *Rann, conj. Mason;*
not mad *F;* but mad *Collier*³, *conj. Staunton.*

185. *fangs*] Shakespeare associates
malice with poisonous serpents, e.g.
Tit., v. iii. 13, 'venomous malice'.
Some (Wilson, Mahood) interpret
the oath as taxing Olivia with malice;
others (Wright, Furness) as asserting
that even malice could charge Viola
with nothing worse than playing a
part. I suppose that 'Fortune's
malice' (cf. *3H6,* IV. iii. 46, IV. vi. 28),
which compels Viola to engage in 'a
barful strife' (I. iv. 41), is meant;
cf. Hilda M. Hulme, '"Malice"
and "Malicious" in Shakespearean
usage', *English Studies,* 47 (1966), pp.
190–9.

187. *usurp myself*] impersonate myself (a paradoxical joke).

188–9. *usurp yourself*] misappropriate
yourself (by withholding yourself
from marriage); cf. Sonnets 1–17.

190. *from my commission*] not part
of my message.

197. *feigned*] Renaissance critical
theory habitually distinguished the
factual nature of history from the
fictitious nature of poetry. Shakespeare refers to this distinction in
AYL., III. iii. 16–17.

200. *be mad*] F's 'be not mad' has
been debated since 1785, when
Mason argued that it was wrong
because synonymous with, not antithetical to, 'have reason': the antithesis is continued in 'be gone' and
'be brief'. His emendation is accepted
here on the supposition that the eye
of scribe or compositor caught 'not'
from l. 201 and he introduced it here
in error. The alternative emendation, 'be but mad', postulates a misreading of 'not' for 'but', which is
graphically doubtful; 'but mad' also
weakens the antithesis. To explain
F's 'not mad' as 'not quite mad'
wrests the phrase from its evident
sense of 'sane'.

201–2. *'tis not . . . me*] I am not
myself lunatic enough. 'The emphatic
word is "me"' (Wilson). The allusion

moon with me to make one in so skipping a
dialogue.

Maria. Will you hoist sail, sir? Here lies your way.

Viola. No, good swabber, I am to hull here a little   205
longer. Some mollification for your giant, sweet
lady! Tell me your mind, I am a messenger.

Olivia. Sure you have some hideous matter to deliver,
when the courtesy of it is so fearful. Speak your
office.   210

Viola. It alone concerns your ear. I bring no overture
of war, no taxation of homage; I hold the olive
in my hand: my words are as full of peace, as
matter.

Olivia. Yet you began rudely. What are you? What   215
would you?

Viola. The rudeness that hath appeared in me have I
learned from my entertainment. What I am, and
what I would, are as secret as maidenhead: to
your ears, divinity; to any other's, profanation.   220

207. lady! Tell ... mind, I] *As* F (Ladie, tell ... minde, I); lady. | *Oli.*
Tell ... mind. | *Vio.* I *Warburton.*   220. other's] F (others), *Pope.*

is to the theory that madness (lunacy)
was associated with the changes of
the moon.

202. *skipping*] 'wild, frolic, mad'
(Johnson); cf. *Ham.*, III. iv. 143–4,
'which madness / Would gambol
from'.

205. *swabber*] one who 'swabs'
(cleans) the decks. Derogatory.

hull] lie with sails furled (replying
to 'hoist sail', l. 204).

206. *Some mollification for your giant*]
Pray pacify your aggressive protector.
Johnson pointed out the allusion to
giants in romances who prevented
access to ladies, Steevens the allusion
to Maria's small size (cf. II. v. 13,
III. ii. 64).

207. *tell me your mind . . . messenger*]
i.e., Are you willing to hear my message? (alluding generally to Olivia's
and Maria's dismissive remarks, and
with direct reference to her own

request that Olivia pacify Maria).
'Tell me your mind' is not synonymous with 'Speak your office' (ll.
209–10), i.e., 'Deliver your message'.
Editors who emend (with Warburton)
suppose that Viola corrects Olivia,
who then ('Speak your office')
corrects herself.

209. *fearful*] terrible. Olivia ironically refers to Viola's complimentary
'poetical' preface.

211. *overture*] declaration (literally,
opening).

212. *taxation*] claim.

olive] olive-branch (figuratively),
as emblem of 'peace' (l. 213).

215. *Yet you began rudely*] alluding
to Viola's being 'saucy' at the gates
(l. 198), not to her reply to Maria
or to any 'scuffle' with her (as
Wilson most implausibly conjectures).

218. *entertainment*] reception (by Sir
Toby and Malvolio).

220. *divinity*] religious discourse.

Olivia. Give us the place alone: we will hear this
 divinity.   [*Exeunt Maria and Attendants.*]
 Now, sir, what is your text?

Viola. Most sweet lady—

Olivia. A comfortable doctrine, and much may be said   225
 of it. Where lies your text?

Viola. In Orsino's bosom.

Olivia. In his bosom? In what chapter of his bosom?

Viola. To answer by the method, in the first of his
 heart.   230

Olivia. O, I have read it: it is heresy. Have you no more
 to say?

Viola. Good madam, let me see your face.

Olivia. Have you any commission from your lord to
 negotiate with my face? You are now out of   235
 your text: but we will draw the curtain and show
 you the picture. [*Unveiling*] Look you, sir, such
 a one I was this present. Is't not well done?

Viola. Excellently done, if God did all.

Olivia. 'Tis in grain, sir, 'twill endure wind and   240
 weather.

Viola. 'Tis beauty truly blent, whose red and white
 Nature's own sweet and cunning hand laid on.
 Lady, you are the cruell'st she alive

221–3. Give . . . text?] *As Rowe; two lines* (Giue . . . alone, / We . . . text?), *F.*
222. [*Exeunt Maria and Attendants.*]] *Capell; Exit Maria. Rowe; not in F; after l.
221 alone. Mahood (subst.).*   224. lady—] *F* (Lady.), *Theobald.*   237. [*Unveiling*]] *Rowe; not in F.*   238. was this present] *F; wear this present Theobald,
conj. Warburton; was, this presents conj. Becket.*

---

225. *comfortable*] bringing (religious)
comfort; cf. *Meas.*, IV. ii. 65, 'Heaven
give your spirits comfort!'

229. *by the method*] in the same
style.

235–6. *out of your text*] straying
from your theme.

237–8. *such a one I was this present*]
'Olivia is pretending to unveil a
portrait, and portraits at this period
were usually inscribed with the age of
the sitter and the date of the painting'
(Wilson). Olivia's inconsistent juxta-

posing of 'was' and 'this present' (the
'common form in dating letters',
Wilson) is humorously intended.

239. *if God did all*] if it is unaided
by cosmetics.

240. *in grain*] indelible, in fast
colours.

242–3. *'Tis beauty . . . hand laid on*]
For the metaphor, cf. Sonnet 20,
ll. 1–2 (addressed to a young man),
'A woman's face, with Nature's own
hand painted, / Hast thou, the Master
Mistress of my passion.'

If you will lead these graces to the grave   245
And leave the world no copy.

Olivia. O sir, I will not be so hard-hearted: I will give
out divers schedules of my beauty. It shall be
inventoried, and every particle and utensil
labelled to my will. As, item, two lips indifferent   250
red; item, two grey eyes, with lids to them;
item, one neck, one chin, and so forth. Were you
sent hither to praise me?

Viola. I see you what you are, you are too proud:
But if you were the devil, you are fair.   255
My lord and master loves you: O, such love
Could be but recompens'd, though you were crown'd
The nonpareil of beauty!

Olivia.   How does he love me?

Viola. With adorations, fertile tears,
With groans that thunder love, with sighs of fire.   260

Olivia. Your lord does know my mind, I cannot love him.
Yet I suppose him virtuous, know him noble,
Of great estate, of fresh and stainless youth;
In voices well divulg'd, free, learn'd, and valiant,
And in dimension, and the shape of nature,   265

---

259. adorations] *F;* [   ] adorations *conj. Walker;* earthward [*or* earthly]
adorations *conj. Camb.*   fertile] *F* (fertill); with fertile *Pope.*

246. *copy*] i.e., a child; cf. Sonnet
11, ll. 13–14.

248. *schedules*] lists; cf. 'inventoried',
l. 249.

249–50. *particle . . . will*] every
single item written on a slip of paper
and pasted (as a codicil) to my will
(continuing the idea of 'leave', l.
246).

251. *lids*] literally, eye-lids, but in
the context playing on 'lids' of pans,
etc.

253. *praise*] appraise, value (following on her list of 'items').

255. *devil*] alluding to Lucifer's
beauty in heaven, and his fall through
pride.

257. *Could be but recompens'd*] would
receive no more than its due reward
(if you accepted it).

258. *nonpareil*] unequalled.

259. *With . . . tears*] F's metrically
defective line is retained, not because it is satisfactory (though
Furness argued for a pause after
'adorations', the line should surely
be as fluent as its fellow, l. 260), but
because it is impossible to recover
Shakespeare's text except by conjecture: the alternatives are two
epithets (making 'adorations' four
syllables) or four 'with's (making
'adorations' five syllables).

fertile] copious: Walker compares
Ham., I. ii. 80, 'the fruitful river in the
eye'.

264. *In voices well divulg'd, free*] well
spoken of [as] magnanimous, etc.;
but 'well divulg'd' may stand alone.

265. *in dimension, and the shape of*

A gracious person. But yet I cannot love him:
He might have took his answer long ago.
Viola. If I did love you in my master's flame,
With such a suff'ring, such a deadly life,
In your denial I would find no sense, 270
I would not understand it.
Olivia. Why, what would you?
Viola. Make me a willow cabin at your gate,
And call upon my soul within the house;
Write loyal cantons of contemned love,
And sing them loud even in the dead of night; 275
Halloo your name to the reverberate hills,
And make the babbling gossip of the air
Cry out 'Olivia!' O, you should not rest
Between the elements of air and earth,
But you should pity me.
Olivia. You might do much. 280
What is your parentage?
Viola. Above my fortunes, yet my state is well:
I am a gentleman.
Olivia. Get you to your lord:
I cannot love him: let him send no more,
Unless, perchance, you come to me again, 285
To tell me how he takes it. Fare you well:
I thank you for your pains: spend this for me.
Viola. I am no fee'd post, lady; keep your purse;
My master, not myself, lacks recompense.

---

276. Halloo] *F* (Hallow), *Collier;* Holla *Malone.* 280–1. You ... parentage?]
As F; one line Capell. 288. fee'd] *Rowe* (fee'd-)*;* feede *F.*

nature] in his physical form (cf. v. i.
235): the terms are used synonymously.

266. *gracious*] graceful.

269. *deadly*] dying (intensifying 'suf-
f'ring'; and, with 'flame', suggesting
that Orsino is love's martyr).

272. *a willow cabin*] a dwelling of
willow-branches (the emblem of sor-
rowful love; cf. *Ado,* II. i. 166, 194).

273. *my soul*] i.e., Olivia.

274. *cantons*] songs (see *OED,* can-
ton, *sb.*², 1).

276. *Halloo*] F's spelling 'conveys
also the idea of "bless"' (Mahood):
used in that sense, as verb and participle, eight times by Shakespeare.

reverberate] reverberating, resound-
ing: cf. Jonson, *The Masque of
Blackness,* l. 237.

277. *babbling gossip of the air*] Echo,
the nymph.

282. *state*] present social rank.

288. *fee'd post*] messenger who takes
rewards.

Love make his heart of flint that you shall love,   290
And let your fervour like my master's be,
Plac'd in contempt. Farewell, fair cruelty.   *Exit.*
Olivia. 'What is your parentage?'
          'Above my fortunes, yet my state is well;
I am a gentleman.' I'll be sworn thou art: 295
Thy tongue, thy face, thy limbs, actions, and spirit
Do give thee five-fold blazon. Not too fast: soft! soft!
Unless the master were the man. How now?
Even so quickly may one catch the plague?
Methinks I feel this youth's perfections   300
With an invisible and subtle stealth
To creep in at mine eyes. Well, let it be.
What ho, Malvolio!

Enter MALVOLIO.

Mal.   Here, madam, at your service.
Olivia. Run after that same peevish messenger
          The County's man: he left this ring behind him,   305
Would I or not; tell him, I'll none of it.
Desire him not to flatter with his lord,
Nor hold him up with hopes: I am not for him.
If that the youth will come this way to-morrow,
I'll give him reasons for't. Hie thee, Malvolio.   310
Mal. Madam, I will.   *Exit.*
Olivia. I do I know not what, and fear to find

291. master's be,] *As F;* master's, be *Theobald.*   305. County's] *Capell;*
Countes *F;* Counts *F2.*

290. *Love make*] may Cupid make
(with his leaden arrow; cf. I. i. 35
note).
291. *master's be,*] I follow Turner in
keeping F's punctuation, which rightly
stresses the rhyme-word; he paraphrases 'let your fervour be like my
master's, that is, held in contempt.'
295. *thou*] 'Note the dawning of love
in this change from *you* to *thou*'
(Furness).
297. *blazon*] literally, armorial
bearings; hence, marks of gentility.
298. *Unless . . . man*] a half-

uttered wish that Cesario were in
Orsino's place, as her lover.
300. *perfections*] (four syllables)
beauties, graces.
305. *County's*] Count's. Capell's
emendation restores the metre.
Shakespeare frequently uses the word,
especially of Paris in *Rom.*
307. *flatter with*] encourage: synonymous with the next phrase.
308. *I . . . him*] 'Him' is to be
stressed, not 'for'; cf. the stress on
'you' in l. 285, which is recalled by
ll. 309–10.

Mine eye too great a flatterer for my mind.
Fate, show thy force; ourselves we do not owe.
What is decreed, must be: and be this so.   [*Exit.*]   315

315. [*Exit.*]] *Rowe; Finis, Actus primus. F.*

313. *Mine eye . . . mind*] that my
eye (cf. l. 302) has misled my mind
(into love).

314–15. *Fate . . . and be this so*] The
couplet amplifies 'Well, let it be' (l.

302) into a maxim (see Tilley,
M1331, 'What must [shall, will] be
must [shall, will] be').

314. *owe*] own.

ACT II

SCENE I

Enter ANTONIO *and* SEBASTIAN.

Ant. Will you stay no longer? nor will you not that I go
with you?

Seb. By your patience, no: my stars shine darkly over
me; the malignancy of my fate might perhaps
distemper yours; therefore I shall crave of you   5
your leave that I may bear my evils alone. It
were a bad recompense for your love, to lay any
of them on you.

Ant. Let me yet know of you whither you are bound.

Seb. No, sooth, sir: my determinate voyage is mere   10
extravagancy. But I perceive in you so excellent a
touch of modesty, that you will not extort from me
what I am willing to keep in: therefore it charges
me in manners the rather to express myself. You
must know of me then, Antonio, my name is   15
Sebastian, which I called Roderigo; my father was

ACT II

Scene 1

ACT II SCENE 1] F (*Actus Secundus, Scæna prima.*).   [*Location.*]   *The Street.*
Rowe; The Sea-coast. Capell; At the door of Antonio's house. N.C.S.   16. Roderigo]
F (*Rodorigo*).

4. *malignancy*] evil influence (astrological, cf. preceding phrase): referring to his shipwreck and the loss of
his sister.

5. *distemper*] infect.

10–11. *my determinate . . . extravagancy*] i.e., my only plan of travel is to
have no plan.

11. *extravagancy*] wandering.

11–14. *But I perceive . . . myself*] But
I see you are so polite that you will

not burden me with questions that I
would rather not answer: therefore
good manners oblige me the more to
tell you who I am.

15–16. *my name . . . called Roderigo*]
Shakespeare requires to impress on
the audience who this new person is,
so, although he has been staying with
Antonio, Sebastian must now for
the first time disclose his identity and
his relationship to Viola.

38

that Sebastian of Messaline whom I know you have
heard of. He left behind him myself and a sister,
both born in an hour: if the heavens had been
pleased, would we had so ended! But you, sir,   20
altered that, for some hour before you took me
from the breach of the sea was my sister drowned.

Ant. Alas the day!

Seb. A lady, sir, though it was said she much resembled
me, was yet of many accounted beautiful: but   25
though I could not with such estimable wonder
overfar believe that, yet thus far I will boldly
publish her, she bore a mind that envy could not
but call fair. She is drowned already, sir, with
salt water, though I seem to drown her remem-   30
brance again with more.

Ant. Pardon me, sir, your bad entertainment.

Seb. O good Antonio, forgive me your trouble.

Ant. If you will not murder me for my love, let me be
your servant.   35

Seb. If you will not undo what you have done, that is,
kill him whom you have recovered, desire it not.
Fare ye well at once; my bosom is full of kindness,
and I am yet so near the manners of my mother,

---

17. *Messaline*] probably derived
from the Latin for Marseilles, but
essentially a Shakespearean invention. 'The inhabitants of Marseilles
and of Illyria are mentioned together ("Massilienses, Hilurios") in
a speech about one twin looking for
another twin in Plautus's *Menaechmi*,
l. 235' (Mahood: see L. G. Salingar,
'Messaline in *Tw.N.*', *TLS*, 3 June
1955).

19. *in an hour*] at the same time, i.e.,
as twins.

21. *some hour*] an hour or so.

22. *breach*] surf, breakers.

26. *estimable wonder*] wonder and
esteem. Sebastian modestly disclaims
his own handsomeness, having just
said his twin sister was considered
beautiful.

29–31. *She is drowned . . . with*

more] Cf. *Ham.*, IV. vii. 186–7, 'Too
much of water hast thou, poor
Ophelia, / And therefore I forbid my
tears.'

32. *your bad entertainment*] my limited
hospitality.

33. *your trouble*] the pains you have
taken as my host.

34–5. *If you . . . servant*] Let me be
your servant, or I shall die of grief
at losing you.

36–7. *If you . . . desire it not*] Sebastian's reply, like his previous one,
vies with Antonio's speech in courtesy: he cannot endure Antonio's
taking further trouble for his sake.

37. *recovered*] rescued, restored to
life.

38. *kindness*] tenderness.

39. *manners of my mother*] womanly
readiness to weep; cf. *H5*, IV. vi. 31–2,

that upon the least occasion more mine eyes will tell   40
tales of me. I am bound to the Count Orsino's
court: farewell.   *Exit.*

Ant. The gentleness of all the gods go with thee!
I have many enemies in Orsino's court,
Else would I very shortly see thee there: 45
But come what may, I do adore thee so,
That danger shall seem sport, and I will go.   *Exit.*

SCENE II

Enter VIOLA *and* MALVOLIO, *at several doors.*

Mal. Were not you ev'n now with the Countess Olivia?

Viola. Even now, sir; on a moderate pace, I have since
arrived but hither.

Mal. She returns this ring to you, sir: you might have
saved me my pains, to have taken it away yourself.   5
She adds, moreover, that you should put your lord
into a desperate assurance she will none of him.
And one thing more, that you be never so hardy to
come again in his affairs, unless it be to report
your lord's taking of this. Receive it so.   10

Scene II

SCENE II] F (*Scæna Secunda.*).   [*Location.*] *A Street. Capell.*   S.D.] *F; Enter
Viola, Malvolio following. Capell.*

'And all my mother came into mine
eyes / And gave me up to tears.'

40–1. *tell tales of me*] betray my
feelings.

43. *gentleness*] favour.

Scene II

S.D. at several doors] at separate
entrances to the stage. Although
Malvolio has been told to 'run after'
the messenger, it is dramatically
more effective to bring them on as
meeting than to give Viola a mute
entry and to allow Malvolio to enter
by the same door shortly afterwards.
We may suppose, if we demand

realism, that Malvolio has intercepted
her by taking a short cut.

7. *desperate assurance*] hopeless certainty.

8. *hardy*] bold.

10. *this*] this message, not this ring.

Receive it so] Take the ring with
these accompanying commands. Collier explained the phrase as 'understand it so' (with reference to the
message); cf. 'receiving', III. i. 122.
But despite the ambiguity of 'this'
and 'it', of 'taking', 'receive', and
(in Viola's reply) 'took', the stage
action makes the sense clear. Malvolio holds out the ring for Viola to
take: hence her reply.

Viola. She took the ring of me, I'll none of it.

Mal. Come sir, you peevishly threw it to her: and her
    will is, it should be so returned. If it be worth
    stooping for, there it lies, in your eye: if not, be it
    his that finds it.   *Exit.*   15

Viola. I left no ring with her: what means this lady?
    Fortune forbid my outside have not charm'd her!
    She made good view of me, indeed so much,
    That methought her eyes had lost her tongue,
    For she did speak in starts distractedly.   20
    She loves me, sure; the cunning of her passion
    Invites me in this churlish messenger.
    None of my lord's ring? Why, he sent her none.
    I am the man: if it be so, as 'tis,
    Poor lady, she were better love a dream.   25
    Disguise, I see thou art a wickedness,
    Wherein the pregnant enemy does much.
    How easy is it for the proper false

---

11. the] *F; no Dyce², conj. Malone.*   19. That] *F;* That sure *F2;* That, as
Dyce², conj. Walker.   28. proper false] *F;* proper-false *Malone.*

11. *She took the ring of me*] F's
reading is usually (and rightly)
accepted, and interpreted as Viola's
ready invention to cover Olivia's in-
discretion (see Introduction, p. lxvii).
The supposed inconsistency with the
following soliloquy is unimportant:
she there thinks the matter out for
the audience's benefit. Further, if
we accept Dyce's reading ('no')
here, Viola's l. 16 becomes pointless
duplication.

12. *you peevishly threw it to her*]
Malvolio's assumption allows him
to throw it down after 'so returned'.
He recalls Olivia's epithet from
I. v. 304.

14. *in your eye*] in your sight.

17. *outside*] exterior, hence appearance; cf. *AYL.*, I. iii. 116, 'We'll have
a swashing and a martial outside.'

have not] A verb of negation (here
'forbid') is often followed by 'not'.

charm'd] enchanted (cf. III. i. 114,
referring to this occasion).

19. *That methought*] The metre, and

presumably the text, is defective, but
(cf. I. v. 259) it is impossible to choose
between 'sure' (F2's emendation,
perhaps suggested by l. 21) and 'as'
(Walker's conjecture); Furness (again
cf. I. v. 259) defends the irregularity.

her eyes . . . tongue] her eyes' pre-
occupation distracted her tongue
(from fluent speech, l. 20).

23. *None . . . ring?*] Viola quotes,
not from Malvolio's message (l. 7),
but from Olivia's speech to Malvolio
(I. v. 306).

24. *I am the man*] i.e., of her choice;
cf. *AYL.*, III. iii. 2–3, 'And how,
Audrey, am I the man yet?'

26–7. *Disguise . . . does much*] The
pregnant enemy is 'the dexterous
fiend, or enemy of mankind' (Johnson); cf. *Ham.*, II. ii. 594–5, 'and the
devil hath power / T'assume a
pleasing shape'.

28. *the proper false*] handsome and
deceitful men; cf. III. iv. 378, 'the
beauteous evil'.

In women's waxen hearts to set their forms!
Alas, our frailty is the cause, not we,   30
For such as we are made of, such we be.
How will this fadge? My master loves her dearly,
And I, poor monster, fond as much on him,
And she, mistaken, seems to dote on me:
What will become of this? As I am man,   35
My state is desperate for my master's love:
As I am woman (now alas the day!)
What thriftless sighs shall poor Olivia breathe?
O time, thou must untangle this, not I,
It is too hard a knot for me t'untie.   [*Exit.*] 40

SCENE III

Enter SIR TOBY *and* SIR ANDREW.

Sir To. Approach, Sir Andrew; not to be abed after
  midnight, is to be up betimes; and *diluculo surgere,*
  thou know'st—

30. our] *F2;* O *F.*   31. made of,] *Rann, conj. Thirlby, Tyrwhitt (independently);*
made, if *F.*   40. [*Exit.*]] *Rowe; not in F.*

Scene III

SCENE III] *F (Scæna Tertia.).*   [*Location.*] *Olivia's House. Rowe.*   2. *diluculo*]
Rowe; Deliculo F; Diliculo F2.   3. know'st—] *Theobald;* know'st. *F.*

29. *In women's . . . forms*] i.e., the handsome person of a man imprints itself on a woman's receptive heart, as a seal imprints itself on wax.

30–1. *Alas, our frailty . . . such we be*] This ed. follows F2 in emending F's 'O', and Rann in emending F's 'if' and transposing the comma. The sense is then, 'for, being made of weak material, we are necessarily weak'; cf. *Meas.,* II. iv. 127–30, 'Women, help heaven! Men their creation mar / In profiting by them. Nay, call us ten times frail; / For we are soft as our complexions are, / And credulous to false prints.' Mahood defends F's l. 31, paraphrasing 'Alas, women's frailty is the cause, not women themselves, for what happens to us—if we are like that,' but admits that the lines, so interpreted, are 'not

easy to get across in a theatre'. There is also the objection that 'the cause for' is un-Shakespearean. He always uses 'the cause of', except (as Turner notes) in *Wiv.,* III. i. 44, where Sir Hugh Evans is given the line 'There is reasons and causes for it' (in order to emphasize his un-English way of speaking).

32. *fadge*] turn out.

33. *monster*] being both 'man' (l. 35) and 'woman' (l. 37).

fond] dote (cf. l. 34).

36. *desperate*] hopeless (cf. l. 7 above).

38. *thriftless*] unprofitable.

Scene III

2. diluculo surgere] '*Diluculo surgere saluberrimum est*' (to rise early is very healthy): a sentence from William

Sir And. Nay, by my troth, I know not: but I know, to be
up late, is to be up late.　　　　　　　　　　　　　5

Sir To. A false conclusion: I hate it as an unfilled can.
To be up after midnight, and to go to bed then, is
early: so that to go to bed after midnight, is to
go to bed betimes. Does not our life consist of
the four elements?　　　　　　　　　　　　　10

Sir And. Faith, so they say, but I think it rather consists
of eating and drinking.

Sir To. Th'art a scholar; let us therefore eat and drink.
Marian, I say! a stoup of wine!

Enter CLOWN.

Sir And. Here comes the fool, i' faith.　　　　　　15

Clown. How now, my hearts? Did you never see the
picture of 'we three'?

Sir To. Welcome, ass. Now let's have a catch.

Sir And. By my troth, the fool has an excellent breast. I
had rather than forty shillings I had such a leg,　20
and so sweet a breath to sing, as the fool has.
In sooth, thou wast in very gracious fooling last
night, when thou spok'st of Pigrogromitus, of the

9. life] *Rowe*³; liues *F.*

Lilly's Latin grammar (1513, but
in use much later).

10. *the four elements*] fire, air, water,
and earth: the supposed compounds
of all matter, and represented in the
human body by the 'humours' of
choler, blood, phlegm, and melancholy, each of which is a compound
of the qualities of two elements, e.g.,
choler is hot and dry like fire and
melancholy is cold and dry like
earth. The connection with the preceding lines is tenuous. Shakespeare
seems merely to be preparing for Sir
Andrew's remark and the rejoinder.

14. *stoup*] large drinking vessel.

S.D.] Sir Toby having called for
Maria, the Clown's entrance (by the
opposite door, since he is first seen by

Sir Andrew) has the effect of realism
as contrasted with contrivance.

17. *picture of 'we three'*] picture of
two fools or two asses, the caption
hence including the spectator. Popular
as an inn sign, and also (Mahood)
existing in the form of a picture
which represented, when looked at
from different angles, two fools and
an ass. Feste offers a genially insulting
greeting, to which Sir Toby as genially retorts.

19. *breast*] singing voice.

19-20. *I had . . . forty shillings*]
Wilson compares Slender's use of the
phrase in *Wiv.*, I. i. 179; cf. below,
v. i. 175, 'forty pound'.

23-4. *Pigrogromitus . . . Vapians . . .
Queubus*] extravagant invented names

Vapians passing the equinoctial of Queubus: 'twas
very good, i' faith: I sent thee sixpence for thy   25
leman: hadst it?

Clown. I did impeticos thy gratillity: for Malvolio's
nose is no whipstock, my lady has a white hand,
and the Myrmidons are no bottle-ale houses.

Sir And. Excellent! Why, this is the best fooling, when   30
all is done. Now a song!

Sir To. Come on, there is sixpence for you. Let's have
a song.

---

26. leman] *Theobald;* Lemon *F.*   27. impeticos . . . gratillity] *F;* impeticoat
[*sic*] . . . gratuity, *Var '78, conj. Johnson.*   29. Myrmidons] *F* (Mermidons),
Theobald.

(cf. I. v. 33 'Quinapalus'), recalling
Rabelais but not found in his writings.
Since 'the equinoctial' means the
celestial equator, Queubus may be
an alphabetical sequel to Phoebus,
the sun.

26. *leman*] sweetheart. This remark
(coming from Sir Andrew) offers no
firm foundation for discussing the
Clown's private life.

27–9. *I did impeticos . . . houses*]
This speech begins as a kind of sense,
and then sinks, or rises, into 'the best
fooling'. The Clown acknowledges
Sir Andrew's present ('gratillity'=
gratuity; 'impeticos'=pocket in my
long coat, the usual wear of fools, cf.
Hotson, *Shakespeare's Motley*, frontispiece); then, with a pseudo-logical
'for' (which should have discouraged
further explication), he utters a trio
of unrelated remarks. 'My lady'
is obviously Olivia rather than his
'leman', since it follows upon mention
of Malvolio's nose; the Myrmidons
are the followers of Achilles, cf. *Troil.,*
v. iii. 33. There is no evidence whatever for a London tavern called the
Myrmidons (nor, if there had been
such a tavern, would it be referred to
with a plural verb and noun). The
explanations offered by Steevens and

Hutson (given by Furness) have been
extended by Wilson, Ribner,
Mahood, and Charney; other explanations, relating to contemporary
persons (Knollys, Queen Elizabeth,
the Yeomen of the Guard), are proposed by Hotson (p. 150). All one
can usefully say is that the reference
to Malvolio is derogatory, the reference to Olivia is complimentary, and
the reference to the Myrmidons is
pure nonsense. It seems probable that
this final phrase grew out of Shakespeare's recollection of *2H4,* II. iv. 123,
where Doll Tearsheet calls Pistol
'you bottle-ale rascal', and where
Pistol's ranting speech, ll. 154–7,
derives from a passage in John Eliot's
Ortho-epia Gallica (1593), quoted by
J. W. Lever in 'Shakespeare's French
Fruits', *Shakespeare Survey,* 6 (1953)
and by A. R. Humphreys in the New
Arden ed. of *2H4,* Appendix I, pp.
231–2, where a braggart exclaims,
inter alia, 'Where is Achilles the Grig,
Captaine of the Mirmidons, I would
send his soule by and by into hell.'

28. *whipstock*] handle of a whip,
possibly implying that, though Malvolio may look down his nose in disapproval, he cannot punish the Clown
(with a whipping): H. Jenkins's suggestion.

Sir And. There's a testril of me too: if one knight give
   a—   35
Clown. Would you have a love-song, or a song of good
   life?
Sir To. A love-song, a love-song.
Sir And. Ay, ay. I care not for good life.

Clown sings.

O mistress mine, where are you roaming?   40
O stay and hear, your true love's coming,
   That can sing both high and low.
Trip no further, pretty sweeting:
Journeys end in lovers meeting,
   Every wise man's son doth know.   45

Sir And. Excellent good, i' faith.
Sir To. Good, good.

35. a—] *F2* (a-), *Rowe;* a *F;* another should. *conj. Singer;* away sixpence so will I give another: go to, a song. *Collier².*   44. *lovers] F;* lovers' *Theobald².*

34. *testril*] diminutive of 'tester' (*OED*, 3)—sixpence.

34–5. *give a*—] In F, the 'a' is at the end of a line of type, suggesting that the compositor intended to complete the speech but, being somehow distracted, instead began the next. F2 added a hyphen (intended as a dash?), which seems to explain the nineteenth-century edd.'s completions ('another', 'away'); one would rather expect the next word following the 'a' to be 'testril'. There is no reason why Sir Andrew should come to a halt or be interrupted.

36–7. *a song of good life*] a drinking song, not, as Sir Andrew thinks, a virtuous one: hence his miscomprehending and unconsciously self-accusing remark.

40. O mistress mine] The words of the song are generally agreed to be Shakespeare's. Whether he fitted them to Morley's tune (see Appendix II, pp. 181–2) or to some other, and whether he and Morley collaborated,

are debatable: for details see Seng, pp. 96–100. The general sense of the song is similar to that of 'It was a lover and his lass', *AYL.*, v. iii. 14–31, with its theme 'How that a life was but a flower . . . And therefore take the present time', though the song in *Tw.N.* is addressed by a lover to his beloved and is more poignant (though not melancholy) in mood. J. Hollander ('*Tw.N.* and the Morality of Indulgence', *Sewanee Review*, 67 (1959), pp. 220–38) takes it to be 'a direct appeal' to Olivia, 'made on behalf of everyone in the play', to marry; the 'true love . . . that can sing both high and low' he interprets as 'Viola-Sebastian, the master-mistress of Orsino's and Olivia's passion.' I think this explanation strained, though I would agree that the song adds much to the otherwise very different mood of the scene, and is in tune with the play as a whole.

45. wise man's son] 'In allusion to the saying that wise men have fools for their sons' (Mahood).

Clown.   *What is love? 'Tis not hereafter,*
           Present mirth hath present laughter:
           What's to come is still unsure.   50
           In delay there lies no plenty,
           Then come kiss me, sweet and twenty:
           Youth's a stuff will not endure.

Sir And. A mellifluous voice, as I am a true knight.

Sir To. A contagious breath.   55

Sir And. Very sweet and contagious, i' faith.

Sir To. To hear by the nose, it is dulcet in contagion. But shall we make the welkin dance indeed? Shall we rouse the night-owl in a catch that will draw three souls out of one weaver? Shall we   60 do that?

Sir And. And you love me, let's do't: I am dog at a catch.

---

50. still] always.

52. sweet and twenty] 'a vocative term of endearment' (Furness, who cites, p. 418, the accurate form of a quotation, slightly altered by Steevens who first drew attention to it, in the prose story-collection *The Merry Devil of Edmonton* (S.R. 1608): 'his little wanton wagtailes, his sweet and twenties, . . . as hee himselfe used commonly to call them'.) Not, therefore, a reference to the lady's age or to the number of kisses, but synonymous with 'pretty sweeting', l. 43.

54. *mellifluous*] Wilson amusingly notes that as recently as 1598 Meres (in his *Palladis Tamia*) had praised 'mellifluous and honey-tongued Shakespeare'.

55. *contagious*] literally, catching, as of a sickness, and, when coupled with 'breath', suggesting 'foul' (the opposite of the word Sir Andrew has just used). Sir Andrew (as Sir Toby intends) adopts the word and absurdly couples it with 'sweet', Sir Toby then enlarging on the absurdity in a statement which Wilson paraphrases as 'If we could hear with our nose, we might call it sweet in stench.' Mahood notes that 'contagious' is used affectedly in 'Apolonius and Silla', to mean 'consuming' or 'powerful': see Appendix I, p. 160, l. 130.

59. *catch*] song in canon form.

60. *three souls*] alluding to the three-part catch; cf. 'hale souls out of men's bodies', *Ado*, II. iii. 61, and Falstaff's reference to weavers ('I could sing psalms or anything', *1H4*, II. iv. 147). Weavers did not only sing psalms ('singing catches with cloth-workers', Jonson, *Silent Woman*, III. iv. 10–11) but perhaps some such incongruity is intended by Sir Toby's reference to souls: Mahood points out that many weavers were 'Calvinist refugees from the Low Countries'. Deighton reminds us that tailors (as sedentary workers, like weavers) also sang at their work; cf. *1H4*, III. i. 260, 'Come, sing . . . 'Tis the next way to turn tailor, or be redbreast teacher.'

62. *dog at*] good at (colloquial); cf. *Gent.*, IV. iv. 14, 'to be, as it were, a dog at all things' (Launce speaking of Crab his dog), and Tilley, D506.

Clown. By'r lady, sir, and some dogs will catch well.
Sir And. Most certain. Let our catch be, 'Thou knave'.   65
Clown. 'Hold thy peace, thou knave', knight? I shall be
  constrained in't to call thee knave, knight.
Sir And. 'Tis not the first time I have constrained one to
  call me knave. Begin, fool: it begins, 'Hold thy
  peace'.   70
Clown. I shall never begin if I hold my peace.
Sir And. Good, i' faith. Come, begin.   *Catch sung.*

Enter MARIA.

Maria. What a caterwauling do you keep here? If my
  lady have not called up her steward Malvolio and
  bid him turn you out of doors, never trust me.   75
Sir To. My lady's a Cataian, we are politicians, Malvolio's a Peg-a-Ramsey, and [*Sings*] *Three merry men*

66. knight?] *Capell;* knight. *F.*   77. [*Sings*]] *N.C.S.; not in F.*

64. *some dogs will catch well*] Cf. *Ado*, v. ii. 10–11, 'Thy wit is as quick as the greyhound's month; it catches', which reinforces the literal sense here, though H. M. Hulme, *Explorations in Shakespeare's Language* (1962), p. 54, gives 'dog' as the name of a gripping device.

65. '*Thou knave*'] See Appendix II, pp. 182–4, for the music.

66, 67. *knave, knight*] playing on the antithesis.

68–9. '*Tis not . . . knave*] Sir Andrew means either (1) that he has often sung this catch with others, or (2) that he has often picked quarrels (cf. Maria's remark, I. iii. 30), but not (3) that he *is* a knave and has often been recognized as such (the comic sense here).

76–8. *My lady's a Cataian . . . merry men be we*] This may well be mostly nonsensical drunken expostulation. Furness suggests that 'Cataian' may have been prompted by the first syllable of 'caterwauling'.

76. *Cataian*] a variant form of 'Cathayan' (*OED*), a native of

Cathay (China). Used in *Wiv.*, II. i. 128, where the context suggests 'rogue'; cf. Onions, and William Watreman's *Fardle of Facions*, 1555 (part II, ch. viii), 'the Cathaiens . . . knowe not what we meane, when we speake of faithfulnesse, or trusti-nesse.' Sir Toby may therefore be implying that Olivia will not keep her word about turning him out, since he is 'consanguineous' (l. 78).

we are politicians] 'politician' appears four other times in Shakespeare (including Sir Andrew's III. ii. 31), always in a derogatory sense. Wilson's interpretation, 'So we (i.e., you) are up to our little schemes, are we?', though at first sight strained, does have the merit of referring to Maria: otherwise, with his 'three merry men', Sir Toby refers to himself and his companions twice, and not at all to Maria. Or it may mean 'we are shrewd enough, we'll manage her.'

77. *Peg-a-Ramsey*] the title of two dance tunes of Shakespeare's time (Chappell, p. 218; Naylor, p. 188). The ribald lyric given in T. D'Urfey's

be we. Am not I consanguineous? Am I not of her blood? Tilly-vally! 'Lady!' [*Sings*] *There dwelt a man in Babylon, Lady, Lady.*   80

Clown. Beshrew me, the knight's in admirable fooling.

Sir And. Ay, he does well enough, if he be disposed, and so do I too: he does it with a better grace, but I do it more natural.

Sir To. [*Sings*] *O' the twelfth day of December—*   85

Maria. For the love o' God, peace!

79. 'Lady!'] *N.C.S.;* Ladie, *F.*   [*Sings*]] *N.C.S.* (*as Rowe, subst.*); *not in F.*
85. [*Sings*]] *N.C.S.* (*as Rowe, subst.*); *not in F.*   O'] *N.C.S.*, *conj. Walker;*
O | *F.*   *December—*] *Theobald; December. F.*

Wit and Mirth, or Pills to Purge Melancholy (London, 1719, Vol. v, 139–40, quoted by Charney) seems to be of later date and Scottish origin: it is called 'Bonny Peggy Ramsey'. Wilson takes the term as equivalent to 'scarecrow'. J. O. Wood (*English Language Notes,* September 1967) argues that in ballads a Peg-a-Ramsey is 'a watchful hovering woman', and suggests that Sir Toby alludes to Malvolio's 'spoil-sport' nature. Hotson (p. 106) notes that a lyric to the tune of Peg-a-Ramsey (a married man's regrets for his bachelor days) includes the refrain 'Give me my yellow hose again', but this is probably rather coincidental than significant: Shakespeare may be subconsciously looking ahead to II. v, but Sir Toby can have no such connection in mind, since the letter is devised by Maria.

77–8. Three merry men be we] the final phrase of several songs (one in Peele's *Old Wives Tale,* 1595, Ind.). See Appendix II, p. 185.

78. *consanguineous*] 'of her blood': characteristic tipsy tautology.

79. *Tilly-vally!*] exclamation of contempt; cf. fiddle-faddle.

'*Lady!*'] scornful repetition of Maria's word, as Wilson stresses by his punctuation, though his interpretation of 'My lady's a Cataian' as

'This "my lady" of yours is a mere trick to put us off' is strained.

79–80. There dwelt . . . Lady, Lady] the opening line and the refrain of a popular ballad of *Constant Susanna* (i.e., Susanna and the Elders: Apocrypha, The History of Susanna, i), licensed 1562. Naylor, p. 182, sets the words to a version of the well-known tune 'Greensleeves', but see Appendix II, pp. 185–6. Wilson quotes the first stanza of *Susanna* and irresponsibly says that 'it is so apt to the situation between Sir Toby and Maria that Shakespeare probably intended him to sing it all, substituting "Maria" for "Susanna".'

82–3. *and so do I too*] the first appearance of what will become one of Sir Andrew's mannerisms; cf. l. 164, and II. v. 183, 186, 189, 192, 208.

84. *natural*] naturally; with an unconscious ambiguity (natural=idiot, cf. I. iii. 29).

85. O' the twelfth day of December] Kittredge regards this as the opening of the ballad on the battle of Musselburgh Field (Child, no. 172). The ballad was still popular in the mid-seventeenth century (cf. Seng, p. 103, where a version of 1656 begins, as here, with 'On the twelfth Day of December', instead of 'the tenth day' as in Child's version. But I. B. Cauthen's suggestion (*Studies in Biblio-*

Enter MALVOLIO.

Mal. My masters, are you mad? Or what are you?
　　Have you no wit, manners, nor honesty, but to
　　gabble like tinkers at this time of night? Do
　　ye make an ale-house of my lady's house, that ye　90
　　squeak out your coziers' catches without any
　　mitigation or remorse of voice? Is there no respect
　　of place, persons, nor time in you?
Sir To. We did keep time, sir, in our catches. Sneck up!
Mal. Sir Toby, I must be round with you. My lady bade　95
　　me tell you, that though she harbours you as her
　　kinsman, she's nothing allied to your disorders.
　　If you can separate yourself and your misde-
　　meanours, you are welcome to the house: if not, and
　　it would please you to take leave of her, she is　100
　　very willing to bid you farewell.
Sir To. [*Sings*] *Farewell, dear heart, since I must needs be gone.*
Maria. Nay, good Sir Toby.
Clown. [*Sings*] *His eyes do show his days are almost done.*
Mal. Is't even so?　　　　　　　　　　　　　　　　　　105
Sir To. [*Sings*] *But I will never die.*
Clown. [*Sings*] *Sir Toby, there you lie.*
Mal. This is much credit to you.
Sir To. [*Sings*] *Shall I bid him go?*
Clown. [*Sings*] *What and if you do?*　　　　　　　　　110

102, 104, 106, 107, 109, 110, 111, 112. [*Sings*]] *N.C.S.* (*as Hanmer*); *only ll. 109–112 in italic in F.*
107. *lie*] F (lye); [*Falls down drunkenly.*] Halliwell, conj. Capell.

graphy, 2 (1949), pp. 182–5) that
Sir Toby misquotes the first line of
the familiar carol called 'The Twelve
Days of Christmas', which traditionally begins 'On the twelfth day', is
attractive, since it combines an obli-
que reference to Twelfth Night (6
January) with a comic error ('December' for 'Christmas'). The tune of
Musselburgh Field is not known.
　88. *wit*] common sense.
　honesty] decency.
　91. *coziers*'] cobblers'; cf. 'tinkers',
l. 89, and 'weaver', l. 60.

92. *mitigation . . . voice*] considerate
lowering of your voices.
　94. *Sneck up!*] Be hanged! (*OED*,
snick, *v.*[1]; cf. Weber's quotation from
John Taylor the Water-Poet's *Praise
of Hempseed* (Var. '21), 'Snickup,
which is in English Gallow-grasse').
　95. *round*] plain.
　102–12. Farewell, dear heart . . .
you dare not] from Robert Jones's
The First Book of Songes and Ayres,
1600, sigs D4[v]–E1, adapted by
Shakespeare from the first two stanzas,
so that they can be sung to the tune

Sir To. [*Sings*] *Shall I bid him go, and spare not?*
Clown. [*Sings*] *O no, no, no, no, you dare not.*
Sir To. Out o' time, sir? ye lie! Art any more than a
    steward? Dost thou think because thou art virtuous,
    there shall be no more cakes and ale?   115

113. time, sir?] *Theobald;* tune sir, *F.*

of one complete stanza. (1) Farewel dear loue since thou wilt needs be gon, | mine eies do shew my life is almost done, | nay I will neuer die, | so long as I can spie, | there be many mo | though that she do go | there be many mo I feare not, | why then let her goe I care not. | (2) Farewell, farewell, since this I finde is true, | I will not spend more time in wooing you: | But I will seeke elsewhere, | If I may find her there, | Shall I bid her goe, | What and if I doe? | Shall I bid her go and spare not, | Oh no no no no I dare not. For music, see Appendix II, p. 187.

103. *Nay, good Sir Toby*] Like her l. 86, an attempt to bring Sir Toby to order (he has picked up Malvolio's last word, just as he picked up Maria's 'lady', ll. 79–80). Furness's suggestion (followed by Wilson) that Sir Toby's line is sung 'personally to her, accompanied with some tipsy demonstrations of affection' is a mere flight of fancy.

107. Sir Toby, there you lie] Many edd. and producers have followed Capell and Halliwell in wrenching this remark into a pun on interpolated stage business, which breaks the continuity of the improvised version of the song. The Clown's line is no more than a common-sense retort to Sir Toby's, since that is nonsense when removed from its original context.

113. *Out o' time, sir? ye lie*] I revert to Theobald's emendation because (1) it is consistent with Sir Toby's retort 'we did keep time', l. 94 (and

the humour is improved if Sir Toby originally intended a mere quibble but now drunkenly recollects Malvolio's remark as musical criticism); (2) the time/tune error is very easily made in reading MS. (cf. *Mac.*, IV. iii. 235, 'This tune [F time] goes manly'); (3) no satisfactory defence of 'tune' has been made. Dyce[2] (who followed Theobald), replying to Collier's suggestion that the Clown had sung 'out of tune' and that those three words are addressed to him, is conclusive: 'The whole of this line is obviously spoken to Malvolio. *The Clown* would hardly *sing out of tune*; he is *the* singer of the play.' Furness endeavours to show that the whole line is spoken to the Clown, who has reflected on Sir Toby's courage (and is therefore given the lie), and has added an extra 'no' to the song (and is therefore declared to be out of tune): but (1) he is wrong about the 'extra "no"' because he took his text from Richard Johnson's poetical anthology *The Golden Garland of Princely Pleasures and Delicate Delights* (1620, sigs. F5–F5[v]), where one 'no' is accidentally omitted; (2) 'out of tune' does not mean 'you have altered the tune'; (3) Sir Toby probably would not call the Clown 'sir', even in jest, whereas he uses it aggressively to Malvolio in both his other speeches to him, ll. 94, 118.

115. *cakes and ale*] traditionally associated with festivity, and disliked by Puritans both on this account and because of their association with weddings, saints' days, and holy-days.

Clown. Yes, by Saint Anne, and ginger shall be hot i' th'
　　mouth too.　　　　　　　　　　　　　　　　*[Exit.]*

Sir To. Th'art i' th' right. Go sir, rub your chain with
　　crumbs. A stoup of wine, Maria!

Mal. Mistress Mary, if you prized my lady's favour at　120
　　anything more than contempt, you would not give
　　means for this uncivil rule; she shall know of it,
　　by this hand.　　　　　　　　　　　　　　　　*Exit.*

Maria. Go shake your ears.

Sir And. 'Twere as good a deed as to drink when a　125
　　man's a-hungry, to challenge him the field, and
　　then to break promise with him and make a fool
　　of him.

Sir To. Do't, knight. I'll write thee a challenge; or
　　I'll deliver thy indignation to him by word of　130
　　mouth.

Maria. Sweet Sir Toby, be patient for to-night. Since
　　the youth of the Count's was today with my lady,

117. *[Exit.]] This ed.; not in F.*

116. *Saint Anne]* mother of the
Virgin Mary. Perhaps mentioned
to underline Sir Toby's anti-Puritan
remark, but still a common oath in
Shakespeare's time; cf. *Shr.*, I. i. 243.

ginger] used to spice ale.

117. *[Exit].]* The fact that the
Clown takes no further part in the
scene (combined with Maria's 'and let
the fool make a third', ll. 173–4, which,
taken alone, might be addressed to
the two gentlemen even if the Clown
were present) implies that he leaves
the stage some time during it. He
has no marked exit, and the final
Exeunt (l. 191) is applicable only to
Sir Toby and Sir Andrew. In some
productions he falls asleep (without
dramatic motivation), but this would
be an impracticable solution on the
stage without a front curtain or
lighting that can be 'blacked out'; or
(as Mahood reports) follows Malvolio out, which seems unconvincing
stage business. I therefore make his
final speech his exit line.

118–19. *rub your chain with crumbs]*
to clean it: alluding provocatively
to Malvolio's officiousness as steward.

121–2. *give means . . . rule]* supply
the drink which encourages this dis-
orderly conduct.

124. *Go shake your ears]* a common
dismissive insult (cf. Tilley, E16),
not always implying that the hearer
is an ass, but probably so here.
Furness gives several instances, and
H. M. Hulme, *Explorations*, p. 198,
quotes Udall (1542). 'When men doe
mocke any bodie, thei wagge their
handes up and down by their eares
at the sides of their hed and do
counterfeact the facion of an Asses
eares.'

125. *as good a deed as to drink]* a
common phrase; cf. *1H4*, II. i. 28.
Sir Andrew's foolish amplification
makes nonsense of it.

126. *challenge him the field]* call him
to a duel. Sir Andrew's genius for
bathos is shown in what he considers
the height of the jest.

she is much out of quiet. For Monsieur Malvolio,
let me alone with him. If I do not gull him into   135
a nayword, and make him a common recreation,
do not think I have wit enough to lie straight in
my bed: I know I can do it.

Sir To. Possess us, possess us, tell us something of him.

Maria. Marry sir, sometimes he is a kind of Puritan.   140

Sir And. O, if I thought that, I'd beat him like a dog.

Sir To. What, for being a Puritan? Thy exquisite
reason, dear knight?

Sir And. I have no exquisite reason for't, but I have
reason good enough.   145

Maria. The devil a Puritan that he is, or anything
constantly, but a time-pleaser, an affectioned
ass, that cons state without book, and utters it
by great swarths: the best persuaded of himself,

---

136. a nayword] *Rowe;* an ayword *F.*
conj. Walker.

139. *Sir To.*] *F (To.); Sir And. Dyce²,*

135-6. *gull him into a nayword*] play
such a trick on him as will make his
name synonymous with 'fool'. Nayword here=byword; in *Wiv.*, II. ii.
113, v. ii. 5 (its only other occurrences in Shakespeare) it=password,
code-word.

137-8. *wit enough . . . bed*] seemingly
proverbial (cf. I. iii. 73-4), but not in
Tilley.

139. Sir To.] Walker suggests that
this line should be Sir Andrew's,
since 'Sir Toby needed no information respecting Malvolio', and points
out that in her reply Maria calls the
speaker 'Sir' (cf. I. iii. 47, 53, 65, 68,
72, 75, 77), not 'Sir Toby', her invariable way of addressing him.
Walker's conjecture is attractive, the
only dissuasions being that the line
has too positive a tone to be characteristic of Sir Andrew, and that at
l. 141 Sir Andrew's explosion is more
comic if he then breaks into the
dialogue for the first time.

Possess us] Give us information.

140. *sometimes*] This is to be taken

with ll. 146-7 ('or anything constantly').

142. *exquisite*] Mahood notes that
this is a difficult word to pronounce
when drunk, and that it is given twice
to Cassio in his drunken scene, *Oth.*,
II. iii. 18 (when sober), 93 (when
drunk). Sir Toby has it again (when
sober) at IV. ii. 64. Sir Andrew, as
usual, snatches at Sir Toby's fine
word without quite understanding it,
hence his puzzled reply, ll. 144-5.

147. *time-pleaser*] time-server (not
used by Shakespeare); cf. *Cor.*, III.
i. 45.

affectioned] affected.

148-9. *cons state . . . swarths*] learns
by heart expressions appropriate to
high position and uses them profusely;
swarth (spelled *swath* in *Troil.*, v. v. 25,
its only other use in this sense by
Shakespeare)=swathe, the width of
standing grass or grain that is cut
down by one swing of the mower's
scythe.

149. *the best . . . himself*] extremely
self-conceited.

so crammed (as he thinks) with excellencies, that   150
it is his grounds of faith that all that look on
him love him: and on that vice in him will my
revenge find notable cause to work.

Sir To. What wilt thou do?

Maria. I will drop in his way some obscure epistles of   155
love, wherein by the colour of his beard, the
shape of his leg, the manner of his gait, the
expressure of his eye, forehead, and complexion,
he shall find himself most feelingly personated.
I can write very like my lady your niece; on a   160
forgotten matter we can hardly make distinction
of our hands.

Sir To. Excellent, I smell a device.

Sir And. I have't in my nose too.

Sir To. He shall think by the letters that thou wilt drop   165
that they come from my niece, and that she's in
love with him.

Maria. My purpose is indeed a horse of that colour.

Sir And. And your horse now would make him an ass.

Maria. Ass, I doubt not.   170

Sir And. O, 'twill be admirable!

Maria. Sport royal, I warrant you: I know my physic
will work with him. I will plant you two, and let
the fool make a third, where he shall find the
letter: observe his construction of it. For this   175

---

157. gait] *F* (gate), *Johnson.*

151. *grounds*] foundations. Plural
noun with singular verb is not unusual in Shakespeare: cf. III. iv. 283.

158. *expressure*] expression.

159. *most feelingly personated*] described with perfect exactitude.

160–2. *on a forgotten matter . . .
hands*] When neither of us remembers
which of us wrote a thing, we cannot
easily discover it from the writing.

168. *a horse of that colour*] proverbial
(Tilley, H665).

169–70. *your horse . . . doubt not*] Sir
Andrew's uncharacteristic wit (noted

by Capell and others: Dyce[2] gave the
line to Sir Toby) allows Maria to call
him an ass, whether by repeating
the word (=you ass) or by punning
on 'as' (cf. *Ham.*, v. ii. 43, 'as-es
[F Assis] of great charge', where
'charge'=(1) moral weight, (2) literal
burden, so that in the second sense
Hamlet's phrase means 'asses heavily
laden').

173–4. *let the fool make a third*] Cf.
note to l. 117.

175. *construction*] interpretation
(from 'construe').

night, to bed, and dream on the event. Farewell.   *Exit.*

Sir To. Good night, Penthesilea.

Sir And. Before me, she's a good wench.

Sir To. She's a beagle, true-bred, and one that adores
    me: what o' that?   180

Sir And. I was adored once too.

Sir To. Let's to bed, knight. Thou hadst need send for
    more money.

Sir And. If I cannot recover your niece, I am a foul way
    out.   185

Sir To. Send for money, knight; if thou hast her not i'
    th' end, call me cut.

Sir And. If I do not, never trust me, take it how you
    will.

Sir To. Come, come, I'll go burn some sack, 'tis too late   190
    to go to bed now. Come, knight, come, knight.   *Exeunt.*

---

176. *event*] outcome.

177. *Penthesilea*] Queen of the Amazons: 'half in admiration, half in jest at Maria's diminutive size' (Wilson).

178. *Before me*] a mild oath, often substituted for 'Before God'.

179. *beagle*] a small hunting dog, also sometimes kept as a pet (cf. Gervase Markham (1611), quoted by Furness and Wilson); cf. l. 177.

182–3. *Thou had . . . money*] Cf. III. ii. 52–3 ('some two thousand strong, or so').

184. *recover*] get (without any sense of 'get back').

184–5. *I am a foul way out*] i.e., I have wasted my time and money; literally, I have lost my way and am in the mire: cf. *LLL.*, v. ii. 903, 'ways be foul'; *Shr.*, iv . i. 2, 'foul ways'; *1H4*, II. i. 81, 'will [boots] hold out water in foul way?'

187. *cut*] (1) docked [horse], with tail cut short: cf. *Wiv.*, III. iv. 46, 'Cut and long-tail' (=all and sundry, cf. Tilley, C938), (2) gelding, (3) female genital organ (cf. II. v. 88–91). As term of abuse, see *OED*, *sb.*² VI. 29, where a much earlier example of the phrase 'call me cut' is given. Falstaff's 'call me horse', *1H4*, II. iv. 215, suggests that either (1) or (2) is the sense here, though in *Gammer Gurton's Needle*, III. iii. 25, the abusive term is applied to an old woman ('Thou slut! thou kut!' etc.).

190. *burn some sack*] warm and spice some sherry.

190–1. *too late to go to bed*] Cf. l. 182, and ll. 1–9: a perfect end to the scene.

SCENE IV

Enter DUKE, VIOLA, CURIO, *and others.*

Duke. Give me some music. Now good morrow, friends.
   Now, good Cesario, but that piece of song,
   That old and antic song we heard last night;

Scene IV

SCENE IV] F (*Scena Quarta.*).   [*Location.*] *The Palace. Rowe.*   1. Give . . .
music. Now] F (Giue . . . Musick: Now); Give . . . music now. *Johnson.* Give . . .
music. [*To Viola*] Now,—[*Enter Musicians*]   *conj. Blair apud Camb.²;* [*to Viola*]
Give . . . music . . . Now— [*musicians enter*] *N.C.S.;* Give . . . music—[*to others*]
Now *conj. this ed.*   friends.] F; friends—*N.C.S., conj. Blair;* friends—[*to
Viola*] *conj. this ed.*   2. Cesario,] F; Cesario—*conj. this ed.*   3. antic] F
(Anticke), *N.C.S.;* antique *Pope.*

1–2. *Give me some music . . . good
Cesario*] The text as printed here is
(for the reader's convenience) essentially that of F. The various conjectures and emendations of punctuation reflect various views as to the
sense of the lines, the persons
addressed, and the accompanying
action. Whether the 'friends' are
the Duke's courtiers, or his musicians,
depends partly on the meaning of
F's S.D.; '*and others*' probably cor-
responds to '*and other Lords*' (I. i. S.D.)
and to '*and Lords*' (v. i. 6. S.D.),
but still admits the possibility that
musicians enter after his first four
words. One's social equals and social
inferiors can both be addressed as
'friends' (e.g., III. i. 1, Viola to the
Clown; v. i. 7, the Duke to Fabian
and the Clown). As in I. i, it is not
clear where the musicians are placed
or what instruments they play, and
(again as in I. i) no special provision
is made for getting them off stage if
they do enter, though on both
occasions they can leave with others
(I. i. 41, II. iv. 80). Johnson was concerned simply to avoid beginning
two sentences with 'Now'. Blair and
N.C.S. both interpret 'good morrow,
friends' as the Duke's 'courteous

side-remark' (Furness; though, unlike them, he would include courtiers
as well as musicians in it), interpolated in his words to Viola. Much
depends on whether the Duke enters
with his courtiers or is meeting them:
there is no reference to 'several
doors', as there is at II. ii. S.D., but
this does not exclude the possibility
that 'Now good morrow, friends' is his
greeting to them. I would include
'Now, good Cesario' in this greeting
(see collation above); for 'Now' in
this sense, still commonly used in
the north of England, cf. *Caes.,*
II. ii. 120 ('Now, Cinna. Now,
Metellus.'), following l. 117 ('Good
morrow, Antony'). If this conjecture
is adopted, the Duke's request is
'Give me some music—but [i.e.,
only] that piece of song', etc., Viola
is singled out for an individual
greeting, and it is unnecessary to
assume that she is being asked to
sing. For further discussion, regarding
the possibility that Shakespeare revised the text, see Introduction, pp.
xxii–xxiii.

   3. *old and antic*] quaint and old-
fashioned; possibly synonymous, for
emphasis, cf. l. 18, 'Unstaid and skittish'.

Methought it did relieve my passion much,
More than light airs and recollected terms   5
Of these most brisk and giddy-paced times.
Come, but one verse.

Curio. He is not here, so please your lordship, that should
sing it.

Duke. Who was it?   10

Curio. Feste the jester, my lord, a fool that the Lady
Olivia's father took much delight in. He is about
the house.

Duke. Seek him out, and play the tune the while.

                    [*Exit Curio.*] *Music plays.*

Come hither, boy. If ever thou shalt love,   15
In the sweet pangs of it remember me:
For such as I am, all true lovers are,
Unstaid and skittish in all motions else,
Save in the constant image of the creature
That is belov'd. How dost thou like this tune?   20

Viola. It gives a very echo to the seat
Where love is thron'd.

Duke.   Thou dost speak masterly.
My life upon't, young though thou art, thine eye
Hath stay'd upon some favour that it loves.
Hath it not, boy?

Viola.   A little, by your favour.   25

Duke. What kind of woman is't?

Viola.   Of your complexion.

---

6. giddy-paced] *F*; giddy-pated *Hanmer*.   14. [*Exit Curio.*]] *Pope*; *not in F.*
18. motions] *F*; notions *Warburton.*

4. *passion*] suffering (from unrequited love); cf. l. 95.

5. *recollected terms*] studied (artificial)
phrases.

11–12. *a fool . . . delight in*] Cf.
All's W., IV. v. 57–60 (the Countess,
speaking of the Clown), 'My lord
that's gone made himself much sport
out of him.'

18. *motions*] emotions.

21–2. *It gives . . . is thron'd*] 'It is an
exact echo to the deepest feelings of
the heart' (Luce).

22. *masterly*] with masterly expres-
siveness.

24. *favour*] face.

25. *by your favour*] if it please you.
The repetition of 'favour', in a different sense from l. 24, leads on to the
dramatic irony of the following
exchange, but the phrase cannot,
without straining it, be made into a
pun and interpreted as 'like you in
feature' (as by Mahood).

Duke. She is not worth thee then. What years, i' faith?
Viola. About your years, my lord.
Duke. Too old, by heaven! Let still the woman take
　　An elder than herself; so wears she to him,　　　　　30
　　So sways she level in her husband's heart:
　　For boy, however we do praise ourselves,
　　Our fancies are more giddy and unfirm,
　　More longing, wavering, sooner lost and worn
　　Than women's are.
Viola. 　　　　　　　I think it well, my lord.　　　　35
Duke. Then let thy love be younger than thyself,
　　Or thy affection cannot hold the bent:
　　For women are as roses, whose fair flower
　　Being once display'd, doth fall that very hour.
Viola. And so they are: alas, that they are so:　　　　40
　　To die, even when they to perfection grow!

---

34. worn] *F* (worne); won *Hanmer.*　　　38. flower] *F* (flowre).

30. *wears she to him*] 'adapts herself to him (as clothes to the wearer)' (Luce).

31. *sways she level*] exercises consistent influence. 'A quibble, "sways" = (a) holds sway, (b) swings. Hence "level", which means in perfect equipoise' (Wilson). Orsino's notion is that men become stable later than women and should therefore marry women younger than themselves, whose beauty will last longer and hence retain wavering affection.

34. *worn*] Much has been said on behalf of both F's reading and Hanmer's emendation *won*. Wilson, who takes 'worne' as a misreading of 'wonne', maintains that a contrast with 'lost' is wanted to suit the idea of inconstancy, and that '"worn" after "lost and" would be so violent a wrench from the expected as to constitute affectation'; Turner adds that 'the masculine affection that "cannot hold the bent" of love with an older woman presumably would be won by the beauty of another and younger rose', and that '"worn" as "consumed, worn out" (Malone) carries a sense of duration, however short, that does not accord with the context.' On the other hand, 'won', by the very fact of its antithesis with 'lost', suggests 'won back', an optimistic turn, whereas 'lost and worn' has a drooping movement in tune with the Duke's next speech and Viola's despondent reply. (Yet, again, such an optimistic turn might be Shakespeare's preparation for Orsino's final change of love from Olivia to Viola.) I retain 'worn' chiefly because of its pathetic tone and because Peele, *David and Bethsabe*, (Yale Edition, *Life and Works*, III) ll. 1061-2, has 'But if he [God] say my wonted love is worne, / And I have no delight in David now'.

37. *hold the bent*] literally, stand the strain ('bent' = the degree to which a bow can be bent without breaking); figuratively, remain ardent.

39. *display'd*] open, in full bloom.

Enter CURIO *and* CLOWN.

Duke. O, fellow, come, the song we had last night.
        Mark it, Cesario, it is old and plain;
        The spinsters and the knitters in the sun,
        And the free maids that weave their thread with bones
        Do use to chant it: it is silly sooth,   46
        And dallies with the innocence of love,
        Like the old age.
Clown. Are you ready, sir?
Duke. Ay, prithee sing.   *Music.* 50

                The [*Clown's*] *Song.*

        Come away, come away death,
        And in sad cypress let me be laid.
        Fie away, fie away breath,
        I am slain by a fair cruel maid:
                My shroud of white, stuck all with yew,   55
                O prepare it.

50. Ay, prithee] *F* (I prethee), *Theobald* (*subst.*), *conj. Thirlby²*.   53. Fie ...
fie] *F;* Fly ... fly *Rowe*.   55–8. *As Pope;* two lines in *F, ending* it. / it. /

43. *Mark it, Cesario*] Many have
contended that if Viola had 'heard'
(l. 3) 'the song we had last night',
and especially if she had sung it,
the Duke should not describe it now.

44. *spinsters*] women spinning flax
or wool.

45. *free*] care-free.

bones] bone bobbins for lace-
making.

46. *silly sooth*] simple truth.

47. *dallies with*] dwells lovingly on.

48. *the old age*] the golden age, when
all was simplicity and sincerity.

50. S.D. The [Clown's] Song] No
contemporary musical setting is
known.

51. Come away] Make haste hither.

52. sad cypress] (1) a coffin of
cypress wood. More probable than
(2) a bier strewn with branches of
cypress (but cf. 'my black coffin', l.
60), or (3) a shroud of Cyprus

(spelled cypress) lawn (but cf. 'my
shroud of white', l. 55; 'sad cypress'
would be black).

53. Fie away] Hotson (p. 144)
defends F's 'Fye' as meaning 'Get
thee gone, loathsome life!' as opposed
to 'Come, sweet death!' In a footnote
he gives other instances of the idiom.
Seng (p. 112) notes that 'in Thomas
Ravenscroft's *Melismata* (1611, sig.
C2) occurs a song titled "The
Mistris to the Courtier" which begins
with a line that may support the
Folio reading: "Fie away, fie away,
fie, fie, fie."' Doubtless Rowe was
unaware of the fact that 'Fie away'
(i.e., begone, for shame) was Elizabethan usage. His reading has the
merit of giving an antithetical verb
('Fly away') after 'Come away',
but, since both 'Come away' and 'Fie
away' are idiomatic, there is sufficient
antithesis to justify retaining the
reading of F.

> *My part of death no one so true*
> *Did share it.*

> *Not a flower, not a flower sweet,*
> *On my black coffin let there be strewn:*   60
> *Not a friend, not a friend greet*
> *My poor corpse, where my bones shall be thrown:*
> *A thousand thousand sighs to save,*
> *Lay me, O where*
> *Sad true lover never find my grave,*   65
> *To weep there.*

Duke. There's for thy pains.   [*Giving him money.*]

Clown. No pains, sir, I take pleasure in singing, sir.

Duke. I'll pay thy pleasure then.

Clown. Truly sir, and pleasure will be paid, one time or   70
another.

Duke. Give me now leave to leave thee.

Clown. Now the melancholy god protect thee, and the
tailor make thy doublet of changeable taffeta, for

63–6.] *As Pope; two lines in F, ending* where | there. | 65. true lover] *F;* true-
love *Capell.*   67. [*Giving him money.*]] *Collier²; not in F.*   72. Give . . .
thee.] *F (reading* leaue, to)*; I give thee now leave to leave me. Harness;* Give
me now leave. | *Clo.* To leave thee!—*conj. Macdonald apud Camb.²*   73. *Clown.*
Now] *F (reading* Clo.)*; Now conj. Macdonald loc. cit.*

57–8. My part of death . . . share
it] No one so true as I did ever share
my allotted portion, death (=I am
the truest lover who ever died of love).

60. strewn] pronounced to rhyme
with 'thrown'.

61. greet] salute. Mahood explains as 'bewail', and regards its
already archaic use in a transitive
sense as an 'antique' feature of the
song, but this makes it incongruous
with the rest of the diction.

65. Sad true lover] Though Capell's
emendation regularizes the metre,
the F reading could no doubt be
fitted to whatever tune was used.

70. *paid*] paid for (with pain);
proverbial (cf. Tilley, P408, 412,
413, 419, 420).

72. *Give . . . leave thee*] a polite

dismissal, Orsino being not in the
mood to listen to the Clown's replies.
Hence Feste's jest about 'the melancholy god' (=Saturn).

74. *changeable taffeta*] shot silk, its
contrasted colours of warp and woof
producing an opalescent effect of
changing colour with the light. H. F.
Brooks points out to me that in
Lyly's prose works 'changeable silk'
is associated with love and with
changes of mind: *Euphues* (Lyly, I,
225), 'you haue giuen vnto me a
true loues knot wrought of chaunge-
able silke'; *Euphues and his England*
(Lyly, II, 93), 'as our changeable silk, turned to yᵉ Sunne hath
many coulours, and turned backe the
contrary, so wit shippeth [*for* shapeth]
it self to euery conceit being constant
in nothing but inconstancie.'

thy mind is a very opal. I would have men of   75
such constancy put to sea, that their business
might be everything, and their intent everywhere,
for that's it that always makes a good voyage of
nothing. Farewell.   *Exit.*
Duke. Let all the rest give place.   [*Exeunt Curio and others.*]
      Once more, Cesario,   80
Get thee to yond same sovereign cruelty.
Tell her my love, more noble than the world,
Prizes not quantity of dirty lands;
The parts that fortune hath bestow'd upon her,
Tell her I hold as giddily as fortune: 85
But 'tis that miracle and queen of gems
That nature pranks her in, attracts my soul.
Viola. But if she cannot love you, sir?
Duke. I cannot be so answer'd.
Viola.   Sooth, but you must.
Say that some lady, as perhaps there is,   90
Hath for your love as great a pang of heart
As you have for Olivia: you cannot love her:
You tell her so. Must she not then be answer'd?
Duke. There is no woman's sides
Can bide the beating of so strong a passion   95
As love doth give my heart; no woman's heart
So big, to hold so much: they lack retention.

80. [*Exeunt Curio and others.*]] *Capell (subst.)*; not in F.   89. I] *Hanmer*; It F.

75–9. *I would . . . nothing*] ironical, meaning that men so variable in their moods would suit the variable moods of the sea, which would take them hither and thither about their profitable business. 'Makes a good voyage of nothing' is ambiguous: (1) turns 'nothing' to good account, (2) turns everything to bad account. Kittredge quotes Guazzo, *Civile Conversation* (1586): 'The Proverbe, That he is not any where, who is everie where' (cf. Tilley, E194).

82. *the world*] the mass of mankind, with their worldly values.

84. *parts*] endowments (wealth and nobility).

85. *giddily*] lightly; Fortune so regards them because she is fickle.

86. *that miracle . . . gems*] her beauty.

87. *pranks*] adorns.

89. *I*] Viola's reply shows that Hanmer's emendation is right.

94–104. *There is no . . . And that I owe Olivia*] Lyly (*Endimion*, v. i. 147–9) similarly makes Eumenides affirm man's superior capacity for love (in this case for a male friend): 'doe not that wrong to the setled friendship of a man, as to compare it with the light affection of a woman.' I owe this reference to H. F. Brooks.

97. *retention*] (medical metaphor)

Alas, their love may be call'd appetite,
No motion of the liver, but the palate,
That suffers surfeit, cloyment, and revolt;   100
But mine is all as hungry as the sea,
And can digest as much. Make no compare
Between that love a woman can bear me
And that I owe Olivia.
Viola.   Ay, but I know—
Duke. What dost thou know?   105
Viola. Too well what love women to men may owe:
In faith, they are as true of heart as we.
My father had a daughter lov'd a man,
As it might be perhaps, were I a woman,
I should your lordship.
Duke.   And what's her history?   110
Viola. A blank, my lord: she never told her love,
But let concealment like a worm i' th' bud
Feed on her damask cheek: she pin'd in thought,
And with a green and yellow melancholy
She sat like Patience on a monument,   115
Smiling at grief. Was not this love indeed?
We men may say more, swear more, but indeed

---

100. suffers] *Rowe;* suffer *F.*   104. know—] *Rowe;* know. *F.*

'the body's power to retain its proper contents' (Wilson: cf. *OED*, 1a, b); cf. 'digest', l. 102.

99. *motion*] emotion; cf. l. 18, and, for 'liver', I. i. 37.

100. *surfeit, cloyment, and revolt*] a revulsion from the food on which it has fed till it is full and weary of it; cf. *2H4*, I. iii. 88, 'Their over-greedy love hath surfeited', etc.

104. *owe*] have for; cf. l. 106.

113. *damask cheek*] an image of colour (as always in Shakespeare) not of texture: in *AYL.*, III. i. 119–22, Phebe describes the colour of Rosalind's lip as 'A little riper and more lusty red / Than that mix'd in his cheek; 'twas just the difference / Betwixt the constant red and mingled damask'. Hence a pink produced by mixing 'red and white'; cf. I. v. 242–3. *thought*] sadness.

114. *green and yellow*] pallid; cf. 'greensickness', *Rom.*, III. v. 157.

115–16. *like Patience . . . grief*] It is Patience, not the pining girl, who smiles; cf. *Per.*, v. i. 137–8, 'Like Patience gazing on kings' graves, and smiling / Extremity out of act'. Renaissance representations of Patience, sometimes as a funerary monument, are reproduced in W. S. Heckscher, 'Shakespeare in his Relationship to the Visual Arts', *Research Opportunities in Renaissance Drama: the Report of the Modern Language Association Seminar* (ed. S. Schoenbaum), nos. 13–14 (1970–1), esp. pp. 35–56.

Our shows are more than will: for still we prove
Much in our vows, but little in our love.
Duke. But died thy sister of her love, my boy?   120
Viola. I am all the daughters of my father's house,
And all the brothers too: and yet I know not.
Sir, shall I to this lady?
Duke.   Ay, that's the theme.
To her in haste; give her this jewel; say
My love can give no place, bide no denay. *Exeunt.*   125

SCENE V

Enter SIR TOBY, SIR ANDREW, *and* FABIAN.

Sir To. Come thy ways, Signior Fabian.
Fabian. Nay, I'll come: if I lose a scruple of this sport,
let me be boiled to death with melancholy.
Sir To. Would'st thou not be glad to have the niggardly
rascally sheep-biter come by some notable shame?   5

Scene v
SCENE v] F (*Scena Quinta.*).   [*Location.*] *Olivia's Garden.* Pope.

118. *Our shows are more than will*]
we profess more than we feel.
   still] always.
   121. *I am . . . father's house*] H. F.
Brooks compares the riddling dialogue in Lyly's *Gallathea*, III. ii, between Phillida and Gallathea, both
disguised as boys, and each in love
with the other supposed boy but
fearing that he may be (like herself)
a girl disguised: '*Phil.* My father
had but one daughter, and therefore
I could have no sister.'
   125. *give . . . denay*] not hold itself
back, endure no denial.

Scene v
1. *Come thy ways*] Come along,
come on; cf. II. iv. 51, 'Come away',
and I. v. 25, 'go thy way'.

3. *boiled . . . melancholy*] 'Fabian
jests; melancholy being a cold
humour' (Wilson).
   5. *sheep-biter*] *OED* gives four senses:
(1) 'A dog that bites or worries
sheep', (2) (figuratively) (a) '? A
malicious or censorious fellow', (b)
'A shifty, sneaking, or thievish
fellow', (3) 'A great mutton-eater'
(literally), (4) 'One who runs after
"mutton"; a woman-hunter, whore-
monger'. The *Tw.N.* quotation is
given under (2), following one from
Nashe, both probably intended in
the sense (2a); for 'sheep-biting face',
Meas., v. i. 352, see J. W. Lever's
note on this in his Arden ed., p. 141,
which suggests that 'sheep-biter' was
applied to a hypocritical Puritan,
and therefore this may be Sir Toby's
meaning (cf. II. iii. 140).

Fabian. I would exult, man: you know he brought me
out o' favour with my lady, about a bear-baiting
here.

Sir To. To anger him we'll have the bear again, and we
will fool him black and blue—shall we not,   10
Sir Andrew?

Sir And. And we do not, it is pity of our lives.

Enter MARIA.

Sir To. Here comes the little villain. How now, my
metal of India?

Maria. Get ye all three into the box-tree. Malvolio's   15
coming down this walk; he has been yonder i' the
sun practising behaviour to his own shadow this
half hour: observe him, for the love of mockery;
for I know this letter will make a contemplative
idiot of him. Close, in the name of jesting! [*As the men*   20
hide, she drops a letter.] Lie thou there: for here comes
the trout that must be caught with tickling.   *Exit.*

---

14. metal] *F* (Mettle), *Malone;* Nettle *F2.*   20. jesting!] *Theobald;* ieasting, *F.*
20-1. [*As the men hide, she drops a letter.*]] *Alexander; Men hide themselves.* [*after*
jesting!] *Capell; Throws down a letter, and | Theobald* [*before l. 22 Exit.*]; *not in F.*

7. *bear-baiting*] of which Puritans
(cf. II. iii. 140) disapproved.

10. *fool him black and blue*] be-
labour Malvolio with our mockery
(by means of the letter: preparing for
Maria's entry), besides angering him
by restoring bear-baiting: cf. (literally) 'beaten black and blue', *Wiv.,*
IV. v. 104, 'pinch us black and blue',
Err., II. ii. 191, and (figuratively)
Wiv., IV. v. 92, 'whip me with their
fine wits'. This note is needed only
because Wilson takes the phrase to
refer to the bear.

12. *it is pity of our lives*] It is a shame
that we should live; cf. *MND.,* III. i.
41.

14. *metal of India*] gold (complimentary metaphor); cf. *1 H4,* III. i.
168-9, 'bountiful / As mines of India';

Donne, 'The Sun Rising', st. 2,
where he calls his mistress 'both
th'Indias, of spice and mine' (i.e.,
the East and West Indies); and *Wiv.,*
I. iii. 65 (Falstaff of Mistress Page),
'She bears the purse too; she is a
region in Guiana, all gold and
bounty . . . they shall be my East and
West Indies, and I will trade to them
both.'

19-20. *contemplative idiot*] vacuous
fool.

20. *Close*] Keep close, lie hidden.

22. *trout . . . tickling*] Trout can be
literally so caught. For the proverbial
sense, cf. Tilley, T537, and Marston,
Antonio and Mellida, II. i. 115-17,
'How he tickles yon trout under the
gills! You shall see him take him by
and by with groping flattery.'

Enter MALVOLIO.

Mal. 'Tis but fortune, all is fortune. Maria once told
me she did affect me, and I have heard herself
come thus near, that should she fancy, it should   25
be one of my complexion. Besides, she uses me
with a more exalted respect than any one else that
follows her. What should I think on't?

Sir To. Here's an overweening rogue!

Fabian. O, peace! Contemplation makes a rare turkey-   30
cock of him: how he jets under his advanced
plumes!

Sir And. 'Slight, I could so beat the rogue!

Sir To. Peace, I say!

Mal. To be Count Malvolio!   35

Sir To. Ah, rogue!

Sir And. Pistol him, pistol him!

Sir To. Peace, peace!

Mal. There is example for't. The Lady of the Strachy

29. *Sir To.*] F; *Sir To. [Aside.] Capell (subst.), and so for Sir Toby, Sir Andrew,
Fabian, to l. 138.*   34. *Sir To.*] F (*To.*); *Fabian. N.C.S., conj. Camb.*   38. *Sir To.*]
F (*To.*); *Fabian. N.C.S., conj. Camb.*   39. the Strachy] F (the *Strachy*); the
Starchy *conj. Steevens (Var. '78)*; the Strozzi *conj. Collier*; the Duchy *conj. Bailey*;
the Stracci *Douai MS., conj. Lloyd apud Camb.*

24. *she*] Olivia.

did affect me] admired me.

25. *fancy*] fall in love.

26. *complexion*] colouring; cf. II. iii.
158, II. iv. 26. The word can also
mean 'temperament, disposition', but
the parallel passages show that this
is not so here.

28. *follows her*] is in her service.

29. *Here's . . . rogue*] Though this
and the other hearers' interjections
are not heard by Malvolio, they constitute so complete a dialogue that
to treat them as 'asides' would be
somewhat misleading.

30–2. *a rare turkey-cock . . . advanced
plumes*] a proverbial image of self-
importance (cf. Tilley, T612, and
H5, v. i. 14, 'swelling like a turkey-
cock').

31. *jets*] struts.

advanced] uplifted. In stage productions Malvolio is often given a tall
hat with a large feather for this out-
door scene, to make the imagery
visual.

34, 38. Sir To.] Wilson regarded
the conjectural assignment of these
speeches to Fabian as 'only logical'.
This is precisely the objection to it:
it is *merely* logical to give Fabian all
the calls for quiet, and it destroys
the humour of Sir Toby's insisting
on quiet from Sir Andrew and finally
even (ll. 85–6) from Fabian. Wilson
likewise conjectured that the prefixes
of ll. 84 and 85 should be trans-
posed but did not press his case to its
logical conclusion by making the
transposition.

39–40. *The Lady . . . wardrobe*]
This 'example' was possibly in-

married the yeoman of the wardrobe.   40

Sir And. Fie on him, Jezebel!

Fabian. O peace! now he's deeply in: look how imagination blows him.

Mal. Having been three months married to her, sitting
in my state—   45

Sir To. O for a stone-bow to hit him in the eye!

Mal. Calling my officers about me, in my branched
velvet gown, having come from a day-bed, where
I have left Olivia sleeping—

Sir To. Fire and brimstone!   50

Fabian. O peace, peace!

Mal. And then to have the humour of state; and after a
demure travel of regard, telling them I know my
place, as I would they should do theirs, to ask for
my kinsman Toby.   55

Sir To. Bolts and shackles!

Fabian. O peace, peace, peace! Now, now!

45. state—] *Pope; state.F.*   49. sleeping—] *Capell; sleeping.F.*   53. travel]
F (trauaile).   55. Toby.] *F* (*Toby*.); Toby—*Rowe.*

vented by Shakespeare to supply
Malvolio's need for one, since no
satisfactory historical or literary
allusion has been traced, despite every
conceivable conjecture that 'Strachy'
may be an error for some other word.
It is most unlikely that some socially
unequal marriage should be universally familiar to Shakespeare's
audience and totally undiscoverable
now. Sisson's suggestion, 1, 188–91
(summarized by Wilson, N.C.S. ed.
1949), that the allusion is to some
association between the wife of
William Strachy, a shareholder in
the Blackfriars theatre in 1606, and to
David Yeomans, at that time 'tireman' of the same theatre, is no more
probable than the rest. Cf. I. iii. 124,
'Mistress Mall's picture'.

41. *Jezebel*] King Ahab's proud
widow, who 'painted her face, and
tired her head, and looked out at a
window' to abuse Jehu, but was by
his command thrown down and

killed, and was eaten by dogs (2
Kings, ix. 30–7). Sir Andrew has
evidently picked up the phrase 'as
proud as Jezebel' but knows nothing
of the story.

43. *blows*] swells, puffs up.

45. *state*] chair of state, throne.

46. *stone-bow*] cross-bow which
shoots small stones, catapult.

47. *branched*] ornamented with em-
broidery representing leafy branches.

48. *day-bed*] couch.

52. *to have . . . state*] to indulge my
taste for authority.

53. *demure travel of regard*] grave
survey of those present.

55. *Toby*] familiarly dropping the
'Sir', cf. l. 61; and l. 68, where Sir
Toby uses this form to mark his indignation (see N.C.S. reading, which
emphasizes this).

56. *Bolts and shackles*] fetters (for
Malvolio); cf. *Meas.*, v. i. 345, 'Away
with him to prison! Lay bolts enough
upon him.'

Mal. Seven of my people, with an obedient start, make
　　out for him. I frown the while, and perchance
　　wind up my watch, or play with my [*Touching his*　60
　　chain]—some rich jewel. Toby approaches; curtsies
　　there to me—

Sir To. Shall this fellow live?

Fabian. Though our silence be drawn from us with cars,
　　yet peace!　　　　　　　　　　　　　　　　　65

Mal. I extend my hand to him thus, quenching my
　　familiar smile with a austere regard of control—

Sir To. And does not Toby take you a blow o' the
　　lips then?

Mal. Saying, 'Cousin Toby, my fortunes having cast me　70
　　on your niece give me this prerogative of speech'—

Sir To. What, what?

Mal. 'You must amend your drunkenness.'

Sir To. Out, scab!

Fabian. Nay, patience, or we break the sinews of our　75
　　plot.

Mal. 'Besides, you waste the treasure of your time with
　　a foolish knight'—

Sir And. That's me, I warrant you.

Mal. 'One Sir Andrew.'　　　　　　　　　　80

Sir And. I knew 'twas I, for many do call me fool.

60–1. my—some] *Collier;* my some *F;* some *F3.*　　[*Touching his chain*]] *N.C.S.*
(*subst.*), *conj. Nicholson apud Furness; not in F.*　62. me—] *Capell;* me. *F.*
64. cars] *F;* carts *conj. Johnson;* cords *White.*　67. control—] *Capell;* con-
troll. *F.*　　68. Toby] *F* (*Toby*); 'Toby' *N.C.S.*　71. speech'—] *Rowe;*
speech. *F.*　　78. knight'—] *Rowe;* knight. *F.*　80. Andrew.'] *F* (*Andrew.*);
Andrew'—*Theobald.*

60–1. *my*—] Malvolio almost for-
gets that, as 'Count Malvolio', he
will no longer be wearing his steward's
chain.

64. *with cars*] with chariots or carts
(and horses). Johnson (conjecturing
carts) compares III. ii. 57–8, 'oxen and
wainropes cannot hale them together', and *Gent.*, III. i. 265, 'but a
team of horse shall not pluck that
from me.' Musgrove compares

Plautus, *Menaechmi*, l. 862. The
humour lies in the idea of silence's
being extorted by torments; contrast
Oth., v. ii. 308, 'Torments will ope
your lips'.

74. *scab*] a familiar insult; cf. *Ado*,
III. ii. 93, where Borachio puns on the
literal sense.

75. *break the sinews of*] figuratively,
hamstring or disable; not connected
with l. 64.

Mal. [*Seeing the letter*] What employment have we
    here?

Fabian. Now is the woodcock near the gin.

Sir To. O peace! and the spirit of humours intimate   85
    reading aloud to him!

Mal. [*Taking up the letter*] By my life, this is my lady's
    hand: these be her very C's, her U's, and her T's,
    and thus makes she her great P's. It is in contempt
    of question her hand.   90

Sir And. Her C's, her U's, and her T's: why that?

Mal. [*Reads*] *To the unknown beloved, this, and my good*
    wishes.

    Her very phrases! By your leave, wax. Soft! and
    the impressure her Lucrece, with which she uses   95

---

82. [*Seeing the letter*]] *This ed.; after l. 83 N.C.S. (subst.); not in F.*   87. [*Taking up the letter*]] *This ed.; after l. 83 Rowe (subst.); not in F.*   92. [*Reads*]] *Capell; not in F.*

82. *employment*] business; i.e., what is this paper doing here?

84. *woodcock*] a proverbially stupid bird (cf. Tilley, W746, 'As wise as a woodcock').

    gin] trap.

85–6. *the spirit . . . to him!*] May the impulse that governs eccentric behaviour inspire him to read aloud! Shakespeare is aware that it is unlikely that Malvolio would do so, and therefore demands a willing suspension of disbelief from his audience.

88–9. *her very C's . . . great P's*] There is no C or P in the superscription of the letter. This fact, and the emphasis given by Sir Andrew's unanswered question, show that (as Wilson points out, N.C.S. ed. 1949, with examples) in order to make Malvolio ridiculous an indecent joke was introduced, 'cut' being the female genital organ (probably derived not from Lat. *cunnus* or Fr. *con*, but from Engl. 'cut', *OED*, *sb.*², iv. 20.b, a narrow passage for water, a strait; cf. 'water gap', used with indecent innuendo in

Angel Day's *English Secretorie* 1586, quoted by J. G. McManaway in *N. & Q.* (1951), p. 134), and 'pee' being a long-established euphemism for 'piss'. Though not explained in print till the twentieth century, the joke was clear much earlier: 'I am afraid some very coarse and vulgar appellations are meant to be alluded to by these capital letters' (Blackstone, in Var. '93). Wilson, who departed from F in printing c, u, and t as lower-case letters, showed that he still missed the full sense of 'her great P's', 'great' meaning 'copious' in the innuendo.

89–90. *in contempt of question*] so certainly as to make any doubt ridiculous.

94. *Soft!*] an exclamation of surprise or caution as he examines the seal.

95. *her Lucrece*] a seal-ring bearing the image of Lucretia, probably in the act of stabbing herself (having been raped by Tarquin); cf. l. 107, 'a Lucrece knife'.

to seal: 'tis my lady! To whom should this be?

[*He opens the letter.*]

Fabian. This wins him, liver and all.

Mal. [*Reads*]   *Jove knows I love;*
                        But who?
                        Lips, do not move,   100
                        No man must know.

'No man must know'! What follows? The numbers
altered! 'No man must know'!—If this should
be thee, Malvolio!

Sir To. Marry, hang thee, brock!   105

Mal. [*Reads*]   *I may command where I adore;*
                   But silence, like a Lucrece knife,
                   With bloodless stroke my heart doth gore;
                   M.O.A.I. doth sway my life.

Fabian. A fustian riddle!   110

Sir To. Excellent wench, say I.

Mal. 'M.O.A.I. doth sway my life.'—Nay, but first
let me see, let me see, let me see.

Fabian. What dish o' poison has she dressed him!

Sir To. And with what wing the staniel checks at it!   115

---

96. [*He opens the letter.*]] *N.C.S.; not in* F.   98. [*Reads*]] *Capell; not in* F.
98–101. *Jove knows . . . must know*] *As Capell; prose* (*who, Lips*) F.   106. [*Reads*]]
Capell; not in F.   106–9. *I may . . . my life*] *As Capell; two lines* (*knife: | With*) F.
114. *dish o'*] F (*dish a*) *; a dish of* Rowe.   115. *staniel*] *Hanmer; stallion* F.

97. *liver and all*] with passionate
conviction; cf. I. i. 37, and II. iv.
99.

102. *numbers*] versification.

105. *brock*] badger, a proverbially
stinking beast (cf. Tilley, B679).

109. *M.O.A.I.*] a sequence of letters
expressly designed to make Malvolio
interpret them as he does, thus pro-
longing the comic scene. Attempts to
wring further meaning from them
are misplaced (e.g., L. S. Cox in
Sh. Q., XIII (1962), p. 360, who finds
an anagram of 'I am O[livia]', or
Hotson (p. 166), who finds in them
the initials of 'the four elements':
'*Mare*—Sea [why not *Aqua*—Water?

ed.], *Orbis*—Earth [why not *Terra*?
ed.], *Aer*—Air, and *Ignis*—Fire').

110. *fustian*] bombastic, highflown
(*OED*, fustian, B., *adj.*, 2); cf. *2H4*,
II. iv. 203, 'fustian rascal'. Fabian is
commending the riddle as one fitted to
its recipient; Sir Toby is not disputing
but reinforcing his comment.

115. *staniel*] kestrel. F's 'stallion'
may have had dialectal currency
(*OED*, under staniel, this example
only), but it is unsafe to assume so, or
to propose a quibble on 'stallion'
(*OED*, 2.b.=a man of lascivious life),
which would not be in Sir Toby's
style.

checks at it] turns to fly at it (fal-
coners' term); cf. III. i. 65.

Mal. 'I may command where I adore.' Why, she may
   command me: I serve her, she is my lady. Why,
   this is evident to any formal capacity. There
   is no obstruction in this. And the end: what
   should that alphabetical position portend? If   120
   I could make that resemble something in me!
   Softly! 'M.O.A.I.'—

Sir To. O ay, make up that! He is now at a cold scent.

Fabian. Sowter will cry upon't for all this, though it be
   as rank as a fox.   125

Mal. 'M'—Malvolio! 'M'! Why, that begins my
   name!

Fabian. Did not I say he would work it out? the cur is
   excellent at faults.

Mal. 'M'—But then there is no consonancy in the   130
   sequel; that suffers under probation: 'A' should
   follow, but 'O' does.

Fabian. And 'O' shall end, I hope.

Sir To. Ay, or I'll cudgel him, and make him cry 'O'!

Mal. And then 'I' comes behind.   135

Fabian. Ay, and you had any eye behind you, you

---

119. this.] *N.C.S.;* this, *F.*   120. portend?] *Theobald;* portend, *F.*   121.
me!] *N.C.S.;* me? *F;* me—*Capell.*   131. sequel;] *Rowe;* sequell *F.*

118. *formal capacity*] right reasoning, normal intelligence.

119. *obstruction*] hindrance.

120. *position*] arrangement.

123. *O ay*] a punning repetition of two of the letters in the riddle.

a cold scent] a point where the scent (of the quarry) becomes imperceptible.

124–5. *Sowter . . . fox*] The hound will 'give tongue' as though he had made a great discovery, though the scent (i.e., the clue to the riddle) is as strong as a fox's. *Sowter* = cobbler, and, as a dog's name, is not necessarily derogatory.

128–9. *the cur . . . faults*] referring to the proverb (Tilley, D460) 'The dog who hunts foulest hits [i.e., takes

the right course] at most faults.' A 'fault' is 'a cold scent' (l. 123).

131. *sequel; that . . . probation*] In F the lack of punctuation after 'sequel' is probably due to lack of space (the word ends the line). Wilson defends F's reading by interpreting 'suffers' as 'allows', but he overlooks the word 'under'. Punctuation is therefore required, making 'that' a pronoun standing for 'sequel', and giving the sense 'There is no consistency in what follows. That breaks down when one tests it' (Kittredge's paraphrase).

133. *And 'O' shall end*] Johnson interprets *O* as a hangman's noose (cf. l. 105). This is probable, since Sir Toby's next line gives the letter another sense.

might see more detraction at your heels than
fortunes before you.

Mal. 'M.O.A.I.' This simulation is not as the former:
and yet, to crush this a little, it would bow to   140
me, for every one of these letters are in my name.
Soft! here follows prose.

[*Reads*] *If this fall into thy hand, revolve. In my
stars I am above thee, but be not afraid of greatness.
Some are born great, some achieve greatness, and some*   145
*have greatness thrust upon 'em. Thy fates open their hands,
let thy blood and spirit embrace them, and to inure thyself
to what thou art like to be, cast thy humble slough, and
appear fresh. Be opposite with a kinsman, surly with
servants. Let thy tongue tang arguments of state; put*   150
*thyself into the trick of singularity. She thus advises
thee, that sighs for thee. Remember who commended thy
yellow stockings, and wished to see thee ever cross-*

---

143. [*Reads*]] *Capell; not in F.*   143–57. *In my stars . . . Farewell*] *F (in roman);
F3 (in italic).*   145. *born*] *Douai MS., Rowe; become F.   achieve*] *F2
(atcheeve); atcheeues F.*

---

137. *detraction at your heels*] mis-
fortune following you (as contrasted
with the fortunes you are pursuing).
Also, perhaps, referring literally to
the group of overhearers behind him.

139. *simulation*] disguise, hence
puzzle.

143. *revolve*] reflect. In stage performance the actor often pensively
turns round while reading this, to
get an easy laugh. Whether Shakespeare intended a visual pun cannot
be known.

145. *born*] Rowe's emendation is
proved correct by III. iv. 40 and
v. i. 369.

146. *open their hands*] make you a
generous offer.

147. *blood and spirit*] (synonymous)
ready courage.

148. *cast thy humble slough*] throw
off your humility (as a snake its old
skin).

150. *tang arguments of state*]
clang forth (as a bell) dignified sub-
jects (cf. II. iii. 148), especially those

discussed by 'politic authors' (ll. 161–
162). For the imagery, cf. *Ado*, III.
ii. 10–12, 'he hath a heart as sound
as a bell, and his tongue is the clapper;
for what his heart thinks, his tongue
speaks.'

150–1. *put thyself . . . singularity*]
assume the affectation of peculiar
conduct or dress; cf. *Wint.*, IV. iv.
740–2 (the Clown, of Autolycus in
Florizel's clothes), 'He seems to be
the more noble in being fantastical.
A great man, I'll warrant; I know by
the picking on's teeth.'

152–4. *Remember . . . I say,
remember*] These lines, and ll. 166–
168 below, are obviously inconsistent
with ll. 199–200. 'Probably the only
commendation is in this letter, and
Shakespeare shows us how Malvolio's
imagination does the rest' (Mahood).
Cf. ll. 23–6 above, where Malvolio
seems to be already indulging his
fancy.

153, 153–4. *yellow stockings, . . .
cross-gartered*] Cross garters were

*gartered: I say, remember. Go to, thou art made, if thou
desir'st to be so. If not, let me see thee a steward still,* 155
*the fellow of servants, and not worthy to touch Fortune's
fingers. Farewell. She that would alter services with
thee,*

> *The Fortunate Unhappy.*

Daylight and champaign discovers not more! 160
This is open. I will be proud, I will read politic
authors, I will baffle Sir Toby, I will wash off
gross acquaintance, I will be point-device the very
man. I do not now fool myself, to let imagination
jade me; for every reason excites to this, that 165
my lady loves me. She did commend my yellow
stockings of late, she did praise my leg being
cross-gartered, and in this she manifests herself
to my love, and with a kind of injunction
drives me to these habits of her liking. I thank 170
my stars, I am happy. I will be strange, stout, in
yellow stockings, and cross-gartered, even with

158–60. *thee,* | *the ... Unhappy.* | Daylight] *As Capell;* thee tht fortunate vnhappy
daylight *F.*   160. champaign] *Dyce* (champain)*;* champian *F.*

'hose garters, going acrosse, or over-
thwart, both above and beneath
the knee' (Junius, *Nomenclator*, 1585).
Both articles of dress seem chosen
for their conspicuousness rather than
for their significance. If both were
'probably old-fashioned' (Wilson),
Malvolio would not have worn them;
more probably they were associated
with jolly young bachelors. Hence
the incongruity in the often-quoted
remarks from Overbury's *Characters*,
1616 ('If he [a country gentleman]
goe to Court, it is in yellow stockings')
and Ford's *The Lover's Melancholy*,
1629, III. i ('As rare an old youth as
ever walked cross-gartered'); cf. also
the reference to 'yellow hose' in note
to II. iii. 77 *Peg-a-Ramsey.*

154. Go to] an emphatic exclamation, here equivalent to 'I tell you'.

thou art made] thy fortune is made;
you are a 'made man' (cf. *MND.*,
IV. ii. 18).

157. alter services] change social
places, i.e., take him for her 'lord
and husband' (cf. *Shr.*, Ind. ii. 104).
Thus Viola finally becomes her
'master's mistress', v. i. 325.

160. *champaign*] Flat open country
(*OED*, A. *sb.*, 2). The word comes
ultimately from Old French and is
accented on the first syllable, 'ch'
being pronounced as in 'church'.

discovers not more] shows things no
more clearly; i.e., the letter's meaning
is as clear as daylight.

162. *baffle*] treat with contempt;
literally, degrade from knighthood
by formal ceremony.

163–4. *point-device the very man*] the
very man described in the letter,
to the point of perfection (for deriva-
tion of 'point-device' see *OED*).

165. *jade*] deceive (as an unruly
horse which throws its rider).

170. *habits*] clothes.

171. *strange, stout*] firmly aloof.

the swiftness of putting on. Jove and my stars be
praised!—Here is yet a postscript. [*Reads*] *Thou
canst not choose but know who I am. If thou entertain'st*   175
*my love, let it appear in thy smiling, thy smiles become
thee well. Therefore in my presence still smile, dear
my sweet, I prithee.* Jove, I thank thee, I will smile,
I will do every thing that thou wilt have me.   *Exit.*

Fabian. I will not give my part of this sport for a   180
pension of thousands to be paid from the Sophy.

Sir To. I could marry this wench for this device.

Sir And. So could I too.

Sir To. And ask no other dowry with her but such
another jest.   185

Enter MARIA.

Sir And. Nor I neither.

Fabian. Here comes my noble gull-catcher.

Sir To. Wilt thou set thy foot o' my neck?

Sir And. Or o' mine either?

Sir To. Shall I play my freedom at tray-trip, and be-   190
come thy bond-slave?

Sir And. I' faith, or I either?

Sir To. Why, thou hast put him in such a dream, that
when the image of it leaves him he must run mad.

Maria. Nay, but say true, does it work upon him?   195

Sir To. Like aqua-vitae with a midwife.

Maria. If you will then see the fruits of the sport, mark
his first approach before my lady: he will come

---

173. Jove] *F* (Ioue,); God *Hudson coju. Halliwell.*   174. praised!—Here] *F*
(praised. Heere), *Theobald.*   [*Reads*]] *Collier; not in F.*   177. *dear*] *F2* (*deere*);
deero F; dear, O *N.C.S., conj. Daniel*   178. Jove,] *F* (Ioue.); *Hudson conj.*
Halliwell.

174. *praised!— Here*] so punctuated   See Introduction, pp. xxx–xxxi.
to show that it is the letter's message,
not the fact of its having a postscript,   190. *play*] wager.
for which he gives thanks.   *tray-trip*] a dice-game in which one
   177. dear] F's *deero* is a misprint.   must throw a three ('tray') to win.
   181. *pension . . . Sophy*] probably
suggested by the favours Sir Anthony   196. *aqua-vitae*] spirituous liquor.
Sherley and his brothers claimed they   Juliet's nurse found it necessary in
had received from the Shah of Persia.   situations of stress, *Rom.*, III. ii. 88,
                                                 IV. v. 16.

to her in yellow stockings, and 'tis a colour she
abhors, and cross-gartered, a fashion she detests:　200
and he will smile upon her, which will now be so
unsuitable to her disposition, being addicted to a
melancholy as she is, that it cannot but turn him
into a notable contempt. If you will see it, follow
me.　　　　　　　　　　　　　　　　　　　　　　　205

Sir To. To the gates of Tartar, thou most excellent
devil of wit!

Sir And. I'll make one too.　　　　　　　　　*Exeunt.*

208. *Exeunt.*] *Exeunt.* | *Finis Actus secundus. F.*

206. *Tartar*] Tartarus, hell; cf. *H5*,
ɪɪ. ii. 123.

ACT III

SCENE I

Enter VIOLA, *and* CLOWN [*playing on pipe and tabor*].

Viola. Save thee, friend, and thy music! Dost thou
    live by thy tabor?
Clown. No, sir, I live by the church.
Viola. Art thou a churchman?
Clown. No such matter, sir. I do live by the church,   5
    for I do live at my house, and my house doth stand
    by the church.
Viola. So thou may'st say the king lies by a beggar, if a
    beggar dwell near him; or the church stands by thy
    tabor, if thy tabor stand by the church.   10
Clown. You have said, sir. To see this age! A sentence

ACT III

Scene I

ACT III SCENE I] F (*Actus Tertius, Scæna prima.*).   [*Location.*] *A Garden. Rowe;*
Olivia's Garden. Pope.   S.D. [*playing on pipe and tabor*]] *Collier²; not in F.*
5. sir.] *Munro;* sir, *F.*   5–6. church, for] *This ed.;* Church: For *F.*   8. king]
F2; Kings *F.* lies] *F* (lyes)*; lives conj. Capell.*

S.D.] Most edd. add 'with a tabor'
(small side-drum); Collier adds the
pipe (which traditionally was played
with one hand while the other beat
time on the tabor; cf. the picture of
the clown Richard Tarlton in
Shakespeare's England, II, 259). Wilson
suggests that the Clown may entertain the audience with his music
before Viola enters.

2. *live by*] make your living by
(playing).

4. *churchman*] 'Viola is deliberately
[and playfully (ed.)] ironical, for
Feste must have been in motley'
(Ludowyk).

5. *do*] not emphasized (as Furness
argues) but part of a simple statement, as in next phrase.

8. *lies by*] lies with (sexually); cf.
OED, lie, *v.*, B.I. If, and 5 (=dwell).
Not a direct allusion to King
Cophetua, but probably indirectly
suggested by his story (mentioned by
Shakespeare, *LLL.*, IV. i. 65, *Rom.*,
II. i. 14, *2H4*, V. iii. 101). Capell's
'lives', sometimes defended as continuing the pun, is to be rejected,
because 'lies by' and 'stands by' are
new examples of play on words.

9. *stands by*] is maintained by.

74

is but a chev'ril glove to a good wit—how quickly
the wrong side may be turned outward!

Viola. Nay, that's certain: they that dally nicely with
words may quickly make them wanton.   15

Clown. I would therefore my sister had had no name, sir.

Viola. Why, man?

Clown. Why, sir, her name's a word, and to dally with
that word might make my sister wanton. But
indeed, words are very rascals, since bonds dis-   20
graced them.

Viola. Thy reason, man?

Clown. Troth, sir, I can yield you none without words,
and words are grown so false, I am loath to prove
reason with them.   25

Viola. I warrant thou art a merry fellow, and car'st for
nothing.

Clown. Not so, sir, I do care for something; but in my
conscience, sir, I do not care for you: if that be to
care for nothing, sir, I would it would make you   30
invisible.

Viola. Art not thou the Lady Olivia's fool?

Clown. No indeed sir, the Lady Olivia has no folly. She
will keep no fool, sir, till she be married, and fools
are as like husbands as pilchards are to herrings,   35

---

35. pilchards] *F* (Pilchers), *Capell.*

12. *chev'ril*] kid leather (Fr. *chevreau*),
which is soft and flexible (cf. *Rom.*,
II. iv. 80, where its stretchable quality
is mentioned, again in connection with
'wit').

14. *dally nicely*] play subtly. 'Dally'
leads on to 'wanton' because it was
sometimes used in amorous contexts,
e.g., 'Not dallying with a brace of
courtezans' (*R3*, III. vii. 74).

15. *wanton*] equivocal, licentious
(cf. 'wrong side', l. 13). Wilson prints
'want-one' at l. 19, alleging a pun on
'wanton' (unchaste) and 'want one'
(i.e., lack a name, i.e., a reputation):
improbable.

16. *had had*] had been given.

20-1. *words . . . disgraced them*]

'because now we have to make a
man give his bond if we are to feel
sure that he will keep his promise'
(Kittredge); cf. Tilley, M458 ('An
honest man's word is as good as his
bond').

33-4. *She will keep . . . be married*]
Wilson regards this as 'a hit at Cesario,
whose long interviews with Olivia
were the subject of domestic gossip'
(cf. II. i ii. 132-4), and 'your wisdom'
(l. 42) in the same light. But since
the spectators always think of Cesario
as Viola, they are not likely to see
things so much through the Clown's
eyes as this. More probably it is a
generalized allusion to marriage as
folly, cf. I. v. 19.

the husband's the bigger. I am indeed not her fool,
but her corrupter of words.

Viola. I saw thee late at the Count Orsino's.

Clown. Foolery, sir, does walk about the orb like the sun,
it shines everywhere. I would be sorry, sir, but   40
the fool should be as oft with your master as with
my mistress: I think I saw your wisdom there.

Viola. Nay, and thou pass upon me, I'll no more with
thee. Hold, there's expenses for thee.   [*Giving a coin.*]

Clown. Now Jove, in his next commodity of hair, send   45
thee a beard!

Viola. By my troth, I'll tell thee, I am almost sick for
one, [*Aside*] though I would not have it grow on
my chin.—Is thy lady within?

Clown. Would not a pair of these have bred, sir?   50

Viola. Yes, being kept together, and put to use.

Clown. I would play Lord Pandarus of Phrygia, sir, to
bring a Cressida to this Troilus.

Viola. I understand you, sir, 'tis well begged. [*Giving another
coin.*]

---

44. [*Giving a coin.*]] *Hanmer* (*subst.*); *not in F.*   48. [*Aside*]] *Camb.; not in F.*
54. [*Giving another coin.*]] *Collier*[2] (*subst.*); *not in F.*

39. *Foolery . . . like the sun*] developed from the proverb 'The sun
shines on all alike' (Tilley, S985).

40–2. *I would . . . mistress*] 'would'=
should: he means (1) that he enjoys
visiting Orsino's house, (2) that
Orsino is as given to foolishness as is
Olivia; cf. *1H4*, v. iii. 22, 'A fool go
with thy soul, whither it goes!' This
second meaning is emphasized by
'your wisdom', an ironic courtesy
title, implying that his hearer is yet
another fool.

43. *pass upon me*] 'the emphatic
word is "me"' (Wilson); he interprets
'make a fool of me', comparing v. i.
350 (where, however, the subject is
'This practice'). The phrase may
mean (1) pass judgment on me (cf.
Meas., II. i. 23, 'thieves do pass on
thieves'), or (2) make a thrust (here
figuratively): cf. *Ham.*, v. ii. 289–91,

Hamlet to Laertes, 'you do but dally; /
I pray you pass with your best
violence; / I am afeard you make a
wanton of me', where we have 'dally',
'wanton', and 'pass' in close association as in this scene, ll. 14, 15, 43.

45. *commodity*] consignment.

50–1. *Would not . . . put to use*] For
the metaphor of breeding money
like beasts, cf. *Mer.V.*, I. iii. 90–1;
'use'=usury, lending money for re-
payment with interest.

52–3. *Lord Pandarus . . . Troilus*]
alluding to the role of Pandarus,
Cressida's uncle, as go-between in
Troilus' courtship; cf. Shakespeare's
Troil. (written shortly after *Tw.N.*,
the story being familiar from
Chaucer's *Troilus and Criseyde*); and
All's W., II. i. 96–7, 'I am Cressid's
uncle / That dare leave two together.'

Clown. The matter, I hope, is not great, sir, begging but 55
    a beggar: Cressida was a beggar. My lady is
    within, sir. I will conster to them whence you
    come; who you are and what you would are out of
    my welkin. I might say 'element', but the word is
    overworn.   *Exit.* 60

Viola. This fellow is wise enough to play the fool,
    And to do that well, craves a kind of wit:
    He must observe their mood on whom he jests,
    The quality of persons, and the time,
    And like the haggard, check at every feather 65

65. And] *F;* Not *Rann, conj. Johnson.*

55–6. *begging but a beggar*] to introduce his next remark; not 'a reflec-
tion on the size of Cesario's coins'
(Wilson).

56. *Cressida was a beggar*] In Henry-
son's *Testament of Cresseid* (printed in
the sixteenth-century editions of
Chaucer's works) she became a leper
and joined a lazar-house. This theme
was used in Dekker and Chettle's lost
play *Troilus and Cressida* (1599) of
which only the 'plot' (or sequence of
stage-entrances) is extant, and includes 'Enter Cressida with beggars'.
Cf. *H5*, II. i. 74, 'the lazar kite of
Cressid's kind'.

57. *conster to them*] construe to them
(i.e., to those 'within' the house).

58–60. *out of my welkin . . . overworn*] 'Element' (as used here) meant
'particular region to which a thing
or creature belongs', as fish to water.
It had also come to be widely used
for air, hence 'sky' (cf. I. i. 26) or
'welkin' (cf. II. iii. 58). In Dekker's
Satiromastix (1601) the expression
'out of [one's] element', i.e., not one's
affair, or beyond one's capacity, is
twice ridiculed in I. ii, and also in
v. ii. See Introduction, pp. xxxi–xxxii.
'Welkin' can be, of course, an equally
affected synonym for 'sky' (cf. *LLL.*,
III. i. 62, Don Armado's 'By thy
favour, sweet welkin, I must sigh in
thy face'), and, since it lacks the

other sense of 'element', is deliberately
inappropriate here.

61–9. *This fellow . . . taint their wit*]
probably 'expressly written to compliment the actor who played Feste,
i.e., Robert Armin' (Wilson). Armin
replaced Kempe in *c.* 1599, and it is
probable, though not established,
that he was the original Clown in
Tw.N.

61. *wise enough . . . fool*] a compli-
mentary application of the proverb
'No man can play the fool so well as
the wise man' (Tilley, M321): cf.
Guazzo's *Civile Conversation* (1586),
'To plaie the foole well, it behooueth
a man first to be wise' (quoted by
Furness).

65–6. *And like the haggard . . . his
eye*] A haggard is a wild, untrained
hawk. Johnson comments on F's
reading: 'He must catch every
opportunity, as the wild hawk strikes
every bird. But perhaps it might be
read more properly, "*Not* like the
haggard". He must choose persons
and times, and observe tempers; he
must fly at proper game, like the
trained hawk, and not fly at large
like the unreclaimed "haggard" to
seize all that comes in his way.'
Others have argued that Viola
draws a distinction between the fool's
being continually on the look-out
for jests and his being discreet in

That comes before his eye. This is a practice
As full of labour as a wise man's art:
For folly that he wisely shows is fit;
But wise men, folly-fall'n, quite taint their wit.

Enter SIR TOBY *and* SIR ANDREW.

Sir To. Save you, gentleman.   70
Viola. And you, sir.
Sir And. Dieu vous garde, monsieur.
Viola. Et vous aussi: votre serviteur.
Sir And. I hope, sir, you are, and I am yours.
Sir To. Will you encounter the house? My niece is   75
   desirous you should enter, if your trade be to her.
Viola. I am bound to your niece, sir; I mean, she is the
   list of my voyage.
Sir To. Taste your legs, sir, put them to motion.
Viola. My legs do better understand me, sir, than I   80
   understand what you mean by bidding me taste my
   legs.

69. wise men, folly-fall'n, quite taint] *Capell* (folly-faln), *conj. Theobald²;* wise-mens folly falne, quite taint *F;* wise men's, folly fall'n, quite taints *Theobald;* wise men's folly, fall'n, quite taints *Malone.*   70. *Sir To.*] *F (subst.); Sir And. Theobald.*   72. *Sir And.*] *F (subst.); Sir Tob. Theobald.*   74. *Sir And.*] *F (subst.); Sir Tob. Theobald.*   75. *Sir To.*] *F (subst.); not in Theobald.*

uttering them. Her indulgent treatment of his jests at her expense, in their dialogue, lends support to this argument: directed at someone less indulgent, they would have been unseasonable. For 'check', cf. II. v. 115.

66. *practice*] profession.

68–9. *For folly . . . taint their wit*] His playing the fool with discretion is appropriate; but men reputedly sane, who fall into folly, give cause to call their intelligence in question.

74. *I hope, sir, . . . I am yours*] Sir Andrew is here allowed to understand French (contrast I. iii. 90–3, wherefore Theobald transferred his lines to Sir Toby) so that he can make this awkward and paradoxical reply.

75. *encounter the house*] 'This mock-ceremony is contemptuous. Viola gives as good as she gets' (Wilson, following Furness); but Sir Toby is naturally given to extravagant language (cf. I. iii. 129–31, II. iii. 55, III. iv. 222–56, etc.). Here he speaks as though the house itself were capable of motion.

77. *bound to*] ambiguous: (1) bound for, (2) obliged to. Viola's explanation confirms the first sense; otherwise she might be merely thanking Olivia for her invitation to enter.

78. *list*] boundary, furthest point (*OED,* list, *sb*³., II. 8).

79. *Taste*] try; cf. *1H4,* IV. i. 119, 'Come, let me taste my horse'.

80. *understand*] stand under, support (with quibble on 'comprehend', l. 81); cf. *Gent.,* II. v. 21–8.

Sir To. I mean, to go, sir, to enter.

Viola. I will answer you with gait and entrance; but we
 are prevented.   85

Enter OLIVIA *and* MARIA.

Most excellent accomplished lady, the heavens rain
 odours on you!

Sir And. That youth's a rare courtier: 'rain odours'—
 well.

Viola. My matter hath no voice, lady, but to your own   90
 most pregnant and vouchsafed ear.

Sir And. 'Odours', 'pregnant', and 'vouchsafed': I'll get
 'em all three all ready.

Olivia. Let the garden door be shut, and leave me to my
 hearing.   [*Exeunt Sir Toby, Sir Andrew, and Maria.*] 95
 Give me your hand, sir.

Viola. My duty, madam, and most humble service.

Olivia. What is your name?

Viola. Cesario is your servant's name, fair princess.

---

84. gait] *F* (gate), *Johnson*.   85. S.D. *Maria*] *Rowe; Gentlewoman. F.*   88–9.
courtier: 'rain odours'—well.] *F* (Courtier, raine odours, wel.), *Camb.* (*subst.*);
courtier—'Rain odours'—well! *N.C.S.*   93. all ready] *Malone;* already *F;*
[*Writing in his table-book*] add. *Collier*[2].   95. [*Exeunt . . . Maria.*]] *Rowe* (*subst.*);
Exeunt Sir Toby and Maria, Sir Andrew lingering before he, too, leaves. Mahood;
not in F.

84. *gait and entrance*] nouns corresponding to Sir Toby's verbs, l. 83.
It seems pointless to seek (with
Wilson) a pun on gate, *OED*, II. 8,
legal right to pasturage.

85. *prevented*] anticipated.

89. *well*] not an exclamation but
an indication that he has noted
(perhaps even written down) the
phrase; cf. *Mer.V.*, I. iii. 1, 2, 6,
where Shylock uses it to show that he
has mentally recorded the terms of
the bond.

91. *pregnant*] receptive.
 vouchsafed] kindly granted.

93. *all ready*] by heart, to use on a
suitable occasion.

95. S.D.] Mahood's direction prepares for III. ii. 4–8; but in practice

Sir Andrew's presence can distract
the audience from Olivia and Viola,
and it is hard to fix a point at which
he leaves. The scene works better if
ll. 96–7 are spoken as the others
move toward the exit.

96–7. *Give me . . . humble service*]
Olivia treats Cesario with unusual
courtesy, by offering to take his hand;
Viola insists on keeping her distance,
and probably kisses Olivia's hand,
perhaps kneeling to do so.

99–104. *servant*] Olivia's ll. 100–2
imply that it is a lie to call oneself
another's servant out of mere courtesy: she is wishing that Cesario
were her 'servant' in the romantic
sense (=lover); cf. Viola's description of Orsino as 'your servant'.

Olivia. My servant, sir? 'Twas never merry world   100
    Since lowly feigning was call'd compliment:
    Y'are servant to the Count Orsino, youth.
Viola. And he is yours, and his must needs be yours:
    Your servant's servant is your servant, madam.
Olivia. For him, I think not on him: for his thoughts,   105
    Would they were blanks, rather than fill'd with me.
Viola. Madam, I come to whet your gentle thoughts
    On his behalf.
Olivia.   O, by your leave, I pray you!
    I bade you never speak again of him;
    But would you undertake another suit,   110
    I had rather hear you to solicit that,
    Than music from the spheres.
Viola.   Dear lady—
Olivia. Give me leave, beseech you. I did send,
    After the last enchantment you did here,
    A ring in chase of you. So did I abuse   115
    Myself, my servant, and, I fear me, you.
    Under your hard construction must I sit,
    To force that on you in a shameful cunning
    Which you knew none of yours. What might you think?
    Have you not set mine honour at the stake,   120

---

112. lady—] *Theobald;* Lady. *F.*   114. you did here] *F* (you did heare),
Warburton, conj. Thirlby; (you did hear) *Hanmer.*

---

100. *'Twas never merry world*] a
conventional Elizabethan phrase for
contrasting unhappy present with
happier past.

101. *Since lowly . . . compliment*] Cf.
Tilley, C581 ('Complimenting is
lying').

106. *blanks*] either (1) blank sheets
of paper (cf. II. iv. 111, where the
empty sheet contrasts with the written
'history'), or (2) 'the metal discs
at the mint, known as blanks, which
when stamped with the royal face
became coin' (Wilson).

108. *by your leave*] Olivia politely
but firmly refuses to hear the Duke's
suit, and (l. 113, 'Give me leave')

insists upon speaking her thoughts
and wishes.

112. *music from the spheres*] heavenly
music inaudible to mortals (cf. *Mer.V.*,
v. i. 60–5), produced by the rotation
of the eight concentric spheres containing the planets and fixed stars;
cf. Plato, *Republic*, x, 14.

114. *enchantment . . . here*] See
Introduction, p. xlii, for a parallel
phrase in Belleforest's version of the
story. F's 'heare' was a common
spelling of 'here'.

115. *abuse*] wrong.

117. *hard construction*] adverse judgment.

120–2. *Have you not . . . think?*] The

And baited it with all th' unmuzzled thoughts
That tyrannous heart can think? To one of your
  receiving
Enough is shown; a cypress, not a bosom,
Hides my heart: so, let me hear you speak.
Viola. I pity you.
Olivia.   That's a degree to love.   125
Viola. No, not a grize: for 'tis a vulgar proof
That very oft we pity enemies.

122–6.] *As F;* That ... think? / To ... shown, / A ... heart: / So ... you. /
That's ... grize; / For ... proof, *N.C.S.*   124. Hides] *F;* Hideth *Globe, conj.*
Delius. my] *F;* my poore *F2.*

metaphor is from bear-baiting (cf.
Mac., v. vii. 1–2), the 'tyrannous
heart' being Viola's, who (Olivia
suggests) must despise her for the
openness of her passion.

  122–7. *That tyrannous . . . enemies*]
The lineation of F is followed here,
because, though it is almost certainly
wrong, its redistribution raises problems. Walker (subst.) proposed the
lineation adopted in N.C.S. for ll.
122–5. Furness (as usual) defends the
irregularity of metre on grounds of
Olivia's strong emotion. The emendations of Delius and F2 (l. 124) are
generally agreed to weaken the
passage. Turner (whose lineation
resembles that of N.C.S., except in
taking 'So, let me hear you speak' as
a short line) comments that, since the
passage 'is found in mid-column
z 1 b, where Compositor B would have
been under no obvious compulsion
to re-line to save space', the error 'is
probably the responsibility of the
scribe, who was misled by the shortness of [l. 122]'. Wilson's N.C.S.
arrangement creates a short line
('For 'tis a vulgar proof'), l. 126.
Hence his preceding and following
lines suggest that Shakespeare may
have intended 'grize' and 'enemies' to
rhyme: a couplet could be formed by
omitting ' 'tis a vulgar proof / That',
but there can be no justification for
making the omission, though the idea

of a couplet may have passed through
Shakespeare's mind, as a way of
concluding Viola's statement of the
situation, which Olivia (l. 128)
evidently takes as a final refusal. The
metrical problem suggests that
Shakespeare may have revised the
lineation in the 'copy' from which the
scribe worked. See Introduction, p.
xxi.

  122. *receiving*] perception.
  123. *cypress*] piece of thin (Cyprus)
linen or gauze.
  bosom] either (1) the part of the
dress which is worn over the bosom
(*OED, sb.,* 3. b), or (2) the bosom of
the body itself. Though it is possible
that Olivia is wearing 'cypress' of dark
colour in mourning for her brother,
it is preferable to take 'cypress'
metaphorically and 'bosom' in the
second sense: i.e., Olivia's heart is as
visible to Viola as if it were not concealed by flesh and blood but merely
by a thin veil, or as if she were wearing it 'on her sleeve' (cf. *Oth.,* I. i.
62–6). Wilson aptly compares *MND.,*
II. ii. 104–5, 'Transparent Helena!
Nature shows art, / That through thy
bosom makes me see thy heart'.

  125, 126. *degree, grize*] step (synonymous: cf. *Oth.,* I. iii. 200, 'a grise or
step').
  126. *vulgar proof*] common experience: cf. *Ado,* II. i. 160, 'This is an
accident of hourly proof'.

Olivia. Why then methinks 'tis time to smile again.
    O world, how apt the poor are to be proud!
    If one should be a prey, how much the better   130
    To fall before the lion than the wolf!   *Clock strikes.*
    The clock upbraids me with the waste of time.
    Be not afraid, good youth, I will not have you,
    And yet when wit and youth is come to harvest,
    Your wife is like to reap a proper man.   135
    There lies your way, due west.
Viola.   Then westward ho!
    Grace and good disposition attend your ladyship!
    You'll nothing, madam, to my lord, by me?
Olivia. Stay:
    I prithee tell me what thou think'st of me.   140
Viola. That you do think you are not what you are.
Olivia. If I think so, I think the same of you.
Viola. Then think you right; I am not what I am.
Olivia. I would you were as I would have you be.

139–40. Stay: / I] *Capell;* Stay: I *F.*   144. were as] *F* (were, as), *Pope.*

128. *Why then . . . smile again*] If my
love is hopeless, I must accept the fact
as cheerfully as I can.

129–31. *O world . . . the wolf!*]
'Olivia refers to herself rather than to
Viola—"Though you reject me, I've
something to be proud of—I have
fallen for a king among men"'
(Mahood).

133. *I will not have you*] Furness
conjectured 'have—', believing that
'Olivia's sentence, owing to her
emotion, is unfinished. To give these
words the meaning "I will not marry
you" represents Olivia as refusing an
offer before it is made.' But her line is
poignant half-jest: 'Be not afraid—I
won't [can't] force you to marry me.'

136. *There lies your way, due west.
. . . Then westward ho!*] Cf. Maria's
remark, I. v. 204, and Viola's answer.
'Westward ho!' was the Thames
watermen's call for passengers from
the City to Westminster. Wilson's
interpretation of 'due west' is perhaps

sentimental ('Cesario is the sun of her
life—about to set') and his explanation of 'Westward ho!' as directly
referring to her 'returning to her
king' over-elaborate. Hotson (p. 139)
explains 'due west' as alluding to the
supposed location of Olivia's and
Orsino's 'houses' in the great hall at
Whitehall, but this is mere specula-
tion.

137. *Grace . . . ladyship*] May God
bless you and give you peace of mind.

141. *That you . . . you are*] either (1)
That you think you are not in love
with a woman, but you are, or (2)
That you are behaving (in loving a
page) as though you thought you
were less nobly born than you are.

142. *If I think so . . . you*] Granted
that I may be wrong about myself, I
think you are not what you seem to be
(i.e., not a page but a young lord; cf.
I. v. 293–7).

144. *I would . . . you be*] I wish you
would return my love.

Viola. Would it be better, madam, than I am?   145
    I wish it might, for now I am your fool.

Olivia. [*Aside*] O what a deal of scorn looks beautiful
    In the contempt and anger of his lip!
    A murd'rous guilt shows not itself more soon
    Than love that would seem hid. Love's night is noon.—
    Cesario, by the roses of the spring,   151
    By maidhood, honour, truth, and everything,
    I love thee so, that maugre all thy pride,
    Nor wit nor reason can my passion hide.
    Do not extort thy reasons from this clause,   155
    For that I woo, thou therefore hast no cause;
    But rather reason thus with reason fetter:
    Love sought is good, but given unsought is better.

Viola. By innocence I swear, and by my youth,
    I have one heart, one bosom, and one truth,   160
    And that no woman has; nor never none
    Shall mistress be of it, save I alone.
    And so adieu, good madam; never more

---

147. [*Aside*]] *Staunton; not in* F.   157. thus with] F (thus, with), *Rowe.*

146. *for now . . . fool*] for now you are treating me like a fool (i.e., wasting my time). Wilson's further suggestion that Viola implies 'now I am fooling you' (i.e., presumably, by my false appearance) seems strained.

147–8. *O what a deal . . . his lip*] Similarly Demetrius' outright denial that he does or can love Helena increases her passion for him ('And even for that do I love you the more', *MND.*, II. i. 202), and Hermia's discouragement of Demetrius increases his love for her ('The more I hate, the more he follows me', I. i. 198). In Lyly's *Love's Metamorphosis*, III. i. 78, Montanus, speaking of Celia, makes it a principle that 'disdain increaseth desire'.

149–50. *A murderous guilt . . . noon*] Love, no more than murder, can be concealed. Both proverbial notions, 'Murder will out' and 'Love cannot be hid' (Tilley, M1315 and L500); dark-ness is (as usual) associated with obscurity and daylight with lucidity (cf. II. v. 160).

153. *thee*] Olivia's avowal of love is accompanied by a change to the second personal singular pronoun. *maugre*] despite. *thy pride*] the 'contempt and anger' of l. 148.

155–6. *Do not extort . . . cause*] Do not perversely seek out, in the fact that I am wooing you, an argument against your wooing me.

155. *clause*] premise (here only in Shakespeare).

156. *For that*] because.

157. *reason . . . fetter*] overcome that argument by this argument.

161. *And that no woman has*] Cf. Rosalind's 'And I for no woman', *AYL.*, v. ii. 81, 86, 96. But Viola proceeds to refine on the statement, making Olivia think one thing and the audience another.

Will I my master's tears to you deplore.
Olivia. Yet come again: for thou perhaps mayst move   165
    That heart which now abhors, to like his love.   *Exeunt.*

SCENE II

Enter SIR TOBY, SIR ANDREW, *and* FABIAN.

Sir And. No, faith, I'll not stay a jot longer.
Sir To. Thy reason, dear venom, give thy reason.
Fabian. You must needs yield your reason, Sir Andrew.
Sir And. Marry, I saw your niece do more favours to the
    Count's serving-man than ever she bestowed upon   5
    me: I saw't i' th' orchard.
Sir To. Did she see thee the while, old boy, tell me that?
Sir And. As plain as I see you now.
Fabian. This was a great argument of love in her toward
    you.   10
Sir And. 'Slight! will you make an ass o' me?
Fabian. I will prove it legitimate, sir, upon the oaths of
    judgment and reason.

Scene II

SCENE II] *F* (*Scæna Secunda.*).   [*Location.*] *Olivia's House. Rowe.*   7. thee the]
F3; the *F.*   that?] *F2;* that. *F.*

2. *dear venom*] cajoling Sir Andrew out of his deadly resolution.

thy] 'Note Sir Toby's familiar second person, in which he always addresses Sir Andrew, and the respectful, and equally invariable, *you* of Fabian' (Furness).

6. *orchard*] garden.

9. *argument*] proof.

11. *'Slight*] by God's light.

12. *prove it legitimate*] make good my case, show it to be 'authorized by law' (*OED, a.,* 2).

13. *judgment and reason*] here apparently synonymous, since Fabian goes on to allege that Olivia's behaviour is capable, rightly judged, of the interpretation he puts on it.

Wilson offers the explanation, 'Three conditions were required, according to the theologians, of every lawful oath, viz. truth, judgment and reason or justice. Fabian purposely omits the condition of "truth".' He bases this upon his earlier reference (pp. 98–9) to a passage in a *Treatise of Equivocation,* where St Jerome is quoted as requiring 'truth, iudgement, and iustice' (following Jeremiah, iv. 2, 'in truth, in judgment, and in righteousness'). Wilson's interpretation seems strained, especially since it depends on his own use of 'reason' as a synonym for 'justice' in the quotation from St Jerome. Fabian, moreover, cannot be charged with suppressing 'truth',

Sir To. And they have been grand-jurymen since before
    Noah was a sailor.   15

Fabian. She did show favour to the youth in your sight
    only to exasperate you, to awake your dormouse
    valour, to put fire in your heart, and brimstone
    in your liver. You should then have accosted her,
    and with some excellent jests, fire-new from the   20
    mint, you should have banged the youth into dumb-
    ness. This was looked for at your hand, and this was
    balked: the double gilt of this opportunity you let
    time wash off, and you are now sailed into the north
    of my lady's opinion, where you will hang like an   25
    icicle on a Dutchman's beard, unless you do redeem
    it by some laudable attempt, either of valour or
    policy.

Sir And. And't be any way, it must be with valour, for
    policy I hate: I had as lief be a Brownist as a   30
    politician.

Sir To. Why then, build me thy fortunes upon the basis
    of valour. Challenge me the Count's youth to fight

since no one but Olivia could know as a fact what her motive was.

14–15. *And they . . . a sailor*] Grand-jurymen were required to decide whether the evidence before them warranted a trial by judge and jury. But there is still some inconsistency between Sir Toby's personification and 'oaths' (l. 12), since oaths come from witnesses: his word is therefore to be understood simply as a heightened synonym for 'true witnesses'; cf. his grand and comic hyperbole for 'from time immemorial'.

17–18. *dormouse valour*] 'Dormouse' not only intensifies 'awake' but is in comic juxtaposition with 'valour'; cf. *2H4*, III. ii. 158, Feeble as 'most magnanimous mouse'.

19. *accosted*] This can be made very comic if Sir Andrew visibly recalls what he thought he was told the word meant in I. iii. 58.

23. *double gilt*] double gilding (as of

gold-plated metal): Mahood compares the familiar phrase 'golden opportunity', which is humorously refined upon in Fabian's persuasive speech.

24–6. *sailed into the north . . . beard*] alluding metaphorically to Olivia's cold indifference, and topically to the Arctic voyage of the Dutchman, William Barentz, to Nova Zembla in 1596–7 (see Introduction, p. xxxii).

28, 30. *policy*] Fabian means 'clever stratagem', Sir Andrew 'despicable intrigue'; cf. 'politician', l. 31, and II. iii. 76.

30. *Brownist*] Robert Browne (*c.*1550–*c.*1633: see *D.N.B.*) had founded by 1581 a sect which became the Independents. Sir Andrew once again indulges his prejudice against Puritans (cf. II. iii. 141).

32. *build me*] build, found; the 'me' is merely intensive, cf. 'Challenge me', l. 33, and 'scout me', III. iv. 177.

with him, hurt him in eleven places: my niece
shall take note of it; and assure thyself there is no   35
love-broker in the world can more prevail in man's
commendation with woman than report of valour.

Fabian. There is no way but this, Sir Andrew.

Sir And. Will either of you bear me a challenge to him?

Sir To. Go, write it in a martial hand, be curst and   40
brief: it is no matter how witty, so it be eloquent
and full of invention. Taunt him with the licence of
ink. If thou thou'st him some thrice, it shall not
be amiss, and as many lies as will lie in thy sheet of
paper, although the sheet were big enough for the   45
bed of Ware in England, set 'em down. Go, about it.
Let there be gall enough in thy ink, though thou
write with a goose-pen, no matter: about it.

Sir And. Where shall I find you?

Sir To. We'll call thee at thy cubiculo. Go! *Exit Sir Andrew.*

---

46. down. Go, about it] *Capell;* downe, go about it *F.*   50. thy] *Hanmer, conj.*
Thirlby; the *F.*   cubiculo] *F (Cubiculo);* cubicle *N.C.S.*

---

40. *Go, write . . . hand*] Johnson
suggested that the martial hand
might be an unceremonious careless
scrawl, and Furness that it might be
one with aggressive flourishes.

40–1. *curst and brief*] fierce and curt.

41–2. *eloquent . . . invention*] power-
fully written and full of matter.

42–3. *with . . . ink*] (1) as freely as
can be done in writing, and also (2)
more freely than you would dare to
speak (probably Sir Toby's primary
meaning here).

43. *thou'st*] call him 'thou' (in-
sultingly); Sir Toby has just so called
Sir Andrew (in familiarity).

44. *lies*] charges of lying (the
unforgivable insult, automatically
provoking a duel).

46. *bed of Ware*] a famous large
carved-oak bedstead 10 feet 9 inches
square, now in the Victoria and
Albert Museum, London.

Go,] Capell's emendation is justified by the parallel command 'about
it' (l. 48); the meaning is the same as

in F (i.e., 'set about it'), but 'Go' gives
an additional impulse to the order
(i.e., 'begone').

47. *gall*] (1) oak-galls (of which ink
was made), (2) bitterness.

48. *goose-pen*] (1) goose-quill, (2)
the pen used by a 'goose', i.e., fool
(so usually in Shakespeare, sometimes
with the further imputation of
cowardice, as in *Lr.*, II. ii. 78, *Mac.*,
v. ii. 12).

50. *at thy cubiculo*] at your bedroom.
OED explains 'cubiculo' as 'either a
humorous use of Latin, from the
phrase *in cubiculo*, or affected use of
Ital. "*cubiculo*"'. Since Sir Andrew does
not go on to ask 'What's that?', the
word is probably meant to be current
Illyrian usage, and there seems no
need to emend to 'cubicle'. Hanmer's
emendation 'thy' does seem necessary,
since there would be more than one
such room in Olivia's house; and there
is nothing to suggest that Cubiculo is
the name of an inn or an inn-room
(Kittredge), since Sir Andrew appears

Fabian. This is a dear manikin to you, Sir Toby.　　　51

Sir To. I have been dear to him, lad, some two thousand
　　　strong, or so.

Fabian. We shall have a rare letter from him; but you'll
　　　not deliver't.　　　55

Sir To. Never trust me then: and by all means stir on the
　　　youth to an answer. I think oxen and wainropes
　　　cannot hale them together. For Andrew, if he were
　　　opened and you find so much blood in his liver as
　　　will clog the foot of a flea, I'll eat the rest of th'　60
　　　anatomy.

Fabian. And his opposite, the youth, bears in his visage
　　　no great presage of cruelty.

Enter MARIA.

Sir To. Look where the youngest wren of nine comes.

55. deliver't.] *F;* deliver't? *Dyce.*　　　64. nine] *Theobald;* mine *F.*

to be staying in Olivia's house (in
spite of I. iii. 16).

51. *a dear manikin to you*] a puppet
whom you enjoy manipulating.

52. *dear*] costly. Justice Shallow
had lent Falstaff 'a thousand pound',
2H4, v. iv. 74; Sir Toby claims to
have had twice the sum from Sir
Andrew (cf. II. iii. 182–6), unless he
means two thousand ducats (cf.
I. iii. 22).

57. *oxen and wainropes*] waggon-ropes
pulled by oxen.

59. *blood in his liver*] The liver was
supposed to be the source of the blood
(cf. *Shakespeare's England*, I, 146). Lack
of blood in the liver was therefore a
sign of cowardice; cf. *2H4*, IV. iii. 111,
Mac., v. iii. 15.

61. *anatomy*] body, considered as a
subject for anatomical demonstration;
cf. 'opened', l. 59. Perhaps also
referring to Sir Andrew's leanness;
cf. v. i. 205, 'a thin-faced knave,' and
Err., v. i. 237–8, where Pinch is called
'a hungry, lean-fac'd villain, / A mere
anatomy'.

64. *the youngest wren of nine*] 'The

last hatched, and therefore the tiniest,
of a brood of nine' (Wilson). Theobald's emendation. Though sometimes wrens lay as many as twice that
number of eggs (Willoughby, quoted
by Furness), Shakespeare elsewhere
mentions litters of nine ('her nine
farrow', *Mac.*, IV. i. 65; 'her nine-fold',
Lr., III. iv. 119). A weaker argument in
favour of 'nine' is that the phrase
'least (i.e., smallest) of nine' may have
been proverbial, but only one instance
has been produced, viz., 'Syr, that is
the lest care I have of nyne, / Thankyd
be God, and your good doctrine'
(John Heywood, *Johan Johan*, pr.
1533, ll. 353–4, in J. Q. Adams,
Chief Pre-Shakespearean Dramas, 1924:
see R. Chapman, *TLS*, 15 June 1946,
p. 283): there is every probability
that Heywood used it merely for its
rhyme (Turner notes that it is not
included in Heywood's *Proverbs* or
his *Epigrams*, pr. together in their
final enlarged form in 1562). Heywood's phrase may be contrasted
with Medwall's, the least care of
fifteen' (*Fulgens and Lucrece*, pr. *c.* 1519;

Maria. If you desire the spleen, and will laugh your-   65
  selves into stitches, follow me. Yond gull Malvolio
  is turned heathen, a very renegado; for there is no
  Christian that means to be saved by believing
  rightly can ever believe such impossible passages of
  grossness. He's in yellow stockings!   70
Sir To. And cross-gartered?
Maria. Most villainously; like a pedant that keeps a
  school i' th' church. I have dogged him like his
  murderer. He does obey every point of the letter
  that I dropped to betray him: he does smile his   75
  face into more lines than is in the new map with
  the augmentation of the Indies: you have not seen
  such a thing as 'tis. I can hardly forbear hurling

---

67. renegado] F (Renegatho), *Rowe.*   76. is] *F*; are *Var.* '93.

Part I, l. 1183, in F. S. Boas, *Five Pre-Shakespearean Comedies*, 1934). The objection to F's 'mine' is that Sir Toby has no other wrens; if 'of mine' is used without the sense of personal possession (cf. Fabian's 'Here comes my noble gull-catcher', II. v. 187), it sounds insufficiently idiomatic.

65. *spleen*] a fit of laughter. The spleen was supposed, among its other emotional functions, to govern laughter. See Furness for contemporary references, and cf. *LLL.*, III. i. 71, *Meas.*, II. ii. 122.

67. *renegado*] a deserter of his faith, especially of Christianity. The F spelling reflects the word's Spanish origin and Elizabethan pronunciation.

69–70. *impossible passages of grossness*] gross impossibilities. 'Impossible' seems to be a transferred epithet, whether 'passages' means (1) 'something that "passes", goes on, takes place, . . . an act . . .' (*OED*, sb., III. 13, citing this reference), or (2) an indefinite portion of a discourse or writing (*OED*, sb., III. 14, first in c. 1611). The reference is clearly to what Malvolio believed from reading the letter, i.e., that Olivia had written

it, was in love with him, and wished him to follow her instructions.

72.   *villainously*]   abominably. Shakespeare was fond of this colloquial sense of 'villainous' about this time (cf. its frequency in *1H4*, esp. II. iv. 392, 'a villainous trick of thine eye'; and cf. *Ham.*, III. ii. 42, of clowns' misbehaviour on stage, 'That's villainous.'

72–3. *pedant . . . i' th' church*] 'Schoolmaster who, having no school-house of his own, teaches in the church' (Mahood, who agrees with Wilson that such a custom was probably obsolescent). It suggests rusticity, the opposite to the smart appearance that Malvolio thinks he has.

76–7. *more lines . . . of the Indies*] the 'new map' of 1599 (see Introduction, p. xxxii), in which 'the Indies' (i.e., the East Indies) are 'augmented' (i.e., shown more fully than before), and which is covered with rhumb lines (hence Maria's striking comparison with the wrinkles produced by Malvolio's smiling; cf. *2H4*, v. i. 81–2, 'O, you shall see him laugh till his face be like a wet cloak ill laid up!').

things at him. I know my lady will strike him: if she
do, he'll smile, and take't for a great favour.   80
Sir To. Come bring us, bring us where he is.   *Exeunt omnes.*

SCENE III

Enter SEBASTIAN *and* ANTONIO.

Seb. I would not by my will have troubled you,
But since you make your pleasure of your pains,
I will no further chide you.
Ant. I could not stay behind you: my desire,
More sharp than filed steel, did spur me forth: 5
And not all love to see you (though so much
As might have drawn one to a longer voyage)
But jealousy what might befall your travel,
Being skilless in these parts: which to a stranger,
Unguided and unfriended, often prove   10
Rough and unhospitable. My willing love,
The rather by these arguments of fear,
Set forth in your pursuit.
Seb.   My kind Antonio,
I can no other answer make, but thanks,

Scene III

SCENE III] F (*Scæna Tertia.*).   [*Location.*] *The Street.* Rowe.   7. one] *F;*
me *Rann, conj. Heath.*

79. *strike him*] not at all probable, but the necessary build-up to the laugh-line that follows, and itself introduced by ll. 78–9.

Scene III

7. *one*] Dyce, who later emended to 'me', observed (1844, quoted by Furness) that 'one' for 'me' is a frequent error, giving an instance from Fletcher's *The Bloody Brother*, I. i. The emendation improves the passage (which is much concerned with Antonio's personal feelings), 'but, inasmuch as "one" makes tolerable

sense, the propriety of change is doubtful' (Furness).

8. *jealousy*] anxiety.

9. *skilless in*] unfamiliar with, a stranger in.

11. *Rough and unhospitable*] Hotson (pp. 151–2) points out that Illyria was noted for 'the lawless profession of piracy', and refers to ' "Bargulus, the strong Illyrian pirate" [*2H6*, IV. i. 108] and the Ragusan "Ragozine, a most notorious pirate" [*Meas.*, IV. iii. 67]', as well as to Orsino's addressing Antonio as 'Notable pirate, thou salt-water thief', v. i. 67.

And thanks, and ever thanks; and oft good turns   15
Are shuffled off with such uncurrent pay:
But were my worth, as is my conscience, firm,
You should find better dealing. What's to do?
Shall we go see the relics of this town?

Ant. To-morrow, sir; best first go see your lodging.   20

Seb. I am not weary, and 'tis long to night.
I pray you, let us satisfy our eyes
With the memorials and the things of fame
That do renown this city.

Ant.   Would you'd pardon me:
I do not without danger walk these streets.   25
Once in a sea-fight 'gainst the Count his galleys,
I did some service, of such note indeed,
That were I ta'en here it would scarce be answer'd.

15–16.] *Not in F2.*   15. thanks, and ever thanks; and] *Theobald;* thankes:
and ever *F;* thanks, and ever. Oft *Var. '73;* thanks, still thanks; and very *Collier²*.
20. lodging.] *F2;* lodging? *F.*   24. you'd] *F* (youl'd).   26. Count his] *F;*
County's *conj. Malone.*

---

15. *thanks, and ever thanks; and*] F's
line, defective in metre and in sense
('ever oft'), is obviously corrupt (as
the omission of ll. 15–16 in F2 and its
successors confirms). The three chief
forms of emendation are (1) simple repunctuation (Var. '73) which leaves
the metre defective; (2) emendation
of 'ever' to 'very' (Collier), which
retains F's punctuation (Collier also,
by adding 'still thanks', emends the
metre, but offers no explanation of
F's omission of 'still', a word which
does not appear elsewhere in F's line);
(3) repunctuation and insertion of
'thanks; and' (Theobald, on the
grounds of F's accidental omission of
two words that already occur twice
in the line). Theobald is followed in
this ed.; the error could have been
made either by scribe or by compositor, despite Sisson's assertion that
such a compositor would be 'entirely
incompetent' (I, 192: he adopts
emendation (1)).

16. *uncurrent pay*] worthless payment, as of counterfeit or debased
coin. Sebastian's whole expression of
gratitude (ll. 13–18) indirectly introduces the lending of Antonio's purse,
with the consequent complications in
III. iv. 342ff.

17. *worth*] wealth (cf. III. iv. 353,
'having').

conscience] sense of what I owe.

firm] real.

19. *relics*] antiquities (cf. ll. 22–3).

26. *Count his*] a familiar Elizabethan
form of the possessive, cf. Abbott,
§217: had Shakespeare written 'Duke
his', no one would have thought the
text defective.

28. *it would scarce be answer'd*]
scarcely any reparation I could make
would be accepted (cf. l. 33), i.e.,
they would insist on my death:
'answer'd' here has the double sense
of (1) atoned for, (2) defensible at
law; cf. 'answer it', III. iv. 341
(=stand my trial).

Seb. Belike you slew great number of his people.

Ant. Th' offence is not of such a bloody nature,   30
    Albeit the quality of the time and quarrel
    Might well have given us bloody argument.
    It might have since been answer'd in repaying
    What we took from them, which for traffic's sake
    Most of our city did. Only myself stood out,   35
    For which, if I be lapsed in this place,
    I shall pay dear.

Seb.   Do not then walk too open.

Ant. It doth not fit me. Hold, sir, here's my purse.
    In the south suburbs, at the Elephant,
    Is best to lodge: I will bespeak our diet,   40
    Whiles you beguile the time, and feed your knowledge
    With viewing of the town: there shall you have me.

Seb. Why I your purse?

Ant. Haply your eye shall light upon some toy
    You have desire to purchase: and your store,   45
    I think, is not for idle markets, sir.

---

29. people.] *F; people? Dyce.*

29. *Belike . . . people*] Sebastian, according to F's punctuation, is drawing an inference (natural enough after Antonio's speech), not asking a question, though it is equally natural that Antonio should explain the circumstances in his reply. He is thus shown to be a peaceable man by temperament (necessary in view of his intervention at III. iv. 319–25).

32. *bloody argument*] a subject for bloodshed.

34. *for traffic's sake*] for the sake of trade; more exactly, to restore the freedom of passage necessary to trade.

36. *be lapsed*] i.e., be apprehended. *OED*, lapse, *v.*, II. 8, conjectures that 'lapse' may here be a transitive verb, = 'to pounce upon as an offender, apprehend', with cross-ref. to 'Lap' *sb.*[1] 8 (error for 6), which seems to have the sense of 'trap', though sometimes written as 'lapse' in the plural. This is possible, and is accepted by Onions; but since Shakespeare else-

where normally uses the noun 'lap' in the sense of *OED*, *sb.*[1]5 (e.g., *Mac.*, I. iii. 4, 'had chestnuts in her lap'), and the verb 'lapse' in the sense of *OED*, I (intransitive verb, = to fall), the idea here is perhaps 'be fallen (into the hands of my foes)'. The sense is, in any case, the same however one accounts for the construction.

39. *the Elephant*] a common inn sign. Often (unnecessarily) taken as suggested by the Elephant and Castle at Newington 'in the south suburbs' of London, though Wright could not trace its existence further back than the middle of the seventeenth century. A. C. Southern, *TLS*, 12 June 1953, p. 381, informs us that an Oliphant Inn existed in 1598–9, in Southwark.

40. *bespeak our diet*] order our board: perhaps in playful antithesis to 'feed your knowledge', l. 41.

44. *toy*] trifle (as opposed to the necessities of life).

45–6. *your store . . . idle markets*] You

Seb. I'll be your purse-bearer, and leave you for
    An hour.
Ant.   To th' Elephant.
Seb.   I do remember.
                                    Exeunt [separately].

SCENE IV

Enter OLIVIA *and* MARIA.

Olivia. [*Aside*] I have sent after him, he says he'll come:
    How shall I feast him? What bestow of him?
    For youth is bought more oft than begg'd or borrow'd.
    I speak too loud.—
    Where's Malvolio? He is sad and civil,   5
    And suits well for a servant with my fortunes:
    Where is Malvolio?

47–8. you for | An] *Theobald;* you | For an *F.*   48. [*separately*]] *Mahood; not in F.*

Scene iv

SCENE iv] *F* (*Scæna Quarta.*).   [*Location.*] *Olivia's House. Rowe; Olivia's Garden. Capell.*   1. [*Aside*]] *Staunton; not in F.*   4–5.] *As Pope; as one line, F.*
5. Where's] *F;* Where is *Pope.*

have not enough ready money to spend on casual purchases.

Scene iv

1. *he says he'll come*] i.e., suppose he says he'll come (Theobald's explanation, though in fact he altered his text to 'say, he will come'). The messenger sent to seek Cesario does not return till l. 55. Yet it is quite possible to interpret Olivia's words literally, and ignore the inconsistency, in the theatre: in fact it is easier to speak them so, and difficult to make the conditional sense clear to an audience.

3. *bought . . . borrow'd*] proverbial; cf. Tilley, B783, 'Better to buy than to borrow [*or* to beg, *or* to beg or borrow]', who cites R. Taverner, *Proverbs* (translated from Erasmus), 1539, f. 13*v.*: '*Emere malo quam rogare.* I had lever bye, then begge', with comment 'Herby is signifyed that a thynge obteyned with moche sute and prayer, is in dede derely bought.' Tilley gives Shakespeare's form of the proverb ('better to buy than to beg or borrow') as first recorded in 1639.

4. *I speak too loud*] The shortness of the line emphasizes its character as an aside.

5. *Where's*] Pope's emendation 'Where is', though doubtless made for the sake of metrical regularity, is perhaps supported by the fact that the line almost fills the column in F; the compositor may have used the contraction to save space. Yet since F's reading cannot be disproved it is retained.

sad and civil] serious and well-governed.

6. *fortunes*] Olivia is thinking possibly of her bereavement, but principally of the 'sad . . . madness' of her unrequited passion, l. 15. We

Maria. He's coming, madam, but in very strange
    manner. He is sure possessed, madam.

Olivia. Why, what's the matter? Does he rave?   10

Maria. No, madam, he does nothing but smile: your
    ladyship were best to have some guard about you if
    he come, for sure the man is tainted in's wits.

Olivia. Go call him hither. [*Exit Maria.*] I am as mad as
    he
    If sad and merry madness equal be.   15

                Enter MALVOLIO [*with* MARIA].

    How now, Malvolio?

Mal. Sweet Lady, ho, ho!

Olivia. Smil'st thou? I sent for thee upon a sad occasion.

Mal. Sad, lady? I could be sad: this does make
    some obstruction in the blood, this cross-gartering;   20
    but what of that? If it please the eye of one, it is
    with me as the very true sonnet is: 'Please one,
    and please all'.

8–9.] *As Pope (prose); as verse* (He's . . . Madame: / But . . . Madam.) *F.*   14.]
As Capell; as two lines (Go . . . hither. / *Enter Maluolio.* / I . . . hee,) *F.* [*Exit
Maria.*]] *Dyce; Enter Maluolio. F.*   15. merry] *F3;* metry *F;* mercy *F2.*   S.D.
Enter Malvolio [*with Maria*].] *Dyce (subst.).*   18. Smil'st thou? . . . occasion] *As
F (prose); as verse* (thou? / I) *Capell.*   19–21. Sad . . . that?] *As Pope (prose);
as verse* (Sad . . . sad: / This . . . blood: / This . . . that?) *F.*

---

have heard nothing of her mourning
for her brother since I. v.

9. *possessed*] by the devil (preparing
for the development later in this scene
and in IV. ii).

14–15. *I am as mad . . . equal be*]
Since Malvolio 'does nothing but
smile', his madness is merry, hers sad;
cf. l. 6, and II. iii. 134 ('she is much
out of quiet') and II. v. 202–3
('addicted to a melancholy as she is').

18. *upon a sad occasion*] about serious
business (i.e., how to entertain
Cesario, cf. ll. 1–7).

19. *sad*] (1) serious, (2) melancholy
(which might be a result of 'obstruction in the blood', causing it to flow
slowly).

22. *sonnet*] lyric; cf. *Wiv.,* I. i. 180,

Slender's 'book of songs and sonnets'.

22–3. '*Please one, and please all*'] If
Malvolio can please one (Olivia), that
is for him as good as if he pleased all.
Halliwell identified the 'sonnet' as one
(S.R., 18 Jan. 1592) called 'A prettie
new Ballad, intytuled: The Crowe
sits vpon the Wall / Please one and
please all. To the tune of, *Please one
and please all.*' Nineteen stanzas follow
the heading, signed R. T. (Richard
Tarlton ?). Furness quotes six. The
first is: 'Please one and please all, / Be
they great be they small, / Be they
little be they lowe, / So pypeth, the
Crowe, / Sitting vpon a wall: / Please
one and please all. / Please one and
please all.' The theme is that all
women want one and the same thing

Olivia. Why, how dost thou, man? What is the matter
     with thee?   25
Mal. Not black in my mind, though yellow in my legs.
     It did come to his hands, and commands shall be
     executed. I think we do know the sweet Roman
     hand.
Olivia. Wilt thou go to bed, Malvolio?   30
Mal. To bed? Ay, sweetheart, and I'll come to thee.
Olivia. God comfort thee! Why dost thou smile so, and
     kiss thy hand so oft?
Maria. How do you, Malvolio?
Mal. At your request? Yes, nightingales answer daws!   35

24 *Olivia.*] F2 (*Ol.*); *Mal. F; Mar. conj. Collier.*   24–5.] *As Pope* (*prose*); *as*
verse (man? / What) *F.*   35. *As Capell* (*prose*); *as two lines* (request: / Yes) *F.*
request?] *Rowe*[3]; request: *F.*   daws!] *Theobald;* Dawes. *F.*

(unspecified: hence possibly = their
own will, but more probably with
coarse innuendo, as Malvolio is made
to talk unconscious bawdry in
II. v. 88–9).

24. Olivia] F2's alteration of F's
wrong prefix at I. iii. 51 is obviously
correct, but here the speaker could
be either Olivia (F2) or Maria
(Collier's conjecture). This ed. follows
F2 because 'Maria nowhere else
"thou's" Malvolio' (Wilson) and
because she seems not to enter the
dialogue till l. 34 (when Malvolio
treats her question, similar to that
asked in l. 24, with contempt and
refuses to reply to it).

26. *Not black . . . legs*] an absurd
antithesis, perhaps parodying Lyly's
mannerism of style, and also with
allusion to a then popular ballad tune
called 'Black and Yellow' (Collier);
'black in my mind' = melancholy
(which was supposedly caused by
black bile), one of the four 'humours'
of the body.

28–29. *sweet Roman hand*] italic
calligraphy, as contrasted with the
traditional cursive English script.

30. *to bed*] i.e., to sleep off his mental
disturbance (cf. IV. ii. 99, 'endeavour
thyself to sleep'). Malvolio under-

stands it as an amorous invitation (cf.
II. v. 48–9, 'having come from a day-
bed', etc.).

31. *Ay, sweetheart . . . to thee*] quoted
from a popular song printed in
Tarlton's Jests (1601) (Mahood).

35. *At your request . . . daws!*] It is
difficult to decide whether both
phrases are to be understood as
spoken to Maria or whether only the
second is to her and the first to Olivia.
Turner argues that 'At your request' is
Malvolio's answer to Olivia's question
because (1) he has replied to her other
questions and it would be strange if he
did not reply to this, and (2) the two
phrases occupy separate lines in F.
On the other hand, H. F. Brooks
points out to me that (1) all Malvolio's
other replies (except the outrageous
one to l. 30) are enigmatic in comparison, (2) a direct answer might be
expected to produce a direct denial,
whereas the audience must feel that
Olivia's continuing bewilderment is
convincing, and (3) 'Yes, nightingales
answer daws!' seems to need the
earlier phrase to connect Malvolio's
contempt with Maria's question. I
incline to the latter opinion, which
makes the whole speech a scornful
reply ('What! Am I (a nightingale)

Maria. Why appear you with this ridiculous boldness
    before my lady?
Mal. 'Be not afraid of greatness': 'twas well writ.
Olivia. What mean'st thou by that, Malvolio?
Mal. 'Some are born great'—   40
Olivia. Ha?
Mal. 'Some achieve greatness'—
Olivia. What say'st thou?
Mal. 'And some have greatness thrust upon them.'
Olivia. Heaven restore thee!   45
Mal. 'Remember who commended thy yellow stock-
    ings'—
Olivia. Thy yellow stockings?
Mal. 'And wished to see thee cross-gartered.'
Olivia. Cross-gartered?   50
Mal. 'Go to, thou art made, if thou desir'st to be
    so:'—
Olivia. Am I made?
Mal. 'If not, let me see thee a servant still.'
Olivia. Why, this is very midsummer madness.   55

Enter SERVANT.

Servant. Madam, the young gentleman of the Count
    Orsino's is returned; I could hardly entreat him

48. Thy] *F;* My *Dyce², conj. Lettsom.*

to answer questions from such as you (a daw)?') with the 'Yes' spoken sarcastically.

48. *Thy yellow stockings?*] Since Olivia is ignorant of the letter's contents, she may possibly understand 'thy' (l. 46) and 'thee' (l. 49) as relating to herself. Some editors who hold this view emend to 'My yellow stockings', while others retain 'Thy' and interpret it as her surprised repetition of his familiar form of address. Alternatively (and more probably), since she has Malvolio's yellow stockings and cross garters before her eyes, she is repeating his phrase with reference to him, and wondering who could have commended his present dress, since she never did so (cf. II. v. 152–4 and note).

53. *Am I made?*] repeating his statement 'in utter bewilderment over the assurance that she had but to wish and her fortune would be "made"' (Furness); cf. II. v. 154. Her change of pronoun to 'I' (contr. l. 48) implies that, whereas she assumed that Malvolio was quoting before (he had said ''twas well writ', l. 38), she now assumes that he is addressing her directly; cf. her equal bewilderment at his next remark, l. 54. There are no substantial grounds for believing that Olivia mistakes 'made' for 'maid' or for 'mad'.

55. *midsummer madness*] proverbial; cf. Tilley, M1117 ('It is midsummer moon with you').

back. He attends your ladyship's pleasure.

Olivia. I'll come to him. [*Exit Servant.*] Good Maria,
let this fellow be looked to. Where's my cousin   60
Toby? Let some of my people have a special care
of him; I would not have him miscarry for the half
of my dowry.   [*Exeunt Olivia and Maria different ways.*]

Mal. O ho, do you come near me now? No worse man
than Sir Toby to look to me! This concurs directly   65
with the letter: she sends him on purpose, that I
may appear stubborn to him; for she incites me to
that in the letter. 'Cast thy humble slough,' says
she; 'be opposite with a kinsman, surly with
servants, let thy tongue tang arguments of state, put   70
thyself into the trick of singularity': and consequently sets down the manner how: as, a sad face, a
reverend carriage, a slow tongue, in the habit of
some sir of note, and so forth. I have limed her,
but it is Jove's doing, and Jove make me thankful!   75

59. [*Exit Servant.*]] *Capell; not in F.*   63. [*Exeunt Olivia and Maria different ways.*]]
Mahood; exit | F; Exeunt Olivia and Maria. Capell.   70. tang] *Capell;* langer
with *F;* tang with *F2.*   75. Jove's . . . Jove] *F (*Ioues . . . Ioue*);* God's . . .
God *Hudson, conj. Halliwell.*

62. *miscarry*] come to harm.

64. *do you . . . now?*] Do you begin
to understand me (i.e., show that you
appreciate my merit)? Spoken by
way of apostrophe to Olivia, who
(he thinks) has merely been feigning
surprise at his speeches because Maria
was present.

70. *tang*] Turner notes that *OED*'s
only example of 'tang with' is this
line; he therefore concludes that
'tang' should be the reading here, as
at II. v. 150, and conjectures that the
compositor either carried over the
'with' from his previous line (which
contains the word twice) or introduced it in the attempt to make better
sense in conjunction with the word
which he misread as 'langer'.

71–2. *consequently*] subsequently.

73. *in the habit*] literally 'in the
dress', but here probably used
figuratively for 'in the fashion', and

referring back to the mannerisms 'a
sad face', etc. (since Malvolio's actual
dress has already been prescribed and
assumed); cf. *AYL.*, III. ii. 257–9
(Rosalind, in her youth's disguise, of
Orlando), 'I will speak to him like a
saucy lackey, and under that habit
play the knave with him.'

74. *limed*] caught (as a bird with
sticky bird-lime); often used (always
metaphorically) in Shakespeare, e.g.,
Ado, III. i. 109, and (more seriously, of
Claudius' soul) *Ham.*, III. iii. 68–9.

75. *Jove's, Jove*] Halliwell's supposition that, here and elsewhere,
Shakespeare's original text read
'God's' and 'God', and that 'Jove's'
and 'Jove' were substituted to comply
with the statute of 1606 forbidding
profanity in plays, is not probable,
since 'Jove' occurs frequently in
Shakespeare's plays before as well as
after the statute, and since 'God'

And when she went away now, 'Let this fellow be
looked to'—'fellow'!—not Malvolio, nor after my
degree, but 'fellow'. Why, everything adheres
together, that no dram of a scruple, no scruple of a
scruple, no obstacle, no incredulous or unsafe cir-   80
cumstance—what can be said?—nothing that can
be can come between me and the full prospect of my
hopes. Well, Jove, not I, is the doer of this, and he is
to be thanked.

Enter SIR TOBY, FABIAN, *and* MARIA.

Sir To. Which way is he, in the name of sanctity? If   85
all the devils of hell be drawn in little, and Legion
himself possessed him, yet I'll speak to him.
Fabian. Here he is, here he is. How is't with you, sir?
How is't with you, man?

83. Jove] *F* (Ioue); God *Hudson, conj. Halliwell.*   88–9. sir? / How] *F;* sir? /
Sir Toby. How *N.C.S., conj. anon. apud Camb.*

occurs several times in this play (e.g.,
I. v. 14, 76, 239), most strikingly in
Sir Andrew's challenge (III. iv. 167–9),
to which Johnson objected on the
grounds of its 'profaneness'. Yet
Luce's comparison of Psalm cxviii. 23,
'This is the Lord's doing; it is
marvellous in our eyes', is worth
recording.

76. *fellow*] Malvolio interprets the
word (with an Olympian disdain for
its context) as 'equal' (cf. *H5,* v. ii. 38,
'fellow with the best king'). Its only
use in this sense in *Tw.N.* is in the
letter, II. v. 156, 'the fellow of
servants'. Generally, here as in the
rest of Shakespeare, it is either
patronizing (Orsino to the Clown,
II. iv. 42, v. i. 10) or derogatory
(Orsino to Antonio, v. i. 96).

77–8. *after my degree*] Malvolio can
no longer bring himself to use the
word 'steward'.

79–80. *no dram of . . . of a scruple*] 'To
understand this phrase, we must take
the first and last "scruple" in the
moral sense, the second as the weight,
the third part of a dram' (Keightley,

N. & Q., 3rd series, XII (1867), 61,
acknowledging J. J. A. Boase's information). Furness, citing Keightley,
compares *2H4,* I. ii. 123–4: 'But how
I should be your patient to follow
your prescriptions, the wise may make
some dram of a scruple, or indeed a
scruple itself', where the reference to
apothecaries' weights is clear.

80. *incredulous or unsafe*] incredible or
undependable.

86. *drawn in little*] a quibble on (1)
'made the subject of a miniature
portrait' (cf. *AYL.,* III. ii. 130; *Ham.,*
II. ii. 362, 'his picture in little'), and
(2) contracted into small compass
(i.e., one man's body).

86–7. *Legion himself*] carrying on the
idea of l. 86. The reference is to
Mark, v. 8–9, where the 'unclean
spirit', being asked what his name
was, replied 'My name is Legion;
for we are many.' Charney points out
that the side-note in the Geneva Bible
(1560) is 'A Legion conteined more
than 6000 in nomber.'

89. *How is't with you, man?*] Wilson
gives this line to Sir Toby, because

Mal. Go off, I discard you. Let me enjoy my private.   90
  Go off.
Maria. Lo, how hollow the fiend speaks within him!
  Did not I tell you? Sir Toby, my lady prays you to
  have a care of him.
Mal. [*Aside*] Ah ha! does she so?   95
Sir To. Go to, go to: peace, peace, we must deal gently
  with him. Let me alone. How do you, Malvolio?
  How is't with you? What, man, defy the devil!
  Consider, he's an enemy to mankind.
Mal. Do you know what you say?   100
Maria. La you, and you speak ill of the devil, how he
  takes it at heart! Pray God he be not bewitched!
Fabian. Carry his water to th' wise woman.
Maria. Marry, and it shall be done to-morrow morn-
  ing, if I live. My lady would not lose him for more   105
  than I'll say.

95. [*Aside*]] *This ed.; not in F.*   97. me] *F;* him *Rowe.*

(1) 'with its "man" in place of the
more respectful "sir", it certainly
belongs to a different speaker from
the first query'; (2) there may have
been confusion between the *Tob.* and
Fab. prefixes (he compares II. v. 34,
38, where I am sure that his redistribution is wrong: actually the
variant forms *To./Tob.* and *Fa./Fab.*
are used with about equal frequency
throughout F); (3) it is printed on the
line following the previous question.
Turner, who adopts Wilson's arrangement, points out nevertheless that the
previous line is nearly full, and that
the type would require considerable
tightening if 'How' were to be
included; but he endorses Wilson's
first point by noting that (1) Sir
Toby addressed Malvolio as 'man'
in l. 98, and (2) Malvolio's 'I discard
you' in l. 90 'sounds precisely as
though he is being opposite with a
kinsman.' I retain F's arrangement,
on the grounds that (1) Fabian may
well, after getting no answer to his
question, repeat it in more insistent

form; (2) Malvolio's reply is just as
surly with servants as it is opposite
with a kinsman; and (3) the comic
effect is the greater if Sir Toby enters
the dialogue only at l. 96, adopting a
gentle and persuasive tone which
completely enrages Malvolio.
  90. *private*] privacy, own company.
  97. *Let me alone*] Leave me to
manage the business.
  101. *La you*] Look you.
  102. *bewitched*] 'Not the same condition as "possessed", and needing
different treatment' (Wilson). The
notion seems to be introduced by
Shakespeare in order to prompt the
next two speeches.
  103. *Carry his . . . woman*] Diagnosis
was often made by inspecting the
patient's urine; cf. *2H4,* I. ii. 1–5. A
'wise woman' was one who claimed to
cure illnesses, undo witchcraft, etc., by
means of charms and herbal remedies.
  105–6. *My lady . . . I'll say*] Though
Maria's remark parallels Olivia's at
l. 62–3, the suggestion is that Malvolio
is a valuable possession, like livestock,

Mal. How now, mistress?

Maria. O Lord!

Sir To. Prithee hold thy peace, this is not the way. Do
　　you not see you move him? Let me alone with　　110
　　him.

Fabian. No way but gentleness, gently, gently: the fiend
　　is rough, and will not be roughly used.

Sir To. Why, how now, my bawcock? How dost thou,
　　chuck?　　115

Mal. Sir!

Sir To. Ay, biddy, come with me. What, man, 'tis not
　　for gravity to play at cherry-pit with Satan. Hang
　　him, foul collier!

Maria. Get him to say his prayers, good Sir Toby, get　　120
　　him to pray.

---

114. thou] *F* (y^u).

which were often supposed to be bewitched. Malvolio's exclamation may
imply that he is incensed by the
implied comparison.

114. *bawcock*] fine fellow (Fr. *beau
coq*).

115. *chuck*] chicken. For both terms
as comic endearments, cf. *H5*, III. ii.
24 (Pistol to Fluellen, who is chasing
Falstaff's followers to the siege of
Harfleur), 'Good bawcock, bate thy
rage. Use lenity, sweet chuck.'
Generally applied to children (cf.
Wint., I. ii. 121, 'bawcock' used by
Leontes to Mamillius) or to women
('chuck' in *Mac.*, III. ii. 45; *Ant.*,
IV. iv. 2; *Oth.*, III. iv. 46, IV. ii. 24).
Armado, *LLL.*, v. i. 97, v. iii. 653,
uses 'chuck' in an affected way, first
to Holofernes and later to the men
in the royal audience.

117. *biddy*] yet another childish
endearment (=chicken). Here only
in Shakespeare. Some edd. have
accepted Ritson's suggestion (*Remarks, Critical and Illustrative, etc.*,
1783) that 'this seems to be a fragment

of some old song, and should be
printed as such.' But it is most unlikely that Sir Toby would sing here,
as he did in II. iii. It would be
thoroughly at variance with his
clumsy attempt (or artful pretence of
an attempt) to cajole Malvolio into a
good temper.

118. *gravity*] dignity, sobriety.
Shakespeare, here and in *1H4*,
II. iv. 285 ('What doth gravity out of
his bed at midnight?') seems to be
thinking of a personification, Gravity,
such as might appear in a morality
play.

play at cherry-pit] i.e., be on familiar
terms; referring to a children's game
of throwing cherry-stones into a hole.

119. *foul collier*] dirty coalman.
Coalmen were proverbially associated
with the devil for their blackness and
dishonest dealing; cf. Tilley, L287,
which is also the title of Ulpian
Fulwell's play, *Like Will to Like, quoth
the Devil to the Collier*, pr. 1568; it
contains the lyric 'Tom Collier of
Croydon hath sold his coals, / And

Mal. My prayers, minx!

Maria. No, I warrant you, he will not hear of godliness.

Mal. Go hang yourselves all: you are idle, shallow things, I am not of your element: you shall   125
know more hereafter.   *Exit.*

Sir To. Is't possible?

Fabian. If this were played upon a stage now, I could condemn it as an improbable fiction.

Sir To. His very genius hath taken the infection of the   130
device, man.

Maria. Nay, pursue him now, lest the device take air, and taint.

Fabian. Why, we shall make him mad indeed.

Maria. The house will be the quieter.   135

Sir To. Come, we'll have him in a dark room and bound. My niece is already in the belief that he's mad: we may carry it thus for our pleasure, and his penance, till our very pastime, tired out of breath, prompt us to have mercy on him; at   140
which time we will bring the device to the bar, and crown thee for a finder of madmen. But see, but see!

---

made his market today, / And now he danceth with the Devil, / For like will to like alway.' The term was also in use to mean 'coal-miner' in Shakespeare's time, but Wilson's elaborations on coal-miners' connections with the devil are not relevant to the proverb or to this passage.

122. *minx*] hussy, impudent woman.

125. *I am not of your element*] i.e., I belong to a higher order of creation.

130. *genius*] i.e., soul, spirit; literally, familiar or guardian spirit; cf. *Err.*, v. i. 331–3.

132–3. *take air, and taint*] i.e., become known, and be spoiled (*OED*, air, I. 11. 'to take air': this passage); or perhaps, grow stale through being neglected. Fabian's reply suggests that Maria has spoken with enthusiasm rather than with apprehension.

136–7. *in a dark room and bound*] the customary treatment; cf. *Err.*, IV. iv. 91, 'They must be bound, and laid in some dark room.'

138. *carry it thus*] maintain this pretence.

141. *bring the device to the bar*] i.e., bring the trick into open court, 'the bar' being the barrier at which the prisoners stand, hence 'tribunal', 'court' (Onions, 3).

142. *finder of madmen*] '"Finders of madmen" are those who formerly acted under the writ *De Lunatico inquirendo*; in virtue whereof they *found* the man *mad*' (Ritson, quoted in Furness; see *OED*, find, *v.*, II.17.b).

Enter SIR ANDREW.

Fabian. More matter for a May morning!

Sir And. Here's the challenge, read it: I warrant there's   145
vinegar and pepper in't.

Fabian. Is't so saucy?

Sir And. Ay, is't, I warrant him: do but read.

Sir To. Give me. [*Reads*] *Youth, whatsoever thou art,
thou art but a scurvy fellow.*   150

Fabian. Good, and valiant.

*Sir To. Wonder not, nor admire not in thy mind, why I do
call thee so, for I will show thee no reason for't.*

Fabian. A good note; that keeps you from the blow of
the law.   155

*Sir To. Thou com'st to the Lady Olivia, and in my sight she
uses thee kindly: but thou liest in thy throat; that is not
the matter I challenge thee for.*

Fabian. Very brief, and to exceeding good sense [*Aside*]
-less.   160

*Sir To. I will waylay thee going home, where if it be thy
chance to kill me—*

Fabian. Good.

---

149. [*Reads*]] Rowe (subst.); not in F.   159–60. sense [*Aside*] -less] N.C.S.
(subst.); sence-lesse F.

144. *More matter for a May morning!*]
i.e., more 'sport fit for a holiday'
(Mahood) or 'for a May-game or
pageant (cf. Chambers, *Mediaeval
Stage*, ch. viii)' (Wilson).

147. *saucy*] (1) insolent, (2) highly
seasoned (cf. 'vinegar and pepper',
l. 146).

149. *thou*] Cf. Sir Toby's advice,
III. ii. 43.

152. Wonder not . . . mind]
tautology characteristic of Sir
Andrew; cf. I. iii. 83.

154. *A good note*] i.e., well said.
that] that sentence.

154–5. *the blow of the law*] legal
punishment (for causing a breach of
the peace); cf. *Wint.*, IV. iv. 426, 'the
dead blow of it [royal displeasure].'

157. *thou liest in thy throat*] an
emphatic form of 'thou liest', very
frequent in Shakespeare, and in
general use (Tilley, T268). Again Sir
Andrew is following instructions; cf.
III. ii. 44.

159–60. *sense-less*] It is senseless
because he has just denied the only
reason he could have for challenging
Cesario.

163. *Good*] Fabian's praise of this
half-sentence is probably brought in
for its ambiguous sense, i.e., that it
would be a good thing if Sir Andrew's
opponent killed him. The point is
easily made in performance if an
expression of puzzled outrage momen-
tarily appears on Sir Andrew's face.

Sir To. Thou kill'st me like a rogue and a villain.

Fabian. Still you keep o' th' windy side of the law: 165
good.

Sir To. Fare thee well, and God have mercy upon one of our
souls! He may have mercy upon mine, but my hope is better,
and so look to thyself. Thy friend, as thou usest him,
and thy sworn enemy,   170

Andrew Aguecheek.

If this letter move him not, his legs cannot. I'll
give't him.

Maria. You may have very fit occasion for't: he is now
in some commerce with my lady, and will by and   175
by depart.

Sir To. Go, Sir Andrew: scout me for him at the corner
of the orchard, like a bum-baily. So soon as ever
thou see'st him, draw, and as thou draw'st, swear
horrible: for it comes to pass oft, that a terrible   180
oath, with a swaggering accent sharply twanged
off, gives manhood more approbation than ever
proof itself would have earned him. Away!

Sir And. Nay, let me alone for swearing.   *Exit.*

Sir To. Now will not I deliver his letter: for the   185
behaviour of the young gentleman gives him out to
be of good capacity and breeding: his employment between his lord and my niece confirms no
less. Therefore this letter, being so excellently
ignorant, will breed no terror in the youth: he   190

180. horrible] *F;* horribly *F2.*

164. like a rogue and a villain] unconscious ambiguity, since it could
relate to 'me' as well as to 'thou'.

165. *o' th' windy side*] to windward
(nautical metaphor), i.e., at a distance
from the law, which, to come up to
him, would have to sail against the
wind; cf. *Ado,* II. i. 283, 'It [Beatrice's
"merry heart"] keeps on the windy
side of care.'

168. He may have mercy . . . my
hope is better] Sir Andrew means to
say 'I hope I shall survive', but in-
felicitously says 'I hope I shall be

damned.' For Johnson's censure, see
note on l. 75.

169–70. Thy friend . . . sworn
enemy] typically self-contradictory.

178. *bum-baily*] a bailiff (sheriff's
officer) who comes up *behind* his
quarry.

180. *horrible*] used adverbially (cf.
Lr., IV. vi. 4, 'horrible steep'), so no
need to emend with F2.

182. *approbation*] credit, reputation.

183. *proof*] trial.

187. *of good capacity and breeding*]
sensible and refined.

will find it comes from a clodpole. But, sir, I
will deliver his challenge by word of mouth, set
upon Aguecheek a notable report of valour, and
drive the gentleman (as I know his youth will
aptly receive it) into a most hideous opinion of　195
his rage, skill, fury, and impetuosity. This will
so fright them both that they will kill one another
by the look, like cockatrices.

Enter OLIVIA *and* VIOLA.

Fabian. Here he comes with your niece: give them way
　　till he take leave, and presently after him.　　200
Sir To. I will meditate the while upon some horrid
　　message for a challenge.　　[*Exeunt Sir Toby, Fabian,*
　　　　　　　　　　　　　　　　　　　and Maria.]
Olivia. I have said too much unto a heart of stone,
　　And laid mine honour too unchary out:
　　There's something in me that reproves my fault:　205
　　But such a headstrong potent fault it is,
　　That it but mocks reproof.

---

202. [*Exeunt . . . and Maria.*]] *Capell; not in F; Exeunt. F2; Exit Maria. Sir Toby
and Fabian stand aside. Mahood.*　　204. out] *Theobald;* on't *F.*

191. *clodpole*] blockhead: literally,
having a head (poll) made of a lump
of earth (clod).

198. *cockatrices*] fabulous serpents
said to 'slay by sight' (Tilley, C495),
also called basilisks. Shakespeare's
idea of a pair of them killing each
other thus is a fine comic fancy.

200. *presently*] immediately; cf.
ll. 175–6, 'by and by'.

204. *laid . . . ou't*] expended.
Theobald's emendation is is supported
by what is agreed to be an error (F's
'on't' for 'out' in *Wint.,* IV. iv. 159–60,
'He tels her something / That makes
her blood looke on't'. Wright, who
first noted this, says: ' "Unchary" is
unsparingly, lavishly. The word
etymologically signifies heedlessly,

carelessly; but that Shakespeare
understood it in the other sense is
evident from *Ham.,* II. iii. 36–7:
"The chariest maid is prodigal
enough / If she unmask her beauty
to the moon"; where "chariest" and
"prodigal" are contrasted.' The
passage in *Ham.* may be influenced
by reminiscence of *Tw.N.,* I. i. 26–8.
Those who retain F's reading understand Olivia as saying either (1) that
she has *placed* her honour on Cesario's
heart of stone, 'as it were, on an altar'
(Collier[3]) or as paying a debt by
putting money upon a known stone
in a church (an Elizabethan custom,
Sisson, I, 193), or (2) that she has
wagered it on a heart which proved
stony (Schmidt, quoted but not accepted by Furness).

Viola. With the same 'haviour that your passion bears
　　Goes on my master's griefs.
Olivia. Here, wear this jewel for me, 'tis my picture: 210
　　Refuse it not, it hath no tongue to vex you:
　　And I beseech you come again to-morrow.
　　What shall you ask of me that I'll deny,
　　That honour sav'd may upon asking give?
Viola. Nothing but this, your true love for my master.   215
Olivia. How with mine honour may I give him that
　　Which I have given to you?
Viola.　　　　　　　　　　I will acquit you.
Olivia. Well, come again to-morrow. Fare thee well;
　　A fiend like thee might bear my soul to hell.   [*Exit.*]

　　　　　Enter SIR TOBY *and* FABIAN.

Sir To. Gentleman, God save thee.   220
Viola. And you, sir.
Sir To. That defence thou hast, betake thee to't. Of
　　what nature the wrongs are thou hast done him, I
　　know not: but thy intercepter, full of despite,
　　bloody as the hunter, attends thee at the orchard-   225
　　end. Dismount thy tuck, be yare in thy prepara-
　　tion, for thy assailant is quick, skilful, and deadly.

209. Goes . . . griefs] *F* (*reading* greefes)*;* Goes . . . grief *Rowe;* Go . . . griefs
Malone.   219. [*Exit.*]] *F2; not in F.*   S.D.] *F* (*Enter Toby and Fabian.*)*; Sir
Toby and Fabian come forward. Mahood.*

210. *jewel*] a miniature in a rich
setting.

214. *That honour . . . give*] 'that
honour may grant without compro-
mising itself' (Mahood), i.e., without
giving up her chastity.

217. *acquit*] release (from your
contract), i.e., refund to you the love
you have given me, so that you can
give it to Orsino.

225. *bloody as the hunter*] 'hunter'
may be either (1) a 'huntsman'
(Shakespeare's usual term) or (2) a
hunting-dog (cf. *Mac.*, III. i. 97: as
part of a categorical description, not
as imagery). The former sense seems

to be used in *Troil.*, IV. i. 19, 'By
Jove, I'll play the hunter for thy life',
and is certainly intended in *Caes.*,
III. i. 266–7, 'and there thy hunters
stand / Sign'd in thy spoil and
crimson'd in thy lethe'; cf. also *H5*,
III. iii. 41, 'At Herod's bloody-hunting
slaughtermen'. I therefore take the
word in its human, not its canine,
sense.

226. *Dismount thy tuck*] Draw your
sword from its sheath. 'Tuck' is from
Fr. *estoc*, Ital. *stocco*, a rapier (referred
to by Falstaff as a type of slenderness,
1H4, II. iv. 240, 'you vile standing
tuck').

yare] quick.

Viola. You mistake, sir; I am sure no man hath any
    quarrel to me: my remembrance is very free and
    clear from any image of offence done to any man.   230
Sir To. You'll find it otherwise, I assure you. There-
    fore, if you hold your life at any price, betake
    you to your guard: for your opposite hath in him
    what youth, strength, skill, and wrath, can
    furnish man withal.   235
Viola. I pray you, sir, what is he?
Sir To. He is knight, dubbed with unhatched rapier,
    and on carpet consideration, but he is a devil in
    private brawl. Souls and bodies hath he divorced
    three, and his incensement at this moment is so   240
    implacable that satisfaction can be none but by
    pangs of death and sepulchre. Hob, nob, is his
    word: give't or take't.
Viola. I will return again into the house, and desire
    some conduct of the lady. I am no fighter. I have   245
    heard of some kind of men that put quarrels
    purposely on others to taste their valour: belike
    this is a man of that quirk.
Sir To. Sir, no: his indignation derives itself out of a

---

228. sir; I am sure no] *Theobald (subst.)*; sir I am sure, no *F*; sir, I am sure, no
F3; sir, I am sure no *Rowe*; sir, I am sure; no *Knight*; sir. I am sure no *N.C.S.*;
sir, I am sure. No *Honigmann*.   237. unhatched] *F* (vnhatch'd); unhack'd
Pope.

237. *unhatched*] unhacked (synonymous, as *OED* explains under
Unhatched, *ppl.a.*: from French verb
hacher, to cut, hew). The sense of the
whole passage 'dubbed . . . consideration' is clearly that Sir Andrew was
knighted at court and not on the
battlefield; hence the contrast with
his alleged ferocity 'in private brawl'.
H. F. Brooks points out that Shakespeare would find the phrase 'the
coward carpet knyght' (of Paris
slaying Achilles) in Golding's Ovid,
XII. 673, XIII. 123.

242. *Hob, nob*] have or have not
(*OED* derives it from M.E. *habbe,*

nabbe); synonymous with 'give't or
take't' ('it' being death).

243. *word*] motto.

245. *some*] Turner points out that
though Shakespeare has 'safe conduct'
in *Troil.*, III. iii. 272, 283 and *H5*,
I. ii. 297, he has 'some conduct' only
here. However, he follows F, since
its reading is understandable as
'someone to safeguard me', and since
the 'some' of l. 246 'seems a little too
far away to have been a contamin-
ating influence'. Cf. 'some guard', l.
12.

247. *taste*] try; cf. III. i. 79.

248. *quirk*] peculiarity.

very competent injury; therefore get you on, and   250
give him his desire. Back you shall not to the
house, unless you undertake that with me which
with as much safety you might answer him;
therefore on, or strip your sword stark naked:
for meddle you must, that's certain, or forswear   255
to wear iron about you.

Viola. This is as uncivil as strange. I beseech you, do
me this courteous office, as to know of the knight
what my offence to him is: it is something of my
negligence, nothing of my purpose.   260

Sir To. I will do so. Signior Fabian, stay you by this
gentleman till my return.   *Exit Sir Toby.*

Viola. Pray you, sir, do you know of this matter?

Fabian. I know the knight is incensed against you, even
to a mortal arbitrement, but nothing of the   265
circumstance more.

Viola. I beseech you, what manner of man is he?

Fabian. Nothing of that wonderful promise, to read
him by his form, as you are like to find him in the
proof of his valour. He is indeed, sir, the most   270
skilful, bloody, and fatal opposite that you could
possibly have found in any part of Illyria. Will
you walk towards him, I will make your peace
with him if I can.

Viola. I shall be much bound to you for't. I am one   275

---

250. competent] *F4;* computent *F.*   258. as to] *F;* to *Capell.*

250. *competent*] sufficient (to justify a
demand for satisfaction), *OED, a.,* 6.b.
H. M. Hulme, *Explorations,* p. 165,
defends F's 'computent' by quoting
Cooper's *Thesaurus* (1578), where
'Computationem expostulare'='To
ask an account, to require a reckon-
ing'.

252. *that*] i.e., a duel.

255–6. *forswear . . . about you*] give
up wearing a sword, i.e., admit to
cowardice.

258. *as to*] common Elizabethan

usage; cf. Abbott, §280, and l. 269 'as
you'.

265. *a mortal arbitrement*] a trial
(i.e., fight) to the death.

269. *form*] outward appearance.

273. *him,*] The punctuation of F is
retained in this ed., in order to show
that the remainder of Fabian's speech
follows directly without a pause, such
as there might be if an interrogation
mark were introduced. It may also be
argued that Fabian's phrase means 'If
you will walk towards him'.

that had rather go with sir priest than sir knight:
I care not who knows so much of my mettle.   *Exeunt.*

277. *Exeunt.*] F; *not in Capell; Exeunt.* | *Scene V* | *Dyce.*

276. *sir priest*] in antithesis with 'sir knight'. A clergyman who had taken his first degree was called 'Sir' as the English equivalent of *Dominus*.

277. Exeunt. 277 S.D. Enter . . . Andrew] The staging of the action from this point to l. 296 S.D. has been much debated (see, besides the comments quoted by Furness, the notes of Wilson, Mahood (following Olivia's couplet, ll. 218–19), and Turner, and J. L. Styan's *Shakespeare's Stagecraft* (1967), pp. 125–6), the chief question being whether Fabian and Viola (1) do, or (2) do not, leave the stage. The opinion that they do is based on (1a) F's stage directions; (1b) the theatrical awkwardness of Sir Andrew's entry on the stage so soon after Fabian has invited Viola to 'walk towards him' (l. 273), if they have not left the stage, since this awkwardness could have been so easily avoided by giving Fabian some such speech as 'But here he comes, and Sir Toby with him', after which they might quite reasonably remain standing where they are; (1c) the arranged place of the duel, 'at the corner of the orchard' (ll. 177–8) and 'at the orchard-end' (ll. 225–6) (i.e., at some distance from the place where Viola parts from Olivia and encounters Sir Toby and Fabian); (1d) Sir Toby's ll. 286–7, 'Fabian can scarce hold him yonder' (interpreted as off stage, visible to Sir Toby and Sir Andrew but not to the audience: a corollary of this is that if Fabian and Viola do leave by a stage door, they must leave it open and not close it after them). The opinion that they do not is based on (2a) the fact that F does not begin a new scene after l. 277, though the stage is cleared by the *Exeunt*; (2b) the theatrical awkwardness of Fabian's and Viola's leaving the stage to 'walk

towards' Sir Andrew, when he immediately afterwards enters; (2c) Sir Toby's ll. 261–2, 'Signior Fabian, stay you by this gentleman till I return' (interpreted as meaning that Fabian and Viola are not to leave the stage); (2d) Sir Toby's ll. 286–7, 'Fabian can scarce hold him yonder' (interpreted as on stage, visible to the audience as well as to Sir Toby and Sir Andrew). I think that, in view of F's frequent omission of stage directions, those which are present are likely to be derived from copy and not to be additions by the scribe, since there is no evidence that he took any interest in visualizing the stage action or in making it clear to the reader. The directions of F are therefore all retained in this ed., even though it is unlikely that Viola and Fabian are to leave the stage; in modern productions they seldom, if ever, do so. It may be that Shakespeare was in two minds about the stage action while writing the scene, and that the possible discrepancy between (1b) and (2c) reflects this authorial indecision, which was sorted out in the theatre but not in his foul papers. The incident, however staged, demands some willing suspension of disbelief when Sir Toby leaves Sir Andrew ('Stand here', l. 293) and proceeds to confer with Fabian (ll. 297–300) without being overheard by Viola, who is in Fabian's company (and, according to some productions, actually in his grasp); the only practical way of managing this (on an Elizabethan or any other stage) is for Sir Toby to meet Fabian for their confidential exchange at the front centre (leaving Sir Andrew and Viola standing at opposite extremes of the stage), after which, instead of returning to Sir Andrew, Sir Toby crosses to

Enter SIR TOBY *and* SIR ANDREW.

Sir To. Why, man, he's a very devil, I have not seen
such a firago. I had a pass with him, rapier,
scabbard, and all: and he gives me the stuck in   280
with such a mortal motion that it is inevitable;
and on the answer, he pays you as surely as your
feet hits the ground they step on. They say he
has been fencer to the Sophy.

Sir And. Pox on't, I'll not meddle with him.   285

Sir To. Ay, but he will not now be pacified: Fabian can
scarce hold him yonder.

Sir And. Plague on't, and I thought he had been
valiant, and so cunning in fence, I'd have seen
him damned ere I'd have challenged him. Let   290

283. hits] *F;* hit *Rowe.*

Viola, while at the same time, instead of returning to Viola, Fabian crosses to Sir Andrew. This is in practice a very effective piece of comic stage action.

279. *firago*] virago (female warrior). *OED*, virago, 2.b, records the word, as applied to a man, only here and in *The Blind Beggar of Bethnall Green, Part I* (Chettle and Day [and Haughton?]), 1600, ed. W. Bang, *Materialien*, 1902, l. 1748: Act IV): 'Come then, my mad Viragoes . . .' In this latter context it seems a mistake of the speaker (Tom Strowd, a rustic), but in *Tw.N.* Viola's disguise gives it some point, either 'I never saw one that had so much the look of a woman with the prowess of a man' (Johnson) or (Kittredge) 'Sir Toby applies this feminine term, for comic effect, to one whom he supposes to be a man; but the audience, aware that Cesario is a woman, enjoys both the joke and the mistake.' Since *v* was often pronounced *f* (as in *fat* for *vat*), there is no need to associate Sir Toby's word with 'fire-eater', 'fire-drake', etc., as Wilson suggests.

pass] here, a bout, by extension from its sense of a thrust (cf. *Wiv.*, II. i. 202, 'your passes, stoccadoes, and I know not what'): Ital. *passado*; cf. *Rom.*, II. iv. 25, III. i. 82.

280. *stuck*] another thrust in fencing; cf. 'stock', *Wiv.*, II. iii. 23, and *Ham.*, IV. vii. 161, 'If he by chance escape your venom'd stuck'. Ital. *stoccata*; cf. *Rom.*, III. i. 72, 'Alla stoccata carries it away'.

in] home, direct to the body; cf. *Rom.* III. i. 87, *Tybalt under Romeo's arm thrusts Mercutio in.*

282. *on the answer, he pays you*] As you return his thrust, he gives it you (i.e., stabs you). For 'pay'=kill, cf. *1H4*, II. iv. 185, 'two I am sure I have paid', and 210, 'seven of the eleven I paid.'

283. *hits*] Cf. II. iii. 151.

284. *Sophy*] Cf. II. v. 181.

286–7. *Fabian . . . yonder*] Furness (p. 239, in his note on the stage directions) remarks that this assertion is 'perhaps the pernicious source of the conversion of Viola's exquisite bearing throughout, into low farce' in some performances.

him let the matter slip, and I'll give him my horse,
grey Capilet.

Sir To. I'll make the motion. Stand here, make a good
show on't: this shall end without the perdition
of souls. [*Aside*] Marry, I'll ride your horse as   295
well as I ride you.

Enter FABIAN *and* VIOLA.

[*To Fabian*] I have his horse to take up the quarrel.
I have persuaded him the youth's a devil.

Fabian. He is as horribly conceited of him, and pants
and looks pale, as if a bear were at his heels.   300

Sir To. [*To Viola*] There's no remedy, sir, he will
fight with you for's oath sake. Marry, he hath
better bethought him of his quarrel, and he finds
that now scarce to be worth talking of. Therefore
draw for the supportance of his vow; he protests   305
he will not hurt you.

Viola. [*Aside*] Pray God defend me! A little thing
would make me tell them how much I lack of a
man.

Fabian. [*To Sir Andrew*] Give ground if you see him   310
furious.

292. Capilet] *F;* Capulet *Dyce.*   295. [*Aside*]] *Theobald; not in F; Aside, as he
crosses to Fabian. Mahood.*   296. S.D. *Enter Fabian and Viola.*] *F; not in Capell.*
297. [*To Fabian*]] *Rowe; not in F.*   301. [*To Viola*]] *Capell; not in F.*   302.
oath sake] *F;* oath's sake *Douai MS., Capell.*   307. [*Aside*]] *Capell; not in F.*
310. [*To Sir Andrew*]] *This ed.; not in F.*

292. *Capilet*] Wright suggests that
this may be a diminutive form of
'capul', a horse (*OED*, caple, capul),
but one would suppose that it was
rather a variant of the Italian surname Capulet, as in *Rom.* Hence
Dyce's emendation. This is confirmed
by the use of 'Capilet' as the surname
of Diana in *All's W.*, v. iii. 144, 157.

297. *take up the quarrel*] make up the
dispute.

299. *is as horribly conceited*] has as
terrifying a notion.

303. *his quarrel*] his grounds of
offence.

307-9. *A little thing . . . man*] (1) It
would not take much to make me
admit how afraid I am. (2) I am almost frightened enough to reveal that
I am a woman in disguise. Cf. *Mer.V.*,
III. iv. 60-3, where Portia, preparing
to disguise herself and Nerissa as men,
tells her that their husbands will see
them 'in such a habit / That they shall
think we are accomplished / With that
we lack'. The sexual innuendo in

Sir To. Come, Sir Andrew, there's no remedy, the
gentleman will for his honour's sake have one bout
with you; he cannot by the duello avoid it: but
he has promised me, as he is a gentleman and a   315
soldier, he will not hurt you. Come on, to't.
Sir And. Pray God he keep his oath!

Enter ANTONIO.

Viola. I do assure you, 'tis against my will.   [*Sir Andrew and
Viola draw.*]
Ant. [*Drawing*] Put up your sword! If this young
gentleman
Have done offence, I take the fault on me: 320
If you offend him, I for him defy you.
Sir To. You, sir? Why, what are you?
Ant. One, sir, that for his love dares yet do more
Than you have heard him brag to you he will.
Sir To. Nay, if you be an undertaker, I am for you.   325
[*Draws.*]

---

317. S.D. *Enter Antonio.*] *F; after l. 321, Capell (Enter Antonio; draws, and runs
between).*   318. [*Sir Andrew and Viola draw.*]] *This ed.; after l. 316 Rowe (subst.);
They draw, and back from each other. Collier*[2] *not in F.*   319. [*Drawing*]] *Rowe
(after l. 321); not in F.*   325. [*Draws.*]] *Rowe; not in F.*

Mer.V., is obvious, that in *Tw.N.*
slight, if indeed intended at all.

314. *by the duello*] by the rules
governing the conduct of a duel.
Several books on the subject were
printed in the last decade of the
sixteenth century, including *The
Booke of Honor and Armes, wherein is
discoursed the Causes of Quarrell and the
Nature of Injuries with their Repulses*
(Sir W. Segar ?), 1590; *The Practice
Proceedings and Lawes of Armes [etc.]*
(Matthew Sutcliffe), 1593; and *Vin-
centio Saviolo, His Practise, in two
bookes: the first intreating of the use of the
Rapier and Dagger, the second of Honour
and Honourable Quarrels*, 1595.

317. S.D. Enter Antonio] Shakespeare now ignores his earlier location
of the duel in Olivia's 'orchard' or

garden, since his plot requires
Antonio's intervention and his subsequent arrest by the Officers, who
later report to Orsino that the
'private brabble' took place 'Here in
the streets' (v. i. 62–3). There is, of
course, no need to reconsider the
stage action of the present scene in
order to accommodate this casual
change of place.

325. *undertaker*] Evidently Sir Toby
quibbles. The most likely senses are:
(1) one who takes upon himself the
business of another, a helper (*OED*,
1), (2) one who takes up a challenge
(*OED*, 3c: this passage only), (3) one
who undertook to hold Crown lands
in Ireland in the sixteenth and seventeenth centuries (*OED*, 4a: first in
1586). Wilson suggests 'a contractor

Enter OFFICERS.

Fabian. O good Sir Toby, hold! here come the
　officers.
Sir To. [*To Antonio*] I'll be with you anon.
Viola. [*To Sir Andrew*] Pray sir, put your sword up, if
　you please.　　　　　　　　　　　　　　　　330
Sir And. Marry, will I, sir: and for that I promised
　you, I'll be as good as my word. He will bear you
　easily, and reins well.
First Off. This is the man; do thy office.
Second Off. Antonio, I arrest thee at the suit　　335
　Of Count Orsino.
Ant.　　　　　　You do mistake me, sir.
First Off. No, sir, no jot: I know your favour well,
　Though now you have no sea-cap on your head.
　Take him away, he knows I know him well.
Ant. I must obey. [*To Viola*] This comes with seeking you;
　But there's no remedy, I shall answer it.　　341
　What will you do, now my necessity
　Makes me to ask you for my purse? It grieves me
　Much more for what I cannot do for you,
　Than what befalls myself. You stand amaz'd,　　345
　But be of comfort.
Second Off. Come, sir, away.
Ant. I must entreat of you some of that money.
Viola. What money, sir?

328. [*To Antonio*]] *Capell; not in* F.　　329. [*To Sir Andrew*]] *Rowe; not in* F.
335-6. Antonio . . . Orsino] *As Capell (verse); one line in* F.　　340. [*To Viola*]]
Collier; not in F.　　342. do, now] *Dyce;* do: now *F;* doe? now *F2.*
344. purse?] *Dyce;* purse. *Ff.*

who had bought up his [Sir Toby's]
debts for the purpose of making him
pay them' (not recorded in *OED*),
and thus explains Sir Toby's l. 328;
but more probably Sir Toby has a
reputation for 'private brabble' (cf.
Olivia's IV. i. 46–56) and wishes to
'keep o' th' windy side of the law'.

331-3. *and for that . . . reins well*] Sir
Toby having kept this part of the
transaction to himself, Sir Andrew's

speech adds to Viola's mystification,
and prepares for the greater mystification of Antonio's.

338. *Though now . . . on your head*]
Shakespeare's masterly economy of
style: he here recalls to us the whole
dialogue of III. iii.

341. *answer it*] Cf. III. iii. 28.

345. *amaz'd*] bewildered, con-
founded (a sense stronger than the
modern).

For the fair kindness you have show'd me here,   350
And part being prompted by your present trouble,
Out of my lean and low ability
I'll lend you something. My having is not much;
I'll make division of my present with you.   354
Hold, there's half my coffer.   [*Offers Antonio money.*]
Ant. Will you deny me now?   [*Refuses it.*]
Is't possible that my deserts to you
Can lack persuasion? Do not tempt my misery,
Lest that it make me so unsound a man
As to upbraid you with those kindnesses   360
That I have done for you.
Viola.   I know of none,
Nor know I you by voice or any feature.
I hate ingratitude more in a man
Than lying, vainness, babbling drunkenness,
Or any taint of vice whose strong corruption   365
Inhabits our frail blood.
Ant.   O heavens themselves!
Second Off. Come sir, I pray you go.
Ant. Let me speak a little. This youth that you see here

---

355. Hold, there's] *F*; Hold, / There's *conj. Walker.* [*Offers Antonio money.*]]
N.C.S. (*subst.*); *not in F.*   356. [*Refuses it.*]] *N.C.S.; not in F.*   364. lying,
vainness, babbling] *Punctuated as F;* lying vainness, babbling *Collier;* lying,
vainness, babbling, *Var. '93.*

354. *my present*] such money as I
have at the present time.

355–6. *Hold . . . now?*] much more
effective as two short lines than as one
line, with or without an extra first
syllable. A strong pause is required
between Viola's offer and Antonio's
reaction.

355. *coffer*] literally, chest; here
used, with rueful exaggeration, of the
few coins in her purse.

357–8. *Is't possible . . . persuasion?*]
Can you, of all people, be unmoved
when you remember what consideration I deserve?

359. *unsound*] morally weak (since
kindnesses should be done for their
own sake, not in expectation of a

return). Wilson interprets theo-
logically as 'losing faith' (in friendship), which may well be the sense in
view of ll. 371–4.

364. *lying, vainness, babbling*] F's
punctuation is retained as being more
natural than the alternatives (both
of which give the line a self-conscious
neatness that comes too pat from
Viola in her surprise), and as giving
better sense: 'lying vainness' as a unit
is hard to define (Shakespeare's other
use of 'vainness', *H5*, v., Prol., 20,
means 'vain-glory', while 'vain', as
applied to persons, usually means
'foolish'), and 'babbling' will hardly
stand alone as a vice. The sense is,
therefore, 'lying, vain-gloriousness,
babbling drunkenness'.

I snatch'd one half out of the jaws of death,
Reliev'd him with such sanctity of love;   370
And to his image, which methought did promise
Most venerable worth, did I devotion.
First Off. What's that to us? The time goes by. Away!
Ant. But O how vile an idol proves this god!
Thou hast, Sebastian, done good feature shame.   375
In nature there's no blemish but the mind:
None can be call'd deform'd but the unkind.
Virtue is beauty, but the beauteous evil
Are empty trunks, o'er-flourish'd by the devil.
First Off. The man grows mad, away with him! Come,
come, sir.   380
Ant. Lead me on.   *Exit [with Officers].*
Viola. Methinks his words do from such passion fly
That he believes himself; so do not I:
Prove true, imagination, O prove true,

---

370. such] *F;* all *Hudson.*   love;] *F* ([?] Ioue;); love,— *Capell.*   371. his]
F; this *Hudson, conj. Walker.*   374. vile] *Pope;* vild *F* (vilde), *Mahood.*   378.
beauteous evil] *F;* beauteous-evil *Malone.*   380. As *Dyce;* as two lines (him: |
Come), *F;* him. 2 *Off.* Come, *Capell.*   381. [with Officers]] *Theobald;* not in *F.*
383. himself;] *Rowe³;* himselfe, *F.*   so do not I:] *F;* so do not I? *N.C.S.;* So!
do not I? *Honigmann.*

370. *such sanctity of love*] intense
devotion (cf. l. 372), as of religious
worship. For 'such' as adding emphasis to 'sanctity', cf. *Cym.,* v. v. 44
(Wright). Turner points out to me that
he reads F's last word as 'Ioue' and
that Giles Dawson and Charlton
Hinman confirm this reading. If it is
in fact an 'I' it is a very damaged one,
and was almost certainly used by
mistake for 'l'. Ff 2–4 read 'loue'.

371. *image*] appearance (i.e., of a
noble mind in a handsome person):
prepares for 'idol', l. 374.

374. *vile*] This ed. modernizes F's
'vilde' in accordance with general
editorial policy, but Mahood's retention of it for euphony deserves
consideration.

377. *unkind*] (1) unnatural, not
according to nature ('kind'), (2) hard-
hearted.

379. *empty trunks . . . devil*] The
metaphor is from trunks or chests
elaborately carved or painted with
'flourishes' (ornaments).

383. *so do not I*] either (1) 'I do not
yet believe myself, when, from this
accident, I gather hope of my
brother's life' (Johnson), or (2) 'I
know that his belief is a mistaken one'
(Deighton). I prefer the second and
simpler interpretation, which does
not 'spoil the effect' (Wilson), but by
its very obviousness ('I know I am not
Sebastian') leads straight into the
hopeful impulse of the next couplet,
and thence to the almost positive
conviction of Viola's next speech.
Wilson, reading 'so do not I?',
interprets it as 'Viola's dawn of hope'.
Mahood, adopting the same punctuation, explains 'why do I not believe
myself (my hope that my brother is

That I, dear brother, be now ta'en for you!   385
Sir To. Come hither, knight, come hither, Fabian.
     We'll whisper o'er a couplet or two of most sage
     saws.
Viola. He nam'd Sebastian. I my brother know
     Yet living in my glass; even such and so   390
     In favour was my brother, and he went
     Still in this fashion, colour, ornament,
     For him I imitate. O if it prove,
     Tempests are kind, and salt waves fresh in love! [*Exit.*]
Sir To. A very dishonest paltry boy, and more a coward   395
     than a hare; his dishonesty appears in leaving his
     friend here in necessity, and denying him; and for
     his cowardship, ask Fabian.
Fabian. A coward, a most devout coward, religious in it.
Sir And. 'Slid, I'll after him again, and beat him.   400
Sir To. Do, cuff him soundly, but never draw thy
     sword.
Sir And. And I do not—   [*Exit.*]

---

394. [*Exit.*]] *F2; not in F.*   403. not—] *F* (not.), *Theobald.*   [*Exit.*]]
Theobald; not in F.

alive)?', which suffers from the
absence of 'why' from the text.
Honigmann's punctuation, which
varies most of all from that of F, gives
undue prominence to 'so', which he
seems to understand in the sense 'very
well!'

387–8. *We'll whisper ... saws*] The
stress is on 'We', and Sir Toby is
clearly deriding some of the couplets
recently uttered. Deighton thinks he
refers both to 'Antonio's moralizing
and Viola's soliloquizing', whereas
Furness argues that Viola's soliloquy
is supposed to be unheard by Sir
Toby. Wilson (here as elsewhere
postulating revision) suggests that
not only is Sir Toby mocking Viola
but also Shakespeare may be 'mocking at verse which he originally took
seriously'. I do take both Antonio's
and Viola's couplets seriously and
regard Sir Toby's remark as un-

consciously reflecting on his super-
ficial view of the situation, which
comes out in the final prose dialogue
of this scene and leads into the comic
catastrophe of IV. i.

389–90. *I my brother know ... glass*] 'I
know my brother to be mirrored to
the life in my person, in myself who
am the glass' (Deighton). That this is
the right interpretation is confirmed
by her following lines, 'even such ...
for him I imitate'.

397. *denying*] refusing to recognize.

399. *religious in it*] as though he had
made a religion of cowardice.

400. *'Slid*] by God's eyelid.

403. *And I do not—*] i.e., 'cuff him
soundly', not 'draw my sword'. Sir
Andrew's speech, unfinished in his
haste to pursue Cesario, may be
completed in either of his familiar
ways: 'never trust me' (II. iii. 188),
or 'it is pity of our lives' (cf. II. v. 12).

Fabian. Come, let's see the event.
Sir To. I dare lay any money 'twill be nothing yet.   405
                                                    Exeunt.

405. *Exeunt.*] *Rowe; Exit | F.*

  404. *event*] outcome.

ACT IV

SCENE I

Enter SEBASTIAN *and* CLOWN.

Clown. Will you make me believe that I am not sent for
    you?
Seb. Go to, go to, thou art a foolish fellow,
    Let me be clear of thee.
Clown. Well held out, i' faith! No, I do not know you,   5
    nor I am not sent to you by my lady, to bid you
    come speak with her; nor your name is not Master
    Cesario; nor this is not my nose neither. Nothing
    that is so, is so.
Seb. I prithee vent thy folly somewhere else,   10
    Thou know'st not me.
Clown. Vent my folly! He has heard that word of some

ACT IV

Scene i

ACT IV SCENE I] F (*Actus Quartus, Scæna prima.*).   [*Location.*] *The Street.*
Rowe; The Street before Olivia's house. Capell.   10–11.] *As Capell; prose in F.*

5. *held out*] persisted in, kept up.
Their dialogue has been going on for
some time; hence Sebastian's growing
irritation.

8. *nor this . . . nose neither*] the ultimate argument against the supposed
Cesario's denial of the self-evident;
cf. Tilley, N215, 'As plain as the nose
on a man's face'.

10–11. *I prithee . . . know'st not me*]
Since Sebastian speaks verse elsewhere throughout the scene, Capell's
re-lining here and at ll. 18–20 is
justified. The contrast between his
verse and the prose of the Clown,
Sir Andrew, and Sir Toby is evidently
intentional. His dialogue with Olivia
is entirely in verse.

10. *vent*] give vent to, let out; cf.
Jaques on Touchstone's observation
'the which he vents / In mangled
forms' (*AYL.*, II. vii. 41–2). Used both
literally and in a variety of figurative
senses in the sixteenth century (*OED*,
2, 3, 4, 5): cf. *Shr.*, I. ii. 175 'Gremio,
'tis now no time to vent our love' (i.e.,
utter it in boastful rivalry). Hence,
though Sebastian is not speaking
incorrectly or affectedly, the Clown
is enabled to retort as if he were, and
to use the word in contexts that make
it sound absurd; cf. his criticism of
'element', III. i. 59–60.

12–13. *He has heard . . . great man*]
Cf. *LLL.*, v. i. 33–4 (of Armado and
Holofernes), 'They have been at a

great man, and now applies it to a fool. Vent
my folly! I am afraid this great lubber, the world,
will prove a cockney. I prithee now, ungird thy   15
strangeness, and tell me what I shall vent to my
lady. Shall I vent to her that thou art coming?

Seb. I prithee, foolish Greek, depart from me.
There's money for thee: if you tarry longer,
I shall give worse payment.   20

Clown. By my troth, thou hast an open hand. These
wise men that give fools money get themselves a
good report—after fourteen years' purchase.

Enter SIR ANDREW, SIR TOBY, *and* FABIAN.

Sir And. Now sir, have I met you again? There's for you!
[*Strikes Sebastian.*]

18–20.] *As Capell; prose in* F.   23. report—] *Staunton;* report, *F.*   24. [*Strikes
Sebastian.*]] *Rowe* (*subst.*)*; not in* F.

great feast of languages and stol'n the
scraps'.

14–15. *I am afraid . . . cockney*] I am
afraid this great awkward fool, the
world, will adopt the affectations of
an effeminate fop. 'Cockney' originally meant a small egg, and then came
to mean a child pampered by its
parents (*OED*, 2), a milksop.

15–16. *ungird thy strangeness*] The
Clown adopts in mockery what he
takes to be Cesario's affectation of
speech: 'put off your pretence of not
knowing me.'

16. *vent*] perhaps giving the word
an indecent application; cf. *Tp.*,
II. ii. 98–9 (Stephano to Trinculo),
'How cam'st thou to be the siege
[i.e., excrement] of this moon-calf
[Caliban]? Can he vent Trinculos?'

18. *foolish Greek*] silly merry-maker.
'Merry Greek' was a familiar expression (Tilley, M901); cf., in
Nicholas Udall's *Roister Doister*,
Matthew Merrygreek, a parasite
who mocks his foolish master. John
Minsheu, *The Guide into Tongues*
(1617), has 'a merrie Greeke . . . a
jester'. Wilson rightly rejects the

suggestion of Warburton and of
Douce (supported by Furness) that
Sebastian calls the Clown a pander,
'corresponding to the Clown, Pompey,
in *Meas.*' (Furness): Pompey is never
called a Greek, and his name, of
course, is Roman.

20. *worse payment*] blows.

21. *thou . . . open hand*] You are
generous, not tight-fisted. Perhaps
(1) because he thinks Cesario is giving
him money twice in a day (cf. III. i.
44), and (2) because Sebastian has
raised his hand, as if to give him a
box on the ear, at l. 20.

23. *a good report . . . purchase*] a
good reputation, provided they pay
well for it. The marketable value
('purchase') of land was equal to
twelve years' rent; 'after'=after
(according to) the rate of. The Clown
expresses his thanks ironically with
the usual ambiguous antithesis between 'wise men' (cf. 'your wisdom',
III. i. 42) and fools. There is no need
to find (with Wilson) a pun on
'report', the official record of a
decision in a legal case.

Seb. Why, there's for thee, and there, and there!   25

                    [*Beats Sir Andrew.*]

          Are all the people mad?

Sir To. Hold, sir, or I'll throw your dagger o'er the
          house.

Clown. This will I tell my lady straight: I would not be
          in some of your coats for twopence.   [*Exit.*]   30

Sir To. Come on, sir, hold!

Sir And. Nay, let him alone, I'll go another way to work
          with him: I'll have an action of battery against
          him, if there be any law in Illyria; though I
          struck him first, yet it's no matter for that.   35

Seb. Let go thy hand!

Sir To. Come, sir, I will not let you go. Come, my young

25-6. there! / Are] *F*; there, and there! / Are *Capell.*   25. [*Beats Sir Andrew.*]]
Rowe (subst.); *not in F*; *He beats Sir Andrew with the handle of his dagger. Mahood.*
30. [*Exit.*]] *Rowe; not in F.*   35. struck] *F* (stroke).

---

25. *Why, there's . . . there!*] Capell's
additional 'and there!' (followed by
some nineteenth-century edd. but no
modern ones) is ironically commended by Furness: 'It would be shocking
and disgraceful if Sir Andrew were
not beaten according to metre.'

27-8. *throw your dagger o'er the house*]
Hotson (pp. 140-1) suggests that Sir
Toby refers to part of the (hypothetical) stage-set, Olivia's house
being 'a little, free-standing roofed
house—over which Sir Toby *could*
throw a dagger with a simple twist of
the wrist'. This destroys Sir Toby's
hyperbole, which (along with the
Clown's exit speech) suddenly estab-
lishes the hitherto unlocalized scene
as outside Olivia's house, and prepares
for her intervention.

33-5. *I'll have an action of battery . . .
no matter for that*] Shakespeare's three
references to 'an action of battery' are
all in plays of this period and all
comic in different ways: the others
are in *Ham.*, v. i. 99 (the lawyer's skull
and the grave-digger's shovel) and
Meas., II. i. 171-3 (where Elbow
confuses slander and battery).

37-8. *Come, my young soldier . . . well
fleshed*] This is surely spoken to
Sebastian, not to Sir Andrew (first
suggested by C. Badham, 1856). I
suppose (1) that Sebastian has drawn
his dagger to beat Sir Andrew
(Kittredge conclusively compares
Rom., IV. v. 115, 'Then will I lay the
serving-creature's dagger on your
pate', 120-2, 'Then have at you with
my wit! I will dry-beat you with an
iron wit, and put up my iron dagger'
and *H5*, IV. i. 54-7); and (2) that he
does not draw his sword till he breaks
free from Sir Toby (ll. 40-1). 'My
young soldier' is, of course, said in
mockery, but this is very apt, since
Sir Toby thinks Cesario has suddenly
got some courage (cf. l. 43, 'this
malapert blood', i.e., saucy, impudent), and has 'flesh'd / [His] maiden
sword' (in this instance his dagger),
1H4, v. iv. 129-30. Since Badham's
opinion has been followed by Furness,
Luce, and Wilson, it had better be
formally refuted. Furness thinks that
Sir Andrew draws his sword when he
sees Sebastian held by Sir Toby, and
that Sir Toby's command to him is

soldier, put up your iron: you are well fleshed.
Come on!

Seb. I will be free from thee. What would'st thou now?   40
   If thou dar'st tempt me further, draw thy sword.

                                                 [*Draws.*]

Sir To. What, what! Nay, then, I must have an ounce or
   two of this malapert blood from you.   [*Draws.*]

                    Enter OLIVIA.

Olivia. Hold, Toby! on thy life I charge thee, hold!
Sir To. Madam!   45
Olivia. Will it be ever thus? Ungracious wretch,
   Fit for the mountains and the barbarous caves,
   Where manners ne'er were preach'd! Out of my sight!
   Be not offended, dear Cesario.
   Rudesby, be gone!   [*Exeunt Sir Toby, Sir Andrew,*
                                          and Fabian.]
                    I prithee, gentle friend,   50
   Let thy fair wisdom, not thy passion, sway
   In this uncivil and unjust extent
   Against thy peace. Go with me to my house,
   And hear thou there how many fruitless pranks
   This ruffian hath botch'd up, that thou thereby   55

41. [*Draws.*]] *Capell* (*subst.*); *not in* F.   43. [*Draws.*]] *Capell* (*subst.*); *They draw and fight. Rowe; not in* F.   48. *preach'd!] Dyce; preach'd:* F.
50. [*Exeunt Sir Toby, Sir Andrew, and Fabian.*]] *Capell; not in* F.

designed to save his life if Sebastian should get loose; Wilson thinks Sir Andrew entered with sword in hand and that it fell 'some yards off' when Sebastian knocked him down. But (1) Sir Toby told Sir Andrew not to draw his sword (III. iv. 401–2) and there is nothing but editorial conjecture to suggest that he ever did; (2) Sir Andrew has already turned from physical action to his absurd legal remedy; and (3) all Sir Toby's other commands are to Sebastian, including certainly the first and presumably the third in this speech.

49. *dear Cesario*] Olivia, like the Clown, uses Cesario's name so that the audience fully appreciates the dramatic irony. See note on IV. iii. 28.

50. *Rudesby*] ruffian. In common use in Shakespeare's time (and, as H. F. Brooks informs me, found in Golding's Ovid, v. 713); cf. *Shr.*, III. ii. 10.

52. *uncivil and unjust*] barbarous and lawless.

extent] 'In law, a writ of execution [*extendi facias*], whereby goods are seized for the king. It is therefore taken here for violence in general.' (Johnson.)

55. *botch'd up*] clumsily contrived (literally, patched together).

May'st smile at this. Thou shalt not choose but go:
Do not deny. Beshrew his soul for me,
He started one poor heart of mine, in thee.
Seb. What relish is in this? How runs the stream?
Or I am mad, or else this is a dream: 60
Let fancy still my sense in Lethe steep;
If it be thus to dream, still let me sleep!
Olivia. Nay, come, I prithee; would thou'dst be rul'd by
me!
Seb. Madam, I will.
Olivia.   O, say so, and so be.   *Exeunt.*

SCENE II

Enter MARIA *and* CLOWN.

Maria. Nay, I prithee put on this gown, and this beard;
make him believe thou art Sir Topas the curate;
do it quickly. I'll call Sir Toby the whilst.   [*Exit.*]

Scene II

SCENE II] F (*Scæna Secunda.*).   [*Location.*] Olivia's House. Rowe.   3. [*Exit.*]]
Theobald; not in F.

57. *Beshrew . . . for me*] my curse
upon him (spoken lightly).
58. *He started . . . in thee*] 'heart' and
'hart' (cf. I. i. 17) are played upon in
this hunting metaphor. Technically,
one 'rouses' a hart, and 'starts' a hare,
from cover; but 'start' is used because
of its associations with human
demonstrations of fear. Olivia means
that her heart is figuratively inside
Cesario, and that in attacking him
Sir Toby made her heart leap with
fear.
59. *relish*] taste: literally, what is
this that I am tasting?; figuratively,
how am I to understand this?
60-2. *Or I am mad . . . still let me
sleep!*] Staunton compares the speech
of Antipholus of Syracuse, when
Adriana accosts him as her husband,
Err., II. ii. 211–15. Similar reference
is made to dreaming and madness,

but the element of rapture is missing,
Adriana being a jealous wife, Olivia
an adoring lover.
61. *Let fancy . . . steep*] May love for
ever keep my understanding plunged
in the river of forgetfulness.
63. *be rul'd by me*] do as I would have
you do (cf. III. i. 144).

Scene II

2. *Sir Topas the curate*] For 'Sir', cf.
note on 'sir priest', III. iv. 276. The
name 'Sir Topas' is probably due to
Shakespeare's delight in incongruity,
as the name had been used twice of
'sir knight', by Chaucer in his bur-
lesque romance the *Tale of Sir Thopas*
in his *Canterbury Tales*, and by Lyly
in *Endimion* (pr. 1591), where Sir
Topas is a bragging warrior. There
may also be an allusion, as H. H.

Clown. Well, I'll put it on, and I will dissemble myself
　　in't, and I would I were the first that ever dis-　　5
　　sembled in such a gown. I am not tall enough to
　　become the function well, nor lean enough to be
　　thought a good student; but to be said an honest
　　man and a good housekeeper goes as fairly as to
　　say a careful man and a great scholar. The com-　　10
　　petitors enter.

Enter SIR TOBY [*and* MARIA].

Sir To. Jove bless thee, Master Parson.
Clown. *Bonos dies,* Sir Toby: for as the old hermit of
　　Prague, that never saw pen and ink, very wittily
　　said to a niece of King Gorboduc, 'That that is,　　15
　　is': so I, being Master Parson, am Master Parson;
　　for what is 'that' but 'that'? and 'is' but 'is'?
Sir To. To him, Sir Topas.

---

6. tall] *F;* fat *Var. '03, conj. Farmer;* pale *conj. Tyrwhitt.*　　11. S.D. *Enter Sir Toby* [*and Maria*].] *Theobald; Enter Toby. F.*　　12. Jove] *F;* God *Hudson, conj. Halliwell.*　　Master] *F* (M.).　　15. Gorboduc] *F (Gorbodacke), Capell.*

Furness, Jr, pointed out, to Reginald Scot's *Discoverie of Witchcraft* (1584), p. 294, 'a topase healeth the lunatic person of his passion of lunacie' (quoted by Furness).

4, 5–6. *dissemble, dissembled*] (1) disguise, (2) play the hypocrite. P. Milward, *Shakespeare's Religious Background* (1973), p. 149, observes that 'the gown was generally worn, without a surplice, by Calvinist ministers —the "black gown of a big heart", as it is called by the other Clown in *All's W.* (I. iii. 91). In this case, there is something ironical in the pitting of a Puritan minister against Malvolio, who is "a kind of Puritan".'

6. *not tall enough*] 'to overlook a pulpit' (Steevens). The gown may have been too long for him. Tyrwhitt's conjecture 'pale' is based on the parallel with 'careful', Farmer's 'fat' on the parallel with 'good housekeeper'.

9. *good housekeeper*] a hospitable man; cf. *LLL.,* II. i. 104, 'I hear your Grace hath sworn out housekeeping'.

10. *careful*] painstaking, laborious.

10–11. *competitors*] confederates: cf. *R3,* IV. iv. 506–7, 'And every hour more competitors / Flock to the rebels, and their power grows strong.'

13. Bonos dies] good day. The bad Latin is probably Shakespeare's invention, not an error of scribe or compositor; cf. *LLL.,* v. i. 24–5, where Holofernes corrects Sir Nathaniel's error, '*bone* for *bene*'.

13–15. *for as the old hermit . . . King Gorboduc*] mock authority; cf. I. v. 33, 'Quinapalus'. Gorboduc is from legendary British history, and appears in the Chronicles and in Norton and Sackville's tragedy *Gorboduc* (1562).

15–17. '*That that is, is' . . . but 'is'?*] mock logic. All his speech is in the assumed character of the man of learning.

Clown. What ho, I say! Peace in this prison!
Sir To. The knave counterfeits well: a good knave.   20

MALVOLIO *within.*

Mal. Who calls there?
Clown. Sir Topas the curate, who comes to visit Malvolio
    the lunatic.
Mal. Sir Topas, Sir Topas, good Sir Topas, go to my
    lady.   25
Clown. Out, hyperbolical fiend! how vexest thou this
    man! Talkest thou nothing but of ladies?
Sir To. Well said, Master Parson.
Mal. Sir Topas, never was man thus wronged. Good Sir
    Topas, do not think I am mad. They have laid me   30
    here in hideous darkness.
Clown. Fie, thou dishonest Satan! (I call thee by the
    most modest terms, for I am one of those gentle
    ones that will use the devil himself with courtesy.)
    Say'st thou that house is dark?   35
Mal. As hell, Sir Topas.
Clown. Why, it hath bay-windows transparent as
    barricadoes, and the clerestories toward the

---

32. Satan! (I] *This ed.;* sathan: I *F.*   34–5. courtesy.) Say'st] *This ed.;*
curtesie: sayst *F.*   35. that] *F;* this *Rann, conj. Mason;* that this *Halliwell.*
38. clerestories] *Var. '21, conj. Blakeway* (clear stories)*; cleere stores *F;* cleare
stones *F2*

---

19. *Peace in this prison!*] In the
Elizabethan *Book of Common Prayer*
(1559, in use till 1662), the *Order for
the Visitacion of the Sicke* begins 'The
Priest entryng into the sicke persones
house, shall saye* Peace be in this house,
and to all that dwel in it.'
    26. *hyperbolical*] literally 'exagger-
ated', here used to mean 'vehement'.
    32. *dishonest*] a euphemism for
'lying'. The Clown, as Parson,
absurdly prides himself on his mild
('modest') and courteous behaviour
to the very devil.
    35. *that house is dark*] A 'dark room'
(III. iv. 136) and a 'dark house' (cf.
AYL., III. ii. 369) are synonyms.

37–9. *Why, it hath bay-windows . . .
lustrous as ebony*] triple self-contradic-
tion. Hotson (p. 140) thinks Feste
alludes to the hall in which he
assumes the first performance to have
taken place, 'with its blocked bays,
its covered clerestories due South and
North, and its two scenic "houses"
set due East and West'. But Feste does
not talk of the south and north, he
talks of 'the south-north' as a single
point of the compass, and all his
sentence is in the same vein: his whole
foolery depends on the hearer's
expectation that the two elements in a
simile will be like and not unlike.
    38. *barricadoes*] adapted from Fr.

south-north are as lustrous as ebony: and yet
complainest thou of obstruction?   40
Mal. I am not mad, Sir Topas. I say to you, this
house is dark.
Clown. Madman, thou errest. I say there is no darkness
but ignorance, in which thou art more puzzled than
the Egyptians in their fog.   45
Mal. I say this house is as dark as ignorance, though
ignorance were as dark as hell; and I say there was
never man thus abused. I am no more mad than
you are: make the trial of it in any constant
question.   50
Clown. What is the opinion of Pythagoras concerning
wildfowl?
Mal. That the soul of our grandam might haply inhabit
a bird.
Clown. What think'st thou of his opinion?   55
Mal. I think nobly of the soul, and no way approve
his opinion.

39. south-north] F (South north), *F3* (South-North).   53. haply] F (happily),
Capell.

barricade or Sp. *barricada* (Fr. *barrique*,
Sp. *barrica*, a cask), barricades having
been originally made of casks filled
with earth and stones (*OED*). Here
used as a type of impenetrability.

clerestories] a number of adjacent
windows high in a wall (usually of a
church), and therefore, like bay-
windows, a source of much daylight.

44. *puzzled*] lost, made hopeless.

45. *the Egyptians in their fog*] Exodus,
x. 21–3, the plague of darkness. The
Clown calls it a fog because it is
described as 'darkness which may be
felt' and 'a thick darkness'.

48. *abused*] the first appearance in
the play of a word which is to be
repeated by Malvolio at l. 90, and
used with reference to him by Olivia
at v. i. 378.

49–50. *any constant question*] any test
of consecutive reasoning. See C. J.
Sisson, 'Tudor Intelligence Tests' in
Essays on Shakespeare and Elizabethan

Drama in Honor of Hardin Craig, ed.
R. Hosley (1963): he concludes (not
surprisingly) that Malvolio's examination was at complete variance
with current legal practice.

51. *Pythagoras*] with reference to the
doctrine of transmigration of souls,
much used in Elizabethan literature;
cf. Marlowe, *Doctor Faustus* (in
Faustus' last speech), 'Ah, Pythagoras'
metempsychosis!', and in Shakespeare,
Mer.V., IV. i. 130–8; *AYL.*, III. ii.
163–5.

52. *wildfowl*] not significantly
associated with the Pythagorean
doctrine, but introduced here in order
to give rise to the 'woodcock' jest
(cf. II. v. 84).

56–7. *I think . . . opinion*] Harold
Jenkins points out to me that
Malvolio's objection was often ex-
pressed by Renaissance thinkers: see
M. van Wyk Smith, 'John Donne's
Metempsychosis', *RES* 24 (1973), pp.
17–25.

Clown. Fare thee well: remain thou still in darkness.
    Thou shalt hold th' opinion of Pythagoras ere I
    will allow of thy wits, and fear to kill a woodcock   60
    lest thou dispossess the soul of thy grandam. Fare
    thee well.

Mal. Sir Topas, Sir Topas!

Sir To. My most exquisite Sir Topas!

Clown. Nay, I am for all waters.   65

Maria. Thou might'st have done this without thy beard
    and gown, he sees thee not.

Sir To. To him in thine own voice, and bring me word
    how thou find'st him: I would we were well rid of
    this knavery. If he may be conveniently delivered,   70
    I would he were, for I am now so far in offence
    with my niece that I cannot pursue with any safety
    this sport to the upshot. Come by and by to my

73. sport to the] *Rowe;* sport the *F;* sport' the *conj. Furness.*

60. *allow of thy wits*] certify you to be rational.

65. *Nay, I am for all waters*] The sense is evidently 'I can turn my hand to anything' (Malone), but the origin is obscure. Furness records many conjectures, the most probable being (1) the Ital. proverb '*Tu hai mantello d'ogni acqua*' (Smith, *apud* Z. Gray, *Critical . . . Notes,* 1754: cf. Tilley, C421, 'To have a Cloak for all waters', cf. 'I'm for any weather' in Tourneur, *The Revenger's Tragedy,* v. i.), and (2) able to 'relish all waters', i.e., drink anything (Halliwell, and Staunton, who instances 'brooke all waters' (Nashe's *Lenten Stuff,* 1599) and 'breathe in your watering' (*1H4,* II. iv. 15); cf. Marlowe, *Doctor Faustus* (ed. Greg, 1950, A1157, B1538–9), where the Horse-Courser, being warned by Faustus not to ride his horse into the water, asks 'Why sir, wil he not drinke of all waters?'

66–7. *Thou might'st . . . sees thee not*] 'This suggests an afterthought on Shakespeare's part, and so, rapid composition' (Mahood). This is possible; but perhaps, on the contrary, Shakespeare showed forethought. The Clown puts on the beard and gown, in the first place, to give himself a preliminary joke or two, and to keep the audience firmly in mind that he is impersonating a clergyman; then (he having here returned the beard and gown to Maria) he resumes his own character, but suddenly, and utterly to the audience's surprise, brings back Sir Topas by changing his voice. Who can say whether that was planned in advance or a stroke of inspiration?

69–70. *well rid of this knavery*] safely clear of the consequences of our practical joke.

70. *conveniently delivered*] set free without too much trouble.

73. *the upshot*] the shoot-off to determine the winner of an archery match; hence, figuratively, the outcome. F's reading leaves it doubtful whether the compositor accidentally omitted a word or misread a contraction.

69–74. *I would we were . . . to my chamber*] 'It seems clear that these

chamber.   *Exit [with Maria].*

Clown. [Singing]   *Hey Robin, jolly Robin,*   75
                      Tell me how thy lady does.

Mal. Fool!

Clown.   *My lady is unkind, perdie.*

Mal. Fool!

Clown.   *Alas, why is she so?*   80

Mal. Fool, I say!

Clown.   *She loves another*—Who calls, ha?

Mal. Good fool, as ever thou wilt deserve well at my
    hand, help me to a candle, and pen, ink, and paper:
    as I am a gentleman, I will live to be thankful to   85
    thee for't.

Clown. Master Malvolio?

Mal. Ay, good fool.

---

74. *Exit [with Maria].*] *Theobald; Exit | F.*   75. *[Singing]] Rowe; not in F.*
75–6.] *As Capell; prose in F.*   82. *another*—] *Rowe; another. F.*

words were spoken to Maria alone,
and the last sentence suggests that
the couple are already married'
(Wilson). This is possible, as is also
the idea that they are going to be
married in his chamber *per verba de
praesenti* (see note on v. i. 154,
'contract'), which I think has not
yet been suggested as a variation on
Wilson's. If the last sentence is
spoken to Maria, it has the merit
of motivating her exit (which must
be included in Sir Toby's since she
takes no further part in the scene).
On the other hand, Wilson gives no
special reason why the Clown should
not be included in Sir Toby's
audience, and it can be argued that
the last sentence is directly addressed
to him by way of repeating 'bring me
word how thou find'st him.' The
reader, or producer, must take his
choice.

75. Hey Robin] The Clown identifies himself for Malvolio's benefit
by singing snatches of an old song,
the words of which are attributed to

Sir Thomas Wyatt, found in B.M.
MS. Egerton 2711 (f. 37v.). Wyatt
may have reworked an older lyric,
as J. E. Stevens suggests in *Music
and Poetry at the Early Tudor Court*
(1961), p. 111. A musical setting,
as a round for three voices, is in B.M.
Add. MS. 31,922 (ff. 53v.–4), where
it is attributed to the musician
William Cornyshe, Wyatt's contemporary. (See Appendix II, p. 187).
The opening stanzas of the lyric (ed.
K. Muir, *Collected Poems of Sir Thomas
Wyatt*, 1949, p. 42) are (1) 'A Robyn, /
Joly Robyn, / Tell me how thy leman
doeth, / And thou shall knowe of myn',
(2) 'My lady is vnkynd, perde!' /
'Alack, whi is she so?' / 'She
loveth an othre better then me, /
And yet she will say no.' Seng, p.
119, comments that the song (like
the dialogue song in ii. iii) is directed
at Malvolio in mockery: 'he is the
lover, Olivia the "lady", and the
"other" she loves is Viola disguised
in male habiliments.'

78. perdie] by God (Fr. *par Dieu*).

Clown. Alas, sir, how fell you besides your five wits?

Mal. Fool, there was never man so notoriously abused: 90
I am as well in my wits, fool, as thou art.

Clown. But as well? Then you are mad indeed, if you be
no better in your wits than a fool.

Mal. They have here propertied me: keep me in darkness, send ministers to me, asses, and do all they can   95
to face me out of my wits.

Clown. Advise you what you say: the minister is here.
[*As Sir Topas*] Malvolio, Malvolio, thy wits the
heavens restore: endeavour thyself to sleep, and
leave thy vain bibble babble.   100

Mal. Sir Topas!

Clown. [*As Sir Topas*] Maintain no words with him,
good fellow! [*As himself*] Who, I, sir? not I, sir!
God buy you, good Sir Topas! [*As Sir Topas*]
Marry, amen! [*As himself*] I will, sir, I will.   105

Mal. Fool, fool, fool, I say!

Clown. Alas, sir, be patient. What say you, sir? I am
shent for speaking to you.

Mal. Good fool, help me to some light and some paper:

---

89. besides] *F;* beside *Var. '73, conj. Capell.*   98, 102, 103, 104, 105. [*As Sir Topas*] ... [*As Sir Topas*] ... [*As himself*] ... [*As Sir Topas*] ... [*As himself*]] *As Hanmer (subst.); not in F.*   104. buy] *F;* b'w' *Pope.*

---

89. *how fell you . . . five wits?*]
What has made you lose your
senses? 'besides'=out of (cf. idiomatic 'beside himself'). The five wits
are the mental powers, catalogued
by Stephen Hawes in his long poem
The Passetyme of Pleasure (1509) as
common wit, imagination, fantasy,
estimation, and memory, but they are
usually regarded collectively, as
personified by the character Five
Wits in *Everyman* (n.d., *c.*1495).

90. *notoriously*] the first appearance
in the play of a word which is to be
repeated at v. i. 328, 342, 378.

94. *propertied me*] treated me like a
senseless object; cf. *John,* v. ii. 79–
82, and *Caes.,* vi. i. 39–40.

95. *ministers . . . asses*] referring,

with contemptuous plural, to Sir
Topas. Since the minister was played
by the 'ass' (ii. iii. 18), Malvolio's
words are truer than he knows.

96. *face me out of my wits*] 'cheat me
out of my wits by sheer impudence'
(Wright).

97. *Advise you*] Be careful.

100. *bibble babble*] senseless prattle.
An established expression by the time
of John Bale's *King John* (MS. before 1561) and used by Shakespeare
in *H5,* iv. i. 70.

104. *God buy you*] God be with you.

105. *I will, sir, I will*] 'Spoken after
a pause, as if, in the meantime, Sir
Topas had whispered' (Johnson).

108. *shent*] rebuked.

I tell thee I am as well in my wits as any man in   110
Illyria.

Clown. Well-a-day that you were, sir!

Mal. By this hand, I am! Good fool, some ink, paper,
and light, and convey what I will set down to my
lady. It shall advantage thee more than ever the   115
bearing of letter did.

Clown. I will help you to't. But tell me true, are you
not mad indeed? or do you but counterfeit?

Mal. Believe me, I am not, I tell thee true.

Clown. Nay, I'll ne'er believe a madman till I see his   120
brains. I will fetch you light, and paper, and
ink.

Mal. Fool, I'll requite it in the highest degree: I
prithee, be gone.

Clown. [*Singing*]   *I am gone, sir, and anon, sir,*   125
                I'll be with you again,
            In a trice, like to the old Vice,
                Your need to sustain;

118. indeed?] *Var. '93;* indeed, *F.*   counterfeit?] *F2;* counterfeit. *F.*
125. [*Singing*]] *Rowe; not in F.*   125-32. *I am gone . . . goodman devil!*] *As F;*
I . . . sir, / And . . . sir, / I'll . . . again, / In . . . trice, / Like . . . vice, / Your . . .
sustain; / Who . . . lath, / In . . . wrath, / Cries . . . devil, / Like . . . lad, /
'Pare . . . dad. / Adieu . . . devil.' *Capell.*

117-18. *are you not mad indeed?*]
i.e., You are really mad, are you not?

120-1. *I'll ne'er believe . . . brains*]
alluding to the proverb, 'You will
not believe he is bald (dead) till you
see his brain' (Tilley, B597), but
with additional force, since he seems
to want ocular proof that Malvolio
has brains at all.

125-32. *I am gone, sir . . . Adieu,*
goodman devil!] Though no early
music has survived, this is more likely
to be sung than spoken.

127. *the old Vice*] The Vice was
an important and favourite character
in moralities and interludes of the
sixteenth century. For 'old', cf. *H5*,
IV. iv. 70, where the Boy refers to
Pistol as 'this roaring devil i' th' old
play, that every one may pare his

nails with a wooden dagger', and
Jonson, *The Devil is an Ass* (1631),
I. i. 43-5, where the minor devil Pug
asks for a Vice for his companion
from hell to London, and mentions
'old Iniquity' whose first speech
begins 'What is he, calls upon me,
and would seeme to lack a Vice? /
Ere his words be halfe spoken, I am
with him in a trice.' It is incorrect
to suppose that the Vice always
carried a 'wooden dagger' ('dagger
of lath'), though he does in *The*
Trial of Treasure (1567) and may
have done so in other plays where he
'fighteth', or that with this dagger
he habitually pared the Devil's nails
(in no extant play does he do so,
but Shakespeare either had seen,
or could imagine, one or more in
which he did).

> *Who, with dagger of lath, in his rage*
> *and his wrath,*
> *Cries, 'Ah, ha!' to the devil:*   130
> *Like a mad lad, 'Pare thy nails, dad.*
> *Adieu, goodman devil!'*   Exit.

SCENE III

Enter SEBASTIAN.

Seb. This is the air, that is the glorious sun,
This pearl she gave me, I do feel't, and see't,
And though 'tis wonder that enwraps me thus,
Yet 'tis not madness. Where's Antonio then?
I could not find him at the Elephant,   5
Yet there he was, and there I found this credit,
That he did range the town to seek me out.
His counsel now might do me golden service:
For though my soul disputes well with my sense

---

132. *goodman devil*] *Capell*; good man diuell *F*; good Man Devil *Rowe*; good man Drivel *Rowe³*; mean-evil, *conj.* goodman *Johnson*; good mean-evil *conj. Mason.*

Scene III

SCENE III] *F* (*Scæna Tertia.*).   [*Location.*] *Not in Rowe*; *Olivia's Garden. Capell*; *Another apartment in Olivia's house. Theobald.*   6. credit] *F*; current *Hanmer*; credent *conj. Theobald.*

131. dad] Sometimes, for example in *Lusty Juventus* (n.d., 1565?), the Vice is the Devil's son.

132. Adieu, goodman devil] either part of the Vice's speech to the Devil in the rhyme, or addressed by the Clown to Malvolio by way of exit line. There is no need to emend 'devil' because it has already appeared in l. 130 (Furness justifies the rhyme by the song's extempore nature) or because 'drivel' (idiot) may be applied to Malvolio in his predicament. 'Goodman' (i.e., master, with possible pun on 'good man' as in Dogberry's proverbial 'Well, God's a good man', *Ado*, III.

v. 34; cf. Tilley, G195) is a sufficiently incongruous title for the Devil.

Scene III

6. *was*] had been.
credit] report (*OED*, *sb.* 3, this instance only).

9–16. *For though . . . else the lady's mad*] For though my inmost feelings and reason conclude, in agreement with my senses, that this is no delusion of insanity, but a real experience, though occasioned by some error, yet this good fortune which has befallen me is so abundant, so beyond all precedent and explanation, that I

That this may be some error, but no madness,   10
'Yet doth this accident and flood of fortune
So far exceed all instance, all discourse,
That I am ready to distrust mine eyes,
And wrangle with my reason that persuades me
To any other trust but that I am mad,   15
Or else the lady's mad; yet if 'twere so,
She could not sway her house, command her followers,
Take and give back affairs and their dispatch,
With such a smooth, discreet, and stable bearing
As I perceive she does. There's something in't   20
That is deceivable. But here the lady comes.

Enter OLIVIA *and* PRIEST.

Olivia. Blame not this haste of mine. If you mean well,
Now go with me, and with this holy man,
Into the chantry by: there before him,
And underneath that consecrated roof,   25
Plight me the full assurance of your faith,
That my most jealous and too doubtful soul
May live at peace. He shall conceal it,

---

28. live] *F;* henceforth live *Hanmer.*   it,] *F;* it still, *Keightley.*

am ready to distrust my eyes (i.e., my senses), and argue against my very reason that the only trustworthy solution is that either I am mad or the lady is so.

12. *discourse*] process of reasoning; cf. *Ham.*, I. ii. 150.

17. *sway*] rule.

18. *Take . . . dispatch*] undertake business ('take affairs') and discharge it ('give back their dispatch'). Wright compares the construction in *Wint.*, III. ii. 160–1, 'though I with death and with / Reward did threaten and encourage him', and *Mac.*, I. iii. 60–1, 'Speak then to me, who neither beg nor fear / Your favours nor your hate.'

21. *deceivable*] able to deceive, deceptive.

24. *chantry*] a part of a church, or a chapel attached to a great house or standing alone, which has been endowed to support one or more priests to sing daily mass for the souls of the founders or for others. There is no need to assume that Olivia had endowed this chantry herself for her brother's soul, or (cf. Hotson, p. 140) to identify it with the Chapel Royal which stood beside the Hall where he thinks the play was first performed.

by] near by.

26. *Plight me . . . of your faith*] Reassure me of your complete good faith by a solemn betrothal. See note on 'contract', v. i. 154.

28. *May live . . . conceal it*] possibly a defective line, though (as Furness suggests) the pause may compensate for the missing foot. Hanmer and Keightley emended by different ad-

Whiles you are willing it shall come to note,
What time we will our celebration keep   30
According to my birth. What do you say?
Seb. I'll follow this good man, and go with you,
And having sworn truth, ever will be true.
Olivia. Then lead the way, good father, and heavens so
          shine,
That they may fairly note this act of mine! *Exeunt.* 35

35. *Exeunt.*] *Exeunt. Finis Actus Quartus. F.*

ditions, and a third might be that of 'sir' at the end of the line (for Olivia must not use the name Cesario in this scene, as she did at iv. i. 49, or the audience's attention will be drawn to the impossibility of keeping up the mistake of identity throughout the ceremony).

29. *Whiles*] until.

30. *What time*] at which time.
celebration] marriage celebration.

31. *What do you say?*] Do you agree to this proposal?

35. *fairly note*] look favourably upon, show that they approve. Olivia may possibly be troubled in conscience about her vow to mourn for seven years; but more probably the couplet stresses that her betrothal to Sebastian, though based on a mistake of identity, is not ridiculous but fitting and admirable. Note how 'heavens so shine' (l. 34) picks up Sebastian's 'that is the glorious sun' (l. 1). The 'golden time' of v. i. 381 is already beginning.

ACT V

SCENE I

Enter CLOWN *and* FABIAN.

Fabian. Now as thou lov'st me, let me see his letter.
Clown. Good Master Fabian, grant me another request.
Fabian. Anything.
Clown. Do not desire to see this letter.
Fabian. This is to give a dog, and in recompense desire   5
    my dog again.

Enter DUKE, VIOLA, CURIO, *and Lords.*

Duke. Belong you to the Lady Olivia, friends?
Clown. Ay, sir, we are some of her trappings.
Duke. I know thee well. How dost thou, my good
    fellow?   10
Clown. Truly, sir, the better for my foes, and the worse
    for my friends.
Duke. Just the contrary: the better for thy friends.
Clown. No, sir, the worse.
Duke. How can that be?   15
Clown. Marry, sir, they praise me, and make an ass of
    me. Now my foes tell me plainly I am an ass: so that

ACT V

Scene 1

ACT V SCENE 1] F (*Actus Quintus, Scena Prima.*).   [*Location.*] *Not in Rowe; The Street.* Pope; *Before Olivia's House.* Capell.   1. his] F; this F2.

5–6. *to give a dog . . . again*] F Manningham's *Diary* (see Introduction, p. xxvi, under date 26 March 1602/3 (i.e., two days after the Queen's death), records the following story: 'Mr Francis Curle told me howe one Dr Bullein, the Queenes kinsman, had a dog which he doted on, soe much that the Queene vnderstanding of it requested he would graunt hir one desyre, and he should haue what soeuer he would aske. Shee demaunded his dogge; he gave it, and "Nowe Madame" quoth he, "you promised to give me my desyre." "I will," quoth she. "Then I pray you giue me my dog againe."'

16. *and make*] and thus make.

by my foes, sir, I profit in the knowledge of myself, and by my friends I am abused. So that,
conclusions to be as kisses, if your four negatives   20
make your two affirmatives, why then the worse for
my friends, and the better for my foes.

Duke. Why, this is excellent.

Clown. By my troth, sir, no: though it please you to be
one of my friends.   25

Duke. Thou shalt not be the worse for me: there's gold.

Clown. But that it would be double-dealing, sir, I
would you could make it another.

Duke. O, you give me ill counsel.

Clown. Put your grace in your pocket, sir, for this once,   30
and let your flesh and blood obey it.

Duke. Well, I will be so much a sinner to be a double-
dealer: there's another.

19–20. that, conclusions to be as kisses] *F;* that, conclusion to be asked, is
conj. *Warburton apud Theobald;* the conclusion to be asked is *Hanmer.*

19. *abused*] wronged, hence deceived.

20–1. *conclusions to be . . . affirmatives*]
probably with a casual allusion to
Sidney, *Astrophil and Stella,* Sonnet 63,
where Stella, on his asking a kiss,
'Lest once should not be heard,
twice said "No, no."' Astrophil
therefore concludes that a kiss is his
due by grammatical right, 'For grammar says (to grammar who says
nay?) / That in one speech two negatives affirm.' Farmer, who first
pointed this out, cites a parallel from
Lust's Dominion (*c.*1600, pr. 1657):
'No, no, says *aye,* and twice *away* says
stay.' (This may equally be influenced by *R2,* IV. i. 201–2, 'Ay, no;
no, ay; for I must nothing be; /
Therefore no no, for I resign to thee.')
It seems unprofitable to ask where
are the Clown's 'four negatives'; he
probably means no more than that
what he has logically 'concluded'
is a paradox, and, as such, comparable to the fact that four negatives
are equivalent to two affirmatives.
Wilson's explanation, that 'a kiss is

made by four lips (contraries or
negatives) brought together by two
ardent mouths (affirmatives)', throws
too heavy a figurative sense on the
words 'negatives' and 'affirmatives'.

20, 21. *your*] used indefinitely,
without any possessive sense.

24–5. *though it . . . friends*] artfully
putting the next line into the Duke's
mouth.

27. *double-dealing*] (1) duplicity (the
usual sense), (2) giving twice over
(the special literal sense in this context).

30. *your grace*] (1) your virtue (in
antithesis with 'your flesh and blood',
i.e., your sensual impulses), (2) the
form of address to a Duke.

in your pocket] To put a thing in
one's pocket (a familiar idiom) is to
overlook it deliberately; cf. the
similar quibbles on 'to pocket up
wrongs' in *John,* III. i. 200, *1H4,*
III. iii. 162, *H5,* III. ii. 48. The Clown
here means the Duke's actual pocket,
as the source of money.

31. *obey it*] obey my 'ill counsel'.

Clown. Primo, secundo, tertio, is a good play, and the
old saying is 'The third pays for all'; the triplex,   35
sir, is a good tripping measure; or the bells of
Saint Bennet, sir, may put you in mind—one, two,
three.

Duke. You can fool no more money out of me at this
throw. If you will let your lady know I am here to   40
speak with her, and bring her along with you, it
may awake my bounty further.

Clown. Marry, sir, lullaby to your bounty till I come
again. I go, sir, but I would not have you to
think that my desire of having is the sin of covetous-   45
ness: but as you say, sir, let your bounty take a
nap, I will awake it anon.   *Exit.*

Enter ANTONIO *and* OFFICERS.

Viola. Here comes the man, sir, that did rescue me.
Duke. That face of his I do remember well;
     Yet when I saw it last, it was besmear'd   50
     As black as Vulcan, in the smoke of war.
     A baubling vessel was he captain of,
     For shallow draught and bulk unprizable,
     With which such scathful grapple did he make

35. triplex] *F;* triplet *Johnson.*   37. Saint] *F* (S.).

34. Primo, secundo, tertio] firstly,
secondly, thirdly. Perhaps an allusion
to a children's game (Wilson quotes
Reginald Scot's *Discoverie of Witchcraft* (1584), XI. x. 159, 'Lotterie . . .
is a childish and ridiculous toie, and
like vnto childrens plaie at Primus
secundus, or the game called The
Philosophers table'); or spoken with
reference to the 'old saying' that follows.

35. *The third pays for all*] proverbial:
the third attempt (shot, etc.) is
lucky; cf. Tilley, T319, 'the third
time pays for all'.

triplex] triple time in music.

37. *Saint Bennet*] Saint Benedict.
'The allusion is, perhaps, to some old
rhyme which has been lost: or it may

be to the real bells of St Bennet Hithe,
Paul's Wharf, just opposite the Globe
Theatre' (Wright).

40. *throw*] i.e., of the dice, alluding
to the 'gambler's proverb' just
uttered by the Clown (Mahood).

43. *lullaby to your bounty*] good repose
to your generosity; cf. 'awake' (l. 42),
'take a nap' (ll. 46–7), 'awake it'
(l. 47).

52. *baubling*] contemptibly small,
like a bauble or trifling plaything; cf.
Troil., I. iii. 35, 'shallow bauble
boats'.

53. *unprizable*] relatively of no
value, not worth taking as a 'prize'.

54. *scathful*] harmful.

With the most noble bottom of our fleet,   55
That very envy and the tongue of loss
Cried fame and honour on him. What's the matter?

First Off. Orsino, this is that Antonio
That took the Phoenix and her fraught from Candy,
And this is he that did the Tiger board,   60
When your young nephew Titus lost his leg.
Here in the streets, desperate of shame and state,
In private brabble did we apprehend him.

Viola. He did me kindness, sir, drew on my side,
But in conclusion put strange speech upon me,   65
I know not what 'twas, but distraction.

Duke. Notable pirate, thou salt-water thief,
What foolish boldness brought thee to their mercies,
Whom thou in terms so bloody and so dear
Hast made thine enemies?

Ant.   Orsino, noble sir,   70

---

58. Orsino] *F* (*subst.*); Signior Orsino *or* Noble Orsino *conj. anon. apud Camb²*.

---

55. *bottom*] ship (by extension from the original literal sense, keel or hull).

56. *very envy . . . loss*] even those who had most reason to begrudge him his bravery, we, his enemies, who lost by it.

58. *Orsino*] an abrupt form of address, as Furness notes, but the insertion of 'Signior' or 'Noble' would turn a strong line into a weaker one with a feminine ending. It also helps to suggest that Antonio's 'Orsino, noble sir' is not ceremonious but a sign of his magnanimity.

59. *fraught from Candy*] cargo (cf. freight) from Candia (Crete).

61. *your young nephew Titus*] This, besides being a piece of corroborative detail as to Antonio's prowess in war, suggests that Orsino (like Hamlet) has had moral years added to him by this point of the play. Compare the Duke-like, regal authority with which he addresses Antonio. Both men seem

therefore to be appreciably older than Sebastian and Viola.

62. *desperate . . . state*] reckless of his personal character (cf. Othello's speech to Montano, *Oth.*, II. iii. 181–8) or of public order. Wilson compares *R2*, IV. i. 225, 'Against the state and profit of this land'. Others interpret 'state' as 'the danger in which it would place him' (Mahood), but the emphasis in the passage seems to be on the behaviour of Antonio rather than on his situation.

63. *brabble*] brawl.

65. *put strange speech upon me*] spoke to me in a strange manner.

67. *Notable*] notorious.

pirate . . . salt-water thief] Wright compares *Mer.V.*, I. iii. 20, 'water-thieves . . . —I mean pirates.'

69. *dear*] grievous (*OED*, dear, *a.²*, 2); cf. its near-synonymous conjunction with 'bloody'. So in *R2*, I. iii. 151, 'The dateless limit of thy dear exile'.

Be pleas'd that I shake off these names you give me:
Antonio never yet was thief, or pirate,
Though I confess, on base and ground enough,
Orsino's enemy. A witchcraft drew me hither:
That most ingrateful boy there by your side,   75
From the rude sea's enrag'd and foamy mouth
Did I redeem. A wrack past hope he was.
His life I gave him, and did thereto add
My love, without retention or restraint,
All his in dedication. For his sake   80
Did I expose myself (pure for his love)
Into the danger of this adverse town;
Drew to defend him, when he was beset;
Where being apprehended, his false cunning
(Not meaning to partake with me in danger)   85
Taught him to face me out of his acquaintance,
And grew a twenty years' removed thing
While one would wink; denied me mine own purse,
Which I had recommended to his use
Not half an hour before.
Viola.   How can this be?   90
Duke. When came he to this town?
Ant. Today, my lord: and for three months before

---

77. wrack] *F* (wracke); wreck *Pope.*

71. *shake off*] repudiate; cf. *Ant.*,
III. vii. 34, 'these offers he shakes off'.

73. *base and ground*] sound cause
(synonyms for 'foundation').

74. *witchcraft*] Cf. Olivia's words to
Viola, III. i. 114, 'After the last
enchantment you did here'. Wright
compares *1H4*, II. ii. 18 (Falstaff, of
Poins), 'and yet I am bewitch'd with
the rogue's company'.

77. *wrack*] lost thing. F's invariable
spelling is retained here to show that
the modern 'wreck' is not synonymous, as it is at l. 265.

82. *Into the danger*] Cf. *Mer.V.*, IV.
i. 175, 'you stand within his danger,
do you not?' The word 'danger'
here retains the older meaning of
'power to harm' (cf. 'hostile town'),

as well as carrying the more modern
sense of 'risk of harm'.

86. *face me out . . . acquaintance*] deny
that he knew me (cf. IV. ii. 96). With
ll. 84–8 of this scene, cf. *Err.*, v. i.
320–1 (Aegeon to the wrong Antipholus), 'but perhaps, my son, / Thou
sham'st to acknowledge me in misery.,

92. *for three months before*] Cf.
Orsino's rejoinder, ll. 96–7. Daniel
(*Time-Analysis*, p. 176, quoted by
Furness) finds these statements inconsistent with the 'very few days' that
must have elapsed between the shipwreck and the twins' arrival in Illyria
(cf. I. iv. 2–3, 'he hath known you but
three days', and note). Wilson
rightly comments that 'the spectator
(as distinct from the reader) would

No int'rim, not a minute's vacancy,
Both day and night did we keep company.

Enter OLIVIA *and Attendants.*

Duke. Here comes the Countess: now heaven walks on earth.
But for thee, fellow—fellow, thy words are madness.   96
Three months this youth hath tended upon me;
But more of that anon. Take him aside.
Olivia. What would my lord, but that he may not have,
Wherein Olivia may seem serviceable?   100
Cesario, you do not keep promise with me.
Viola. Madam—   [*Speaking*
Duke. Gracious Olivia—   *together.*]
Olivia. What do you say, Cesario? Good my lord—
Viola. My lord would speak, my duty hushes me.   105
Olivia. If it be aught to the old tune, my lord,
It is as fat and fulsome to mine ear
As howling after music.

---

96. fellow—fellow] *Dyce;* fellow, fellow *F.*   102. Madam—] *F* (Madam:),
this ed.; Madam? *Capell.*   103. Olivia—] *F* (*Oliuia.*), *Theobald* (*subst.*).
102–3. [*Speaking together.*]] *This ed.; not in F.*   104. lord—] *Rowe*[2] (*subst.*)*;*
lord. *F.*

notice nothing wrong.' The three
months are probably specified in
order (1) to give Antonio's regard for
Sebastian a substantial basis, (2) to
emphasize the identical time of the
twins' arrival. Cf. *Err.,* v. i. 325–8,
'*Duke.* I tell thee, Syracusan, twenty
years / Have I been patron to Antipholus, / During which time he ne'er
saw Syracusa. / I see thy age and
dangers make thee dote.'

99–105. *What would my lord . . .
hushes me*] Olivia first addresses the
Duke, who had sent the Clown to ask
her to come and speak with him;
then, seeing Cesario at his side, she
mildly reproaches him (for having
left her house and resumed his
attendance on the Duke). Viola and
the Duke both reply at once; and
Olivia (guided by both duty and inclination) bids her husband speak on,
and asks the Duke (probably hold-
ing up her hand to make the point
implied in her unfinished sentence)
to wait his turn. Viola (whose duty is
wholly to the Duke in every way)
insists on letting him speak first.
Hence Olivia's brusque, and even
rude, dismissal of his suit.

99. *but that he may not have*] except
what he may not have (i.e., her love);
with the further significance, known
to herself but not to the Duke, that
she is another's.

107. *fat and fulsome*] gross and distasteful.

108. *howling after music*] Cf. *Ado,*
II. iii. 74–5 (Benedick of Balthasar's
singing), 'An he had been a dog
that should have howl'd thus, they
would have hang'd him.'

Duke. Still so cruel?

Olivia.   Still so constant, lord.

Duke. What, to perverseness? You uncivil lady,   110
 To whose ingrate and unauspicious altars
 My soul the faithfull'st off'rings hath breath'd out
 That e'er devotion tender'd—What shall I do?

Olivia. Even what it please my lord that shall become him.

Duke. Why should I not, had I the heart to do it,   115
 Like to th' Egyptian thief at point of death,
 Kill what I love?—a savage jealousy
 That sometime savours nobly. But hear me this:
 Since you to non-regardance cast my faith,
 And that I partly know the instrument   120
 That screws me from my true place in your favour,
 Live you the marble-breasted tyrant still.
 But this your minion, whom I know you love,
 And whom, by heaven, I swear I tender dearly,
 Him will I tear out of that cruel eye   125
 Where he sits crowned in his master's spite.
 Come, boy, with me; my thoughts are ripe in mischief:
 I'll sacrifice the lamb that I do love,

---

112. hath] *Capell;* haue *F;* has *Pope.*

116. thief at] *F* (theefe, at), *Collier.*

110. *uncivil*] barbarous; cf. IV. i. 52.

116. *Like to th' Egyptian thief . . . death*] Thyamis, an Egyptian robber-chief in Heliodorus' *Ethiopica*, who, in the story of 'Theagines and Chariclea', tried to kill his loved captive Chariclea when he was beset by a rival band of robbers and seemed likely to lose his life to them; fortunately in the darkness of a cave he mistook someone else for her. The *Ethiopica* was translated by Thomas Underdowne (1569, reprinted 1587). 'If the barbarous people be once in despaire of their own safetie, they have a custome to kill all those by whome they set much, and whose companie they desire after death' (ed. 1587, fol. 20).

121. *screws*] wrenches.

122. *Live you . . . still*] This line, and the remainder of the speech,

mark Orsino's change of plan: he will let Olivia live, but will kill her minion (whom he also loves) to revenge himself on her. The whole speech perfectly prepares the audience for the transference of his love from Olivia to Viola as soon as the latter's identity is disclosed.

marble-breasted tyrant] Cf. III. i. 122, 'tyrannous heart'. The terms are conventional in love-poetry: cf. Sidney, *Certain Sonnets* (pr. 1598 as addition to the *New Arcadia* and *Astrophil and Stella*) 'My mistress' marble heart' (from 'Ring out your bells', l. 24), and *Astrophil and Stella*, Sonnet 47, l. 4, 'yoke of tyranny'.

123. *minion*] darling (Fr. *mignon*).

126. *Where he . . . master's spite*] For 'crowned', cf. I. i. 39, 'one self king'; 'in his master's spite', to the vexation of his master.

   To spite a raven's heart within a dove.
Viola. And I most jocund, apt, and willingly,   130
     To do you rest, a thousand deaths would die.
Olivia. Where goes Cesario?
Viola.   After him I love
   More than I love these eyes, more than my life,
   More, by all mores, than e'er I shall love wife.
   If I do feign, you witnesses above   135
   Punish my life, for tainting of my love.
Olivia. Ay me detested! how am I beguil'd!
Viola. Who does beguile you? Who does do you wrong?
Olivia. Hast thou forgot thyself? Is it so long?
   Call forth the holy father.   [*Exit an Attendant.*]
Duke.   Come, away!   140
Olivia. Whither, my lord? Cesario, husband, stay!
Duke. Husband?
Olivia.   Ay, husband. Can he that deny?
Duke. Her husband, sirrah?
Viola.   No, my lord, not I.
Olivia. Alas, it is the baseness of thy fear
   That makes thee strangle thy propriety.   145

---

140. [*Exit an Attendant.*]] *Capell; not in F.*

129. *a raven's heart within a dove*] the cruel heart within Olivia's beautiful form: alluding primarily to the raven's blackness (cf. *MND.*, II. ii. 114, *Rom.*, I. v. 46, in both which examples doves are contrasted with ravens and crows), and perhaps also to its predatory character. In *Arden of Feversham*, III. v. 96–7, where Mosbie is quarrelling with Arden's wife Alice, his lover, he resolves to reform 'these eyes / That show'd my heart a raven for a dove.'

134. *by all mores*] by all such comparisons.

135–6. *If I do feign . . . love*] If I speak falsely, may the heavens punish with death my disloyalty to the love I feel. Cf. *Oth.*, IV. ii. 161–2, 'And his unkindness may defeat my life, / But never taint my love.'

137. *detested*] hated by, hateful to,

another. Cf. *Lr.*, I. iv. 262, 'Detested kite!', and (for 'hate' in a context of lovers' inconstancy) *MND.*, III. ii. 272, 'Hate me! wherefore? O me! what news, my love?' Wilson glosses 'renounced with an oath', but this use (*OED*, detest, *v.*, 3, rare, only example 1688) is not found elsewhere in Shakespeare, so the obvious meaning seems to be the correct one. Olivia, of course, misunderstands the inner meaning of l. 134, and takes it as a desertion of herself (cf. *All's W.*, III. v. 61–2, ''Tis a hard bondage to become the wife / Of a detesting lord.')

141. *husband*] Cf. note on 'contract', l. 154. Olivia uses the word with reference either to an accomplished marriage or an agreed one.

145. *strangle thy propriety*] suppress your real identity (as my husband).

Fear not, Cesario, take thy fortunes up,
Be that thou know'st thou art, and then thou art
As great as that thou fear'st.

Enter PRIEST.

                                    O welcome, father!
Father, I charge thee by thy reverence
Here to unfold—though lately we intended   150
To keep in darkness what occasion now
Reveals before 'tis ripe—what thou dost know
Hath newly pass'd between this youth and me.

Priest. A contract of eternal bond of love,
Confirm'd by mutual joinder of your hands,   155
Attested by the holy close of lips,
Strengthen'd by interchangement of your rings,
And all the ceremony of this compact
Seal'd in my function, by my testimony;
Since when, my watch hath told me, toward my grave
I have travell'd but two hours.   161

Duke. O thou dissembling cub! What wilt thou be

---

150. unfold—] *F* (vnfold,), *N.C.S.*   152. ripe—] *F* (ripe:), *N.C.S.*   161.
travell'd] *F* (trauail'd).

148. *that thou fear'st*] that of which
you are afraid (the Duke).

151. *occasion*] what has befallen;
present circumstances. For the connection of 'occasion' and 'ripe'
(l. 152), cf. I. ii. 43.

154. *contract*] Cf. *Tp.*, IV. i. 15–19,
where Prospero, giving his daughter
to Ferdinand, distinguishes between
'this contract' and 'all sanctimonious
ceremonies . . . [administered] with
full and holy rite', and *Lr.*, V. iii.
228–9, where Edmund says of
Goneril and Regan, 'I was contracted
to them both. All three / Now marry
in an instant.' J. W. Lever (New
Arden *Meas.*, pp. liii–liv) explains
that 'English common law recognized
two forms of "spousals". *Sponsalia
per verba de praesenti*, a declaration

by both parties that each took the
other at the present time as spouse,
was legally binding irrespective of
any change of circumstances, and,
whether the union was later consecrated or not, amounted to full
marriage. *Sponsalia per verba de futuro*,
a sworn declaration of intention to
marry in the future, was not thus
absolutely binding.'

155. *joinder*] joining; cf. 'rejoin-
dure', *Troil.*, IV. iv. 48 (of lips).

158. *compact*] accented on the
second syllable.

159. *Seal'd . . . function . . . testimony*]
confirmed or ratified through my
performance of my priestly office and
by my formal attestation.

162. *cub*] fox-cub, the fox being proverbial for cunning.

When time hath sow'd a grizzle on thy case?
Or will not else thy craft so quickly grow
That thine own trip shall be thine overthrow?   165
Farewell, and take her, but direct thy feet
Where thou and I henceforth may never meet.
Viola. My lord, I do protest—
Olivia.   O do not swear!
Hold little faith, though thou hast too much fear.

Enter SIR ANDREW.

Sir And. For the love of God, a surgeon! Send one   170
    presently to Sir Toby.
Olivia. What's the matter?
Sir And. 'Has broke my head across, and has given Sir
    Toby a bloody coxcomb too. For the love of God,
    your help! I had rather than forty pound I were   175
    at home.
Olivia. Who has done this, Sir Andrew?
Sir And. The Count's gentleman, one Cesario. We took
    him for a coward, but he's the very devil in-
    cardinate.   180
Duke. My gentleman, Cesario?
Sir And. 'Od's lifelings, here he is! You broke my head
    for nothing; and that that I did, I was set on to
    do't by Sir Toby.

168. protest—] *F* (protest.), *Rowe.*   173. 'Has]'*Dyce²;* Has *F;* He has *Malone.*
179–80. incardinate] *F;* incarnate *Rowe.*

163. *sow'd a grizzle on thy case*]
sprinkled your hair with grey.
    case] fox's skin.
    164–5. *Or will not else . . . over-
throw?*] or possibly your deceitfulness
will grow so fast that it will result
in your undoing, even before you
grow grey.
    165. *trip*] a leg movement by which
one throws one's opponent in wrest-
ling (*OED*, trip, *sb.³* II. 5.b (figuratively)).
    169. *Hold little faith*] Keep at least
a little faith. Antithesis and allitera-
tion with 'too much fear'.

174. *coxcomb*] a jocular term for the
head (*OED*, 2); cf. *H5*, v. i. 39, 49.

175. *forty pound*] Cf. 'forty shillings',
II. iii .20.

179–80. *incardinate*] Sir Andrew's
mistake for 'incarnate' (in the flesh,
in human form); cf. similar mistakings
of 'incarnate' by Launcelot Gobbo,
Mer.V., II. ii. 25, and Mistress
Quickly, *H5*, II. iii. 33.

182. *'Od's lifelings*] The diminutive
plural reduces the force of the oath
('by God's life'); cf. *AYL.*, III. v. 43,
' 'Od's my little life'.

Viola. Why do you speak to me? I never hurt you: 185
    You drew your sword upon me without cause,
    But I bespake you fair, and hurt you not.

Enter SIR TOBY *and* CLOWN.

Sir And. If a bloody coxcomb be a hurt, you have hurt
    me: I think you set nothing by a bloody coxcomb.
    Here comes Sir Toby halting, you shall hear   190
    more: but if he had not been in drink, he would
    have tickled you othergates than he did.
Duke. How now, gentleman? How is't with you?
Sir To. That's all one, 'has hurt me, and there's th'
    end on't. Sot, didst see Dick Surgeon, sot?   195
Clown. O, he's drunk, Sir Toby, an hour agone; his
    eyes were set at eight i' th' morning.
Sir To. Then he's a rogue, and a passy measures pavin:
    I hate a drunken rogue.

196. Sir Toby] *F* (sir *Toby*); sir above *F2*; sir, above *F4*; Sir Toby, above
Theobald.   198. and a passy measures pavin] *Malone;* and a passy measures
panyn *F;* and a past-measure Painim *Pope;* after a passy measures Pavin *F2.*

189. *set nothing by*] make no account
of.
190. *halting*] limping.
192. *othergates*] in another way (i.e.,
he would have put up a better fight).
195. *Sot*] Cf. I. v. 122 and note.
197. *set*] closed. Wilson, comparing
Tp., III. ii. 8, 'thy eyes are almost
set in thy head', interprets 'gone out
like stars in the morning'; but more
probably the metaphor is from the
sun's setting (with consequent paradox, 'at eight i' th' morning'). In
Tp. the expression is used in order to
allow Trinculo's jest, 'He were a
brave monster indeed, if they were
set in his tail.'
198. *passy measures pavin*] passe-
measure pavan (see *OED* under
both words), from Ital. *passemezzo*
pavana. The two words are often
found together: each means a slow
and stately dance, but 'the *passa-*
mezzo [sic] has a two-in-a-bar

rhythm brisker than that of the
standard pavan, and employs twice
the number of steps to each beat,
its name deriving from this latter
fact' (*Grove's Dictionary of Music and
Musicians*, ed. Eric Blom, 1966, vol.
VI, p. 600). Sir Toby may nevertheless be referring to the surgeon's
lethargy, and mentioning the brisker
'passy measures' merely for its alli-
terative mouth-filling quality. He may
also be likening the steps of the dance,
which are 'executed with a peculiar
swaying grace and lilt' (*Grove's Dictionary, ibid.*), to the unsteady walk of
a drunken man. Naylor's explanation
(*Shakespeare and Music*, p. 114) that
'set at eight' (l. 197) suggests to Sir
Toby the pavan, which also is 'set at
eight' (i.e., has a strain consisting of
eight bars), has found general acceptance. It is not, however, conclusive,
for though Thomas Morley (*A Plaine
and Easie Introduction to Practicall*

Olivia. Away with him! Who hath made this havoc   200
        with them?
Sir And. I'll help you, Sir Toby, because we'll be
        dressed together.
Sir To. Will you help? An ass-head, and a coxcomb,
        and a knave, a thin-faced knave, a gull?   205
Olivia. Get him to bed, and let his hurt be looked to.
        [*Exeunt Clown, Fabian, Sir Toby, and Sir Andrew.*]

                Enter SEBASTIAN.

Seb. I am sorry, madam, I have hurt your kinsman:
        But had it been the brother of my blood,
        I must have done no less with wit and safety.
        You throw a strange regard upon me, and by that   210
        I do perceive it hath offended you:
        Pardon me, sweet one, even for the vows

204. help? An] *Malone;* helpe an *F.*   206. [*Exeunt Clown, Fabian, Sir Toby, and
Sir Andrew.*]] *Dyce; not in F.*   210. You throw ... that] *F; (subst.);* You
throw / A ... that *conj. Walker.*   and] *F; not in Pope.*   that] *F; which Pope.*

Musicke, 1597), in the passage Naylor
quotes, says 'fewer than eight
[semibreves] I have not seene in any
pauan', he also says pavans may consist of twelve or sixteen 'as they list';
nor does Naylor show that 'set at
eight' was ever a musical term.
Malone (to whom we owe the
emendation, since he retained F2's
correction of F's misprint while rejecting its substitution of 'after' for
'and', which would make Sir Toby
say that the thing he most disliked
was a pavan, and after this he most
disliked a drunkard) compares Sir
Toby's allusions to dances in I. iii.
125–8, and says 'It is one of Shakespeare's unrivalled excellences that
his characters are always consistent.
Even in drunkenness they preserve
the traits which distinguished them
when sober.'
        204. *coxcomb*] fool (*OED*, 3); cf.
H5, IV. i. 76–9 (Fluellen to Gower),
'If the enemy is an ass, and a fool, and
a prating coxcomb, is it meet, think

you, that we should also, look you,
be an ass, and a fool, and a prating
coxcomb?'
        205. *a thin-faced knave*] Wilson com-
pares Slender's 'little wee face', *Wiv.*,
I. iv. 20.
        208. *the brother of my blood*] a kins-
man of my own, and the closest.
This is artfully introduced by Shakespeare just before Sebastian is to see
Viola; cf. ll. 224–9.
        209. *with wit and safety*] with reason-
able care for my own safety.
        210. *you throw . . . that*] Lettsom
(who was anticipated by Pope except
in retaining F's 'that' where Pope
substituted 'which') explains his
conjecture ('You throw a strange regard on me; by that') by suggesting
that F's 'and' probably 'crept in
from the line above'.
        strange] distant (as if you did not
know me). Sebastian misinterprets
Olivia's feelings (l. 211), but his
observation (l. 210) is correct; cf.
Olivia's l. 223, 'Most wonderful!'

We made each other but so late ago.

Duke. One face, one voice, one habit, and two persons!
A natural perspective, that is, and is not!   215

Seb. Antonio! O my dear Antonio,
How have the hours rack'd and tortur'd me,
Since I have lost thee!

Ant. Sebastian are you?

Seb.   Fear'st thou that, Antonio?

Ant. How have you made division of yourself?   220
An apple cleft in two is not more twin
Than these two creatures. Which is Sebastian?

Olivia. Most wonderful!

Seb. Do I stand there? I never had a brother;
Nor can there be that deity in my nature   225
Of here and everywhere. I had a sister,
Whom the blind waves and surges have devour'd:
Of charity, what kin are you to me?
What countryman? What name? What parentage?

Viola. Of Messaline: Sebastian was my father;   230
Such a Sebastian was my brother too:
So went he suited to his watery tomb.
If spirits can assume both form and suit,
You come to fright us.

---

215. *A natural perspective*] The Duke refers to an artificial 'perspective' (accented on first syllable) or distorting glass, which, by optical illusion, can make one picture or object appear like two or more; the same effect, he says here, is now produced by nature, without the operation of art (i.e., of a 'glass'; cf. l. 263). See *OED*, perspective, *sb.*, I. 2.

217. *hours*] a disyllable here, for the metre.

219. *Fear'st thou that*] Are you in doubt of that? (i.e., Let me reassure you that I am Sebastian).

225-6. *that deity . . . everywhere*] Sebastian refers to 'the divine attribution of ubiquity' (Abbott, §77, quoted in Furness).

227. *blind waves*] i.e., 'pitiless; inas-

much as they could not see the loveliness they were destroying' (Furness).

232. *So . . . tomb*] Clothed in that manner, he went to his watery grave.

233. *If spirits . . . suit*] 'One of the moot questions of Shakespeare's day was whether the souls of the departed could "assume" their mortal forms, and whether ghosts were not rath devils masquerading as the de (Wilson, citing *Ham.*, I. ii. 244, assume my noble father's p and III. iv. 135, 'My father habit as he liv'd!'; his s that *Tw.N.*, II. ii. 26-7, re same question is, in wrong.

234. *You come to frig* a ghost. 'Spirit', bethan usage it ca

Seb.   A spirit I am indeed,
But am in that dimension grossly clad   235
Which from the womb I did participate.
Were you a woman, as the rest goes even,
I should my tears let fall upon your cheek,
And say, 'Thrice welcome, drowned Viola.'

Viola. My father had a mole upon his brow.   240

Seb. And so had mine.

Viola. And died that day when Viola from her birth
Had number'd thirteen years.

Seb. O, that record is lively in my soul!
He finished indeed his mortal act   245
That day that made my sister thirteen years.

Viola. If nothing lets to make us happy both,
But this my masculine usurp'd attire,
Do not embrace me, till each circumstance
Of place, time, fortune, do cohere and jump   250
That I am Viola; which to confirm,
I'll bring you to a captain in this town,
Where lie my maiden weeds; by whose gentle help
I was preserv'd to serve this noble count:

---

254. preserv'd] *F;* preferr'd *Theobald.*

means ghost; cf. *Lr.,* IV. vii. 49 (Lear to Cordelia), 'You are a spirit, I know. Where did you die?' Probably emphasis on the supposed spirit's Sebastian's clothes, as well is meant to lighten the f Viola's words them- ole passage (ll. 214–46) eare's treatment of ene in *Err.,* v. i. 330– ion, p. xlviii.

hat . . . *participate*] ody as my soul since my birth. form.

isn] as every ls.

teen years] , l. 246, e fact This to

suggest that Sebastian is, at least, not younger than Olivia.

244. *record*] (accented on the second syllable) recollection.

247. *lets*] hinders.

250. *cohere and jump*] hold together and fit exactly; cf. *Shr.,* I. i. 185, 'Both our inventions meet and jump in one.'

254. *preserv'd to serve*] Theobald's attractive emendation 'preferr'd to serve' (i.e., helped into the service of) accords with Viola's '*present me as an eunuch to him*'; it also avoids the sameness of sound (to some readers distasteful) in 'preserv'd to serve'. (Walker suggests that the opposite error of 'prefer' a peace (F preferre) for 'preserve' a peace, occurs in *1H6,* III. i. 110, though few editors have adopted his reading.) The reading of F makes satisfactory

All the occurrence of my fortune since   255
Hath been between this lady and this lord.

Seb. [*To Olivia*] So comes it, lady, you have been mistook.
But nature to her bias drew in that.
You would have been contracted to a maid;
Nor are you therein, by my life, deceiv'd: 260
You are betroth'd both to a maid and man.

Duke. Be not amaz'd, right noble is his blood.
If this be so, as yet the glass seems true,
I shall have share in this most happy wreck.
[*To Viola*] Boy, thou hast said to me a thousand times
Thou never should'st love woman like to me.   266

Viola. And all those sayings will I over-swear,
And all those swearings keep as true in soul
As doth that orbed continent the fire
That severs day from night.

Duke.   Give me thy hand,   270

255–6. occurrence ... Hath] *F;* occurrents ... Have *Hanmer.*   257. [*To Olivia*]] *Rowe; not in F.*   264. wreck] *F* (wracke), *Rowe.*   265. [*To Viola*]] *Rowe; not in F.*   267. over-swear] *F* (ouer sweare), *F2.*

sense, however, meaning that the Captain saved her life when the ship was wrecked (even so, one might argue that 'gentle help' suits the idea of preferment better than preservation), and is therefore retained.

255. *All the occurrence of*] everything that has happened to.

258. *But nature ... in that*] The metaphor is from the game of bowls: the 'bias' is (1) the lead weight inserted into a bowl to make it take an indirect course, (2) the consequent tendency of the bowl to describe a curve, and (3) the curve so described. Nature followed its inborn tendency, to mate female with male, and so undo the effects of Viola's misleading disguise.

261. *maid and man*] 'virgin youth' (Mahood).

263. *as yet the glass seems true*] since what seemed to be the delusion of a perspective glass (cf. l. 215) is still turning out to be real.

264. *this most happy wreck*] this shipwreck which has had such fortunate results; for the paradox, cf. Viola's couplet, III. iv. 393–4.

265. *Boy*] Cf. ll. 384–5. Orsino's touches of humour help to give a firm basis to his newly discovered love for Viola as a woman, just as the hyperbole of 'a thousand times' suggests that his different affection for her, as his page, has continued for at least the 'three months' (l. 97) during which Viola has 'call'd [hi̶m̶ master for so long' (l. 323).

266. *like to me*] so well as you me.

267. *over-swear*] swear ove̶ with a further suggestion emphasis.

269–70. *As doth ... .* Though the force of V̶ tion is clear, its pr̶ debatable: 'that̶ may be either (1̶ the sphere in̶

And let me see thee in thy woman's weeds.
Viola. The captain that did bring me first on shore
Hath my maid's garments; he upon some action
Is now in durance, at Malvolio's suit,
A gentleman and follower of my lady's.   275
Olivia. He shall enlarge him: fetch Malvolio hither.
And yet alas! now I remember me,
They say, poor gentleman, he's much distract.

Enter CLOWN *with a letter, and* FABIAN.

A most extracting frenzy of mine own
From my remembrance clearly banish'd his.   280
How does he, sirrah?

279. extracting] *F;* exacting *F2;* distracting *Hanmer.*

Ptolemaic astronomy, the sun was fixed. Shakespeare uses the word 'orb' both for the heavenly bodies (Onions, 4) and for their Ptolemaic spheres (Onions, 2); he also uses 'continent' both for something which contains something else (Onions, 1) and for the solid earth (Onions, 2) or (Onions, 3) the sun in this passage (following *OED*, continent, *sb.,* 11.3.c, which cites this passage and Milton, *Para- Lost,* v. 422, of the moon). The 'orbed' occurs in Shakes- ly here and in *Ham.,* III. ii. ptune's salt wash and ed ground'), where he s the spherical earth. he fire / That severs recalls Genesis, i. 14 let there be lights of the heaven to m the night')— adds weight to this does not firm passage, since (which king either 'the fire rmament. ret the arched e sun omes t as

the sun (and 'the fire' as that which the sun maintains), because (1) the use of 'orbed' in *Hamlet* supports this sense, (2) the only use of 'orb' in *Tw.N.* is at III. i. 39, meaning the round earth which is perambulated by the sun, (3) *'that* orbed continent' suggests that Viola actually points at the sun in the sky (cf. IV. iii. 1, Sebastian's 'This is the air, that is the glorious sun', and Olivia's final couplet, ll. 34–5, in the same scene).

273. *action*] lawsuit.

276. *enlarge*] set free.

279. *A most extracting frenzy*] a madness (cf. III. iv. 14–15) which drew everything else from my mind (or, which drew my own mind away from me). Malone quotes *The Historie of Hamblet* (1608), 'to try if men of great account bee extract out of their wits', and Steevens illustrates from the phrase *'extractus a mente'* used of Henry VI by William of Worcester (both in Furness). Wilson thinks there may be an allusion to 'extracting the quintessence' in alchemy, but this seems irrelevant to the phrase here. Mahood observes the echo of 'dis- tract', l. 278.

280. *his*] ambiguous: either (1) his remembrance, i.e., 'my remem-

Clown. Truly, Madam, he holds Belzebub at the stave's
       end as well as a man in his case may do; 'has here
       writ a letter to you. I should have given't you
       to-day morning, but as a madman's epistles are no   285
       gospels, so it skills not much when they are
       delivered.

Olivia. Open't, and read it.

Clown. Look then to be well edified, when the fool
       delivers the madman. [*Reads*] *By the Lord,*   290
       madam,—

Olivia. How now, art thou mad?

Clown. No, madam, I do but read madness: and your
       ladyship will have it as it ought to be, you must
       allow *vox.*   295

Olivia. Prithee, read i' thy right wits.

Clown. So I do, madonna. But to read his right wits is
       to read thus: therefore, perpend, my princess,
       and give ear.

290. [*Reads*]] *Rowe; not in F.*

brance of him', or (2) his madness,
i.e., '*my* madness made me forget
that *he* was mad.' The use of 'of mine
own' makes (2) the more probable
sense.

282–3. *he holds Belzebub at the
stave's end*] He keeps the devil at a
distance. A proverbial metaphor
from the sport of quarterstaff fighting
(cf. Tilley, S807). Wilson quotes
(from *OED*, staff, *sb.*[1], 1.5b) Arthur
Dent's *Plain Man's Pathway to Heaven*
(1601), 'wee . . . keepe Satan at the
staues end'. 'Belzebub' is the invariable spelling in Shakespeare and his
contemporaries (cf. *H5*, IV. vii. 134,
Mac. II. iii. 5: in the latter case
Alexander prints 'Beelzebub', but F's
spelling is as here).

285–7. *as a madman's epistles . . .
delivered*] There is wordplay on
'epistles' as (1) any letters, (2)
apostolic letters in the New Testament; on 'gospels' as (1) the four
evangelists' histories of Christ's
ministry in the New Testament, (2)

statements to be implicitly received
as true (*OED*, 4; cf. Tilley, A147,
'All is not gospel that comes out of his
mouth'); and on 'delivered' as (1)
taken to the person to whom they are
directed, (2) read aloud in public.

286. *it skills not much*] it matters
little.

290. *delivers*] reports the message
of, speaks for. (He then proceeds to
read like a madman (cf. l. 295, *vox*).)

291. madam] Sisson (I, 194) would
here create a play on words, and
would read 'mad-am', but has found
few if any supporters.

292. *art thou mad?*] The pronoun is
stressed; hence the Clown's reply.

295. *allow* vox] permit me to use
the appropriate 'voice' (Lat.).

297. *his right wits*] his authentic
state of mind (i.e., madness), quibbling on Olivia's command, l. 296.

298. *perpend*] 'A word used only
by Pistol, Polonius and the clowns'
(A. Schmidt, *Shakespeare-Lexicon*).
Shakespeare probably saw its absurd

Olivia. [*To Fabian*] Read it you, sirrah.   300

Fabian. (*Reads*) *By the Lord, madam, you wrong me, and
the world shall know it. Though you have put me into
darkness, and given your drunken cousin rule over me,
yet have I the benefit of my senses as well as your ladyship. I have your own letter, that induced me to the*   305
*semblance I put on; with the which I doubt not but to
do myself much right, or you much shame. Think of me as
you please. I leave my duty a little unthought of, and
speak out of my injury.*

                     The madly-used Malvolio.   310

Olivia. Did he write this?

Clown. Ay, madam.

Duke. This savours not much of distraction.

Olivia. See him deliver'd, Fabian, bring him hither.   [*Exit
                                      Fabian.*]

My lord, so please you, these things further thought on,
To think me as well a sister, as a wife,   316
One day shall crown th' alliance on't, so please you,
Here at my house, and at my proper cost.

Duke. Madam, I am most apt t'embrace your offer.

   [*To Viola*] Your master quits you; and for your service
     done him,   320

300. [*To Fabian*]] *Rowe; not in F.*   314. [*Exit Fabian.*]] *Capell; not in F.*
317. on't, so] *F;* an't so *Rann, conj. Heath;* on's so *Dyce*[2].   320. [*To Viola*]]
Rowe; not in F.

possibilities in Thomas Preston's
Cambises (n.d., pr. *c.* 1570), e.g.,
l. 5, 'My sapient words, I say,
perpend', and l. 1018, 'My queene,
perpend. What I pronounce, I wil
not violate.' (He mentions the play
in *1H4*, II. iv. 376, but actually
parodies its style in *LLL.*, v. ii. 546–51
when Costard recites his part as
Pompey, and in *MND.*, v. i. 268–338
passim, adding internal rhyme to its
'fourteener' couplets.) The Clown,
with his 'Therefore perpend, my
princess, and give ear' (blank verse),
is about to resume his impassioned
and frantic delivery.

308–9. I leave my duty . . .
injury] I omit somewhat the respect
for you which would normally keep

me silent, and speak out of my feeling
of the wrong you have done me.

315. *these things*] all that has happened as a consequence of Sebastian's
arrival, and the discovery of his and
Viola's identities.

316. *To think . . . as a wife*] to
approve me for a sister(-in-law) as
much as you would have approved me
for a wife. (Alluding to her marriage
to Sebastian and recommending
Orsino's marriage to Viola.)

317. *th' alliance on't*] the alliance or
relationship (between you and me)
effected by it (the double marriage
ceremony).

318. *proper cost*] own expense.

320. *quits you*] releases you from his
service.

So much against the mettle of your sex,
So far beneath your soft and tender breeding,
And since you call'd me master for so long,
Here is my hand; you shall from this time be
Your master's mistress.

Olivia.   A sister! you are she.   325

Enter [FABIAN *with*] MALVOLIO.

Duke. Is this the madman?
Olivia.   Ay, my lord, this same.
   How now, Malvolio?
Mal.   Madam, you have done me wrong,
   Notorious wrong.
Olivia.   Have I, Malvolio? No.
Mal. Lady, you have. Pray you, peruse that letter.
   You must not now deny it is your hand: 330

---

325. S.D. *Enter [Fabian with] Malvolio.] As Capell (subst.); Enter Maluolio F.*
326–7. Ay . . . Malvolio?] *As Capell; I my Lord, this same: How now Maluolio?*
(as one line), F.

321. *mettle*] disposition.

322. *soft and tender breeding*] delicate bringing up (as a noble lady).

325. *Your master's mistress*] a paradox prepared by Orsino's reference to himself in the third person in l. 320. Charney compares the conceit in Sonnet 20, l. 2, 'the Master Mistress of my passion'.

A sister! you are she] Olivia is already (by her marriage to Sebastian) Viola's 'sister', whether or not Viola marries Orsino, but his decision to offer her his hand reinforces the family alliance: hence Olivia's exclamation of pleasure and congratulation. Wilson finds the last three words 'not very intelligible', though 'it is of course clear that both Olivia and Orsino are content to find a sister in the original object of their passion'; he conjectures, without much conviction, either that we might read 'Ah Sister!' (which would not increase the intelligibility) or that a line may have been omitted. Honigmann

makes the extraordinary suggestion that Olivia has looked away from the twins and now has to guess which is Viola (perhaps based on *Err.*, v. i. 363, where the Duke, still mistaking one Antipholus for the other, bids them 'Stay, stand apart; I know not which is which', and at l. 407 one of the servants mistakes the wrong twin for his master: but such business would be wholly foreign to the immediate context in *Tw.N.*). Charney proposes to treat the phrase as a proverbial formula, citing Tilley, 188. 'You are Ipse (he, the man)', and may be right (cf. *AYL.*, v. i. 40–1, where Touchstone applies Tilley's proverb to himself in order to discourage William's aspirations to Audrey; and *Tw.N.*, II. ii. 24, where Viola says 'I am the man').

328. *Notorious*] Cf. IV. ii. 90 and note, and ll. 342 and 378 below.

330. *You must not*] you cannot possibly.

Write from it, if you can, in hand, or phrase,
Or say 'tis not your seal, not your invention:
You can say none of this. Well, grant it then,
And tell me, in the modesty of honour,
Why you have given me such clear lights of favour,   335
Bade me come smiling and cross-garter'd to you,
To put on yellow stockings, and to frown
Upon Sir Toby, and the lighter people;
And acting this in an obedient hope,
Why have you suffer'd me to be imprison'd,   340
Kept in a dark house, visited by the priest,
And made the most notorious geck and gull
That e'er invention play'd on? Tell me, why?
Olivia. Alas, Malvolio, this is not my writing,
Though I confess much like the character: 345
But, out of question, 'tis Maria's hand.
And now I do bethink me, it was she
First told me thou wast mad; then cam'st in smiling,
And in such forms which here were presuppos'd
Upon thee in the letter. Prithee, be content;   350
This practice hath most shrewdly pass'd upon thee.
But when we know the grounds and authors of it,
Thou shalt be both the plaintiff and the judge
Of thine own cause.
Fabian.   Good madam, hear me speak,
And let no quarrel, nor no brawl to come,   355

331. *Write from it*] write differently.

332. *invention*] composition, style.

334. *in the modesty of honour*] in the name of decency and propriety.

335. *clear   lights*] evident signs. 'Perhaps a nautical metaphor' (Wilson), but more probably a metaphor from broad daylight: cf. II. v. 160, 'Daylight and champaign discovers not more!'

338. *Sir Toby, and the lighter people*] the 'kinsman' and 'servants' of the letter, II. v. 149–50.

341. *visited by the priest*] Shakespeare obviously distinguishes between 'Sir Topas the curate', whose name (if he exists at all, and is not merely an invention of Maria's) the Clown has assumed in IV. ii, and the 'holy man' of the following scene and the present one. To make Malvolio here eye the priest with indignation is a temptation which wise producers resist.

342. *geck and gull*] synonyms for 'fool'.

343. *invention*] contrivance.

345. *character*] synonymous with 'writing' (l. 344) and 'hand' (l. 346).

349. *presuppos'd*] suggested beforehand.

351. *This practice . . . upon thee*] This trick has been most mischievously played upon you.

Taint the condition of this present hour,
Which I have wonder'd at. In hope it shall not,
Most freely I confess, myself and Toby
Set this device against Malvolio here,
Upon some stubborn and uncourteous parts　　　360
We had conceiv'd against him. Maria writ
The letter, at Sir Toby's great importance,
In recompense whereof he hath married her.
How with a sportful malice it was follow'd
May rather pluck on laughter than revenge,　　　365
If that the injuries be justly weigh'd
That have on both sides pass'd.

Olivia. Alas, poor fool, how have they baffled thee!
Clown. Why, 'Some are born great, some achieve great-
　　　ness, and some have greatness thrown upon them.'　　370

---

361. against] *F;* in *Rann.*　　　369–70, 372–3, 373–5.] *As quotations, Theobald.*
370. thrown] *F;* thrust *Douai MS., Theobald.*

360–1. *Upon some stubborn . . . against him*] because of the resentment aroused in us by his uncompromising incivility. 'Parts' has the double sense of (1) characteristics (Onions, 3), (2) acts (literally, pieces of conduct (Onions, 4)); cf. *2H4,* IV. v. 64, 'This part of his [Prince Henry's act of removing the crown from his dying father's pillow] conjoins with my disease'.

361. *against him*] F's reading is defensible if (cf. Abbott, §244) 'conceived' implies an *enmity* created by the 'parts' which they disliked in Malvolio. But Rann's emendation 'in him' (which simplifies the sense and regularizes the metre) is attractive; 'against' may have been caught from its similar place in l. 359.

362. *importance*] importunity. In fact the letter was Maria's own device, II. iii. 134–8. Fabian shields her behind Sir Toby, whose relationship to Olivia protects him.

363. *In recompense . . . married her*] an announcement prepared, as Wilson notes, by I. v. 25–7, II. v. 182–91, and possibly (though this depends on our

accepting Wilson's interpretation) IV. ii. 69–74. Luce aptly comments that by this time Sir Toby 'has got married, got drunk, received "a bloody coxcomb", and been sent to bed. To pry into the exact sequence of these events is scarcely profitable.'

365. *pluck on*] induce.

368. *poor fool*] poor fellow. This combination is frequent in Shakespeare as an expression of compassion, and sometimes also (though not here) of endearment; cf. *3H6,* II. v. 36 (of ewes), *Ado,* II. i. 283 (by Beatrice of her own heart), *Ven.,* 578 (of Adonis), *Lr.,* v. iii. 305 (of Cordelia), *AYL.,* II. i. 22, 'poor dappl'd fools', and 40, 'hairy fool' (of deer), *Ant.,* v. ii. 303, 'poor venomous fool' (of the asp). 'But "fool" also means "dupe", and it is Olivia's use of the word that brings Feste into the dialogue' (Wilson).

baffled] exposed to ridicule, made mock of.

370. *thrown*] probably not a mistake but Shakespeare's own casual variation, 'from his knowing, by professional experience, the difficulty of

I was one, sir, in this interlude, one Sir Topas, sir,
but that's all one. 'By the Lord, fool, I am not
mad.' But do you remember, 'Madam, why laugh
you at such a barren rascal, and you smile not,
he's gagged'? And thus the whirligig of time   375
brings in his revenges.

Mal. I'll be reveng'd on the whole pack of you!   [*Exit.*]

Olivia. He hath been most notoriously abus'd.

Duke. Pursue him, and entreat him to a peace:
He hath not told us of the captain yet.   [*Exit Fabian.*]

---

373. remember,] *F*; remember? *Malone, conj. Tyrwhitt.* 'Madam, why]
Malone, conj. Tyrwhitt; Madam,—'why *Theobald;* Madam, why *F.*   377.
[*Exit.*]] *Rowe; not in F.*   380. [*Exit Fabian.*]] *This ed.; not in F.*

quoting with perfect accuracy'
(Staunton); cf. the discrepancy between Bertram's letter in *All's W.*,
III. ii. 55–8 and v. iii. 306–7, and also
between the Clown's quotations
from Malvolio, ll. 372–3 and 373–5
below, and their originals in IV. ii.
and I. v. Notice also that though the
Clown was not present in II. v or in
III. iv, he is here supposed to know
the contents of the letter written by
Maria; no one would perceive this
incongruity in the theatre.

371. *interlude*] play (i.e., figuratively,
sport), with an allusion to his assuming the part of Sir Topas (in IV. ii),
whom he mentions as if he were a
character in a play.

372. *that's all one*] that's of no
special consequence (a mere detail
which I mention for the sake of
completeness).

372–3. *By the Lord . . . mad*] 'By
the Lord' is nowhere used by Malvolio in IV. ii. It is in fact the opening
phrase of his letter, ll. 290–1 and 301
above. 'Fool, I am not mad' also
fails to occur in IV. ii, though the
gist of it lies in various speeches to
Sir Topas and to the Clown.

373–5. *Madam . . . he's gagged*] a
fairly close paraphrase of I. v. 81–6,
but again not a precise reproduction
of the lines. The Clown is given

many opportunities of imitating
Malvolio's deep voice (cf. III. iv. 92,
'Lo, how hollow the fiend speaks
within him!') in this scene.

375. *the whirligig of time*] time's
spinning-top. Cf. *Lr.*, v. iii. 174, 'The
wheel is come full circle.'

377. *I'll be reveng'd*] The pronoun
is stressed, Malvolio picking up the
last word of the Clown's speech.
It may be that the Clown is given this
speech, not to show the depth of his
grudge against Malvolio, but to supply
Malvolio with his exit line.

378. *He . . . notoriously abus'd*] Cf.
IV. ii. 48, 90 and v. i. 328, 342.
Olivia's intonation may express
amusement, or amusement mingled
with concern, but in view of its echo
of Malvolio's phrases it can hardly
be spoken with complete seriousness,
still less with positive anger (as in a
BBC television production, 14 May
1974, where, to make matters worse,
she struck the Clown, an action
utterly at variance with the whole
mood of these last minutes of the
play).

380. [*Exit Fabian.*]] Clearly someone should do as Orsino says in ll.
379–80. I give the office to Fabian,
who, although he has just (in Malvolio's hearing) shouldered half the
responsibility for the 'device', has

When that is known, and golden time convents,   381
A solemn combination shall be made
Of our dear souls. Meantime, sweet sister,
We will not part from hence. Cesario, come;
For so you shall be while you are a man;   385
But when in other habits you are seen,
Orsino's mistress, and his fancy's queen.

Exeunt [all except Clown].

387. [*all except Clown*]] *Dyce; not in F.*

also shown himself a diplomatist and (especially in ll. 354–7) a peace-maker.

381. *convents*] Onions, noting that the interpretation is questionable, glosses as 'either "summons" or "is convenient"'. Shakespeare's other uses are all in the former sense, but also all take a direct object, so that (unless 'us' is to be understood) he may be using it in the latter, unique, sense here.

383. *dear*] (1) affectionate, loving and beloved; (2) valuable, precious (i.e., to God; a sense suggested by the adjacent 'solemn').

383–4. *Meantime . . . not part from hence*] Orsino accepts the hospitality offered by Olivia, ll. 315–18, and at the end of his speech the whole company enters her house. All is happiness and harmony.

387. *his fancy's queen*] The word 'fancy' is here used with no dero-gatory sense, but is synonymous with 'love'.

387. Exeunt. 387. S.D. Clown sings] F's directions are ambiguous as to whether the Clown (1) goes out with the others and then returns or, more probably, (2) remains on stage, a procedure clearly adopted in *All's W.*, where F has *Flourish* at the end of the last speech (by the King), after which the King speaks the epilogue and *Exeunt omn[es]*: since the epilogue is usually an appeal for applause, it is natural for an actor 'in character'

to remain behind (otherwise the audience will applaud as the actors move off at the final line). Thus, at the end of *AYL.*, it appears as though the Duke's final couplet and *Exit* are the signal for all the company to leave the stage except Rosalind, who speaks the epilogue and then *Exit*. At the end of *Tp.*, Prospero invites the others to his dwelling, and at his last words 'Please you, draw near' would seem to point the way, afterwards coming forward to speak the epilogue. At the end of *MND.*, the Fairies' song, led by Oberon (v. i. 384–5), ends 'Trip away; make no stay; / Meet me all by break of day,' and Puck (*Robin* in F) speaks the epilogue. The epilogue to *2H4* is spoken by none of the actors 'in character', and is indeed a composite work, requiring Shakespeare him-self to speak the opening paragraph, and someone who can dance (*possibly* Falstaff's page) to speak the re-mainder, with a suitable introduction, on some other occasion (see A. R. Humphreys's note in the New Arden ed.). The epilogue of *H5* is spoken by the Chorus, that of *Pericles* by the choric Gower, and that of *H8* (evidently Fletcher's) by an unidenti-fied person. *Troilus and Cressida* has a patched-on epilogue for Pandarus, presumably for a revival, bringing him incongruously on the battle-field with three lines of dialogue the proper place of which is at the end of v. iii. None of Shakespeare's other plays has an epilogue (excepting perhaps, *LLL.*, where Armado's final sentence after the two songs occupies the place of one), and *Tw.N.* is the only one where the epilogue takes the form of a song.

388–407. When that I was . . . please you every day] For discussion of the music see Appendix II, p. 188, Opinions vary as to whether the words of the song are (1) an original composition by Shakespeare, (2) his adapted version of a traditional song, (3) a traditional song altered by him only by the addition of the last stanza, (4) a composition, by Robert Armin or someone else, added to the play. A related stanza is given to the Fool in *Lr.*, III. ii. 74–7: 'He that has and a little tiny wit, / With heigh-ho, the wind and the rain, / Must make content with his fortunes fit / Though the rain it raineth every day.' This stanza is probably a reminiscence of the *Tw.N.* song, aptly introduced into the storm scene (Lear has just expressed his pity for his 'poor fool and knave', and after the stanza says, 'True, my good boy'). Wilson, on the contrary, believes the *Tw.N.* song to be 'a mere development, and a clumsy one', of the quatrain in *Lr.*, composed by Armin after he had played the Fool in *Lr.*, 'and tacked on to the playhouse version of *Twelfth Night* about 1606'. (For the question of revision of the text, see Introduction, pp. xxii–xxv.) It can fairly be assumed, from *Ham.*, III. ii. 37 ff., that Shakespeare disapproved of clowns who took liberties with the text provided by the playwright, so there is little likelihood that he would have approved of Armin's 'tacking on' a song in this manner. Armin never claimed authorship of the song, nor would he have needed to have it written down if he was to be its singer; its inclusion

in F suggests that the edd. regarded it as Shakespeare's, which is the opinion generally held at present.

Opinions also vary as to the merit of the song. Early edd. (Warburton, Capell, Steevens) regard it as trivial and irrelevant to the play which it concludes. Capell comments briefly on its structure: 'The pursuits of the speaker, and his disappointments in some of them in four stages of life, are severally describ'd in as many stanza's [*sic*] . . . The concluding stanza is a meer badinage.' In the mid-nineteenth century Knight calls it 'the most philosophical Clown's song upon record . . . and the conclusion is, that what is true of the individual is true of the species . . .', to which Weiss (1876) adds that 'the grave insinuation of the song is touched with the vague, soft bloom of the play'. Noble (1923) sees it as an appropriate end to 'this high-spirited comedy' and its 'wise nonsense' as 'a commentary on the events of the play'; he suggests that 'the groundlings' would take up the popular refrain (this seems to me much more likely than MacSweeney's suggestion, *N. & Q.*, Ser. 12, 4 (1918), p. 40., that 'the players, in whole or in part, dance to the music'). Hotson (pp. 167–72) interprets it as ribaldry (see note on l. 390 below) directed to a moral end, a satirical 'song of good life' (II. iii. 36–7) or 'Drunkard's Progress' reminding us 'that the wassailing of the Twelfth Night saturnalia had better not be followed as a way of life'; in its final stanza, 'turning smoothly into Robert Armin the player, Feste is out of his moral and into an Epilogue, to beg a gracious *plaudite* of the hearers.' Seng, pp. 123–8, gives these and other views in longer quotation, as does Furness for the earlier of them.

CLOWN *sings.*

When that I was and a little tiny boy,
    With hey, ho, the wind and the rain,
A foolish thing was but a toy,   390
    For the rain it raineth every day.

But when I came to man's estate,
    With hey, ho, the wind and the rain,
'Gainst knaves and thieves men shut their gate,
    For the rain it raineth every day.   395

But when I came, alas, to wive,
    With hey, ho, the wind and the rain,

388. tiny] *Rowe*[3]; *tine* F.   394. 'Gainst] *F3*; *Gainst* F.

388. and a] Wilson agrees with Furness that the 'and' is introduced to fit the words to the tune. Comparing its similar uses in *Lr.*, III. ii. 74, and *Oth.*, II. iii. 82, he points out that it is in F but not in the Q of either play, and 'is possibly therefore an insertion of the playhouse musician entrusted with the arrangement of the songs.'

little tiny] Cf. *Lr.*, III. ii. 74 (quoted above). Its other two Shakespearean occurrences are both in *2H4* (*c.*1598), v. i. 27, 'any pretty little tiny kickshaws', and v. iii. 57, 'my little tiny thief' (to Falstaff's Page). The latter phrase is perhaps echoed here in 'little tiny boy', and, since Shakespeare's only other use of 'kickshaws' (in its plural form) is in *Tw.N.*, I. iii. 113, it helps confirm the authenticity of the song and suggests that the song formed part of the original text and was not added after the composition of *Lr.* The F spelling 'tine' in all four places follows the word's earliest form (see *OED*, tine, *a.*, A, first in early fifteenth century, apparently always preceded by 'little'; and *OED*, tiny, *a.*, first in 1598 ('little tinie'), first as 'tiny' 1599).

The origin is obscure (see note under *OED*, tine, *a.*).

390. A foolish thing . . . toy] A foolish (i.e., wayward) child was merely looked upon as a trifle (and therefore indulged): 'i.e., my mischievous pranks were not taken seriously' (Wilson). Hotson finds in 'thing' an indecent reference to the fool's 'bauble', which he identifies with the phallus (p. 168).

394. 'Gainst knaves and thieves . . . gate] 'i.e., but when I grew up I found men's doors shut against me as a knave and a thief' (Wilson). 'Shut' (which could be present tense) is past tense in conformity with the other stanzas. Hotson, pursuing his line of interpretation (p. 171), says 'the lecherous knave finds that his goatish vice renders him an outcast, shut out in the rain.' Shakespeare was very capable of writing indecently, but a comparison of this song with the dialogue between Lafeu and the Clown in *All's W.*, IV. v. 20–7, or with Mercutio's simile and the following dialogue in *Rom.*, II. iv. 87–96 (in both of which the indecent sense of 'bauble' is underlined) will show how far Hotson is over-interpreting here.

By swaggering could I never thrive,
  For the rain it raineth every day.

But when I came unto my beds,   400
  With hey, ho, the wind and the rain,
With toss-pots still 'had drunken heads,
  For the rain it raineth every day.

A great while ago the world begun,
  With hey, ho, the wind and the rain,   405
But that's all one, our play is done,
  And we'll strive to please you every day.   [Exit.]

400, 402. beds . . . heads] F; bed . . . head Hanmer.   402. With] F; We conj.
Pollard apud N.C.S.   still 'had] This ed.; still had F; I had Hanmer; still I had
Collier². 404. begun] F (begon), Rowe. 405. With hey] F2; hey F. 407.
[Exit.]] Rowe; FINIS F.

398. swaggering] bullying and
blustering. Cf. 2H4, II. iv. 66–103,
for the Hostess's objection to 'swag-
gerers' like Pistol.
  400–2. But when I came . . .
drunken heads] Wilson denies Shakespeare's authorship of this stanza
because of its 'exceeding clumsiness';
various emendations have been suggested in order to give proper syntax,
but they seem unnecessary if we read
F's 'had' as ''had' ('I had'); cf. the
omission of pronoun 'he' at I. v. 149,
v. i. 173. Wilson paraphrases l. 402
as 'My wife and I always went drunk
to bed together', but for the plural

forms cf. 'knaves and thieves' (l. 394)
which would give the sense of 'like
other tosspots I was always coming
home drunk to bed'. 'Came unto my
beds' may mean 'grew old', since the
first three stanzas have shown increasing age: 'it is bedde time with a
man at three score and tenne'
(Overbury's Characters, quoted by
Furness from Halliwell).

  407. And we'll strive . . . every day]
Cf. All's W., epilogue, ll. 3–4, where
the King asks for applause, 'which
we will pay / With strife to please
you, day exceeding day'.

APPENDIX I

DIRECT SOURCE

From RICHE HIS FAREWELL TO MILITARIE PROFESSION

by Barnabe Riche (1581)

Riche his Farewell to Militarie profession: conteining verie pleasaunt discourses fit for a peaceable tyme. Gathered together for the onely delight of the courteous Gentlewomen bothe of England and Irelande, For whose onely pleasure they were collected together, And vnto whom they are directed and dedicated by Barnabe Riche, Gentleman. *Malui me diuitem esse quam vocari.* Imprinted at London, by Robart Walley. 1581.

Of Apolonius and Silla.

The argument of the second Historie.

Apolonius *Duke, hauyng spent a yeres seruice in the warres against the Turke, returnyng homward with his companie by sea, was driuen by force of weather to the Ile of* Cypres, *where he was well receiued by* Pontus *gouernour of the same Ile, with whom* Silla *daughter to* Pontus, *fell so straungely in loue, that after* Apolonius *was departed to Constantinople,* Silla *with one man followed, and commyng to Constantinople, she serued* Apolonius, *in the habite of a manne, and after many prety accidentes falling out, she was knowne to* Apolonius, *who in requitall of her loue maried her.*

5

Of Apolonius and Silla.] The text is reprinted from the copy in the Bodleian Library, Oxford. Because of the scarcity of the original edition, a literal reprint is given here, excepting only some evident errors. These are listed below, as are the most necessary modernizations of punctuation and the words (mostly conjunctions) which appear to have been omitted either by Riche or by the printer. A few glossarial notes are also added.

There is no child that is borne into this wretched worlde,   10
but before it doeth sucke the mothers Milke, it taketh first a
soope of the Cupp of errour, which maketh vs when we come
to riper yeres, not onely to enter into actions of iniurie, but
many tymes to straie from that is right and reason, but in
all other thinges, wherein wee shewe our selues to bee moste   15
dronken with this poisoned Cuppe, it is in our actions of
Loue, for the louer is so estranged fro[m] that is right, and
wandereth so wide from the boundes of reason, that he is not
able to deeme white from blacke, good from badde, vertue
from vice: but onely led by the apetite of his owne affections,   20
and groundyng them on the foolishnesse of his owne fancies,
will so settle his likyng, on such a one, as either by desert or
vnworthinesse, will merite rather to be loathed then loued.

If a question might be asked, what is the ground in deede
of reasonable loue, whereby the knot is knit, of true and   25
perfect freendship: I thinke those that be wise would
aunswere: Deserte, that is, where the partie beloued, dooeth
requite vs with the like, for otherwise, if the bare shewe of
beautie, or the comelinesse of personage, might bee sufficient to confirme vs in our loue. Those that bee accustomed   30
to goe to Faires and Markettes, might sometymes fall into
loue with twentie in a daie: Desert must then bee (of force)
the grounde of reasonable loue, for to loue them that hate vs,
to followe them that flie from vs, to faune on them that
froune on vs, to currie fauour with theim that disdaine vs, to   35
bee glad to please theim that care not how thei offende vs:
who will not confesse this to be an erronious loue, neither
grounded vppon witte nor reason. Wherfore right curteous
gentilwomen, if it please you with pacience to peruse this
Historie following, you shall se Dame Errour so plaie her   40
parte, with a Leishe of Louers, a male and twoo femalles, as
shall woorke a wonder to your wise iudgement, in notyng
the effecte of their amorous deuises and conclusions of their
actions. The first neclectyng the loue of a noble Dame, yong,
beautifull, and faire, (who onely for his good will, plaied the   45
parte of a seruing manne, contented to abide any maner of
paine onely to behold him[)]. He again setting his loue of a
Dame that despisyng hym, (beeyng a noble Duke) gaue her
self to a seruyng manne (as she had thought) but it otherwise fell out, as the substance of this tale shall better discribe.   50

30. loue. Those] _Read_ loue, those

And because I haue been somethyng tedious in my first discourse, offending your pacient eares, with the hearyng of a
circumstaunce ouer long. From hence forthe, that whiche I
minde to write, shall bee doen with suche celeritie, as the
matter that I pretende to penne, maie in any wise permit   55
me, and thus followeth the Historie.

During the tyme that the famous Citie of *Constantinople*,
remained in the handes of the Christians, emongst many
other noble menne, that kepte their abidyng in that florish-
yng Citie, there was one whose name was *Apolonius*; a wor-   60
thie Duke, who beyng but a verie yong man, and euen then
newe come to his possessions whiche were verie greate,
leuied a mightie bande of menne, at his owne proper
charges, with whom he serued againste the Turke, duryng
the space of one whole yere, in whiche tyme although it were   65
very shorte, this yong Duke so behaued hym self, as well by
prowesse and valiaunce shewed with his owne handes, as
otherwise, by his wisedome and liberalitie, vsed towardes
his Souldiors, that all the worlde was filled with the fame of
this noble Duke. When he had thus spent one yeares seruice,   70
he caused his Trompet to sounde a retraite, and gather-
yng his companie together, and imbarkyng theim selues
he sette saile, holdyng his course towardes *Constantinople*:
but beeyng vppon the Sea, by the extreamitie of a tempest
whiche sodainly fell, his fleete was deseuered some one waie,   75
and some an other, but he hym self recouered the Ile of
Cypres, where he was worthily receiued by *Pontus* Duke and
gouernour of the same Ile, with whom he lodged, while his
Shippes were newe repairyng.

This *Pontus* that was Lorde and gouernour of this famous   80
Ile, was an auncient Duke, and had twoo children, a soonne
and a daughter, his sonne was named *Siluio*, of whom hereafter we shall haue further occasion to speake, but at this
instant he was in the partes of *Africa*, seruyng in the warres.

The daughter her name was *Silla*, whose beautie was so   85
perelesse, that she had the soueraintie emongst all other
Dames, aswell for her beautie as for the noblenesse of hir
birthe. This *Silla* hauing heard of the worthinesse of
Apolonius, this yong Duke, who besides his beautie and good
graces, had a certaine naturall allurement, that beeyng now   90
in his companie in her fathers Courte, she was so strangely

53. long. From] *Read* long, from

attached with the loue of *Apolonius*, that there was nothyng
might content her but his presence and sweete sight, and
although she sawe no maner of hope, to attaine to that she
moste desired: Knowyng *Apolonius* to be but a geaste, and   95
readie to take the benefite of the next Winde, and to departe
into a straunge Countrey, whereby she was bereued of all
possibilitie euer to see hym againe, and therefore striued
with her self to leaue her fondenesse, but all in vaine it
would not bee, but like the foule which is once Limed, the   100
more she striueth, the faster she tieth her self. So *Silla* was
now constrained perforce her will to yeeld to loue, wherefore from tyme to tyme, she vsed so greate familiaritie with
hym, as her honour might well permitte, and fedde him
with suche amourous baites, as the modestie of a maide,   105
could reasonably afforde, whiche when she perceiued, did
take but small effecte, feelyng her self so muche out raged
with the extreamitie of her passion, by the onely countenaunce that she bestowed vppon *Apolonius*, it might haue been
well perceiued, that the verie eyes pleaded vnto hym for pitie 110
and remorse. But *Apolonius* commyng but lately from out the
feelde, from the chasyng of his enemies, and his furie not
yet throughly desolued, nor purged from his stomacke,
gaue no regarde to those amourous entisementes, whiche
by reason of his youth, he had not been acquainted with all.   115
But his minde ranne more to heare his Pilotes, bryng newes of
a merie winde, to serue his turne to *Constantinople*, whiche
in the ende came very prosperously: and giuyng Duke *Pontus*
hartie thankes for his greate entertainment, takyng his leaue
of hym self, and the Ladie *Silla* his daughter, departed with   120
his companie, and with a happie gaale ariued at his desired
porte: Gentlewomen accordyng to my promise, I will heare
for breuities sake, omit to make repetition of the long and
dolorous discourse recorded by *Silla*, for this sodaine departure of her *Apolonius*, knowyng you to bee as tenderly harted   125
as *Silla* her self, whereby you maie the better coniecture the
furie of her Feuer.

But *Silla* the further that she sawe her self bereued of all
hope, euer any more to see her beloued *Apolonius*, so muche
the more contagious were her passions, and made the greater   130
speede to execute that she had premeditated in her mynde,
whiche was this: Emongest many seruauntes that did attend
vppon her, there was one whose name was *Pedro*, who had a
long tyme waited vpon her in her Chamber, wherby she

was well assured of his fidelitie and trust: to that *Pedro*,   135
therefore she bewraied first the ferue[n]cie of her loue borne
to *Apolonius*, coniuring him in the name of the Goddes of
Loue her self, and bindyng hym by the duetie that a
Seruaunte ought to haue, that tendereth his Mistresse safetie
and good likyng, and desiryng hym with teares tricklyng   140
doune her cheekes, that he would giue his consent to aide
and assiste her, in that she had determined, whiche was for
that she was fully resolued to goe to *Constantinople*, where
she might againe take the vewe of her beloued *Apolonius*,
that he accordyng to the trust she had reposed in hym,   145
would not refuse to give his consent, secretly to conuaie her
from out her fathers Courte, accordyng as she should giue
hym direction, and also to make hym self pertaker of her
iourney, and to waite vpon her, till she had seen the ende
of her determination.   150

   Pedro perceiuyng with what vehemencie his Ladie and
Mistresse had made request vnto hym, albeeit he sawe
many perilles and doubtes, dependyng in her pretence notwithstandyng, gaue his consent to be at her disposition,
promisyng her to further her with his beste aduice, and to   155
be readie to obeye whatsoeuer she would please to commaunde him. The match beyng thus agreed vpon, and all
thynges prepared in a readinesse for their departure: It
happened there was a Gallie of *Constantinople*, readie to departe, whiche *Pedro* vnderstandyng came to the Captaine,   160
desiryng him to haue passage for hym self, and for a poore
maide that was his sister, whiche were bounde to *Constantinople* vppon certaine vrgent affaires, to whiche request,
the Captaine graunted, willyng hym to prepare aborde
with all speede, because the winde serued hym presently   165
to departe.

   Pedro now commyng to his Mistres, and tellyng her how
he had handeled the matter with the Captaine: she likyng
verie well of the deuise, disguisyng her self into verie simple
atyre, stole awaie from out her fathers Court, and came   170
with *Pedro*, whom now she calleth brother aboarde the
Galleye, where all thynges beyng in readinesse, and the
winde seruyng verie well, thei launched forthe with their
Oores, and set saile, when thei were at the Sea, the Captaine

153. pretence] *Read* pretence, (*i.e., intention.*)   171. brother] *Read* brother,
174. saile, when] *Read* sail. When

of the Galleye takyng the vewe of *Silla*, perceiuyng her 175
singular beautie, he was better pleased in beholdyng of her
face, then in takyng the height either of the Sunne or Starre,
and thinkyng her by the homelinesse of her apparell, to be
but some simple maiden, callyng her into his Cabin, he
beganne to breake with her after the Sea fashion, desiryng 180
her to vse his owne Cabin for her better ease: and duryng the
tyme that she remained at the Sea, she should not want a
bedde, and then, wisperyng softly in her eare he saied, that
for want of a bedfellow, he hym self would supplie that
rome. *Silla* not beyng acquainted with any suche talke, blus- 185
shed for shame, but made hym no aunswere at all, my
Captaine feelyng suche a bickeryng within him self, the like
whereof he had neuer indured vpon the Sea: was like to bee
taken prisoner aboard his owne Shippe, and forced to yeeld
hym self a captiue without any Cannon shot, wherefore to 190
salue all sores, and thinkyng it the readiest waie to speed, he
began to breake with *Silla* in the waie of mariage, tellyng
her how happie a voiage she had made, to fall into the likyng
of suche a one as hym self was, who was able to keepe and
maintaine her like a gentilwoman, and for her sake would 195
likewise take her brother into his fellowship, whom he would
by some meanes prefarre in suche sorte, that bothe of theim
should haue good cause to think theim selues thrise happie,
she to light of suche a housbande, and he to light of suche a
brother. But *Silla* nothyng pleased with these prefermentes, 200
desired hym to cease his talke, for that she did thynke her
self in deede to bee too vnworthie suche a one as he was,
neither was she minded yet to marrie, and therefore desired
hym to fixe his fancie vppon some that were better worthie
then her self was, and that could better like of his curtesie 205
then she could dooe, the Captaine seeyng hym self thus
refused, beyng in a greate chafe, he saied as followeth.

    Then seeyng you make so little accompte of my curtesie,
proffered to one that is so farre vnworthie of it, from henceforthe I will vse the office of my aucthoritie, you shall knowe 210
that I am the Captaine of this Shippe, and haue power to
commaunde and dispose of thynges at my pleasure, and
seyng you haue so scornfully reiected me to be your loiall
housbande, I will now take you by force, and vse you at my
will, and so long as it shall please me, will kepe you for 215
myne owne store, there shall be no man able to defende you,

186. all, my] *Read* all. My   206. dooe, the] *Read* dooe. The

nor yet to perswade me from that I haue determined. *Silla*
with these wordes beyng stroke into a greate feare, did
thinke it now too late, to rewe her rashe attempte, determined rather to dye with her owne handes, then to suffer   220
her self to be abused in suche sorte, therefore she moste
humbly desired the Captaine so muche as he could to saue
her credite, and seyng that she must needes be at his will
and disposition, that for that present he would depart, and
suffer her till night, when in the darke he might take his   225
pleasure, without any maner of suspition to the residue of
his companie. The Captaine thinkyng now the goole to be
more then half wonne, was contented so farre to satisfie her
request, and departed out leauyng her alone in his Cabin.

Silla, beyng alone by her self, drue oute her knife readie to   230
strike her self to the harrt, and fallyng vpon her knees,
desired God to receiue her soule, as an acceptable sacrifice
for her follies, whiche she had so wilfully committed,
crauyng pardon for her sinnes, and so forthe continuyng a
long and pitifull reconciliation to GOD, in the middest   235
whereof there sodainly fell a wonderfull storme, the terrour
whereof was suche, that there was no man but did thinke
the Seas would presently haue swallowed them, the Billowes
so sodainly arose with the rage of the winde, that thei were
all glad to fall to heauing out of water, for otherwise their   240
feeble Gallie had neuer bin able to have brooked the Seas,
this storme continued all that daie and the next night, and
thei beeyng driuen to put romer before the winde to keepe
the Gallie ahed the Billowe, were driuen vppon the maine
shore, where the Gallie brake all to peeces, there was euery   245
man prouidyng to saue his own life, some gat vpon Hatches,
Boordes, and Casks, and were driuen with the waues to and
fro, but the greatest nomber were drouned, amongst the
whiche *Pedro* was one, but *Silla* her self beyng in the Caben
as you haue heard, tooke holde of a Cheste that was the   250
Captaines, the whiche by the onely prouidence of GOD
brought her safe to the shore, the whiche when she had
recouered, not knowyng what was become of *Pedro* her
manne, she deemed that bothe he and all the rest had been
drouned, for that she sawe no bodie vppon the shore but her   255
self, wherefore, when she had a while made greate lamenta-

219–20. attempte, determined] *Read* attempte, [and] determined   238.
them, the] *Read* them. The   243. put . . . winde] i.e., *sail with a following wind*
(*see* room, *adv.*, 3, *OED*).   245. peeces, there] *Read* peeces. There

tions, complainyng her mishappes, she beganne in the ende
to comforte herself with the hope, that she had to see her
Apolonius, and found suche meanes that she brake open the
Chest that brought her to lande, wherin she found good   260
store of coine, and sondrie sutes of apparell that were the
captaines, and now to preuent a nomber of iniuries, that
might bee proffered to a woman that was lefte in her case,
she determined to leaue her owne apparell, and to sort her
self into some of those sutes, that beyng taken for a man,   265
she might passe through the Countrie in the better safetie,
& as she changed her apparell, she thought it likewise conuenient to change her name, wherefore not readily hap-
penyng of any other, she called her self *Siluio*, by the name of
her owne brother, whom you haue heard spoken of before.   270
    In this maner she trauailed to *Constantinople*, where she
inquired out the Palace of the Duke *Apolonius*, and thinking
her self now to be bothe fitte and able to plaie the seruyng-
man, she presented her self to the duke, crauyng his seruice,
the duke verie willyng to giue succour vnto strangers, per- 275
ceiuyng him to bee a proper smogue yong man, gaue hym
entertainment: *Silla* thought her self now more then satisfied
for all the casualties that had happened vnto her in her
iourney, that she might at her pleasure take but the vew
of the Duke *Apolonius*, and aboue the reste of his seruauntes 280
was verie diligent and attendaunt vppon hym, the whiche
the Duke perceiuyng, beganne likewise to growe into good
likyng with the diligence of his man, and therefore made
hym one of his Chamber, who but *Siluio* then was moste
neate aboute hym, in helpyng of hym to make hym readie   285
in a mornyng, in the settyng of his ruffes, in the keepyng of
his Chamber, *Siluio* pleased his maister so well, that aboue all
the reste of his seruauntes aboute hym, he had the greatest
credite, and the Duke put him moste in trust.
    At this verie instaunt, there was remainyng in the Citie a   290
noble Dame a widowe, whose housebande was but lately
deceased, one of the noblest men that were in the partes of
Grecia, who left his Lady and wife large possessions and
greate liuinges. This Ladies name was called *Iulina*, who besides the aboundance of her wealth, and the greatnesse of   295
her reuenues, had likewise the soueraigntie of all the Dames

258. the hope, that] *Read* the hope that   274-5. seruice, the] *Read* seruice.
The   276. smogue] smug, *i.e., neat.*   284. Chamber, who] *Read* Chamber.
Who   287. Chamber, *Siluio*] *Read* Chamber? *Siluio*

of *Constantinople* for her beautie. To this Ladie *Iulina*, *Apolonius*
became an earnest suter, and accordyng to the maner of
woers, besides faire woordes, sorrowfull sighes, and piteous
countenaunces, there must bee sendyng of louyng letters,   300
Chaines, Bracelettes, Brouches, Rynges, Tablets, Gemmes,
Iuels, and presentes I knowe not what: So my Duke, who
in the tyme that he remained in the Ile of *Cypres*, had no
skill at all in the arte of Loue, although it were more then
half proffered vnto hym, was now become a scholler in   305
Loues Schoole, and had alreadie learned his first lesson, that
is, to speake pitifully, to looke ruthfully, to promise largely,
to serue diligently, and to please carefully: Now he was
learnyng his seconde lesson, that is to reward liberally, to
giue bountifully, to present willyngly, and to write louyngly.   310
Thus *Apolonius* was so busied in his newe studie, that I
warrant you there was no man that could chalenge hym for
plaiyng the truant, he followed his profession with so good
a will: And who must bee the messenger to carrie the tokens
and loue letters, to the Ladie *Iulina*, but *Siluio* his manne, in   315
hym the Duke reposed his onely confidence, to goe betweene
hym and his Ladie.

Now gentilwomen, doe you thinke there could haue been
a greater torment deuised, wherewith to afflicte the harte
of *Silla*, then her self to bee made the instrumente to woorke   320
her owne mishapp, and to plaie the Atturney in a cause,
that made so muche againste her self. But *Silla* altogether
desirous to please her maister, cared nothyng at all to
offende her self, followed his businesse with so good a will,
as if it had been in her owne preferment.   325

Iulina now hauyng many tymes, taken the gaze of this
yong youth *Siluio*, perceiuyng hym to bee of suche excellente
perfecte grace, was so intangeled with the often sight of this
sweete temptation, that she fell into as greate a likyng with
the man, as the maister was with her self: And on a tyme   330
Siluio beyng sent from his maister, with a message to the
Ladie *Iulina*, as he beganne very earnestly to solicet in his
maisters behalfe, *Iulina* interruptyng hym in his tale, saied:
Siluio it is enough that you haue saied for your maister,
from henceforthe either speake for your self, or saie nothyng   335
at all. *Silla* abashed to heare these wordes, began in her
minde to accuse the blindnesse of Loue, that *Iulina* neglect-

315. manne, in] *Read* manne? In   324. followed] *Read* [and] followed

yng the good will of so noble a Duke, would preferre her
loue vnto suche a one, as Nature it self had denaied to
recompence her likyng.   340

And now for a tyme, leauyng matters dependyng as you
haue heard, it fell out that the right *Siluio* indeede (whom
you haue heard spoken of before, the brother of *Silla*,) was
come to his Fathers Courte into the Ile of *Cypres*, where
vnderstanding, that his sister was departed, in maner as   345
you haue heard coniectured, that the very occasion did
proceade of some liking had betwene *Pedro* her man (that
was missyng with her) and her self, but *Siluio* who loued
his sister, as dearly as his owne life, and the rather for that
as she was his naturall sister, bothe by Father and Mother, 350
so the one of theim was so like the other, in countenaunce
and fauour, that there was no man able to descerne the one
from the other by their faces, sauyng by their apparell the
one beyng a man, the other a woman.

Siluio therefore vowed to his Father, not onely to seeke out 355
his sister *Silla* but also to reuenge the villanie, whiche he
conceiued in *Pedro*, for the carriyng awaie of his sister, and
thus departyng, hauyng trauailed through many Cities and
Tounes, without hearyng any maner of newes, of those he
wente to seeke for, at the laste he arriued at *Constantinople*, 360
where as he was walkyng in an euenyng for his owne recreation, on a pleasaunte greene yarde, without the walles of
the Citie, he fortuned to meete with the Ladie *Iulina*, who
likewise had been abroad to take the aire, and as she
sodainly caste her eyes vppon *Siluio*, thinkyng hym to bee 365
her olde acquaintaunce, by reason thei were so like one
an other, as you haue heard before, saied vnto hym, sir
Siluio, if your haste be not the greater, I praie you let me
haue a little talke with you, seyng I haue so luckely mette
you in this place.   370

Siluio wonderyng to heare hym self so rightlie named,
beeyng but a straunger, not of aboue twoo daies continu-
aunce in the Citie, verie courteouslie came towardes her,
desirous to heare what she would saie.

Iulina commaunding her traine somthyng to stande   375
backe, saied as followeth. Seyng my good will and frendly
loue, hath been the onely cause to make me so prodigall to

346. heard coniectured, that] *Read* heard, coniectured that   348–54. but
*Siluio . . . a woman.] This sentence is unfinished; its main verb may be regarded as
being 'vowed' in the next paragraph (l. 355).*

offer, that I see is so lightly reiected, it maketh me to thinke, that men bee of this condition, rather to desire those thynges, whiche thei can not come by, then to esteeme or value of that, whiche bothe largely and liberallie is offered vnto theim, but if the liberalitie of my proffer, hath made to seme lesse the value of the thing that I ment to present, it is but in your owne c[on]ceipt, consideryng how many noble men there hath been here before, and be yet at this present, whiche hath bothe serued, sued, and moste humbly intreated, to attaine to that, whiche to you of my self, I haue freely offred, and I perceiue is dispised, or at the least verie lightly regarded.

Siluio wonderyng at these woordes, but more amazed that she could so rightlie call hym by his name, could not tell what to make of her speeches, assuryng hym self that she was deceiued, and did mistake hym, did thinke notwithstandyng, it had been a poincte of greate simplicitie, if he should forsake that, whiche Fortune had so fauourably proffered vnto hym, perceiuyng by her traine, that she was some Ladie of greate honour, and vewyng the perfection of her beautie, and the excellencie of her grace and countenaunce, did thinke it vnpossible that she should be despised, and therefore aunswered thus.

Madame, if before this tyme, I haue seemed to forgett my self, in neglectyng your courtesie whiche so liberally you haue ment vnto me: please it you to pardon what is paste, and from this daie forewardes, *Siluio* remaineth readie preste to make suche reasonable amendes, as his abilitie maie any waies permit, or as it shall please you to commaunde.

Iulina the gladdest woman that might bee, to heare these ioyfull newes, saied: Then my *Siluio* see you faile not to Morowe at night to Suppe with me at my owne house, where I will discourse farther with you, what amendes you shall make me, to whiche request *Siluio* gaue his glad consente, and thus thei departed verie well pleased. And as *Iulina* did thinke the tyme verie long, till she had reapte the fruite of her desire: So *Siluio* he wishte for Haruest, before Corne could growe, thinkyng the tyme as long, till he sawe how matters would fall out, but not knowyng what Ladie she might bee, he presently (before *Iulina* was out of sight) demaunded of one that was walkyng by what she was, and

380

how she was called, who satisfied *Siluio* in every poincte, and
also in what parte of the toune her house did stande, where-   420
by he might enquire it out.

Siluio thus departing to his lodging, passed the night with
verie vnquiet sleapes, and the nexte Mornyng his mynde ran
so muche of his Supper, that he neuer cared, neither for
his Breakfast nor Dinner, and the daie to his seemyng passed   425
awaie so slowlie, that he had thought the statelie Steedes had
been tired, that drawe the Chariot of the Sunne, or els some
other *Iosua* had commaunded them againe to stande, and
wished that *Phaeton* had been there with a whippe.

Iulina on the other side, she had thought the Clocke   430
setter had plaied the knaue, the daie came no faster forewardes, but sixe a clocke beeyng once stroken, recouered
comforte to bothe parties: and *Siluio* hastenyng hymself to
the Pallace of *Iulina*, where by her he was frendly welcomed,
and a sumpteous supper beeyng made readie, furnished with   435
sondrie sortes of delicate dishes, thei satte them doune,
passyng the Supper tyme with amarous lokes, louyng countenaunces, and secret glau[n]ces conueighed from the one
to the other, whiche did better satisfie them, then the
feedyng of their daintie dishes.   440

Supper tyme beeyng thus spent, *Iulina* did thinke it verie
vnfitly, if she should tourne *Siluio* to goe seeke his lodgyng in
an euenyng, desired hym therefore, that he would take a
bedde in her house for that Night, and bringyng hym vp
into a faire Chamber, that was verie richely furnished, she   445
founde suche meanes, that when all the reste of her hous-
holde seruauntes were a bedde and quiet, she came her
self to beare *Siluio* companie, where concludyng vppon conditions, that were in question betweene them, thei passed
the night with suche ioye and contentation, as might in that   450
conuenient tyme be wished for, but onely that *Iulina*, feedyng
too muche of some one dishe aboue the reste, receiued a
surfet, whereof she could not bee cured in fourtie wekes after,
a naturall inclination in all women whiche are Subiecte to
longyng, and want the reason to vse a moderation in their   455
diet: but the mornyng approchyng, *Iulina* tooke her leaue,
and co[n]ueighed her self into her owne chamber, and
when it was faire daie light, *Siluio* makyng hym self readie,
departed likewise about his affaires in the toune, debatyng

with hymself how thynges had happened, beyng well   460
assured that *Iulina* had mistaken him, and therefore for feare
of further euilles, determined to come no more there, but
tooke his iourney towardes other places in the partes of
Grecia, to see if he could learne any tidynges of his sister *Silla*.

The duke *Apolonius* hauyng made a long sute, and neuer   465
a whit the nerer of his purpose, came to *Iulina* to craue her
direct aunswere, either to accept of hym, and of suche
conditions as he proffered vnto her, or els to giue hym his
laste farewell.

Iulina, as you haue heard, had taken an earnest penie of   470
an other, whom she had thought had been *Siluio* the Dukes
man, was at a controuersie in her self, what she might doe,
one while she thought, seyng her occasion serued so fitt, to
craue the Dukes good will for the mariyng of his manne,
then againe, she could not tell what displeasure the Duke   475
would conceiue, in that she should seeme to preferre his
man before hym self, did thinke it therefore beste to con-
ceale the matter, till she might speake with *Siluio*, to vse
his opinio[n] how these matters should be handled, and
herevpon resoluyng her self, desiryng the duke to pardon   480
her speeches, saied as followeth.

Sir Duke, for that from this tyme forwardes I am no
longer of my self, hauyng giuen my full power and authoritie
ouer to an other, whose wife I now remaine by faithfull
vowe and promise: And albeeit, I knowe the worlde will   485
wonder, when thei shall vnderstande the fondnesse of my
choice, yet I trust you your self will nothyng deslike with
me, sithe I haue ment no other thing, then the satisfiyng of
myne owne contentation and likyng.

The Duke hearyng these woordes, aunswered: Madam,   490
I must then content my self, although against my wil,
hauing the Lawe in your owne handes, to like of whom you
liste, and to make choise where it pleaseth you.

Iulina giuyng the Duke great thankes, that would
content himself with suche pacience, desired hym likewise,   495
to giue his free consent and good will, to the partie whom
she had chosen to be her housebande.

Naie surely Madam (q[uoth] the Duke) I will neuer give
my consent, that any other man shall enioye you then my

471. she] he *1581*.   472. was] *Read* [and] was   472-3. doe, one while]
Read doe: one while   477. did] *Read* [and] did   482-3. I am no longer of
my self] *Read* I am no longer [mistress] of my self

self, I haue made too greate accompt of you, then so lightly   500
to passe you awaie with my good will: But seeyng it lieth not
in me to let you, hauyng (as you saie) made your owne
choise, so from hence forwardes I leaue you to your owne
likyng, alwaies willyng you well, and thus will take my
leaue.   505

The Duke departed towardes his owne house verie sorrowfull, that *Iulina* had thus serued hym, but in the meane space
that the Duke had remained in the house of *Iulina*, some of
his seruantes fell into talke and conference, with the
seruantes of *Iulina*, where debatyng betwene them, of the   510
likelihood of the Mariage, betweene the Duke and the Ladie,
one of the seruantes of *Iulina* saied: that he neuer sawe his
Ladie and mistres, vse so good countenaunce to the Duke
hym self, as she had doen to *Siluio* his manne, and began
to report with what familiaritie and courtesie, she had   515
receiued hym, feasted hym, and lodged hym, and that in his
opinion, *Siluio* was like to speede before the Duke, or any
other that were suters.

This tale was quickly brought to the Duke hymself, who
makyng better enquirie in the matter, founde it to be true   520
that was reported, and better consideryng of the woordes,
whiche *Iulina* had vsed towardes hymself, was verie well
assured that it could bee no other then his owne manne,
that had thrust his Nose so farre out of ioynte, wherefore
without any further respect, caused hym to be thrust into a   525
Dongeon, where he was kept prisoner, in a verie pitifull
plight.

Poore *Siluio*, hauyng gotte intelligence by some of his
fellowes, what was the cause that the Duke his Maister did
beare suche displeasure vnto hym, deuised all the meanes   530
he could, as well by mediation by his fellowes, as otherwise by petitions, and supplications to the Duke, that he
would suspende his Iudgemente, till perfecte proofe were
had in the matter, and then if any maner of thyng did fall
out againste hym, wherby the Duke had cause to take any   535
greef, he would confesse hym self worthie not onely of im-
prisonmente, but also of moste vile and shamefull death:
with these pititions he daiely plied the Duke, but all in
vaine, for the duke thought he had made so good proofe,

502. let] *i.e.,* *hinder.*   525. caused] *Read* [he] caused   531. mediation]
meditation *1581.*

that he was throughlie confirmed in his opinion against his 540
man.

But the Ladie *Iulina*, wonderyng what made *Siluio*, that
he was so slacke in his visitation, and why he absented hym
self so long from her presence, beganne to thinke that all was
not well, but in the ende, perceiuyng no decoction of her 545
former surfette, receiued as you haue heard, and findyng in
her self an vnwonted swellyng in her beallie, assuryng her
self to bee with child, fearyng to become quite banckroute
of her honour, did thinke it more then tyme to seeke out a
Father, and made suche secret searche, and diligent en- 550
quirie, that she learned the truthe how *Siluio* was kepte in
prison, by the Duke his Maister, and mindyng to finde a
present remedie, as well for the loue she bare to *Siluio*, as for
the maintenaunce of her credite and estimation, she speedily
hasted to the Pallace of the Duke, to whom she saied as 555
followeth.

Sir Duke, it maie bee that you will thinke my commyng
to your house in this sorte, doeth somethyng passe the limites
of modestie, the whiche I protest before GOD, proceadeth
of this desire, that the worlde should knowe, how iustly I 560
seke meanes to maintaine my honour, but to the ende I
seeme not tedious with prolixitie of woordes, nor to vse other
then direct circumstaunces, knowe sir, that the loue I beare
to my onely beloued *Siluio*, whom I doe esteeme more then
all the Iewells in the worlde, whose personage I regard more 565
then my owne life, is the onely cause of my attempted
iourney, besechyng you, that all the whole displeasure,
whiche I vnderstand you haue conceiued against hym, maie
be imputed vnto my charge, and that it would please you
louingly to deale with him, whom of my self I haue chosen 570
rather for the satisfaction of mine honest likyng, then for the
vaine preheminences or honourable dignities looked after
by ambicious myndes.

The Duke hauing heard this discourse, caused *Siluio*
presently to be sent for, and to be brought before hym, to 575
whom he saied: Had it not been sufficient for thee, when I
had reposed my self in thy fidelitie, and the trustinesse of
thy seruice, that thou shouldest so traiterously deale with
me, but since y^t tyme haste not spared, still to abuse me
with so many forgeries, and periured protestations, not onely 580

545. decoction] *i.e., digestion.*   548. fearyng] *Read* [and] fearyng

hatefull vnto me, whose simplicitie thou thinkest to bee
suche, that by the plotte of thy pleasaunt tongue, thou
wouldest make me beleeue a manifest vntrothe, but moste
habominable bee thy doynges in the presence and sight of
God, that hast not spared to blaspheme his holy name, by   585
callyng hym to bee a witnesse to maintaine thy leasynges,
and so detestably wouldest forsweare thy self, in a matter
that is so openly knowne.

Poore *Siluio* whose innocencie was suche, y^t he might
lawfully sweare, seing *Iulina* to be there in place, aunswered   590
thus.

Moste noble Duke, well vnderstandyng your conceiued
greefe, moste humbly I beseche you paciently to heare my
excuse, not mindyng thereby to aggrauate or heape vp youre
wrathe and displeasure, protestyng before God, that there is   595
nothyng in the worlde, whiche I regarde so much, or dooe
esteeme so deare, as your good grace and fauour, but
desirous that your grace should know my innocencie, and
to cleare my self of suche impositions, wherewith I knowe
I am wrongfully accused, whiche as I vnderstande should   600
be in the practisyng of the Ladie *Iulina*, who standeth here
in place, whose acquitaunce for my better discharge, now I
moste humbly craue, protestyng before the almightie God,
that neither in thought, worde, nor deede, I haue not
otherwise vsed my self, then accordyng to the bonde and   605
duetie of a seruaunte, that is bothe willyng & desirous,
to further his Maisters sutes, which if I haue otherwise saied
then that is true, you Madame *Iulina*, who can verie well
deside the depthes of all this doubte, I moste humbly beseche
you to certifie a trothe, if I haue in any thyng missaied, or   610
haue otherwise spoke[n] then is right and iust.

Iulina hauyng heard this discourse whiche *Siluio* had
made, perceiuyng that he stoode in greate awe of the
Dukes displeasure, aunswered thus: Thinke not my *Siluio*,
that my commyng hither is to accuse you of any mis-   615
demeanour towardes your Maister, so I dooe not denaie,
but in all suche Imbassages wherein towardes me
you haue been imployed, you haue vsed the office of a
faithfull and trustie messenger, neither am I ashamed to
confesse, that the first daie that mine eyes did beholde,   620
the singuler behauiour, the notable curtesie, and other
innumerable giftes wherwith my *Siluio* is endued, but that
beyonde all measure my harte was so inflamed, that

impossible it was for me, to quenche the feruente loue, or
extinguishe the leaste parte of my conceiued torment,   625
before I had bewraied the same vnto hym, and of my
owne motion, craued his promised faithe and loialtie of
marriage, and now is the tyme to manifest the same vnto
the worlde, whiche hath been doen before God, and
betwene our selues: knowyng that it is not needefull, to   630
keepe secret that, whiche is neither euill doen, nor hurtfull
to any persone, therefore (as I saied before) *Siluio* is my
housbande by plited faithe, whom I hope to obtaine
without offence, or displeasure of any one, trustyng that
there is no manne, that will so farre forget hym self, as to 635
restraine that, whiche God hath left at libertie for euery
wight, or that will seeke by crueltie, to force Ladies to
marrie otherwise, then accordyng to their owne likyng.
Feare not then my *Siluio* to keepe your faith and promise,
whiche you haue made vnto me, and as for the reste: I   640
doubte not thynges will so fall out, as you shall haue
no maner of cause to complaine.

Siluio amased to heare these woordes, for that *Iulina*
by her speeche, semed to confirme that, whiche he moste
of all desired to bee quite of, saied: Who would haue   645
thought that a Ladie of so greate honour and reputation,
would her self bee the Embassadour, of a thyng so preiudi-
tiall, and vncomely for her estate, what plighted promises
be these whiche bee spoken of: Altogether ignoraunt vnto
me, whiche if it bee otherwise then I haue saied, you   650
Sacred Goddes consume me straight with flashyng flames
of fire. But what woordes might I vse to give credite to the
truthe, and innocencie of my cause? Ah Madame *Iulina*, I
desire no other testimonie, then your owne honestie and
vertue, thinkyng that you will not so muche blemishe the   655
brightnesse of your honour, knowyng that a woma[n] is or
should be, the Image of curtesie, continencie, and sham-
fastnesse, from the whiche so sone as she stoopeth, and
leaueth the office of her duetie and modestie, besides the
degraduation of her honour, she thrusteth her self into the   660
pitte of perpetuall infamie, and as I can not thinke you
would so farre forgette your self, by the refusall of a noble
Duke, to dimme the light of your renowne and glorie,

640. reste: I] *Read* reste, I   642. of] af *1581*.   645. quite] quit, *i.e., clear.*
648. estate, what] *Read* estate? What   649. spoken of:] *Read* spoken of?
657–8. shamfastnesse] shamefastness, *i.e., modesty.*

which hetherto you haue maintained, emongest the beste
and noblest Ladies, by suche a one as I knowe my self to   665
bee, too farre vnworthie your degree and callyng, so moste
hu[m]bly I beseche you to confesse a trothe, whereto
tendeth those vowes and promises you speake of, whiche
speeches bee so obscure vnto mee, as I knowe not for my
life how I might vnderstande them.   670

Iulina somethyng nipped with these speeches saied, and
what is the matter that now you make so little accoumpte
of your *Iulina*, that beeyng my housbande in deede, haue
the face to denaie me, to whom thou art contracted by so
many solemne othes: what arte thou ashamed to haue me   675
to thy wife? how muche oughtest thou rather to be ashamed
to breake thy promised faithe, and to haue despised the
holie and dreadfull name of GOD, but that tyme con-
strayneth me to laye open that, whiche shame rather
willeth I should dissemble and keepe secret, behold me   680
then here *Siluio* whom thou haste gotten with childe, who
if thou bee of suche honestie, as I trust for all this I shall
finde then the thyng is doen without preiudice, or any
hurte to my conscience, consideryng that by thy professed
faithe, thou diddest accoumpt me for thy wife, and I   685
receiued thee for my spouse and loyall housbande, swearyng
by the almightie God, that no other then you haue made
the co[n]quest and triumphe of my chastitie, whereof I
craue no other witnesse then your self, and mine owne
conscience.   690

I praie you Gentilwomen, was not this a foule ouersight
of *Iulina*, that would so precisely sweare so greate an othe,
that she was gotten with childe by one, that was altogether
vnfurnishte with implementes for suche a tourne. For
Gods loue take heede, and let this bee an example to you,   695
when you be with childe, how you sweare who is the Father,
before you haue had good proofe and knowledge of the
partie, for men be so subtill and full of sleight, that God
knoweth a woman may quickly be deceiued.

But now to returne to our *Siluio*, who hearyng an othe   700
sworne so deuinely that he had gotten a woman with childe,
was like to beleeue that it had bin true in very deede, but

667. trothe,] *Read* trothe: 668. speake of,] *Read* speake of?   675. what
arte thou] *Read* what, arte thou   683. finde then] *Read* finde, then   684.
thy] the *1581.*   698. subtill] subtilil *1581.*   698-9. God knoweth] *Read*
(God knoweth)

remembryng his owne impediment, thought it impossible
that he should committe suche an acte, and therefore half
in a chafe he saied. What lawe is able to restraine the 705
foolishe indescretion of a woman, that yeeldeth her self to
her owne desires, what shame is able to bridle or with-
drawe her from her mynd and madnesse, or with what
snaffell is it possible to holde her backe, from the execution
of her filthinesse, but what abhomination is this, that a 710
Ladie of suche a house should so forget the greatnesse of her
estate, the aliaunce whereof she is descended, the nobilitie
of her deceased housbande, and maketh no conscience
to shame and slaunder her self, with suche a one as I am,
beyng so farre vnfit and unsemely for her degree, but how 715
horrible is it to heare the name of God so defased, that wee
make no more acompt, but for the maintenaunce of our
mischifes, we feare no whit at all to forsweare his holy
name, as though he were not in all his dealinges moste
righteous true and iuste, and will not onely laie open our 720
leasinges to the worlde, but will likewise punishe the same
with moste sharpe and bitter scourges.

Iulina, not able to indure hym to proceede any farther in
his Sermon, was alreadie surprised with a vehement greefe,
began bitterly to crie out vtteryng these speeches followyng. 725

Alas, is it possible that the soueraigne iustice of God, can
abide a mischiefe so great and cursed, why maie I not
now suffer death, rather then the infamie whiche I see to
wander before myne eyes. Oh happie and more then right
happie had I bin, if inconstant fortune had not deuised 730
this treason wherein I am surprised and caught, am I thus
become to be intangled with snares, and in the handes
of hym, who inioiyng the spoyles of my honour, will
openly depriue me of my fame, by makyng me a common
fable to al posteritie in tyme to come, ah Traitour and dis- 735
courtious wretche, is this the recompence of the honest
and firme amitie which I haue borne thee, wherin haue I
deserued this discourtesie, by louing thee more then thou
art able to deserue, is it I arrant theefe is it I, vppon whom
thou thinkest to worke thy mischiues, doest thou think me 740
no better worthe, but that thou maiest prodigally waste
my honour at thy pleasure, didest thou dare to aduenture

710. filthinesse, but] *Read* filthinesse? But   716. defased] defaced   725.
began] *Read* [and] began

vppon me, hauing thy conscience wounded with so deadly
a treason: ah vnhappie and aboue all other most vnhappie,
that haue so charely preserued myne honour, and now am   745
made a praie to satisfie a yong mans lust, that hath coueted
nothyng but the spoyle of my chastitie and good name.

Here withall the teares so gushed doune her cheekes,
that she was not able to open her mouth to vse any farther
speeche.   750

The Duke who stood by all this while, and heard this
whole discourse, was wonderfully moued with compassion
towardes *Iulina,* knowyng that from her infancie she had
euer so honourably vsed her self, that there was no man able
to detect her of any misdemeanour, otherwise then be-   755
seemed a Ladie of her estate, wherefore beyng fully
resolued that *Siluio* his man had committed this villanie
against her, in a greate furie drawyng his Rapier he saied
vnto *Siluio.*

How canst thou (arrant theefe) shewe thy self so cruell   760
and carelesse to suche as doe thee honour, hast thou so little
regard of suche a noble Ladie, as humbleth her self to suche
a villaine as thou art, who without any respecte either of
her renowme or noble estate, canst be content to seeke the
wracke and vtter ruine of her honour, but frame thy self   765
to make such satisfaction as she requireth, although I knowe
vnworthie wretche, that thou art not able to make her the
least parte of amendes, or I sweare by god, that thou shalt
not escape the death which I will minister to thee with my
owne handes, and therefore aduise thee well what thou   770
doest.

Siluio hauyng heard this sharpe sentence, fell doune on
his knees before the Duke crauyng for mercie, desiryng
that he might be suffered to speake with the Ladie *Iulina*
aparte, promising to satisfie her, accordyng to her owne   775
contentation.

Well (q[uoth] the Duke) I take thy worde, and there
with all I aduise thee that thou performe thy promis,
or otherwise I protest before God, I will make thee suche
an example to the worlde, that all Traitours shall tremble   780
for feare, how they doe seeke the dishonouryng of Ladies.

But now *Iulina* had conceiued so greate greefe againste
Siluio, that there was muche a dooe, to perswade her to

764. renowme] renown   765. honour, but] *Read* honour? But

talke with hym, but remembryng her owne case, desirous
to heare what excuse he could make, in the ende she agreed,   785
and beyng brought into a place seuerally by them selues,
Siluio beganne with a piteous voice to saie as followeth.

I knowe not Madame, of whom I might make complaint,
whether of you or of my self, or rather of Fortune, whiche
hath conducted and brought vs both into so greate aduer-   790
sitie, I see that you receiue greate wrong, and I am condemned againste all right, you in perill to abide the
brute of spightfull tongues, and I in daunger to loose the
thing that I moste desire: and although I could alledge
many reasons to proue my saiynges true, yet I referre my   795
self, to the experience and bountie of your minde. And
here with all loosing his garmentes doune to his stomacke,
and shewed *Iulina* his breastes and pretie teates, sur-
mountyng farre the whitenesse of Snowe it self, saiyng:
Loe Madame, behold here the partie whom you haue   800
chalenged to bee the father of your childe, see I am a
woman the daughter of a noble Duke who, onely for the
loue of him, whom you so lightly have shaken of, haue
forsaken my father, abandoned my Countreie, and in
maner as you see am become a seruing man, satisfiyng   805
my self, but with the onely sight of my *Apolonius*, and now
Madame, if my passion were not vehement, & my tormen-
tes without comparison, I would wish that my fained greefes
might be laughed to scorne, & my dese[m]bled paines to
be rewarded with floutes. But my loue beyng pure, my   810
trauaile continuall, & my greefes endlesse, I trust Madame
you will not onely excuse me of crime, but also pitie my
destresse, the which I protest I would still haue kept
secrete, if my fortune would so haue permitted.

Iulina, did now thinke her self to be in a worse case then   815
euer she was before, for now she knewe not who[m] to
chalenge to be the father of her child, wherfore, when
she had told the duke the very certantie of the discourse,
which *Siluio* had made vnto her, she departed to her owne
house, with suche greefe and sorrowe, that she purposed   820
neuer to come out of her owne doores againe aliue, to be a
wonder and mocking stocke to ye worlde.

But ye Duke more amased, to heare this strau[n]ge dis-

790-1. aduersitie, I] *Read* aduersitie. I   793. brute] bruit   loose] lose
798. and] *Read* he   *Iulina*] *Iuliua/1581*.   803. shaken of] shaken off
818. discourse] discouse *1581*.

course of *Siluio* came vnto him, who[m] when he had
vewed with better consideratio[n], perceiued indeede that   825
it was *Silla* the daughter of Duke *Pontus*, and imbrasing
her in his armes, he saied.

Oh the braunche of all vertue, and the flowre of curtesie
it self, pardon me I beseche you, of all suche discourtesies,
as I haue ignorantlie committed towardes you: desiring   830
you that without farther memorie of auncient greefes, you
will accept of me, who is more ioyful and better contented
with your presence, then if the whole worlde were at my
commaundement. Where hath there euer been founde
such liberalitie in a Louer, whiche hauyng been trained vp   835
and nourished emongest the delicacies and banquettes of
the Courte, accompanied with traines of many faire and
noble ladies liuing in pleasure, and in the middest of
delightes, would so prodigallie aduenture your self, neither
fearing mishapps, nor misliking to take suche paines, as I   840
knowe you haue not been accustomed vnto. O liberalitie
neuer heard of before! O facte that can neuer bee sufficiently rewarded! O true Loue moste pure and vnfained:
here with all sendyng for the moste artificiall woorkmen,
he prouided for her sondrie sutes of sumpteous apparell,   845
and the Marriage daie appoincted, whiche was celebrated
with greate triumphe, through the whole Citie of *Constantinople*, euery one prasing the noblenesse of the Duke,
but so many as did behold the excellent beautie of *Silla*,
gaue her the praise aboue all the rest of the Ladies in the   850
troupe.

The matter seemed so wonderfull and straunge, that the
brute was spreade throughout all the partes of *Grecia*, in so
muche that it came to the hearyng of *Siluio*, who as you
haue heard, remained in those partes to enquire of his sister,   855
he beyng the gladdest manne in the worlde, hasted to
Constantinople, where comming to his sister he was ioyfullie
receiued, and moste louynglie welcomed, and entertained
of the Duke his brother in Lawe. After he had remained
there twoo or three daies, the duke reuealed vnto *Siluio*,   860
the whole discourse how it happened, betweene his sister
and the Ladie *Iulina*, and how his sister was chalenged, for
gettyng a woman with childe: *Siluio* blushyng with these

---

824. *Siluio* came] *Read* | *Siluio,* came   825. perceiued] *Read* he perceiued
829. beseche] besche *1581*.   853. *Grecia*] *Gretia/1581*.   855–6. sister, he]
Read sister. He

woordes, was striken with greate remorse to make *Iulina*
amendes, vnderstanding her to bee a noble Ladie, and was   865
lefte defamed to the worlde through his default, he therefore
bewraied the whole circumstaunce to the Duke, whereof
the Duke beyng verie ioyfull, immediatlie repaired with
Siluio to the house of *Iulina*, whom thei found in her
chamber, in greate lamentation & mournyng. To whom the   870
Duke saied, take courage Madam for beholde here a
gentilman, that will not sticke, bothe to father your child
and to take you for his wife, no inferiour persone, but the
sonne and heire of a noble Duke, worthie of your estate
and dignitie.   875

Iulina seyng *Siluio* in place, did know very well that he
was the father of her childe, and was so rauished with ioye,
that she knewe not whether she were awake, or in some
dreame. *Siluio* imbracyng her in his armes, crauyng
forgiuenesse of all that past: concluded with her the   880
mariage daie, which was presently accomplished with
greate ioye, and contentation to all parties: and thus
Siluio hauyng attained a noble wife, and *Silla* his sister her
desired houseband, thei passed the residue of their daies
with suche delight, as those that haue accomplished the   885
perfection of their felicities.

FINIS.

866. default, he] *Read* default: he   880. all that past: concluded] *Read* all
that [was] past, concluded

APPENDIX II

THE SONGS

The only songs or fragments of songs for which contemporary or near-contemporary settings are known to exist are given here.

1. 'O mistress mine' (II. iii. 40ff.).

The tune given below survives in two instrumental versions, by Thomas Morley (*The First Book of Consort Lessons*, 1599) and William Byrd (in the Fitzwilliam Virginal Book, *c*.1619), and as the melody of Thomas Campion's song 'Long have mine eyes gazed with delight' (John Gamble's Commonplace Book).[1] It

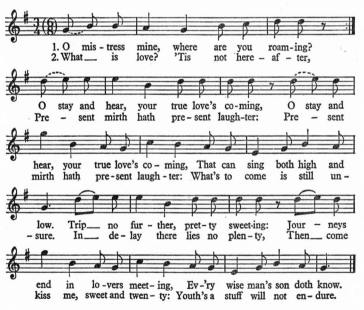

1. O mis - tress mine, where are you roam-ing?
2. What__ is love? 'Tis not here - af - ter,

O stay and hear, your true love's co-ming, O stay and
Pre - sent mirth hath pre-sent laugh-ter: Pre - sent

hear, your true love's co - ming, That can sing both high and
mirth hath pre-sent laugh-ter: What's to come is still un -

low. Trip__ no fur - ther, pret-ty sweet-ing: Jour — neys
– sure. In__ de-lay there lies no plen-ty, Then__ come

end in lo-vers meet-ing, Ev-'ry wise man's son doth know.
kiss me, sweet and twen-ty: Youth's a stuff will not en-dure.

1. Dates are of publication or of first known extant version (not of com-position), and are derived from P. J. Seng, *The Vocal Songs in the Plays of Shakespeare* (Cambridge, Mass., 1967), pp. 94–130, except when otherwise stated. Bibliographical details are to be found in Seng.

probably existed before Morley set it, and, though Morley composed the melody of 'It was a lover and his lass' (*A.Y.L.*, v. iii. 14),
it is unknown whether he had any connection with the use of the
tune in *Twelfth Night*; it is not certain that the words were sung
to this tune, but the correspondence of title makes it probable.[1]
The version given here is edited by Sidney Beck, 'The Case of
"O Mistress Mine"', *Renaissance News*, VI (1953), 19–23, and
reprinted from Mahood.[2]

2. 'Hold thy peace' (II. iii. 66).

Two versions exist, the former (a) printed by Thomas Ravenscroft, *Deuteromelia* (1609), the latter (b) in a manuscript book of
rounds 'collected and gathered by Thomas Lant' (1580).[3] It is
not known in which, if in either, Shakespeare's actors performed
the catch. Version (a) below is reprinted from Mahood; version
(b) is edited by me to correspond with the presentation of (a).

3. 'Three merry men be we' (II. iii. 77–8).

Version (a), a catch by William Lawes from John Hilton's

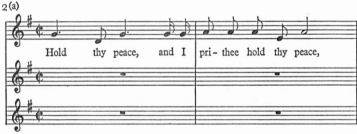

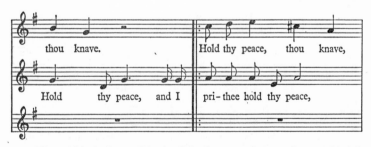

---

1. The subject is discussed in detail by Seng, *op. cit.*, pp. 96–100, with full
reference to the various opinions which have been maintained.
2. All other songs in Mahood are transcribed and edited by F. W. Sternfeld.
3. Jill Vlasto, 'An Elizabethan Anthology of Rounds', *Musical Quarterly*, 40
(1954), 222–34. The description of the catch is on p. 228, a transcript on p. 231
(as example 5).

Catch that Catch Can (1652) is derived from Mahood, but re-edited by me with 3/4 (6/8) tempo added, none being given in Mahood. It should obviously go briskly, and Sir Toby should sing the last phrase of the third part. Version (b) is derived from E. W. Naylor, *Shakespeare and Music* (1932), p. 182, who quotes it from W. Chappell, *Popular Music of the Olden Time* (1855–9), I, 216, where it is cited from 'a MS. common-place book, in the handwriting of John Playford' (c.1650),[1] but nothing further is stated about this MS. I have again shortened the notes to conform with normal modern 4/4 tempo.

1. Seng, *op. cit.*, p. 103.

2(b)

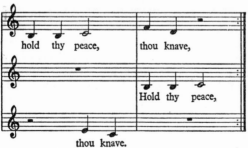

3(a)

1. [The] wise men were but seven,_____ ne'er
   Three mer-ry men, and three mer-ry men, and

2. [The] mu – ses were but nine,_____ the
   Three mer-ry men, and three mer-ry men, and

3. [The] three mer-ry boys, and three mer-ry boys, and
   Three mer-ry men, and three mer-ry men, and

1. more shall be for me._____
   three mer-ry men are we._____

2. worth – ies three times three._____
   three mer-ry men are we._____

3. three mer-ry boys are we._____
   three mer-ry men are we._____

3(b)

Three mer-ry men, and three mer-ry men, and

three mer-ry men_ be we. I in the wood, and

thou on the ground, and Jack sleeps in_ the tree.

4. 'There dwelt a man in Babylon' (ii. iii. 79–80).

The version below is based on the music to William Elderton's ballad 'The pangs of love and lovers' fits', which opens a stanza about 'King Solomon', from whom the tune (composer unknown) took its name. Claude M. Simpson, *The British Broadside Ballad and its Music* (1966), pp. 410–12, points out that several ballads shared its 'Lady, lady' refrain, and argues convincingly that they were sung to this tune.[1] The melody survives in two MSS. of the later sixteenth century, one at the British Museum and the other at Trinity College Dublin, and has here been transcribed and edited by F. W. Sternfeld, who kindly communicated it to me, together with the words sung by Sir Toby, which he has inserted in the appropriate place.

5. 'Farewell dear heart, since I must needs be gone' (II. iii. 102ff.).

The version below, transcribed and adapted to the words of Sir Toby and the Clown, is reprinted from Mahood. The original is in Robert Jones's *First Book of Songs and Airs* (1600).[2]

6. 'Hey, Robin, jolly Robin' (IV. ii. 75ff.).

The words are in B.M. MS. Egerton 2711 (fol. 37ᵛ). The poem

1. Seng, *op. cit.*, p. 104. There seems to be no better authority than theatrical tradition for setting the tune to 'Greensleeves'.

2. Seng, *op. cit.*, p. 106.

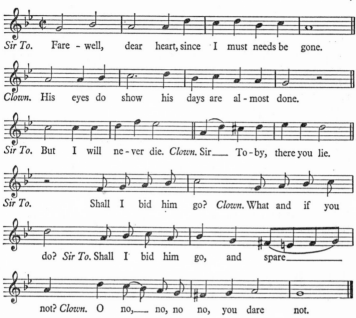

Sir To. Fare - well, dear heart, since I must needs be gone.

Clown. His eyes do show his days are al - most done.

Sir To. But I will ne - ver die. *Clown.* Sir___ To - by, there you lie.

Sir To. Shall I bid him go? *Clown.* What and if you

do? *Sir To.* Shall I bid him go, and spare___

not? *Clown.* O no,___ no, no no, you dare not.

of which they form part is ascribed to Sir Thomas Wyatt, though it is possible that the first two stanzas (from which the quoted words come) are older. The only known setting is for three voices by William Cornyshe (*c.*1485–*c.*1523).[1] This setting is printed in full by Mahood, followed by the fragments of the melodic line which are reprinted here. It is possible that in Shakespeare's play the words were sung to a later setting for solo voice, since lost.

Hey, Ro - bin, jol - ly Ro - bin, Tell me how thy

la - dy does... My la - dy is un - kind, per-die. A -

- las, why is she so? She loves a - no - ther...

1. Seng, *op. cit.*, pp. 117–19, for the Egerton MS. text of the lyric and for further discussion.

7. 'When that I was and a little tiny boy' (v.i. 388ff.).

The version below is reprinted from Mahood. The earliest recorded existence of a setting generally resembling this one is in Joseph Vernon's *The New Songs in the Pantomime of the Witches: the Celebrated Epilogue in the Comedy of Twelfth Night* (etc.) . . . *Sung by Mr. Vernon at Vaux Hall, composed by J. Vernon* (London, n.d. [1772]). It is in G minor, differs in many respects from this version, and is reprinted, together with this version in E minor (the version given by W. Chappell, *op. cit.*, 1, 225) by F. W. Sternfeld.[1] Allusion, in playbills from 1799, to this final song as 'the original epilogue song' may imply that Vernon's term 'composed' was taken to mean 'arranged' and the song regarded as traditional; on the other hand, the song may have been composed (in the usual sense) by Vernon, and the version given by Chappell may be adapted therefrom, not a traditional tune. Nevertheless, it being now traditional in the theatre, and its date being just possibly Elizabethan, it is included in this edition.

1. *Music in Shakespearean Tragedy* (1963), Appendix VII, pp. 189–91 (with reference to the one-stanza song in *Lr.*, III. ii. 74). Seng, *op. cit.*, p. 129.